Great Military Battles

ENDPAPERS

British 25-pounders engaged in a night bombardment of German positions before the Battle of Alamein, October 1942

Great Mili

Edited by
Cyril Falls

tary Battles

Spring Books

London·New York·Sydney·Toronto

Original edition published 1964 and © 1964 by
George Weidenfeld and Nicolson Limited, London

This edition published 1969 by
The Hamlyn Publishing Group Limited
London · New York · Sydney · Toronto
Hamlyn House, Feltham, Middlesex, England

3rd Impression 1972

Printed in Italy by
Arnoldo Mondadori Editore Officine Grafiche, Verona

ISBN 0 600 01652 8

Contents

8   INTRODUCTION
Captain Cyril Falls, sometime Chichele Professor of the History of War, University of Oxford

16   ROCROI, 1643
A brilliant victory gained by the young Duc d'Enghien – the future Great Condé – which destroyed the legend of the 'invincible Spanish infantry'
Captain Cyril Falls, sometime Chichele Professor of the History of War, University of Oxford

30   BLENHEIM, 1704
Marlborough and Eugène, by routing the Franco-Bavarians and capturing Tallard, shattered the reputation for invincibility enjoyed by French armies for sixty years
David Chandler, Senior Lecturer in Military History, Royal Military Academy, Sandhurst

42   POLTAVA, 1709
Peter the Great broke the military power of Sweden, achieving an immense political triumph, which announced the emergence of a new great power in the east
John Adair, Senior Lecturer in Military History, Royal Military Academy, Sandhurst

50   FONTENOY, 1745
The Duke of Cumberland's famous 'British square' penetrated the French centre but, lacking the full support of his allies, he was deprived of a great victory
Jacques Boudet, author of *1918-1948, trente ans d'histoire* (1949)

58   ROSSBACH, 1757
The Prussians' first great victory over the French, in which Frederick the Great inflicted heavy losses, was the most decisive battle of the Seven Years' War
Christopher Duffy, Lecturer in Military History, Royal Military Academy, Sandhurst

66   QUEBEC, 1759
Having scaled the Heights of Abraham by night, Wolfe routed the French under Montcalm, and decided the fate of Canada – both generals were killed
Christopher Hibbert, author of *Wolfe at Quebec* (1959)

78   BUNKER HILL, 1775
The American Colonists, by threatening Boston from Bunker Hill, drew out the British garrison who drove them off, though the city was evacuated nine months later
Brian Connell, author of *The Plains of Abraham* (1959)

90   SARATOGA, 1777
Burgoyne's surrender at Saratoga, mainly the result of inefficient direction of the war from London, brought France and, later, Spain as allies to the Americans
John Terraine, author of *Douglas Haig, The Educated Soldier* (1963)

102   YORKTOWN, 1781
Admiral Graves's failure to defeat de Grasse in Chesapeake Bay enabled Washington and his French allies to complete the stranglehold on Cornwallis at Yorktown
Major Reginald Hargreaves, author of *Red Sun Rising – The Siege of Port Arthur* (1962)

CONTENTS

114   **JENA, 1806**
Jena and Auerstedt were both won by superior French tactics, and Napoleon's determined pursuit of the routed armies ended Prussian participation in the war until 1813
Peter Paret, Professor of History, University of California, Davis

128   **BORODINO, 1812**
Though Napoleon won this stubborn battle and captured Moscow, his army was decimated during its retreat both by the rigours of the Russian winter and persistent harrying
Brigadier Peter Young, Reader in Military History, Royal Military Academy, Sandhurst

140   **WATERLOO, 1815**
The Hundred Days, Napoleon's final gamble, ended in Belgium when he gave battle too late at Waterloo, and lost all to Wellington and Blücher
Antony Brett-James, Deputy Head, Military History, Royal Military Academy, Sandhurst

154   **BALACLAVA, 1854**
This repulse of a Russian attack in the Crimean War is famous for the charge of Lord Cardigan's Light Brigade, which only one-third of his men survived
John Naylor, author of *Waterloo* (1960)

166   **FIRST BULL RUN, 1861**
McDowell's attack on Beauregard's Confederates thirty miles from Washington, the first pitched battle of the American Civil War, failed and the raw Federal troops fled in disorder
Bruce Catton, Senior Editor of *American Heritage* magazine

178   **GETTYSBURG, 1863**
During the three days of the greatest battle in the American Civil War all Lee's attacks, including Pickett's famous charge, were repulsed, and the Confederates had to retire
Hugh Cole, author of *The Lorraine Campaign* (1951)

192   **GRAVELOTTE – SAINT-PRIVAT, 1870**
The French under Marshal Bazaine were outflanked on their right, encircled and severely defeated by King Wilhelm's Germans in this episode of the Franco-Prussian War
The late Major-General J.F.C. Fuller, author of *The Decisive Battles of the Western World* (1954-6)

204   **PORT ARTHUR, 1904**
The six-months' siege of this fortress cost heavy casualties: its fall hastened the end of the Russo-Japanese War upon terms very favourable to Japan
Major Reginald Hargreaves, author of *Red Sun Rising – The Siege of Port Arthur* (1962)

212   **TANNENBERG, 1914**
One of the most complete victories in history was achieved, despite Ludendorff's mistakes, by Russian folly, hunger and disorganization, and the brilliance of General von François
Captain Cyril Falls, sometime Chichele Professor of the History of War, University of Oxford

220   **THE MARNE, 1914**
After the failure of Plan 17, Joffre rallied the French armies and the BEF and, piercing a gap in the German front, gained a great victory
Captain Robert B. Asprey, author of *The First Battle of the Marne* (1962)

228   **SUVLA BAY, 1915**
The landing was successful but, over-cautious, General Hamilton lost a great opportunity, and the Turks, under Liman von Sanders and Mustapha Kemal, easily checked him
General S.L.A. Marshall, Chief Historian of European Theatre

CONTENTS

234 CAPORETTO, 1917
An Austro-German force, breaking through the Italian left on the Isonzo, inflicted a disastrous defeat on General Cadorna, forcing him to retire to the Piave
John Keegan, Senior Lecturer in Military History, Royal Military Academy, Sandhurst

244 THE CROSSING OF THE MEUSE, 1940
Despite the respite of the 'phoney war', France and England were unprepared for the German assault: its success led swiftly to the fall of France
Joachim Röseler, Lecturer in History and Political Science, Staatliche Ingenieurschule, Bielefeld

252 STALINGRAD, 1942
The heroic Russian defence of this city against the Germans, which cost both sides appalling casualties, was one of the turning points in the Second World War
Antony Brett-James, Senior Lecturer in Military History, Royal Military Academy, Sandhurst

260 ALAMEIN, 1942
Ten days' strenuous fighting brought Montgomery victory and forced Rommel – hitherto virtually unbeaten – to retreat: it was the prelude to German expulsion from North Africa
Brian Bond, Assistant Lecturer in Modern History, University of Liverpool

270 GUADALCANAL, 1942
The ejection of the Japanese from this island in the Solomon group by the US Marines and Army with naval and air support ended a hard fought campaign
Neville Brown, Research Associate, Institute for Strategic Studies London

278 SAINT-LÔ – FALAISE, 1944
Following the successful Normandy landings, Eisenhower directed the main American attack towards Saint-Lô, while the British and Canadians trapped 100,000 Germans in the Falaise pocket
Piers Mackesy, Fellow of Pembroke College, Oxford

286 THE ARDENNES, 1944
Von Rundstedt's counter-attack, aimed at Antwerp, achieved initial success, but delayed the main Allied offensive by a mere six weeks, at the cost of heavy German casualties
Charles V.P. von Luttichau, Senior Historian, Office of Military History, US Army, Washington DC

292 THE DEVELOPMENT OF FORTIFICATIONS
David Chandler, Senior Lecturer in Military History, Royal Military Academy, Sandhurst

294 THE DEVELOPMENT OF UNIFORMS
A.E. Haswell Miller, artist and military historian, sometime Keeper, The National Galleries of Scotland

300 THE DEVELOPMENT OF TACTICS
Brigadier Peter Young, Reader in Military History, Royal Military Academy, Sandhurst

302 THE DEVELOPMENT OF ARTILLERY
Brigadier O.F.G. Hogg, author of *British Artillery 1326-1716* (1963)

303 THE DEVELOPMENT OF SMALL ARMS
H.L. Blackmore, author of *British Military Firearms 1650-1850* (1961)

304 Acknowledgments

Introduction

THE INTEREST IN MILITARY HISTORY in Britain, the United States, and several other countries in Europe is at present immense. It does not mean quite the same thing everywhere, however. Our official histories are strictly objective, and the same applies to those of the majority of nations. It is often said of the official historians of the Second World War that they are unduly timid, as was previously urged against those of the First. Is there any official history of any sort or kind of which the same cannot be said? If the writer is what the authorities consider too bold he will find his passage struck out. Yet readers who are alert will often discover neatly veiled but effective criticism. One example of recent and unveiled criticism may be cited: the comments on Orde Wingate in Burma.

On the other side of the Iron Curtain this has been very different: it was not merely that Stalin could do no wrong; virtually no one else could either. Soviet Russia was always right. Even this is changing, not necessarily because the historians have become more conscientious, and this is doubtless to the pleasure of the majority.

During and after each of the wars there was a considerable output of unofficial books; then, after a pause, a spate. These two outputs again differed markedly. The first was highly patriotic, one book at least, *The First Hundred Thousand*, though very readable – or so I then thought with the rest – almost mawkishly so; the second was marked by disillusion, disgust, and fury. There was hardly a leader who came out undamaged. This was even truer, as might be expected, of the multitude of novels and of the verse. How far the spirit of Julian Grenfell

differs from that of Robert Graves! The former came to be derided by admirers of the second, but he was every whit as honest a man.

The earliest of the battles included in this book is Rocroi, in 1643, which I myself have dealt with. It is the only one of the seventeenth century, but thereafter they are more or less evenly spread out: eight in the eighteenth, seven in the nineteenth, and eleven in the twentieth, still the most interesting period to the majority of readers. One of my regrets is that it has proved impossible to include any battle of the English Civil War. Otherwise the list seems to me as representative as it could well have been. The majority of the greatest soldiers appear in it. We have Condé, Saxe, Marlborough, Eugène, Wolfe, Frederick, Washington, Napoleon, Wellington, Lee, Stonewall Jackson, Moltke, Joffre, Mustapha Kemal, Montgomery, Rommel, and Bradley. All the historians have themselves seen warfare, all but one in junior ranks, so that none of them are likely to suppose that generals win battles without stout troops prepared to sacrifice their lives, and that in some battles, e.g. Bunker Hill, the troops play a far larger part than the generals. Sometimes, too, the general who gets the praise is not the one who contributes most to the victory. A good example of this is Tannenberg in 1914, when Hermann von François anticipated the planning of the Hindenburg–Ludendorff combination and increased the force of a devastating

RIGHT *Sieges played a great part in seventeenth- and eighteenth-century warfare: William of Orange (William III of England) recaptured the great fortress of Namur from the French 5 September 1695*

victory by repeated disregard of their orders.

It is often said that strategy is unchangeable, and the statement contains a considerable element of truth. A vital ingredient of the strategy of the seventeenth and eighteenth centuries was the network of fortresses holding stores for the armies. Thus sieges were considered as important as battles in the field and were far more numerous, even in the record of commanders most determined to fight in the open. The position and renown of fortresses owed much to the state of the roads, which were quagmires in bad weather. Thus the opposing armies of both sides invariably went into winter quarters, though the greatest soldiers, such as Condé, might wait till the enemy had done so and then emerge from their own to bring off a coup. Fortresses remained important in the opening phases of the First World War and so were improvised ones such as Stalingrad in the Second. It was Napoleon above all who lowered their status, and this not only through his genius but owing to the change in conditions. Foremost stood the improvement of roads. Secondly, there was the consequent lightening and increase in the mobility of artillery. Third stands the more thorough organization of requisitioning.

The strategy of the Thirty Years War, initiated by Gustavus Adolphus and in lesser degree by Wallenstein, carried on in the latter stages by Condé, Turenne, and Mercy, was as sweeping as any up to the time of the First World War. Napoleon apart, there was little change in the nature of marches, but immense change in the speed of movement of rearward echelons. Railways hastened mobilization, provided armies with unlimited ammunition, stores, and supplies, and carried them to the front or switched them to other theatres of war, with the result that armies became bigger than ever. In succession the telegraph, the field telephone, and wireless improved control. Moltke had the first, but in issuing orders to troops in contact with the enemy had to rely on the mounted officer.

Tactics are another matter and are constantly changing. In the Thirty Years War cavalry was still the decisive arm. It was not only the arm of opportunity but it could also hope to break unshaken infantry. Up to the day of Gustavus, armies had been drawn up with the infantry in the centre and the more numerous cavalry on the wings. He intermingled cavalry with the central block and others, the Spaniards especially, placed musketeers with the cavalry on the wings. The pike had begun to decline well before the period at which we start. It was superseded by a bayonet thrust into the muzzle of the musket. Only when the ring-bayonet was invented, so that fire could continue after it had been fixed, did the mastery of the battlefield switch to the infantry. When steady infantry was given time to form square it had henceforth little fear of being broken by cavalry.

Great tactician as was Marlborough – as well as one of the supreme strategists – an even more interesting tactical innovator was Frederick the Great. His first asset was his *coup d'œil*, his ability to size up the battlefield at a glance and act instantly. The Prussian Army was a highly drilled machine, terrible in attack, rock-like in defence. Its stiffness seldom or never appeared a serious handicap while it remained in Frederick's hands, though after his death it declined into pure stagnation. The consequences were seen when it encountered Napoleon and Davout at Jena and Auerstedt.

One of Frederick's virtues was, strange though it may

General Bonaparte's extraordinary speed was sometimes achieved with the aid of another, less happy innovation – violation of neutrality, as when he crossed the Po at Piacenza in May 1796

An immense gain to speed of mobilization and ease of supply, railways also helped to increase the size of armies, as these German soldiers on their way to the front in 1914 witness

seem to the uninitiated, his moderation. He never forgot, even after great victories, the weaknesses of Prussia, hemmed in between Russia, the Empire, and France, his western flank sometimes precariously covered by British and Hanoverian allies. Not all great soldiers maintain a sense of proportion equal to his while drinking the heady wine of victory. He emerged from the war with what was within his grasp and then sat back while it dragged on for another three years. This aspect, and not alone his skill on the battlefield, entitles him to be remembered as 'the Great'.

Wellington's outstanding contribution to the art of war lay in his liking for what is called strategic offensive with tactical defensive, that is, a swift and often deep advance into hostile territory followed by a defensive battle. It was born of his general inferiority of numbers on the battlefield and perpetual inferiority in the theatre of war during the Peninsular campaigns. He fought on the sort of position which has come to be known as 'Wellingtonian', drawing up his army in two lines behind the crest of gently-sloping ground. After they had driven in his skirmishers, what the French saw was, in the words of the young Bugeaud, the main body which, 'silent and impressive, with ported arms, loomed like a long red wall'. Often enough a single terrific volley decided the issue.

In the First World War both sides started in all the main theatres with equal reliance on the offensive, and the chief reason why it appears that the French were the most addicted to it is that they were defeated in the early collisions. After the Marne, the Aisne, and the so-called race to the sea, the defensive triumphed until March 1918. It was broken partly by the collapse of Russia, which enabled Germany to obtain a great numerical superiority; partly by German tactical skill; in the later stages by the tank, British perseverance, the considerable degree of recovery made by the French since their forces had been rotted by the failure of the Nivelle offensive of 1917; and, finally, the arrival of American troops. Yet, though trenches were dug in all theatres, this was the only one in which stagnation occurred. In all the others vast distances were covered in offensives: witness the Breakthrough of Gorlice in 1915 and its exploitation, in which well over three hundred miles were covered by the Austrians and Germans, and Caporetto in 1917, when Austrians and Germans advanced fifty miles in little over a fortnight and captured 275,000 prisoners and 2,500 guns, far more prisoners than Haig in his final offensive, and in fact more than Haig and Pétain combined.

The Second World War was marked by the triumph of the offensive, though there were brief periods of deadlock. The change was brought about by the improvement in the hitting power and endurance of the tank and by the advance in the speed and range of mechanical transport. To a far greater extent than in the First World War the mobility and fighting power of armies depended on wealth, though even in that war little belligerents were separated from great by a gap wider than any hitherto. In the Second World War the first Russian blow at Stalingrad proved decisive because the armament of the Rumanians was wretched. There was in more important respects a vast contrast between the hostile coalitions: the United States and in lesser degree the United Kingdom were able not only to bridge the interval between the German assault on Russia and the building up of her vast industrial production but to re-equip French forces in Africa and those of a potential ally such as Turkey. Ger-

British infantry (the 28th Regiment at Quatre Bras) demonstrate the ability of a steady square to resist cavalry attack; with their improved weapons, infantry were now (1815) in the ascendant

The 'triumph' of the defensive, trench warfare in the First World War: the desolate scene presented by a British front line trench at Ovillers in July 1916 during the Battle of the Somme

LEFT *Since the early sixteenth century Spanish engineers had been renowned for their expertise in bridge-building: here Philip V and the Duke of Medina Sidonia prepare to cross a pontoon bridge over the Tagus in May 1704.* RIGHT *In the Second World War the British Bailey bridge was a valuable invention: a huge span across the river Santerno in Italy nears completion in October 1944*

many could do nothing of the kind for her allies and was, as in the First World War, prevented by British sea power from trading over the seas, particularly with the United States before she became a belligerent. In the earlier war a single German submarine had filled up with rubber at New York and brought it home. Not even this much was accomplished in the later war. It is pointless to speculate at what stage President Roosevelt would have closed down trade with Germany, but impossible to believe he would have done so from the start. A highly equipped nation, Japan, was utterly defeated by the United States, which was fighting her with one hand, because the latter's production of ships, aircraft, arms, and equipment was so immensely superior.

The development of missile weapons between the seventeenth and the mid-twentieth centuries was prodigious, but if the gunner made very much greater progress than the engineer it was because the latter's skill stood so high to start with. Seventeenth-century engineers in some recorded cases used metal pontoons for bridging and worked with amazing speed. At that time the Spaniards were the cleverest in Europe. As early as the first years of the sixteenth century, the engineers of 'the Grand Captain', Gonzalo de Cordoba, had beams and planks so skilfully measured that after being borne by pack train to the bank of the Garigliano in darkness a whole series of pontoons was assembled from them and three thousand men were able to cross before dawn, to lead the army to a glorious victory.

It is hardly too much to say that little further progress was made until the First World War, though one of the greatest British engineers, General Sir James Pasley, who died in 1860, invented the demi-pontoon with square stern. Two of these, lashed stern to stern, performed the function of a single pontoon but were far easier to transport, each demi-pontoon weighing little more than half as much. However, this experiment, valuable at the time, did not survive. The parts of timber trestle bridges were assembled in advance in the American Civil War. The great achievement of the First World War was the British lock bridge. It was made about twice as long as the span of high-banked, narrow streams and canals, carried across very swiftly, and then reduced to the necessary length. Another British invention, the Bailey bridge of the Second World War, will still be fresh in what are becoming middle-aged memories.

The work of the engineers in the layout of fortifications was far more outstanding. Vauban set a new level, but it is sometimes forgotten that he and some of his contemporaries were as skilled in taking a fortress as in constructing one. As previously mentioned, Napoleon inaugurated a phase in which their importance sank to a much lower level, but it was revived later in the nineteenth century. Here the great figure is the Belgian Brialmont. He did not invent the cupola which raised a gun for each shot, but he elaborated it. The centre, generally a city, was surrounded by a ring of forts to keep the hostile batteries out of range. As artillery increased in power

LEFT *Eighteenth-century artillery, heavy and unwieldy, short-ranged, slow-firing (Swedish guns – Gadebusch, 1710).* CENTRE *Heaviness and unwieldiness in the First World War, combined with long range and hideous devastating power (15-inch howitzer – Ypres, 1917).* RIGHT *The artillery complement to the tank, the self-propelled gun, in the Second World War (Priest guns – Brigassard, France, July 1944)*

this function steadily declined, yet in the First World War the defence of Namur, Antwerp, and Przemysl made them household words. In the Second the Maginot Line fulfilled its functions till it had been uncovered by the disaster sustained by the field armies; otherwise only improvised fortresses such as Stalingrad can be considered worthy of mention.

The progress of artillery has been, first, in mobility; secondly, in the construction of guns; thirdly in the development of shell; fourthly, in rifling and breech-loading; fifthly, in the invention of the rocket battery of the Second World War, though one cannot yet assess the future of this last. While the thirteenth-century monk Roger Bacon may be considered the father of the arm, the second half of the nineteenth century and the first half of the twentieth is the period in which its strides have been most rapid. After Napoleon one may say that the most skilful artilleryman was a relatively junior officer, Prince Krafft zu Hohenlohe-Ingelfingen, commander of the artillery of the Guard Corps. He had distinguished himself in the Seven Weeks' War against Austria in 1866, but his great merit is to be found in the fact that, particularly where his own command was concerned, he corrected all the errors made on that occasion in the Franco-Prussian War of 1870. For example, whereas in Bohemia all the corps artillery had marched at the tail of the columns, so that the Prussians began the action of Nachod with twelve guns against thirty-two and incurred grave risks at Königgrätz because their artillery came

into action so late, at Saint-Privat Prince Krafft actually led the artillery of the Guard foremost into the battle.

I venture to quote my own description of the French counter-attack and its fate:

> Prince Krafft stayed with his best battery commander and gave ranges to all batteries from his trial shots. He first opened fire with thirty guns at 1900 paces. The enemy was enveloped in smoke, but the red trousers came through it. At once he stopped fire. He now fired a trial shot at 1700 paces and re-engaged the French when they reached that line. He did the same thing at 1500, 1300, 1100, and 900 paces. The French displayed great bravery, but at 900 they could stand it no longer. They broke and fled. After the war he met the ADC of General Ladmirault, who had ordered the counter-attack, and the former said to him: 'It was impossible to succeed. You have no notion what it is to advance under the fire of your artillery'.

In the First World War we meet the giant howitzers designed to put the most powerful forts out of action, the French long 155-mm guns which harried and often destroyed them at Verdun, and the streamline shells which increased ranges in the later stages. In the Second infantry divisions were furnished with artillery more powerful than any hitherto conceived. The self-propelled gun, so difficult to knock out that it could be handled with extreme boldness, was even more novel. Again ranges and hitting-power increased. Yet, when the great rolling barrages of 1917 onwards were repeated, the number of pieces used was smaller and the weight of the bombardment less.

Hitherto we have considered cavalry, infantry, and

13

One of the forerunners of perhaps the most powerful weapon (apart from the atomic bomb) which has been put in the hands of the generals in this century: an RE8 biplane ready to take off on a night flight at Savy, October 1917

artillery, old arms using weapons and equipment which to outward view appear to change only gradually through the centuries. The first of the new arms, the aircraft, was truly revolutionary, more so, indeed, than gunpowder because the bow continued alongside the musket well into the reign of Queen Elizabeth I. The early aircraft, slow and vulnerable as they were, soon made their presence felt, but as adjuncts to the forces of land and sea. The stages of their progress were observation pure and simple, photography, ranging of artillery, bombing, and mass attacks from low altitudes. The most important in-

vention came early, towards the end of 1915: it was the synchronizing gear which enabled the machine-gun to fire between the propeller blades. The British took the first step forward in organization – one not imitated by the Americans for a generation – when they formed the Air Ministry. They also, less advisedly, amalgamated their naval and military services in the Royal Air Force. The French did not then go as far as an Air Ministry, but they made an interesting experiment in creating an 'Air Division', which put over six hundred planes into the Battle of Amiens-Montdidier.

In the Second World War the United States took over as pioneer after she had become a belligerent. Both in the solidity gained by substituting metal for wood and the protection of the crew by armour, and in speed, height, and endurance, the advance was startling. The bomber proved a terrific weapon of destruction, even though the claims made for its effects on German industry were later found to be greatly exaggerated. Parachute forces, of which Russia was the progenitor, were exploited to great effect, but the number of occasions on which they were used proved astonishingly few. The transport of troops and supplies by air exercised a great influence on strategy.

The best example comes from Burma. During the Japanese invasion of Assam a British division was moved from Arakan, and in the later advance several columns were supplied on routes where there were virtually no roadways and they were able to seal a pass behind them so that they had little need to fear Japanese threats to their rear.

The tank first employed on the Somme in 1916 was primitive by comparison with that of 1918, slower, and threatened by the armour-piercing bullet speedily introduced by the Germans. At the end of 1917 the tank first fully proved its mettle at Cambrai, but its defensive role was small in the German offensives of 1918 because sufficient numbers could rarely be assembled in time or refilled with shell when they were. Thenceforth British, French, and Germans alike realized that it was a war-winner. The Germans, caught by surprise, produced the clumsiest of tanks and any successes they gained in armoured warfare were achieved with those captured from the British. Very few men relatively were killed by the fire of tanks; they were above all moral weapons and continued in the later war to be so predominantly, though their destructive power against troops and fortifications alike increased enormously. The increase in numbers even in the early stage was notable: Rawlinson employed 36 on the first occasion on which they were used, Allenby 48 on the first day at Arras, Rawlinson in the Battle of Amiens 324 heavy and 96 light, not counting reserves or older types converted to supply vehicles. As regards these last the British record was to be a sorry one. They were never seriously exploited in the Second World War, though the pioneers in armoured warfare had never ceased to advocate their reintroduction.

Here the fiercest struggle was the old one of gun against armour, which means in practice to increase the protection afforded by armour while decreasing speed to the minimum. British tank policy was so vague that it is hardly possible to be sure if one existed. We were saved by the Americans and did not ourselves produce a first-class tank till the war was nearing its end. The Germans opted for weight after their outstanding victories had

New weapons but, 250 years on, Namur in December 1944 is still of great strategic importance: a Sherman tank of the Coldstream Group of the Guards Armoured Division guards the Meuse crossing

been gained with medium or even light tanks. In 1942 they produced a 56-tonner (Tiger I) with maximum armour of 100 mm, and in 1944 a 68·7-tonner with 185 mm. The 1943 Panther was regarded as a medium tank for the Panzer divisions, but weighed 44·8 tons with 110-mm armour. The Tigers carried an 88-mm gun, adapted from the anti-tank version, which had been equally deadly in an anti-aircraft role. These heavy tanks were magnificent in defence, but their weight and size prevented them from using the smaller bridges and thus handicapped them on the offensive. The biggest tank of all was the Russian Stalin, mounting a 122-mm gun. Hitler, ever a megalomaniac, made his designers produce the 'mock-up' of a far greater giant, the Mouse, but it never got beyond that stage.

I have been fortunate in that I have found excellent contributors and that there were only three outstanding writers who had to refuse the task owing to pressure of other work. I should have liked to include more Americans but, though my knowledge of the very fine work now being done in the United States in the field of military history is fairly extensive – two of the best being friends of old standing – it is naturally not as much so as in this country. One great success was in securing the aid of Mr Bruce Catton, who must rank as the foremost historian of the American Civil War and wears, if anyone can be said to do so, the mantle of the late Douglas Southall Freeman. Mine has been a somewhat arduous task, but I have seldom undertaken one more fascinating.

CYRIL FALLS

1643
Rocroi

A brilliant victory gained by the young Duc d'Enghien – the future Great Condé –
which destroyed the legend of the 'invincible Spanish infantry'

'BORN A CAPTAIN' LIKE Caesar and Spinola, as the Cardinal de Retz remarked, the Duc d'Enghien, destined for immortality as Prince de Condé, was twenty-one when he fought the battle of Rocroi and had never held the smallest command. He had been chosen mainly because he was a Prince of the Blood and the King's cousin, but this is not the whole story. Watching his education, planned and carried through by his disreputable but enlightened and affectionate father, Richelieu had marked him as a coming man who would advance his interests. He had forced the lad to marry his niece, Claire-Clémence de Brézé, and thereby condemned him to misery, since she was stunted in mind and body and was eventually to become a mad-woman. Mazarin, on coming to power at his master's death, had been equally convinced that Enghien was a latent genius.

In this last phase of the Thirty Years War the situation had suddenly been reversed in favour of the Empire and Spain. If France had a latent genius of the first order, Spain put into the field an assured genius of the second. At the first of the famous Battles of Nördlingen the Cardinal Infante and his Austrian allies overthrew the Swedes before he marched his picked army into the

Netherlands. In 1635 he took Corbie and would certainly have taken Paris had he not been let down by the Imperialist leader Gallas, who should have invaded France simultaneously through Franche-Comté. Two years before Enghien took the field in 1643 Don Fernando died at the siege of Aire, to be succeeded by a Portuguese nobleman faithful to Spain, Don Francisco de Melo, who in 1642 had utterly defeated the French at Honnecourt. They had suffered previous reverses at Thionville in 1640 and La Marfée in 1641. He was not of the same calibre, but the core of the army, six Spanish tercios, was as formidable as ever. It was the tenth legion which encouraged the Flemish, Walloon, Italian, and mercenary contingents. The trouble was that, since the defeat of the Armada, it had become virtually impossible to reinforce the army by sea, so that time after time normal wastage reduced it to a mere shell. By land reinforcements had to move by a devious route through Italy, where Italian troops from Spain's possessions were recruited, over the Alps, and through territories outside the French frontier either in Spanish hands, in those of allies, or of friendly neutrals. In the day of Alva and later in that of the Cardinal Infante, when it had sunk almost to nothing, new armies had been formed for the purpose, without which the leadership of these commanders would have been of no avail. These soldiers were often ready to mutiny but always ready to die. The cavalry, especially the Netherlanders, was of high quality and well mounted. There were generally a few Spanish officers in its ranks,

17

ROCROY.

An engraving of the battle closely resembling Sauveur Le Conte's painting, but marking the positions of the camps of the Spanish troops and identifying the generals; Enghien is near the centre of the battlefield, while the Comte de Gassion appears to be in two places at once. BELOW *An illustration from de Gheyn's* Différents exercises de l'homme de cheval du dix-septième siècle, *published in 1640*

but its commanders were most often natives. The discipline of the whole was superior to that of the French. Richelieu had relied almost entirely on mercenaries, and though there was now something which could possibly be called a French Army, it was not until Louvois had reorganized it that it really merited the title, while still embodying mercenaries.

On the eve of the encounter Louis XIII died, having woken shortly before to find Enghien's father at his bedside and having said to him: 'Monsieur de Condé, I dreamt your son had won a great victory'. Enghien hid the news till the last possible moment and flatly refused to obey Condé's order to return to Paris and help him secure the future of their house under the rule of Anne of Austria, Regent for the child Louis XIV. As was the custom, he had been given a mentor, François de l'Hôpital, a cautious veteran whose advice he entirely disregarded and who was to prove an incubus rather than an aid. The one man who had his ear was the brilliant Comte de Gassion.

On 12 May Melo was joined outside the walls of Rocroi, held by a small French garrison, by his best cavalry, led by his best cavalryman, the Flemish Comte d'Isembourg. The little fortress was clearly at his mercy, and the question before Enghien's council of war was whether to withdraw the defenders under cover of a small mobile force or bring on a battle. To attack the Spaniards involved entry into a veritable rat-trap, a plateau four miles wide, surrounded by thickets passable only by a narrow defile, marshy and rocky. In the early hours of 17 May Gassion returned after three days spent in reconnaissance, having on his own initiative managed to put a reinforcement into the town, and brought in a luminous report of what he had seen. The debate that followed was sharp but short: l'Hôpital advised that Rocroi should be relieved but a major battle avoided; Gassion was all for fighting; Enghien summed up by saying that Rocroi was a secondary matter and that it was a question of saving France and the child King's throne, forbade further discussion, and closed the council.

Rocroi was fought on 18 May, but there was at least heavy skirmishing on 17 May. The heads of the French columns under Gassion reached the fringe of the plateau at about 8 am., found the approaches unguarded, and met within the woods only outposts which they scattered to the winds. On word from him Enghien moved to his support at the head of two thousand cavalry. Suddenly he caught sight of the whole hostile array in the open space between the surrounding forests, drawn up like his own in the conventional right, centre, and left, but on a slightly narrower front and with musketeers filling the gaps between cavalry squadrons, so that it looked like a single block. The centre was formed mainly of the grim,

The Cardinal Infante Don Fernando of Austria, Melo's predecessor as commander of the Spanish army, who died at the siege of Aire in 1641 (painted by Velázquez)

brown-skinned 'natural Spaniards' under the famous Franche-Comtois veteran Fontaine, often erroneously described as Fuentes in the belief that he was a Spaniard. The French had a slight superiority in strength, 23,000, of which from six to seven thousand were cavalry, while the Spaniards numbered at most 20,000. Galled by their artillery fire, which had come into action first and was heavier than his own, Enghien decided to turn their left. Before he moved he took a quick glance at his own, to see a sight that aroused his anxiety and anger. L'Hôpital, apparently eager to avoid a battle by bringing on an inconclusive skirmish, had moved La Ferté's columns forward. Isembourg had awaited some such opportunity; before Enghien's message could halt La Ferté's advance

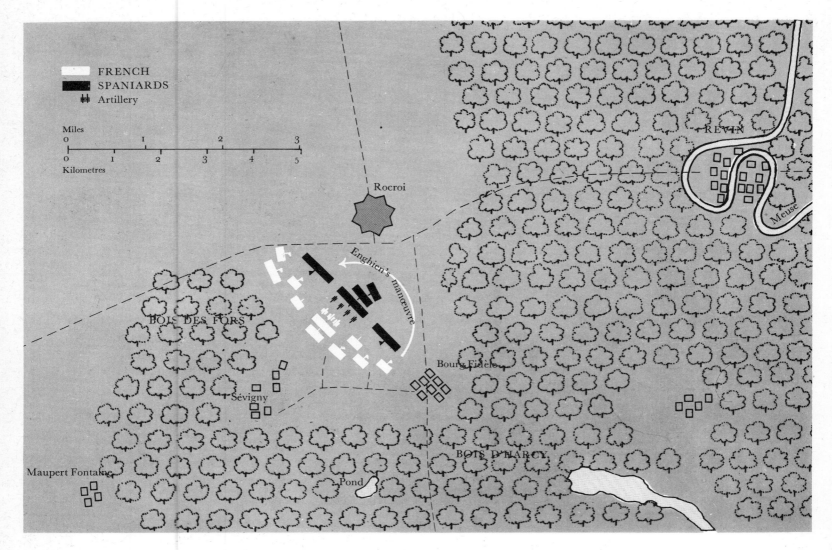

the Flemish cavalry thundered forward. For a few brief moments Enghien's anxiety persisted because in their flight the French skirmishers had thrown their own leading line into grave disorder. Then Isembourg pulled up. His orders from Melo had been to postpone battle. Had the latter been an Enghien, he would have galloped to the scene, driven the charge home, and perhaps laid the foundations of victory.

Late that night Enghien wrapped himself in his cloak, lay down where he stood, and at once fell asleep. He cannot have known that ability to do so was to be a gift that would never forsake him, however heavy the problems facing him, even when he stood on the brink of disaster. He was awakened to speak to a French deserter from the Spanish side. After the man had been granted mercy he remained on his knees to give a very valuable report: Melo was expecting a strong reinforcement, including the sixth Spanish tercio, under command of the German leader Beck.

Sleep was confined to less than three hours. Enghien, called in the darkness, donned a cuirass and a hat with immense white plumes such as had been made famous by Henry IV at Ivry, and for the same purpose, that he

The rat-trap into which Enghien led his army on 17 and 18 May 1643 and where, by brilliant generalship, he won a decisive victory

RIGHT *In Heim's painting of the battle, the Duc d'Enghien halts the slaughter of the Spaniards after their surrender; the French cavalrymen had mistaken a Spanish movement for a renewal of resistance*

OVERLEAF *Enghien and his staff survey the battlefield, a four-mile wide plateau, surrounded by thickets, marshy ground and a small lake (painted by Sauveur Le Conte)*

might be easily recognized. The French advance began at 3 am., and very soon afterwards there was just sufficient light for it to see its way and dress its ranks. Gassion led the way with seven squadrons, Enghien with eight echelonned to his left rear. The Spaniards had prepared an ambuscade of musketeers in the woodlands, but the French had learnt of their presence and surprised them, since they were keeping a very bad watch. They were entirely destroyed, every man being killed or captured.

In their rear the cavalry of the Duc d'Albuquerque.

LEFT ABOVE *Rocroi, which secured the child King of France, Louis XIV's throne, was an even heavier blow to Philip IV of Spain (here painted by Velázquez) than the defeat of the Spanish Armada to his grandfather, Philip II*

FAR LEFT *Enghien issues orders to his officers while, in the thick of the battle, the crippled, veteran Comte de Fontaine, fallen from his chair, lies mortally wounded (painted by Le Paon)*

LEFT *A Musketeer preparing to fire, from de Gheyn's* Maniement d'armes *(1618): the bandolier holds wooden tubes, each containing powder and ball for one shot, and the forked stick supports the weight of the barrel*

ABOVE *A seventeenth-century engraving showing Enghien's conspicuous white plumes, and including the German general Beck who did not, in fact, arrive with his reinforcements for Melo until the morning after the battle*

commanding on this wing, was more alert, but his first line was caught in flank and the single squadron which wheeled to take the shock was scattered to the winds, disappearing with Enghien's wild and ferocious Croats on its heels. Albuquerque, a competent soldier, rallied the second line, but it must have been shaken by what it had seen, for it was almost immediately driven back in confusion and with heavy loss. The battlefield was witnessing on the French side a speed in action hardly paralleled in the Thirty Years War even by Gustavus Adolphus himself.

Enghien had now to consider how the success was to be exploited in the centre and on the left, and rode on to higher ground to see what the effects of the bombardment and counter-bombardment had been. At first all was hidden by dense clouds of smoke from the artillery and musketeers on both sides; then came a brief clearance of the air. In these few seconds he saw an appalling sight. La Ferté was repeating himself. In later campaigns

25

The opposing armies drawn up at the beginning of the battle in strict order according to the rules of seventeenth-century war

A German view of the battle: Fontaine lies dying in the foreground, and La Ferté, unhorsed, is about to be taken prisoner, near the centre

Enghien was often to be savage in reproof, but yesterday he had spoken mildly, which probably explains why the culprit was now advancing in a dangerous diversion to avoid marshy ground and a little lake. This time he paid the full penalty. Instead of returning to his former station, Isembourg had spent the night close up behind the trenches, so that he had a shorter way to go and could jump straight into a gallop. He smashed the French horse, cut it off from the infantry in the centre, and drove it back in disorder. La Ferté was thrice wounded and taken. As so often happened in battles of those days, some of Isembourg's force rode to loot the baggage, but discipline had kept the majority in their ranks as he swerved left-handed, overwhelming the cavalry and musketeers and capturing the artillery. L'Hôpital won back a few guns but lost them again, so that there were thirty pieces

The Spanish commander, Don Francisco de Melo, fleeing before the victorious Enghien

Enghien's horse leaps over the bodies of Visconti and Velandia, the commanders of the two Italian tercios broken by the French cavalry

The Duc d'Enghien presents his victories at Rocroi and Thionville to the young King Louis XIV, in the presence of his father, the Prince de Condé, and the Regent, Anne of Austria

Standards and other trophies captured by the French at Rocroi borne by the Swiss in triumph into Notre-Dame

to bombard the French centre and it had none to hit back with.

Again Enghien acted without hesitation. He bade Gassion remain where he was in case Albuquerque's cavalry rallied. Then he wheeled his cavalry leftward and led it at top pace close behind the enemy's centre, charged the Spanish right, and routed it. Melo too had hurried to the scene, but, blinded by smoke, nearly rode into the French cavalry. He took refuge in the right tercio, an Italian, of the centre, crying out: 'Gentlemen, I seek death amid the Italians!' 'We are all ready to die for our King', replied the gallant Visconti – who died shortly afterwards. All the Italian infantry fought magnificently. When Visconti's tercio broke up, Velandia's moved on to the third to maintain the struggle back to back. It could not last. Velandia also gave his life, and both tercios were likewise broken.

Enghien's men and horses were now exhausted. Would he have time to defeat the five Spanish tercios before Beck arrived? Could he indeed defeat them at all? He drew out the less wearied battalions for support, but it was the cavalry that must do the main job. At this moment Fontaine, a cripple and recognizable by his long white beard, was hoisted on to the shoulders of two soldiers to survey the French. That done, he was lifted on to a chair in front, and raised his cane as a signal for fire. Guns and muskets crashed out together. Enghien's charge was a disastrous failure, as was the second, with very heavy loss. He himself was bruised by a bullet which dented his cuirass and came back on a dying horse. This time he could give men and horses a breather while his guns carried out a final bombardment. He had the best stable in Europe, and it may be supposed he chose a good horse now.

He met a welcome surprise as his third charge began. Not a Spanish gun opened fire, and he was to find out afterwards that the last cannon ball had been expended. His quick eye also saw several gaps in the hostile phalanx made by his own artillery preparation. As the horsemen broke in, these widened and, though the Spaniards fought on gallantly, their situation was impossible, since the French infantry had now had time to close up. On hearing shouts of surrender the French officers signalled that fighting should stop and Enghien rode away. Suddenly a fresh din caused him to look back, and he saw that it had broken out again. The keyed-up French cavalrymen had mistaken some movement among the Spaniards for a renewal of resistance and had begun to kill. Enghien brought this horror to an end, but not soon enough to prevent a grievous rise in the death-roll, to say nothing of great danger to his own person. When he could at last dismount many Spaniards encircled him and blessed him on their knees. The incident was never forgotten. Whether he served with them as a rebel against his King or fought them, Spanish troops always regarded him with admiration, indeed something like affection.

He had much to do before he could make up for lost sleep: his despatch to be written; food and surgeons to be provided for the vanquished; Fontaine, dead in his chair, to be buried with full honours; a triumphal entry into Rocroi. Beck appeared next morning and naturally took himself off at once.

Rocroi was a decisive battle. Its effects were more important than those of Nördlingen, which it reversed. It swung back the ascendancy to France and her allies and made all her adversaries but Spain content to wind up the Thirty Years War on the best terms they could get. It destroyed the *tercios viejos* in the Netherlands. Here, it must be confessed, many excellent historians have gone astray in not making it clear that these troops were eventually replaced and that their successors often fought admirably, but it seems certain that they were never quite as formidable. Spain, in her tremendous efforts in Europe, North and South America, even Asia, was wearing herself out. France, by pressure on the route to the Netherlands already mentioned, by way of Savoy, Franche-Comté, and the 'Three Bishoprics' (Metz, Toul, and Verdun) was able to keep down the passage of reinforcements. At home recruiting was becoming more difficult. An unhappy war with Portugal wasted away resources to no useful end. A long revolt in Catalonia, nourished by the French, was a festering wound. It is just to say that Rocroi struck Spain an even heavier blow than the defeat of the Spanish Armada.

The victory was won by sheer generalship. The calculated risk of the passage behind the Spanish centre, which might have turned about and virtually destroyed Enghien's horse by fire, can rarely have been paralleled in war. The French might indeed have reversed Wellington's words on a famous occasion: 'If the Great Condé hadn't been there we'd have been beat'. Condé was a ready-made genius at an age when some other great captains are still on the square.

CYRIL FALLS

Illustrations from de Gheyn's Différents exercises de l'homme de cheval du dix-septième siècle, *published in 1640*

LA GLOIRE DES ARMEES CONFEDEREES, ILLUSTREE PAR UNE DESCRIPTION BLAZONNEE — commemorative engraving of the Battle of Blenheim (Bleinheim et Hochstad), 2 August 1704, dedicated to Prince George of Denmark.

1704
Blenheim

Marlborough and Eugène, by routing the Franco-Bavarians and capturing Tallard, shattered the reputation for invincibility enjoyed by French armies for sixty years

'FOR THIS CAMPAIGN I SEE so very ill a prospect that I am extremely out of heart', wrote John Churchill, first Duke of Marlborough, to his wife Sarah on 20 February 1704. His pessimism appeared all too justifiable, for the 'Grand Alliance' of England, the United Provinces, and Austria seemed on the verge of collapse as the forces of the 'Two Crowns' (France and Spain) prepared to converge on Vienna. The Imperial capital was already threatened by a Hungarian rising to the east, and only Baden's 35,000 and Styrum's 10,000 soldiers guarded the western approaches. While Villeroi pinned the Anglo-Dutch army in the Netherlands and Vendôme threatened an invasion from North Italy, Marshal Tallard was to join the forces of the Elector of Bavaria and Marsin for the final march down the Danube with a joint army of 71,000 men.

The crises of southern Europe seemed comfortingly remote to many English and Dutch statesmen, and only Marlborough and a few others realized the true implications of the Danube situation. At the age of fifty-four, the Duke was at the height of his powers, and his reputation as a statesman already stood high. He was also widely regarded as a competent soldier, who had seen service on land and sea and had been apprenticed to the great Turenne as a young officer. His record as Captain-General of the Anglo-Dutch forces during the first two years of the War of the Spanish Succession had been good if not outstanding – but the campaign of 1704 was to establish him as a great general. A daring march and one great battle were destined to reverse the fortunes of the war and inflict the first serious reverse for over fifty years on the proud armies and grandiose ambitions of Louis XIV.

All this was still hidden in April when Marlborough secretly revealed his plan to the Lord Treasurer, Godolphin: 'I think it absolutely necessary for the saving of the Empire to march with the troops under my command . . . in order to take measures with Prince Lewis of Baden for the speedy reduction of the Elector of Bavaria'. This bold step was beset by political and military problems which would have appeared insuperable to a lesser general. The cautious and dyke-minded Dutch would never sanction the weakening of the Netherlands' army; the long flank march down the front of two French field armies would afford Louis's generals ample opportunity to intercept Marlborough or at least cut his communications at any point between Coblenz and Philipsburg; the supply problem would be immense. These difficulties made it singularly improbable that Marlborough would reach the Danube in a fit state to force a major engagement. Nevertheless, 21,000 troops left Bedburg on 20 May.

In the event, a combination of strategic deception and brilliant administration enabled the Duke to achieve the apparently impossible. Fooling Dutch and French alike

31

by successive feints against the Moselle and Alsace, Marlborough retained the initiative throughout and successfully transferred his army – eventually 40,000 strong – over the rivers Main and Neckar to link with Baden's forces near Launsheim on 22 June. In just over five weeks the army had covered more than two hundred and fifty miles – and despite the gloomy prophecy of Captain Blackadder that 'this is like to be a campaign of great fatigue and trouble', the Captain-General and his small staff had overcome every administrative problem. New shoes were issued at Heidelberg; sufficient gold was carried to purchase local supplies and – most important of all – an alternative line of communication was opened down the River Main to Nuremberg, avoiding the French-dominated regions of the Rhine valley. Regular rests and careful march-discipline reduced wear and tear. 'Surely never was such a march carried on with more regularity', wrote Captain Parker, 'and with less fatigue to man and horse.'

Marlborough immediately turned to plans for destroying Bavaria before Tallard could transfer his main army to his assistance. The Allies settled their schemes at Gross Heppach on 13 June: the newly-arrived Prince Eugène was to relieve Baden at Stollhofen and shadow Tallard's imminent advance (10,000 reinforcements had already been passed to Ulm in May), whilst Marlborough and the Margrave set out with 80,000 men to seek the Elector. Good fortune, however, now deserted the Allies. In spite of the successful storming of the Schellenberg Heights on 2 July, the Bavarian strongholds of Ulm, Munich and Augsburg proved impregnable to a force lacking heavy cannon. Secure behind his fortifications whilst the Allies ravaged the countryside, the Elector refused either to fight or negotiate, well aware that Tallard had left the Rhine on 1 July and was advancing through the Black Forest, pushing Eugène before him.

The climax of the campaign was approaching: Tallard duly met the Elector near Augsburg on 5 August, and the Franco-Bavarian army, now 56,000 strong, threatened to isolate Marlborough from Eugène and to sever his communications north of the Danube. Marlborough's flexible genius was fortunately equal to the occasion. Detaching the crusty but cautious Baden to besiege Ingolstadt with 15,000 men, the Duke executed a series of brilliant marches to reunite his forces with Eugène at Donauworth on 11 August. The 'Two Princes' immediately agreed to flout the conventions of eighteenth-century warfare and to stake all on an attack against Tallard's army, snugly encamped ten miles to the west in the angle formed by the River Danube and its tributary, the Nebel. Next day the Allies moved to Münster, and before dawn on 13 August 52,000 men advanced on the unsuspecting Marshal Tallard.

To that officer's stupefaction, the lifting mists revealed nine immense columns bearing down on his position. Only an hour before – at 7 o'clock – Tallard had forwarded a despatch to Versailles reporting that the enemy was retreating towards Nördlingen; information cunningly planted by Allied 'deserters', and French over-reliance on the accepted military conventions had resulted in complete surprise. Fortunately for Tallard, Marlborough was unable to launch an attack until after midday as Eugène and the Allied right wing were delayed by difficult country. During this respite, Tallard deployed his army along a three-mile ridge overlooking the Nebel from a distance of eight hundred yards. His position was strong: both flanks were protected, the left by wooded hills, the right by the Danube. Along the ridge stood a line of defensible villages; to their front, the marshes of the Nebel presented a difficult obstacle. Planning to lure Marlborough to attack this sector, Tallard drew up his massed cavalry practically unsupported by infantry in the centre, intending to use Clérambault's and Blainville's battalions from Blenheim and Oberglau against the flanks of the marsh-bound Allies in support of the decisive, frontal cavalry charge of the concentrated French squadrons.

Marlborough did not disappoint Tallard in selecting this apparent death-trap for his main assault, but the Duke's eagle eye had not failed to notice several weaknesses in the French position. If the garrisons of Blenheim and Oberglau could be effectively contained within their positions, Tallard's centre would be dangerously exposed. Moreover the left of the enemy array (Marsin and the Elector) formed a virtually independent army, and it would be difficult for the French commander to ensure full co-operation between his two flanks. It would probably be wrong to credit Marlborough with a clear-cut plan of action before the battle opened, but doubtless he appreciated the opportunity offered by the weak French centre.

By 10 am. the Allied left and centre were in position, the former including the pick of the English battalions under the command of Lord Cutts, the latter drawn up

RIGHT *A ceremonial portrait of Marlborough painted for The Hudson's Bay Company by Sir Godfrey Kneller*

OVERLEAF LEFT *Prince Eugène of Savoy, Marlborough's staunch ally, painted by Johann Kupetsky*

OVERLEAF RIGHT *Two of three episodes depicted by Laguerre in one of his sketches for the murals at Marlborough House: (left) the French Foot in the centre cut in pieces and being abandoned by their cavalry; (right) Prince Eugène directing the attack against the enemy left wing*

in a unique formation, four lines deep, under General Charles Churchill, the Duke's brother. Shortly after midday, Eugène was at last in position and the battle could begin. In overall terms the French enjoyed a slight numerical advantage, 56,000 against 52,000, and a decided superiority in artillery, 90 cannon facing 60. The Allies possessed a slight superiority in cavalry, 160 squadrons against 140, but deployed only 65 infantry battalions to the Franco-Bavarian 79.

About 12.30 Lord Cutts launched the first attack against Blenheim; his leading brigade held its fire until it had advanced within sword distance of the palisades, but the French garrison repulsed the onslaught, killing the brigade commander, Rowe. A bold counter-attack by three squadrons of the élite Gendarmerie was beaten off by the next brigade and, after pausing to extend his front, Cutts ordered a second assault. This, too, was beaten back, but Clérambault was so impressed by the ferocity of these attacks that on his own authority he packed first seven, and then a further eleven, battalions of Tallard's reserve infantry into the already overcrowded village. The Commander-in-Chief meanwhile had been visiting Marsin, and was fully occupied watching the rout of eight squadrons of the Gendarmerie by five English cavalry units under Colonel Palmes. This reverse – though slight in itself – shook Tallard's faith in ultimate victory.

Blenheim safely masked, Marlborough was free to concentrate on Oberglau, where the Prince of Holstein-Beck's initial assault had been halted by Blainville's garrison, foremost amongst them the 'Wild Geese', or Irish units serving in the French pay. This check nearly turned into a rout when Tallard ordered up his first line of cavalry, but the exploitation of their initial success was mishandled, affording Marlborough enough time to lead up three Hanoverian battalions and several batteries to rally the line. Meantime the first and second formations of the Allied centre were steadily negotiating the marshes and forming up on the French side of the Nebel. Tallard had already missed his best opportunity of victory.

The crisis of the battle came at 2.15 pm. when Marsin launched a successful cavalry onslaught against the right flank of the deploying Allied centre. For a time the situation looked ugly, and Marlborough sent an urgent appeal to Prince Eugène for cavalry reinforcement. Despite his own preoccupations, Eugène at once responded to the request and detached Fugger's brigade of Imperial cuirassiers. These horsemen attacked the flank of Marsin's second cavalry charge and scattered it in confusion. Profiting from this success, Holstein-Beck's infantry again attacked the Oberglau garrison, and by 3 o'clock Blainville had been shut within the precincts of the village. Marlborough had surmounted the crisis, and the deploy-

A medal bearing a representation of Queen Anne on the obverse and Marlborough, the Captain-General of the Anglo-Dutch forces, on the reverse

LEFT ABOVE *Beyond Marlborough and his staff Laguerre shows the Allied forces moving into position, while the villages of Blenheim, Sonderheim, Oberglau and Lutzingen are visible on the three-mile ridge beyond the Nebel, where Tallard's army is deployed*

LEFT *Laguerre's sketch of the end of the battle: Marshal Tallard a prisoner and French trophies at the victor's feet; in the left background the French cavalry are making a vain attempt to swim the Danube – 3,000 were reputedly lost*

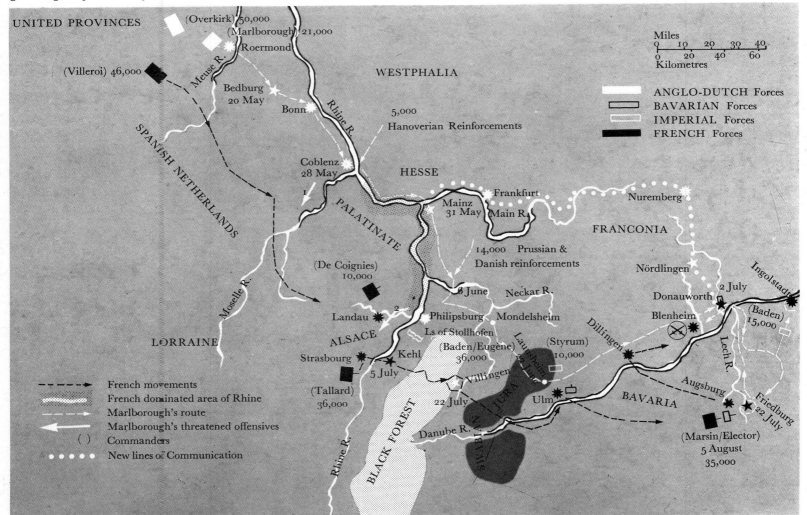

The pencilled note on the back of a tavern bill which Marlborough sent to his wife Sarah on the evening of the Battle of Blenheim, reporting the first news of his victory to the Queen. His letter is transcribed at the foot of page 41

Marlborough's daring march to the Danube, May–July 1704, during which he concealed his intentions from the French and the Dutch, while gathering reinforcements from his German allies, was the prelude to the Battle of Blenheim in August

ment of the centre continued with both its flanks secure.

An hour's lull followed whilst both sides made their final arrangements. By 4 o'clock the Allied centre was firmly in position well over the Nebel, cavalry in front closely supported by infantry battalions and field batteries brought well forward. An anxious Tallard saw fate about to bear down on his centre. He called for infantry reserves to strengthen his cavalry, but only nine battalions of raw recruits were available; Clérambault's earlier folly was now only too evident. Marsin and the Elector refused to send aid on the grounds that their wing was too hard pressed by Eugène, whose Danish and Prussian battalions were working round the Lutzingen flank. This unco-operative attitude contrasts strongly with Eugène's selflessness.

At 4.30 the Allied centre began a deliberate advance. In desperation Tallard ordered his remaining cavalry to charge, thereby earning a temporary respite, for the advance was checked. An hour later, however, the Allied attack again moved inexorably up the ridge, and 80

Marshal Tallard, the commander of the Franco-Bavarian forces, whose loose control and weak authority together with his army's over-confidence, contributed largely to the French defeat

RIGHT *Tallard's centre, deployed along a ridge overlooking the Nebel (above), was exposed to attack and routed (below), after Marlborough had contained the garrisons of Blenheim and Oberglau on Tallard's flanks*

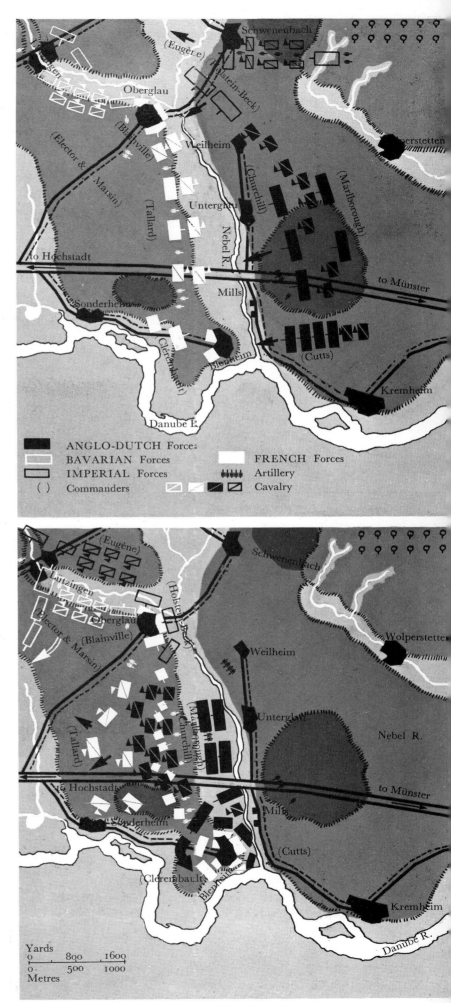

fresh squadrons rapidly routed the weary remnants of Tallard's 60, who vainly tried to stem the tide with pistol and carbine fire. The issue was soon decided: French squadrons broke and fled before the impact of cold steel, and the nine battalions gallantly died where they stood. Tallard's entire centre disintegrated in a flash.

It was almost the end of the battle; possibly 3,000 French horsemen were drowned trying to swim the Danube near Sonderheim, and Tallard himself was taken prisoner. Deprived of even formal leadership, French resistance rapidly deteriorated. On the left, Marsin and the Elector decided that the day was lost, and proceeded to extricate their forces, abandoning the Blenheim garri-son to its fate. By 6 o'clock, Charles Churchill had com-pletely cut off the 27 French battalions in the village, but these practically fresh troops might still have fought their way out had not Clérambault deserted his post unnoticed and perished in the Danube. Leaderless, the garrison hesitated until Major-General Lord Orkney bluffed M. de Blansac into surrendering. Even then the capitulation was not ratified by some units for a further hour, the Regiment of Navarre reputedly burning its colours to save them from falling into enemy hands.

By 9 pm. all was over. At a cost of 12,000 men, the Allies had inflicted 20,000 casualties and captured 14,000 prisoners and at least 60 cannon. The remainder of the

The Blenheim Tapestry (which hangs at Blenheim Palace, presented to Marlborough by the nation) depicts the surrender of Tallard. The Grenadier guardsman (left foreground) is holding the captured standard of the French Maison du Roi. The trophy of arms surrounding the tapestry, although largely symbolic (the jousting lances and armour are, of course, purely decorative), does include several items of considerable interest: the grenadier cap (top right), with stiffened front, long bag and a tassel behind, so shaped to give freedom for throwing the grenade, later evolved into the more familiar 'mitre cap'; a group of hautbois (left panel), a favoured instrument in the bands of Queen Anne's day; cavalry kettle drums and trumpets (top and bottom); holster and holster-cap (bottom panel, left centre and right) – the holsters were fixed at the front of the saddle (Marlborough is equipped with one) and were covered by a decorated cloth, known as the holster cap; the sutler's barrel (top right), representing what was the eighteenth-century equivalent of the modern NAAFI or PX

French and Bavarians retreated towards Hochstadt pursued by the English cavalry and Eugène's battle-worn Imperialists.

It had been a glorious victory. At one stroke, Marlborough had saved Vienna, reversed the tide of the war, and inflicted a grave blow on French military prestige. The battle represented a vindication of English and Dutch fighting techniques over those of France, but Marlborough also owed a great debt to the staunch fighting abilities of Prince Eugène and his Imperialists. In equipment and numbers there had been almost parity: the outcome rested on the tactical employment of flintlock and bayonet, cannon and sabre. The effect of well-controlled platoon fire outclassed the French battalion volleys, and Allied 'fire and movement' contrasted with the static role adopted by the French infantry – a relic of the days of pike and matchlock. Similarly, the English cavalry's use of shock action and cold steel proved far superior to the French preoccupation with their mounted arm as an instrument of sophisticated fire-power. Marlborough's careful siting of his batteries had compensated for their disparity in metal. But above all, the victory was due to Marlborough's ability as a battle commander. His cool grasp of the complete situation was made possible by carefully trained aides-de-camp, who served as his eyes in the more distant or powder-fogged sectors of the line. Marlborough's personal intervention at points of crisis, his firm retention of the initiative and superb control of a multi-national army contrasted strongly with the loose control and weak authority of Marshal Tallard. The French army, made over-confident by two generations of unquestioned success, weakened by a hidebound methodicism based on out-dated tactical conceptions, and betrayed by uninspired leadership, had started down the depressing slope of defeat that was to last for five more years.

Eventual fruits of victory included the fortresses of Ulm, Ingolstadt and Landau. But as night fell on the battlefield a weary Marlborough could only find time to pen a short note to Sarah on the back of a tavern bill, announcing the greatest victory won by English arms for generations: 'I have no time to say more but to beg you will give my duty to the Queen and let her know that her army has had a glorious victory. Monsieur Tallard and two other generals are in my coach and I am following the rest. The bearer, my Aide-de-camp, Colonel Parke, will give her an account of what has passed. I shall do it in a day or two by another more at large'. A new era in the military history of Europe had been inaugurated, and a new name had merited inclusion in the Halls of Fame.

DAVID CHANDLER

1709
Poltava

Peter the Great broke the military power of Sweden, achieving an immense political triumph, which announced the emergence of a new great power in the east

ON 19 AUGUST 1700 TSAR Peter the Great of Russia declared war on Sweden. His central aim was to establish Russian influence in the Baltic. On that same day he heard that one of his allies, Denmark, had already been defeated by the eighteen-year-old King of Sweden, Charles XII. Charles then transferred his troops over the Baltic to Livonia and fell on the Russian army, which had massed against Narva. In a snowstorm the young king led his army of 12,000 blue-coated Swedish soldiers to victory against 40,000 Russians (30 November 1700).

With prodigious energy the Tsar set about reorganizing the Russian military system. With the help of foreign officers his army practised the drill and tactics of contemporary Europe and with this army Peter began to win victories against the Swedes. In 1703, on the Baltic seaboard, near the mouth of the Neva, he was able to found a Russian port, which he called St Petersburg.

In January 1708 Charles marched eastwards, towards Moscow, at the head of 46,000 men. Before the tall and resolute young man and his veteran army the Russians fell back. Armed rebellion among the Don and Dnieper Cossacks diverted the Tsar's attention, and there was a risk that an old enemy, Turkey, would enter the war. Menshikov and his cavalry laid waste the countryside but, unlike the retreat of Tsar Alexander in 1812 before Napoleon, the strategy which Peter adopted had been

LEFT *Tsar Peter the Great of Russia, the victor of Poltava, which established Russia as the great Baltic power (painted by Kneller)*

carefully planned: he intended to use the vast wastes of eastern Poland to wear down the Swedes. However, in September that year King Charles reached the Russian border sixty miles from Smolensk.

At the small town of Tatarsk Charles decided to march south towards the Ukraine, for the Russians had felled an entire forest to block the Smolensk road. However, Mazeppa, the friendly Cossack Hetman of the Ukraine, offered him military support and munitions. With this ally, and the Polish army he expected to join him in Severia, Charles intended to march on Moscow.

Charles believed that Count Lewenhaupt, marching from the Baltic with 16,000 men to reinforce him, had come much further than in fact he had. On 9 October the Russians defeated Lewenhaupt in the battle of Lesnaya, which Peter later described as 'the mother of Poltava'. Lewenhaupt lost over 6,000 men, a supply train of 2,000 wagons, all his artillery, and 42 colours.

At last, Lewenhaupt and the remnants of his army found Charles near the border between Severia and the Ukraine. The taciturn King showed no surprise or anger when he heard Lewenhaupt's report. He divided the surviving infantry among his other regiments, but kept Lewenhaupt's six cavalry regiments intact. His army now numbered over 32,000 men. Menshikov's cavalry, however, arrived at Baturin, Mazeppa's capital, before the Swedes, and burnt it. The Swedish king had no option but to march still further southwards in the hope of finding food and gunpowder.

A tankard lid commemorating Charles XII's victory against the Russians at Narva on 30 November 1700

The winter of 1708–9 proved to be the severest in living memory. Minor actions and skirmishes in the bitter cold caused much suffering among the troops but, as a whole, the army survived the winter tolerably well. Peter, however, ordered a savage campaign against the Dnieper Cossacks, which effectively discouraged them from supporting the invaders. In April Peter's fleet sailed out on the Black Sea and persuaded the Sultan not only to stay out of the war himself, but also to order the Crimean Tartars to give no assistance to the Swedish army.

In the late spring Charles laid siege to the small town of Poltava. He desperately needed the supplies which he believed were stored in the town. While the Swedish engineers dug their elaborate parallels, Field-Marshal Scheremetyev and the Russian field army arrived on the east side of the river.

On 17 June, his twenty-seventh birthday, the Swedish king was riding along the river bank on a reconnaissance, when a Cossack on the other bank fired at him. The musket ball smashed through the King's foot from heel to toe. After some hasty surgery the King lapsed into a coma. Field-Marshal Rehnsköld, took command. Meanwhile, the Tsar decided to relieve Poltava at once. On 19 June he crossed the river north of the town, with 40,000 soldiers and erected a fortified earth-work camp. Five days later, he transferred his army to a second and larger camp nearer to Poltava.

On 27 June Charles announced to Rehnsköld that he would give battle next day. His plan was to outflank Peter's second camp and interpose his army between it and the bridges over the Vorskla. Charles trusted that this move would provoke a battle. South of Peter's position a tributary of the Vorskla divided itself among woods and ravines. East of the camp a thick wood, interspersed with marshes, rendered the ground difficult. Peter linked these two natural obstacles with a line of six diamond-shaped redoubts, and four more were built at an angle from them. On 27 June, however, only two of this second line had been completed. Behind these fortifications Peter placed Menshikov with a strong force of dragoons. Rehnsköld ordered the available Swedish troops to be drawn up in four infantry and six cavalry columns. While some battalions engaged the redoubts the bulk of the infantry would march through them at dawn, disperse the Russian cavalry and continue northwards. Out of the 28,000 Swedish soldiers available, Charles left 1,000 in the trenches opposite Poltava and 2,000 in the fieldworks near the river, to guard his flank. Mazeppa's 2,000 Cossacks and 1,500 Swedes guarded the baggage train and artillery.

At 3 am. the Swedish army set out from their assembly area west of Poltava. In his striking force King Charles had 18 infantry regiments, each composed of two weak battalions of 350 men, and 40 squadrons of cavalry and dragoons of 150 men each. The four centre columns, each

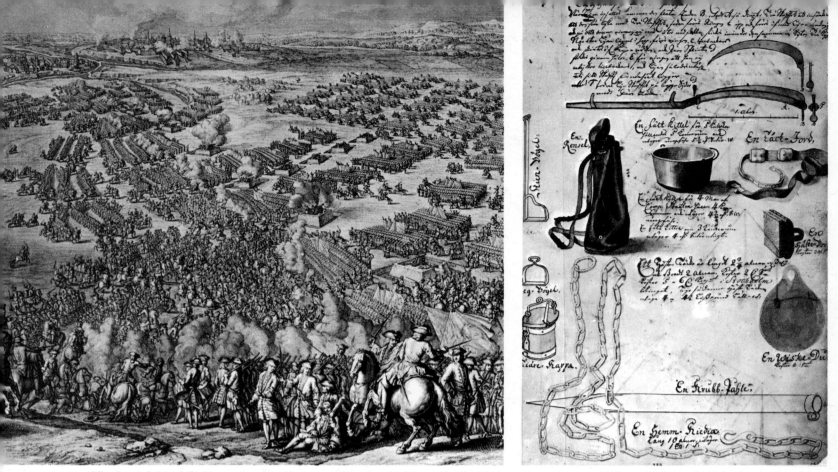

ABOVE *The battlefield of Poltava, showing the strong Russian position: the fortified earth-work camp (left), and (centre) their forward position, a line of six diamond-shaped redoubts, with four more at an angle to them (after the painting by Martin le Jeune).* ABOVE RIGHT *Various items of Swedish equipment of c 1700, including a scythe, boiling-pot (centre) and knapsack*

of six squadrons, were flanked on both sides by two corps of eight squadrons. Sparre and Stackelberg led infantry brigades of five regiments on the left, while Roos and Posse on the right each had four. General Lewenhaupt held command over all the infantry.

As the army groped forward through the dark, Field-Marshal Rehnsköld rode ahead to look at the redoubts. As he came near he could hear the sound of picks and shovels from the nearest redoubts: the Russians had begun their day's work. When he turned to leave, a sentry saw him and fired a pistol. At once drums beat and men rushed to arms inside the redoubts.

Roos led his battalions against the first unfinished redoubt and carried it with the bayonet. As the sun rose, heavy artillery fire swept his ranks. Meanwhile, General Stackelberg captured the second redoubt and returned to his column. Colonel Siegroth, with his Dalecarlian regiment, and Roos then attacked the third redoubt, which had already been fired on by two of Sparre's battalions from the left. The Russians held this successfully. When the smoke cleared, Roos found that the Swedish army had disappeared, taking with it the 3rd and 4th Guards battalions which had been under his command. Siegroth, who apparently had been appointed staff colonel for the day, and who might have been able to explain to him the King's plan, lay on the ground 'with little life in him'. Roos himself had no idea what he should do, and continued to lead his six remaining

battalions in charges against the stubborn defenders of the redoubt.

General Lewenhaupt denied after the battle any knowledge of the King's plan. Field-Marshal Rehnsköld, who disliked him intensely, may not have passed on the plan. Therefore, once through the second line of redoubts, he kept marching forward with Posse's column towards the Russian camp. The King, whose litter had been broken among the redoubts, sent a message to recall him. The aide succeeded in reaching Lewenhaupt with the order before he assaulted the Russian camp, and he rejoined the Swedish army north of the redoubts.

After almost half of his men had fallen, Roos led the remnant into the broken country south of the Russian camp. Peter saw this blunder and sent General Menshikov after him with a large force. The Russians half surrounded Roos in a wood, and General Sparre's column, which Charles had sent to rescue Roos, could not get through to him. When Roos finally surrendered in a fieldwork near Poltava, only 400 out of his original force of 1,400 men remained alive.

Meanwhile, the main Swedish army marched along the edge of a wood to the west of the Russian earthworks. Gyllenkrook, Quartermaster-General, later gave his account of what happened next.

I came to the place not far off where His Majesty was, and with him Major-General Sparre, who told His Majesty that he had not been able to penetrate the enemy force, but that Major-General

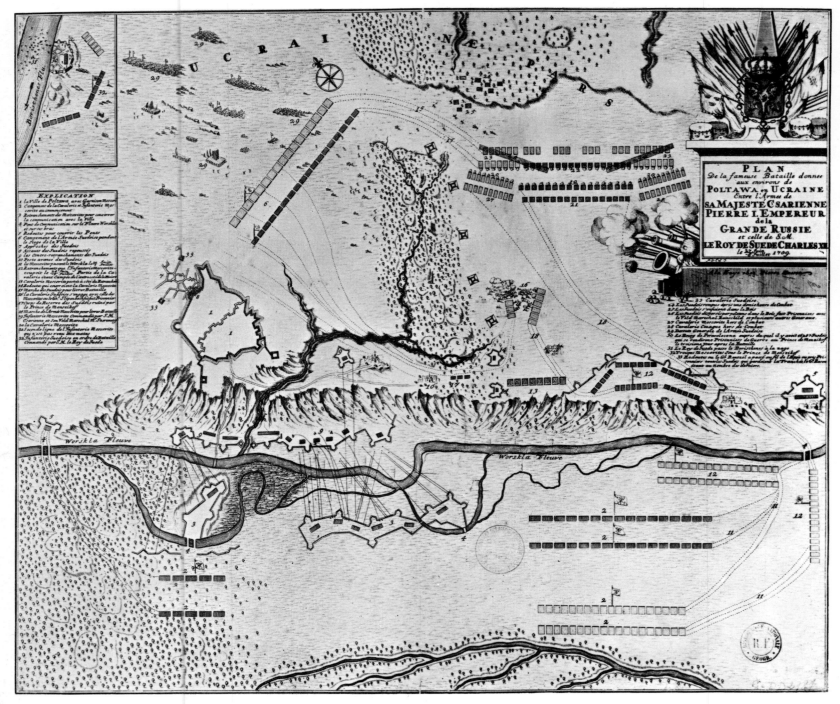

An elaborate and comprehensive plan which tells the whole story of Poltava, from the Swedish siege of the town (1), to the arrival of the Russian army, the battle, its aftermath, the Swedish retreat, Charles's escape (inset) and the capture of most of his army

LEFT TO RIGHT Field-Marshal Rehnsköld (painted by David von Krafft) who took command of the Swedish army after the King was wounded; Count Lewenhaupt (painted by D. Richter), the commander of the infantry; Major-General Roos (painted by Georg Schröder), whose battalions paid the price for the breakdown of command and communications in the Swedish army

Roos was standing fast in a wood and defending himself well. To this I said, 'Ay, ay, General, but 'twere better Roos were here, and I fear it shall go ill'. Sparre answered: 'If he will not defend himself when he has six battalions with him, then he may do what the devil he pleases; I cannot help him'. At that same moment the Field-Marshal approached His Majesty and said that the enemy was bringing out his infantry from the lines. His Majesty answered: 'Had we not best go against their horse, and drive that off first?' His Excellency, the Field-Marshal replied: 'No, Your Majesty, we must go against them'. His Majesty rejoined: 'Well, well, do as you will'. Then all the battalions began to march back again.

While the Swedes retraced their steps, the Russian army formed up in front of their camp. Prince Repnin commanded the centre, which consisted of two lines made up from 39 infantry battalions, averaging 850 men. Menshikov led the Russian cavalry, which comprised 69 squadrons. It is uncertain how many of these had reached their positions on either flank of the infantry. Some still hunted Roos; others stood north of Peter's camp. Lieutenant-General Bruce, a Scot who commanded the artillery, ordered his men to drag many of their 72 guns out of the camp and place them among the infantry battalions. In all the Russian army numbered approximately 44,000 men.

At length the Swedish army halted and formed left to face the enemy. The cavalry, who had marched on the right of the army, struggled through a swamp to reach their stations on the left and right of the infantry. With Roos's battalions lost, the Swedish army had been reduced to 18,000 men. Only 4 iron field-guns had been brought to the field; for want of ammunition the remainder had been left behind in the artillery park. A sense of foreboding spread through the Swedish ranks as they looked at the host before them. Quarrelling between Rehnsköld and Lewenhaupt betrayed some inner fears. At last Rehnsköld gave the signal to advance. The infantry, bayonets fixed and drums beating, marched in line towards the Russians, just as they had done nine years before. But the Russian army had changed since Narva. King Charles's contempt for his enemy betrayed him.

BELOW *A drawing of a Swedish field forge of* c *1700*
RIGHT *An eighteenth-century French engraving of Stockholm, Charles XII's capital*

A Scots mercenary described how the Swedish army moved

directly to the enemy, charged with great Fury and a good Success . . . but the Cannon from the entrench'd Camp advancing, the Troops opening in several Places for their playing upon us, it was impossible our Foot could keep their Order, or the men stand the fire of 70 Pieces of Cannon loaden with Cartouches of small Shot . . .

The Russian guns scythed down the infantry on the left of the Swedish line. A single discharge almost annihilated the Kalmar Regiment. Lewenhaupt on the right fared better. His men broke the first line of Russian battalions with their bayonets, took some cannon and fired a musket volley at the enemy, but their inferior powder caused either misfires or bangs no louder 'than the slapping of two gloves'. Yet the Swedish right carried on until, as Lewenhaupt wrote, 'at last, with pike and bayonet, we came at our enemies' backs'. He could not, however, persuade the battalions on his left to advance against the Russian guns, firing at point-blank range. By the time he returned to the right the tide of battle had turned.

Peter rode to and fro among his men on his Turkish horse, exposing himself fearlessly, shouting encouragement and promising rewards. It is said that musket balls passed through his saddle and his hat, and dented a jewelled cross which he wore beneath his shirt. The Russian battalions in the centre began to press forward, unchecked by cavalry charges from the Nyland Regiment and the East Gothland Horse. In front of them dead 'bluecoats' littered the field but, as one Swedish officer noted, 'even thicker, God be praised, were strewn the green uniforms of the Muscovites'.

The Russians gradually swept the Swedish infantry before them. One eye-witness saw the last of the Upplanders Regiment – 'some hundred men or more lying in a heap, as if fallen or thrown one upon the other, whom the enemy with pike, bayonet and sword was eagerly slaughtering and massacring with all his might'. At this eleventh hour, Creutz charged with his cavalry on the right wing but came up against fresh Russian infantry: they formed squares and beat him off. His charge also

ARX REGIA HOLMENSIS
versus Orientem

exposed him to cannon fire and the threat of a cavalry attack from the redoubts in his rear, and he withdrew.

In the centre chaos reigned as Swedish soldiers ran in panic past their cursing officers: cannon fire killed all but three of Charles's 24 bodyguards and shattered his litter. The King painfully mounted a horse and, escorted by 500 troopers, was led away by his aides. With his departure the battle ended.

The King left behind him 301 officers and 6,600 other ranks dead on the field. Field-Marshal Rehnsköld, four generals, five colonels, 182 officers, and 2,587 other ranks were taken prisoner along with many of the wounded in the Swedish camp. The Russian losses have been estimated at 1,300 dead and missing.

As the King moved south, Peter entertained Rehnsköld and the four captured Swedish generals to lunch on the field of battle and jubilantly toasted 'Teachers in the Art of War'. 'Who are they?', asked Rehnsköld. 'You are, gentlemen', replied the Tsar. 'Then well have the pupils returned thanks to their teachers', commented Rehnsköld.

On 29 June King Charles, with under 16,000 men, reached the Dnieper, only to find that all the boats had been burnt. Using improvised rafts, he crossed himself, with 1,000 selected men, and continued southwards into the lands of the Turk. The next day General Lewenhaupt surrendered to a Russian force his army of 1,161 officers and 13,138 men. After a triumphant procession in Moscow, the Tsar sent many of them to Siberia. In 1718 the Tsar allowed Rehnsköld, who was 68 years old, to return home. Three years later, after the long war with Sweden had drawn to a close, Peter invited the repatriated Swedish officers to a banquet in Moscow, and spoke graciously of their master as having 'more than supernatural courage'.

After his escape from Poltava, King Charles continued to intrigue and fight to preserve the Swedish empire around the Baltic. On 30 November 1718 he was shot through the head while on a reconnaissance during the siege of Fredrikshall in southern Norway and fatally injured.

Poltava revealed how hard Peter the Great had worked at reorganizing the Russian army, and infusing new spirit into it. His strategy of withdrawal and the ruthless devastation of east Poland and the Ukraine reduced the Swedish army to a state in which it could be defeated. How far he was responsible for the direction of the battle may be disputed, but his personal bravery, and the effect it had upon the Russian army, may not.

The battle also demonstrated to his contemporaries the young Swedish king's limitations as a general. The Duke of Marlborough, who had met the King in 1706, wrote in a despatch that Charles's 'continued successes and the contempt he has of his enemies has been his ruin'.

ABOVE LEFT *A company ensign of the regiment of the Dragoons of Scania, of c 1686.* ABOVE RIGHT *The uniform of a Swedish grenadier of c 1700–10 – the model holds a grenade in his right hand, and the 'match' in his left*

OPPOSITE *A portrait of Charles XII, the soldier-king of Sweden, whose contempt for his enemy, in addition to the serious wound which prevented him from directing the battle himself, cost him a disastrous defeat at Poltava (painted by David von Krafft).* BELOW *A medal commemorating the battle of Poltava and the end of hostilities between Russia and Sweden, confirmed by the Peace of Nystadt (1721)*

Tactically, the failure of the King to brief his subordinates led to unnecessary disorder. No doubt had the King not sustained a serious wound he could have galloped about the field and directed the battle himself. Outnumbered though they were, in normal circumstances the Swedes might have defeated the Russians, but once their king was *hors de combat* these excellent Swedish soldiers had only their reckless courage to rely upon. Like Alexander the Great, the young Swedish king had centralized the control of battles in his own person, and his men, like the Macedonians, were lost without their general. Lacking experience in using his generals as anything more than brigade commanders, it is hardly surprising that the King in his litter had difficulty in controlling the battle. Marlborough summed up King Charles's conduct of the battle in one terse sentence – 'ten years of unbroken success, and two hours of mismanagement'.

Politically, the Peace of Nystadt (1721) harvested the fruits of Poltava. Sweden ceded to Russia the provinces of Livonia, Estonia and Ingria. Russia replaced Sweden as the great Baltic power. On the day of his victory on the Vorskla, Peter the Great wrote to Admiral Apraxin, 'Now, with God's help, the last stone has been laid to the foundation of St Petersburg'.

JOHN ADAIR

1745
Fontenoy

The Duke of Cumberland's famous 'British square' penetrated the French centre but, lacking the full support of his allies, he was deprived of a great victory

THE WAR BEGUN IN 1740 over the succession to the Imperial throne of Austria had eventually carried hostilities from Bohemia and Bavaria to the very frontiers of France. In the spring of 1744, an Austrian army was threatening Alsace, while the English, with the help of the Hanoverians and the Dutch, held strong positions from the North Sea to the Meuse, in a region bristling with fortresses. During most of that year, Louis XV was taken up by his campaign on the Rhine, but in December Marshal Saxe received orders to prepare a plan of operations for the army in Flanders.

Maurice de Saxe, on whom the subsequent fate of French arms depended, was a curious figure. A natural son of Augustus II of Poland and Anne of Königsmark, he was only fifty-one but, after a life full of unparalleled political, military and amorous adventures, his health was precarious. Throughout that decisive spring of 1745 he was unceasingly afflicted by dropsy, which prevented him from mounting his horse.

His plan was a simple one: to storm Tournai and through the breach thus opened on the Scheldt to advance into the Austrian Netherlands. By the end of April the town was so vigorously besieged that the allies decided to march to its relief with some 65,000 men –

25,000 English, 30,000 Dutch, 800 Hanoverians and some Austrians – only 46,000 of whom were to take part in the final battle.

Warned of their advance on 5 May, Marshal Saxe sought a suitable spot to block them, while the King and the Dauphin set out from Versailles to take part in the action. Leaving a besieging force of 20,000 in front of Tournai, the Marshal repaired with 50,000 men to the right bank of the Scheldt, about five miles south-east of his chosen battle-field. He had guessed the direction from which the attack would come and had correctly gauged the advantages offered by this position.

On the right bank of the Scheldt lay a broad, gently sloping plateau crossed by a ravine. To the left of the French positions the village of Antoing overlooked the river, while the houses of Fontenoy provided a strong, fortified centre. With the help of the expert engineers, whom he had used at the siege of Tournai, the Marshal skilfully fortified this front in the form of a rectangle two and a quarter miles in length between Ramecroix and Antoing, and a mile and a half between Antoing and the wood of Barry. Two redoubts protected the tip of the wood of Barry; Fontenoy and Antoing were stiff with cannon and crammed with troops; and three redoubts were set up between the two villages. However, the Marshal – and this was his greatest mistake that day – did not think it necessary to fortify the half-mile separating Fontenoy from the wood, through which the rain-

LEFT *Unable longer to withstand the shock of repeated cavalry charges, the British and Hanoverian infantry retires, and the battle is over; Louis XV points to the victor, Marshal Saxe (painted by Lenfant)*

sodden ravine ran. 'I did not think any general would be bold enough to venture along such a road', he was to say later in excuse.

The French Guards were posted in front of the ravine; they were neither as well trained nor as spirited as the English, Scottish and Hanoverian Guards that were to face them, but they were supported by hand-picked brigades of infantry, Swiss, Irish and French, disposed behind the fortified points. The bulk of the 68 squadrons of cavalry were arrayed in two lines parallel to the Scheldt, ready to intervene on the two wings. Three regiments of dragoons were based on Antoing.

The French were cheerful on the 10th. The King – he was thirty-five years old (and the Dauphin barely fifteen) – was in high spirits; he visited the troops, the camp, the stores and the hospitals, tasting the soldiers' bread and the sick men's broth. He gave wholehearted support to the decisions of the Marshal, who was in great pain despite almost daily tappings, and who had difficulty maintaining his authority in the face of experts and a general staff only too eager to take decisions. The eve of battle presented a lively scene. The talk turned on battles in which kings had taken part in person: Poitiers was mentioned, naturally, or better Maupertuis, for since 1356 no King of France had thus fought by his son's side ('Father, keep watch on your right, keep watch on your left'). The reference was not really a happy one, in view of the capture of John the Good, but hitherto no French sovereign had defeated an English army, and Louis XV hoped to be the first.

On 11 May, by 4 a.m., the King had set up his headquarters at Notre-Dame au Bois. The Dauphin and

Not since 1356 had a French king fought by his son's side; here Louis XV assists the Dauphin in donning his cuirass before the battle

Marshal de Noailles were with him. He was strongly protected by picked covering troops, and a bridgehead on the Scheldt was fortified in case of possible retreat. The Duc de Richelieu was in attendance, and the day was to owe much to this forty-nine-year-old eccentric, whose life had been even more richly adventurous than that of Marshal Saxe, but who was endowed with an iron constitution. (A familiar figure at the Court of Louis XIV, he lived on until 1788, the eve of the Revolution.)

About 5.30 in the morning, as the early mists were dispersing, the battle entered its first phase. The Duke of Cumberland tried out the resistance of the three fortified points. The Dutch moved towards Antoing. Harried by dragoons from the right, under fire from the troops at Antoing in front and from six cannon hidden on the left bank of the Scheldt, they refused to fight, and throughout the day stood waiting. Ingoldsby's brigade of Highlanders attacked near the tip of Barry Wood, but behind its undergrowth and felled timber lay concealed French infantrymen, the 'Grassins'. These redoubtable fighters, whose regiments had been formed only the previous year, and who were equally skilled in the use of the musket or, at close quarters, of the sword, easily succeeded in halting their opponents, thus taken by surprise. In the centre, Fontenoy was beleaguered by the English Guards, but the vigorous artillery and musket fire of the French checked the assault. Thus, at 8.30 am., after three hours' fighting, the French still held the upper hand, but the Duke of Cumberland, who had carefully studied the French positions, was preparing one of those daring strokes which frequently decide the fate of battles.

The French Guards, stationed between the redoubts in Barry Wood and Fontenoy, had not so far had to take part in the action, but now suddenly they observed several cannon emerge on the crest of the ravine that divided them from the enemy. Were these isolated units which had ventured too far? No, immediately behind them 15,000 English, Scottish and Hanoverian foot-soldiers, floundering through mud and undergrowth, were making their way stolidly up the slopes and had begun to cut the French position in two. The stupefaction of both sides, brought suddenly face to face, may perhaps contribute to explaining the famous, and much debated, episode that ensued. The English officers in command of the Campbell and Royal Scottish regiments, Lord Albemarle, Robert Churchill and Lord Charles Hay, advanced a few steps farther and took off their hats in salute. The French Guards did the same. Nobody moved. The French were no doubt astounded, the English out of breath. Lord Charles Hay is said to have pulled out a flask and drunk a toast, shouting to the French: 'We hope you will stand still till we come up to you, and not swim the river as you did at Dettingen'. Another saying,

né et levé sur les lieux par le S. Bernard.

Gravé par Guélard A.

UE DE LA BATAILLE DE FONTENOY GAGNÉE PAR LE ROY LOUIS XV SUR L'ARMÉE DES ALLIEZ LE XI MAY 17.

ONTENOY Village reveu d'un Parapet de terre avec un fossé, defendu par la
igade Dauphin, et qui a merité par sa Situation quoiquen angle et par sa defense de
nner le nom à la Bataille.
mp de Bataille, ou Theatre du carnage.
doute defendue par le Regiment d'Eu, aiant 6 pieces de Canon.
doute defendue par le Regiment de l'Aly, aiant 4 p. de Canon.
is Redoutes garnies de pieces de Canon et soutenües par des detachemens du
iment de Bettens.
urg d'Antoin bordant l'Escaut defendu par la Brigade de Piedmont et de
iment de Bettens.
yal la Marine et par 4 a 5 pieces de Canon.
ase de Gueronne.
rtice d'Antoin, Lieu ou etoit le Roy et Monseigneur le Dauphin.
Dame des Bois ou etoit l'Hopital ambulant.

L Chemin de Tournay a Mons qui borde le Corps de reserve.
M Rame-croix.
N Gaurin.
O Bois de Bary.
P Front de l'Armée Françoise composé du Regiment du Roy, des Gardes Françoises et
Suisses et ceux d'Aubeterre, des Irlandois &c.ª
Q 2.ª Ligne composée des Brigades de Normandie, des Vaisseaux et autres R.ª Infanterie.
R 3.ª Ligne composée des Carabiniers et de plusieurs Brigades de Cavalerie.
S 4.ª Ligne composée de la M. du Roy et de differentes Brig. de Cavalerie.
T L'Escadron qui couvre le Roy, composé du Guet de ses Gardes.
V Les Dragons et Crillon Biron et Bettens en avant faisant faceaux Troupes Hollandoises.
X Le Planty des dix Quartiers, Lieu eminent et planté de hautes futayes eloignées, d'ou
les Officiers Generaux Ennemis observoient nos differens mouvemens et autas du-
quel l'on voit les Camps des Ennemis dans les plaines coupées au Village de Vezon.

Y Gros Bataillon d'Infanterie Angloise qui s'est formé en avançant et qui a fait l'
l'effort de l'Action, aiant à droite et à gauche deux autres corps d'Infanterie dont ce
la gauche s'est porté à trois reprises sur le Village de Fontenoy sans aucun suc-
s'est un nulle angros du Centre pour se porter ensemble sur notre front.
Z Cavalerie Hollandoise qui a presque toujours été à la meme distance quelle paroit e
le feu de notre Artillerie.
& Corps d'Infanterie de trois à quatre mil hommes destiné pour se saisir du po
d'Antoin, mais qui n'a pu resister à la vivacité du feu de l'Artillerie qui lui
oppose.
AA Deux Batteries stables des Ennemis les autres étant menées à bras suivant
l'occasion le requeroit.

A PARIS.
Chez Limosin Rüe de Gevres au grand Cœur.

A French print of the battlefield of Fontenoy, showing in detail the dispositions of Marshal Saxe's army in the foreground; the British infantry are in the distance beyond the village of Fontenoy, and the Dutch, who played no part in the battle, are stationed on the right

BELOW LEFT *Louis XV, though Cumberland's success in the morning almost denied him the privilege, became the first French sovereign to defeat an English army (painted by Hyacinthe Rigaud).* CENTRE *Marshal Saxe, the French Commander-in-Chief at the Battle of Fontenoy, whose painful affliction of dropsy prevented him from mounting his horse.* RIGHT *William Augustus, Duke of Cumberland, the British Commander-in-Chief, whose failure to exploit his initial success at this battle has been much censured (painted by D. Morier)*

53

however, is more closely cherished by tradition. Lord Charles Hay is said to have called out to the Comte d'Auteroche, Lieutenant of the Grenadier Guards: 'Tell your men to fire'. 'No, gentlemen, we never shoot first. The honour is yours', came the reply.

Was this singular dialogue dictated by the spirit of chivalry? No, there was a more prosaic explanation, for the French Guards, seized with panic at the Battle of Lens in 1648, after opening fire too soon, had since been under strict orders never to fire first. The complex process of re-charging muskets – in twenty-four movements – did in fact set the combatant who had fired first at his adversary's mercy, enabling the latter to approach within point-blank range.

But this regulation, which could have its advantages where the infantryman was in a sheltered position and ready to withstand the attack, here proved wholly unfavourable to the French Guards, who had been surprised in the open. The French battalions and even the Swiss began to fall back on the two wings, while the allied infantry, 15,000 strong, advanced imperturbably towards the heart of the French 'hedgehog'. At 10, the second phase of the battle was thus concluded in favour of the Duke of Cumberland.

Louis XV and those around him were most perturbed at the situation. Marshal de Noailles advised the King to retire across the Scheldt. Marshal Saxe opposed the suggestion, and set off across the field of battle in his open wicker chariot, while the Duc de Richelieu galloped, hatless, from one group of officers to another. The order was given for the 68 squadrons bearing the finest names in the French cavalry, Royal-Roussillon, Royal-Cravate, Royal-Etranger, Dragons d'Egmont, Brionne, Penthièvre, and more besides, to charge in successive waves.

For this phase of the battle, which was to last four hours, the two Commanders-in-Chief were each to incur criticism. Of Cumberland, who let the opportunity slip by, Frederick the Great declared: 'A quarter-wheel right or a quarter-wheel left, or even both at once, would have brought him victory'. True, but did not the success of his column depend on the massive cohesion of its head? The cavalry that protected its deployment was paralysed a mile away, quite unable to venture through the excessive difficulties of the ravine. The 'infernal column' was thus obliged to remain where it stood all afternoon, keeping up a heavy fire in face of the frenzied charges of the French squadrons. Only one of these managed to get through, but no man of it came back alive, and its commander, the Marquis de Wignacourt, was left on the field with two bayonet wounds in his stomach.

Marshal Saxe has likewise been blamed for these costly cavalry assaults, which failed to penetrate his adversary's

This Saxon Dragoon at the time of Fontenoy wore a green coat trimmed with scarlet, and was armed with a musket, two pistols and a sabre; his horse had a wolf-skin saddle-cloth

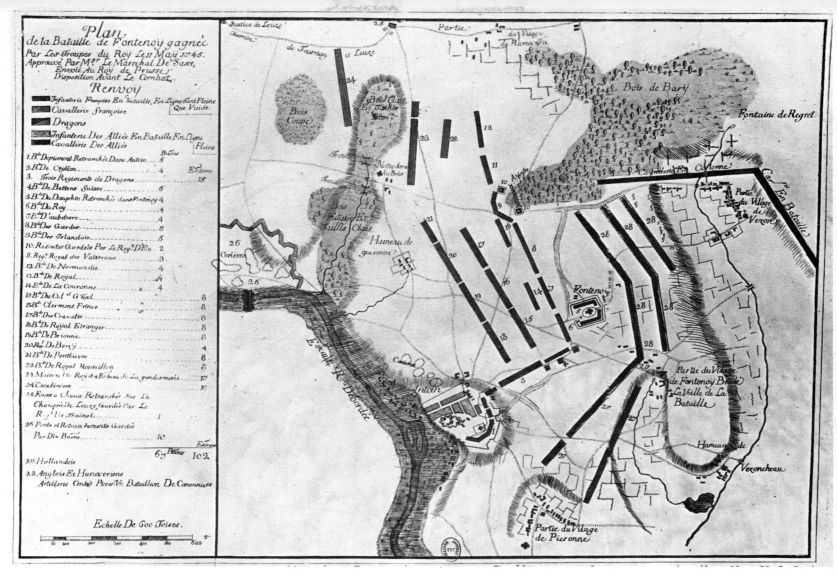

The strong French position at Fontenoy: to the existing defences provided by Antoing on the bank of the river Scheldt on the right, and Fontenoy in the centre, Marshal Saxe added two redoubts at the tip of the wood of Barry, and three more between Antoing and Fontenoy

An officer reports to the King, while the column of British and Hanoverian infantry is fiercely attacked by squadrons of French cavalry, and comes under heavy fire from Fontenoy and one of the redoubts in front of the wood of Barry (painted by van Blarenberghe)

LEFT *The Dauphin is urged to stay by the King's side, while Marshal Saxe, incapacitated by dropsy, sets off to inspect the front in his open wicker chariot.* RIGHT *At 10 o'clock, when the column of British infantry broke through the French centre, the royal headquarters was thrown into alarm, and the King's boots were brought so that he could mount his horse and retire from the battlefield; he refused to do so*

A fierce cavalry engagement near the village of Antoing on the French right; 50,000 French soldiers faced an Allied army of 46,000 at Fontenoy, of which the French suffered more than 5,000 and the Allies more than 7,000 casualties

ranks. He explained them thus: 'So long as the enemy had not taken Fontenoy, his successes in the centre were to his disadvantage, since he lacked any local base of operation. The further forward he advanced, the more he exposed his troops to capture by the French whom he had left in his rear. It was thus essential to pin him down by reiterated charges, which moreover gained time to prepare the main attack'.

At 2 pm. the situation was undecided, but the third and final phase of the battle was about to begin. The French infantry had regrouped themselves on the right flank of the column; the Irish infantry brigades and those of Normandy and Royal-Vaisseaux attacked sharply, careless of their lives. Marshal Saxe decided on a general charge: on the left, the Comte de Lowendal, who had hurried up from Tournai with 15 squadrons, on the right the Duc de Biron, uniting the squadrons which had defended Antoing and battalions of infantry which had retreated but recovered; while in the centre the King had agreed to provide his personal artillery units and the infantry protecting them. Under the Marshal's personal command, Lifeguards, Carabineers, Musketeers, and mounted Grenadiers began to advance, led by Richelieu, sword in hand. 'It was a scene from the days of chivalry, like some great tourney in the reign of Edward or John'; thus in 1884 wrote Comte Pajol, the methodical historian of Louis XV's wars. One should not exaggerate, however, and this cavalry charge against a mass of infantry which, moreover, was under oblique fire from eight guns, has nothing in common with jousts or tourneys.

On the other hand it is undeniable that in 1745, in spite of La Guérinière's famous *Ecole de cavalerie*, published in 1733, French cavalrymen fought as though in a tilt-yard or on a parade-ground. But, this was scarcely a virtue, as the French were to learn in 1757 in the bitter lesson given them by the Prussian squadrons at Rossbach.

Under the terrific shock the English, Scottish and Hanoverian troops were forced to beat a retreat. Without surrendering their colours, they retired along the ravine through which they had come, leaving there 7,000 dead and wounded. The help subsequently provided by the allied cavalry and the presence of the Dutch troops – inactive but still intact – prevented the French from pressing their advantage. Nevertheless, the Duke of Cumberland was forced to abandon a major part of his matériel, and to leave the Austrian Netherlands open to Louis XV.

The losses in both camps were considerable: 7,000–10,000 dead and wounded (according to different historians) on the English side, 5,000–7,000 casualties on the French side, including 53 officers killed, among them the Duc de Gramont and six other generals. The Irish paid dearly for their impetuosity; many of their officers,

Clad in green, with a curious, turban-like helmet, and armed with a lance, a pistol and a sabre, the Saxon Uhlans provided Marshal Saxe with his guard

Dillon and Clare among them, were killed. When the Dauphin, after the battle, hurried to Lally to announce the French King's blessings on his men: 'Monseigneur', replied the officer, whose face was covered in blood, 'they are like the blessings in the Gospel, they fall on the halt and the blind'.

Maurice de Saxe, increasingly crippled by dropsy, was helped on to his horse by his faithful guard of Saxon Uhlans and led to the King, who embraced him. 'Sire, I have lived long enough', said the Marshal, adding: 'You see on what the fate of battles turns'. When night fell at last, the King led the Dauphin to the field of battle and showed him the thousands of dead. 'My son', he said, 'consider this dreadful sight, learn not to play with your subjects' lives, and do not shed their blood in unjust wars.'

King George II, who was about to embark for the Continent, returned to London. He had reason to be dissatisfied with his Dutch allies. But the Dutch, who had indeed been very reluctant to abandon their neutrality, may have believed quite sincerely that the Duke of Cumberland could do without their active help. On 13 May, when the guns were fired at Namur and at Charleroi to announce the safe delivery of the Queen of Hungary, the people of the Low Countries naturally assumed that they announced the victory of the Coalition.

JACQUES BOUDET

1757 Rossbach

The Prussians' first great victory over the French, in which Frederick the Great inflicted heavy losses, was the most decisive battle of the Seven Years' War

KING FREDERICK II OF PRUSSIA has shown himself to posterity in many guises: the Frenchified Brandenburger, the lawgiver and treacherous ally, the philosopher who became the chief clerk and gaoler of his people. Here we must consider the most famous victory of his army, and his reputation as the outstanding commander of his age.

In 1740 Frederick had seized the rich Austrian province of Silesia. This land would eventually give a great accession of strength to the scattered territories that made up Prussia, though it was at the price of decades of war and rivalry with the Empress Maria Theresa of Austria. Frederick managed to cling on to his booty through the War of the Austrian Succession but, by 1756, at the outbreak of the Seven Years' War, the formidable Maria Theresa had reorganized her army on the Prussian model, and was summoning up Russia and France as allies to sustain her cause. In the autumn of 1757 Frederick found that enemies were closing in from every direction in apparently irresistible force. Russians and Swedes threatened the heartland of the Prussian monarchy, while in western Germany the French had defeated the Duke of Cumberland and his British-subsidized force of Hanoverians, Hessians and Brunswickers – the sole friends left to Frederick on the Continent. In addition Louis XV had despatched a force under the Prince de Soubise into Thuringia in order to combine with the German troops led by the Prince of Sachsen-Hildburghausen, and so form a powerful army to busy Frederick on his western front at the same time as the Austrians made ready to overrun Silesia.

Prussia's survival against the might of the enemy coalition constitutes one of the finest episodes of military history. Strategically, Frederick conducted his campaigns on sound principles. Recognizing the folly of scattering his troops in an attempt to hold on to every last yard of territory (*'Wer alles conserviren will, der conserviret nichts'*), he concentrated his energies on a mobile striking-force with which he could dart against each enemy in turn, and defeat him or at least prevent him from joining up with his allies. Frederick's grip on tactics was less sure. He was capable of handling troops on the field in masterly fashion, but more than once he had suffered a failure of nerve and judgment, and seen the day saved by the disciplined valour of his bluecoats, or by the initiative of one of his generals. Such a subordinate accompanied him to Rossbach in 1757. At thirty-six, Seydlitz was the youngest of Frederick's cavalry generals, and still wore the straw-yellow uniform of his old regiment. In appearance he was remarkable only for what might have been taken as signs of a casual and easy-going temperament – the clay pipe that was his constant companion, a full mouth, and light, almost sleepy eyes. Frederick had been among the first to recognize in him the gifts that would make the Prussian cavalry the match of the Imperial Austrian, and the virtuosity that would give him the reputation of perhaps the finest cavalry leader of German history.

RIGHT *Charles de Rohan, Prince de Soubise, who owed his command of the French troops at Rossbach almost entirely to the favour of Madame de Pompadour*

58

Marsch! Marsch!

2 Compagnien.

2 Comp.

Unteroffizier.

If 'Old Fritz' was fortunate in his generals, he was lucky also in the quality of his opponents. Soubise and Hildburghausen would probably be the first with whom he would have to settle accounts. The Frenchman commanded a contingent that made up about half of the *Kombinierte Kaiserliche Reichs-Exekutions-Französische Armee*, the assemblage of 50,000 troops which came together in mid-September at Eisenach in Thuringia. Lacking almost every qualification for command save that of personal courage, Soubise owed his position to the favour of Madame de Pompadour, and was under instructions to leave the main burden of the campaign to the Austrians. In contrast the orders that came from Vienna were positive and simple – to drive the Prussians from Saxony and reduce the Elbe fortresses – and Hildburghausen, the man who was to carry them out, was the superior of Soubise not only in nominal authority, but in ability and experience. Unfortunately, the most inspired generalship could still have achieved little with an army that was admitted by its own officers to be unfit to face the enemy in open battle.

The force assembled by decree of the Imperial Diet was a fitting reflection of eighteenth-century Germany: a congeries of contingents from the states of the southern and western circles, each with its own drill, equipment, uniform, and commissariat arrangements. At best the troops could summon up no more than a mild enthusiasm for the Austrian cause, and many of the Württembergers and Franconians showed a positive inclination towards Prussia. At a camp at Fürth, Hildburghausen had drilled the Imperial troops into the semblance of a unified army, but it was only to see the bonds of discipline broken again as soon as the soldiers came into contact with the French. Saint-Germain, one of Soubise's own generals, has described the state of his command: 'I am leading a band of robbers, of murderers fit to be broken on the wheel, who would take to their heels at the first musket shot, and are perpetually on the verge of mutiny. I have never seen the like. The King has the worst and most indisciplined infantry in the world; with troops like this, there is nothing to be done'. Saxony groaned under the

EXTREME LEFT *Reproductions of Adolph Menzel's drawings of the uniforms of grenadiers in Frederick the Great's army, showing the details of caps and other distinguishing features of the different companies and ranks*

LEFT *A reproduction of Menzel's drawing of the straw-yellow uniform of Seydlitz's regiment*

RIGHT *Frederick the Great of Prussia, the outstanding commander of his age, whose army gained its most famous victory at Rossbach (painted by his court painter, Pesne)*

Boucher's symbolical design for a medallion to commemorate the alliance of France and Austria in 1756; the Allies' attempt to crush the Prussians at Rossbach failed lamentably
Seydlitz, the true victor of Rossbach, was perhaps the finest cavalry leader in German history

ravages of the French, and Hildburghausen heard that half-decayed corpses were being dragged from the coffins in the search for gold.

In the first half of September news came to Frederick of the progress of Soubise and Hildburghausen. Marching at a rate of a dozen miles a day, remarkable for the time, Frederick raced off to deal with the new threat, only to have the allies draw back out of his reach. The King had to hurry back to the north-east, for an Austrian general had taken advantage of his absence to despatch a raiding party against Berlin, but there was time only for a brief gesture in that direction before he learnt that the allies were again on the move, and might well give him the encounter he desired. By 4 November Frederick was back again in western Saxony, facing the enemy army across a swampy valley near the village of Rossbach.

Now, after all these weeks of campaigning, the allies at last summoned up the courage to exploit the great advantage which their numbers seemed to confer upon them (now about 11,000 Imperialists and 30,000 French against 20–22,000 Prussians). Soubise spoke out for an advance around the southern flank of the Prussian position so as to threaten Frederick's communications over the River Saale; Hildburghausen agreed, though in view of the desperate state of the supplies of the Imperial troops he hoped to use this opportunity to finish with Frederick once and for all.

Early on the morning of 5 November, Saint-Germain and the Austrian general Loudon advanced detachments to the heights directly facing the Prussian camp but, since at any given time a large proportion of the French troops were bound to be absent marauding, it was 11.30 before the army lurched off to the beating of drums and the shrilling of trumpets and fifes. The march took the broad allied columns due south to Zeuchfeld, and then eastwards along the row of heights leading by way of Pettstädt to Reichardtswerben. Below them to the left they could see the southern flank of the Prussian camp at Rossbach, and behind it the low swells of the Janus and Pölzen Hills which extended parallel to their own line of march.

The Imperial general was still far from persuading Soubise into changing the flank march into a full-scale attack when, at about 2.30 pm. all was changed by the first signs of a reaction in the enemy camp. In less than two minutes all the Prussian tents collapsed to the ground 'just as if they had been pulled by a cord in some theatrical scene', and the enemy army wound out of sight behind the Janus Hill. A little later reports came in from the light cavalry to the effect that the Prussians were drawing away, and from now on the allies, Soubise as well as Hildburghausen, subordinated everything to the aim of overtaking and crushing the enemy before he

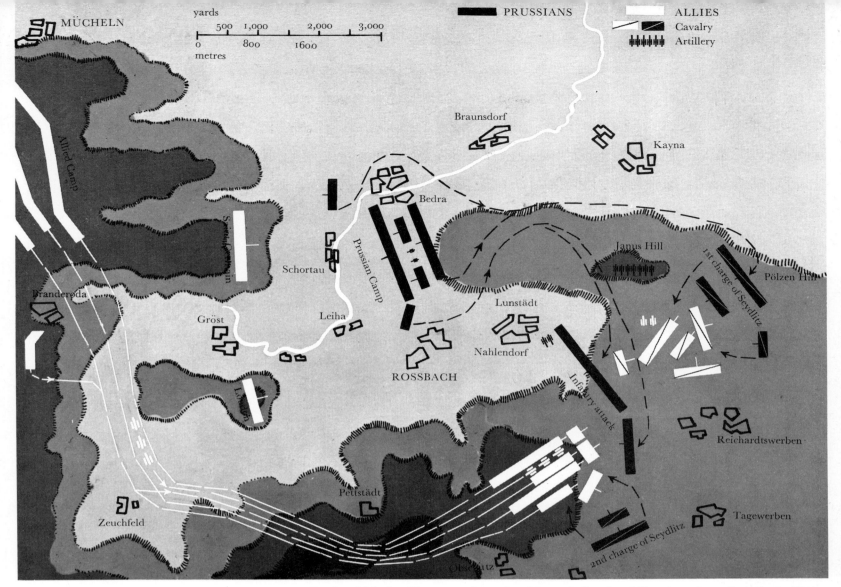

MÜCHELN

yards
500 1,000   2,000   3,000

0   800   1600
metres

PRUSSIANS   ALLIES
Cavalry
Artillery

Braunsdorf

Kayna

Bedra

Janus Hill

1st charge of Seydlitz

Pölzen Hill

Schortau

Lunstädt

Prussian Camp

Brandereda

Gröst

Leiha

Nahlendorf

ROSSBACH

Infantry attack

Reichardtswerben

Pettstädt

Zeuchfeld

Tagewerben

2nd charge of Seydlitz

Obschütz

The battlefield of Rossbach, showing the swampy valley in which the village was situated and its encircling low hills where the undisciplined allied army was scattered before the Prussians

could slip out of their grasp. The five columns of the army accordingly veered to the north-east, plunged down into the shallow valley, and began to mount the further slopes beyond Reichardtswerben.

For hours nothing had been able to persuade Frederick to take more than a mild interest in the movements of the allied army, and early in the afternoon he sat down to lunch with his generals in his quarters in the mediaeval Herrenhaus at Rossbach. Seydlitz for one was disturbed by the reports that came from Captain Gaudi, who had been posted in a vantage point in the garret above, and he quietly sent word to the cavalry to saddle up and hold itself in readiness. The near-by artillery followed the example of the horsemen. At last Frederick was convinced, and delivered the entire cavalry into the hands of Seydlitz with orders to march to the left and head off the enemy thrust. The infantry followed, led by a battery of sixteen heavy cannon and two howitzers under Colonel von Moller.

Seydlitz rode out along the crest of the Janus Hill, from where he could gauge the progress of both the rival armies, then, at the first shot from Moller's guns, he halted his own command behind the cover of the Pölzen

Hill, and assembled the 38 squadrons in two lines facing south. Seydlitz gloried in his control over his excited cavalrymen. Heads were bared for a pastor's blessing – a captain was cursed to the devil by Seydlitz for being unable to keep his horse under control. Seydlitz led his riders forward for a short distance, halted them for a few moments more, then cast his pipe in the air and led them over the swell of land into the charge.

> *Hervor mit seiner Reiterei*
> *Brach Seydlitz mörderlich*
> *Welch ein Gemetzel, welch Geschrei:*
> *'Wer kann, der rette sich!'*
>
> (*Forward with his cavalry*
> *Murderous Seydlitz ran*
> *Such shrieking and such butchery:*
> *'Save yourself if you can!'*)

Out of the cavalry corps leading the heads of the allied columns, the Austrian cuirassier regiments of Brettlach and Trautmannsdorf were alone able to deploy before the shock. The stout-hearted Austrians checked the enemy in bitter hand-to-hand fighting, which gave

63

Frederick the Great at the Battle of Rossbach; the battle scene in the distance appears to represent Seydlitz's second cavalry charge which shattered the remaining allied infantry (after Schadow)

Two engravings of French uniforms of 1756: the Life-guardsman (left) wore a gold-laced scarlet coat with black velvet cuffs. The Musketeer (right) of the 1st Company also wore a scarlet coat and was well armed, with a sword and two pistols, as well as his musket

Broglie time to move to their help with a powerful reserve of French cavalry. A disciplined, homogeneous cavalry might have withstood the impact of the 18 squadrons of Seydlitz's second line, but not the milling mass of the allied horsemen who could find no sense in the bewildering variety of uniforms they saw on every side, or in orders yelled in German, in French, and in the Gaelic of the 'French' regiment of Fitz-James. The allied horse broke away to the south and west under the new onslaught, but Seydlitz showed his stature as a tactician and disciplinarian by calling off the pursuit, and reassembling his squadrons in the hollows near Tagewerben; given the time to recruit strength, he would have the means of delivering still more damaging blows.

From an elm tree at Lunstädt, thenceforward known as the 'Fritzenbaum', Frederick meanwhile directed the march of the infantry over the ridge and back into the view of the enemy. Prince Henry, the commander of the left wing, deployed his battalions into line of battle as soon as the heads of columns came within six hundred paces of Reichardtswerben, and marched south-west against the allies; the extreme left was prolonged into a single line, so as to gain a flanking position, and the pace of these troops was hastened until they found themselves facing west. For the allied infantry, the scenes of the cavalry fight were re-enacted on a larger scale. Once more a few regiments – Piemont, Mailly, Provence and Poitou – contrived to put themselves in order, and moved boldly forward. The Frenchmen marched in formations of line and column to drive back the enemy with the bayonet, but just before the encounter heads began to turn, firing broke out without order, and the soldiers took to their heels. The Franconian regiments in the midst of the allied formations wavered and broke with little attempt to come to grips with the enemy, and only the seven battalions on the far Prussian left had need to employ their muskets at all.

Seydlitz had been observing the course of the infantry fight, and launched his re-formed cavalry from Tagewerben in a new charge as soon as he saw that the confusion had become general. He allowed a bullet wound in the arm to receive only the briefest attention before pressing on again with the pursuit. Two Swiss regiments in the French employ, Diesbach and Planta, compelled Frederick's attention by standing rooted like 'a wall of red bricks', but dusk found the rest of the army scattered in every direction. In their first camp after the battle the Prussian troops gave voice to anthems of thanksgiving, and broke up the great quantities of abandoned muskets to feed the stocks to their fires.

Broken beyond repair, the remnants of the allied army straggled back through Thuringia. They would never trouble Frederick again. The King accepted his success

Part of a British broadside satirizing the defeat of the French and Allies at Rossbach; the Prussian grenadier prepares to sweep the French (who have thrown down arms and plunder) out of the country

in philosophic mood, as giving him the liberty to seek new adventures against the Austrians in Silesia. The next month would bring him a hard-fought victory over the Austrians at Leuthen, but five more years of war were to pass before he could be assured of the survival of Prussia.

Rossbach is a victory almost unexcelled as an example of the superiority of generalship, training and morale over mere weight of numbers. The Prussians had suffered a total of 548 casualties, but 'la bataille amusante' had cost the allies about 5,000 in killed and wounded, and a like number had been taken prisoner in the field or delivered up by the peasants. The shameless Soubise clung to high command until the end of the war, but Hildburghausen chose to retire to private life, thankful at least that his martyrdom was at an end. Gaudi, the living reproach to Frederick's lapse of vigilance, found himself banished to the Jägers with an imputation on his courage: Seydlitz, as the true victor of Rossbach, was admitted to the Order of the Black Eagle and made Lieutenant-General.

Less happily, Rossbach was a foreshadowing of a kind of conflict that was to come. Among the causes of the victory Gaudi makes particular mention of: 'the natural hate which the ordinary man in Germany, but especially the Magdeburgers, inhabitants of the Mark and the Pomeranians, feels in his heart for all who bear the name of Frenchman. It is a feeling which he imbibes with his mother's milk. Our troops were not content merely to do their duty and advance bravely against the enemy, for it must have struck everyone, who observed their conduct, that they were fighting out of real hatred. This was particularly noticeable from the behaviour of the cavalrymen as they hewed their way into the enemy infantry, and the officers found great difficulty in bringing the troopers to grant quarter.'

CHRISTOPHER DUFFY

CONQUESTS in the Glorious 1759, from the London Gazettes Extraordinary.

Basseterre the Capital of Guadalupe taken by Com. Moore & Gen. Hopson. (L.G.E. Mar 7.)

Guadalupe Surrender'd to Gen. Barrington (L.G.E. June 11.

Goree
taken by Commodore Keppel.
(Vide L.G.E. Jan.y 29, 1759)

The Courier riding thro' Cleves,
gives an account of Contades defeat
(L.G.E. Aug. 8.)

SSSS

The thundering Guns proclaim,
Great George's glorious name.

THE TOULON FLEET
of Mons.r De la Clue, destroy'd
by Admiral Boscawen.
(L.G.E. Sep.r 7.th)

Niagara
Surrendred to S.r Will.m Johnson Bar.t
(L.G.E. Sept.r 10.)

The gloomy throngs look terrible from far,
Disclosing slow the horrid face of war;
The thick Battalions move in dreadful forme,
As low'ring Clouds advance before a storm.

Admiral Pocock
defeats Mons.r Lally in the East Indies.
(L.G.E. 12 Octo.r)

The Cannons roar & distant regions scare,
Shake all the shores and torture all the air.

Fire Ships and Rafts
sent down the River S.t Laurence,
by the French with design to
destroy his Majestys Ships, under,
Admirals Saunders Holmes &c.
(L.G.E. Oct. 16.)

On either side the Foe outrageous grew,
And Deaths unseen in dreadful tempests flew;
Destruction they exchange, by turns they give,
Exploded Ruin and by turns receive.

James Cooper
Whitsuntide 1760

QUEBEC
taken by Woolfe, Townsend, Saunders, &c.
(L.G.E. Octo.r 17.)

Brest Fleet
under Conflans, destroy'd by Adm.l Hawke
(L.G.E. Nov. 30.)

Published according to Act of Parliam.t April 30, 1760. & sold by J. Hawkins Printer in Fleet Lane, Temple Bar London.

1759 Quebec

Having scaled the Heights of Abraham by night, Wolfe routed the French under Montcalm, and decided the fate of Canada – both generals were killed

THREE HUNDRED MILES UPSTREAM from its immensely wide mouth, the St Lawrence River narrows to a channel which is less than a mile across. Here in the summer of 1608, Samuel de Champlain, who foresaw a new empire in the silent wilderness that stretched beyond the river banks, founded a trading post which he called Quebec. A hundred and fifty years later the few log cabins of the early settlement had grown into the large and beautiful capital of New France. By then, however, the quarrels and rivalries between the French in Canada and the British colonists along the Atlantic seaboard further south had erupted into war, and the future of Quebec and of the great colony which surrounded it was in the balance.

The war in America – an extension of the Seven Years' War in Europe – began with a series of ignominious defeats for the British expeditionary troops whose rigid tactics were never satisfactorily adapted to the exigencies of forest warfare. And it was not until 1758, when William Pitt and Lord Ligonier, the clever old Commander-in-Chief, turned their attention to the conquest of Canada, that there seemed any hope that the war could be ended in England's favour. In discussions with Lord Anson, the First Lord of the Admiralty, they decided that the previous advances on the French colonial forts had not only

come from the wrong direction but had taken no account of British sea power. Instead of moving overland against the enemy from Virginia in the south or from New England in the east, they suggested an amphibious attack from the north down the St Lawrence River. The suggestion was adopted and preparations began.

The first obstacle to be overcome was Louisbourg, a massive and forbidding fortress of grey rock, whose four hundred cannon guarded the approaches to the Gulf of St Lawrence. But by the end of July 1758, after a long and laboriously conducted siege, Louisbourg lay in ruins and the passage to the river beyond was open. The following year a fleet of creaking, laden ships under Admiral Charles Saunders tacked through fog and ice floes toward Nova Scotia, and the siege of Quebec was about to begin.

The man who had been given the duty of conducting it was lying, exhausted by sea sickness, in a small and stuffy cabin. He had neither the face nor the figure of a soldier. He was extremely tall and excessively thin; his nose was thin and pointed, his jaw undershot to the verge of deformity, his pale blue eyes were strangely prominent; his pallor, emphasized by bright red hair, was alarming. He had no grace of movement and no grace of manner. Indeed, his humourless, pedantic conceit, his priggish disdain of life's pleasures, his contempt for practically all of his fellow officers and the majority of the men who served under them had made him one of the most unpopular officers of his generation. But it was impossible to deny James Wolfe's extraordinary talents, his deter-

mined dedication to his profession, his heroic bravery. At the age of sixteen he had been his battalion's adjutant at Dettingen; before he was twenty-three he was commanding what was universally considered to be England's best trained and best disciplined infantry regiment; now, at the age of thirty-two, he was commanding an army. It was admittedly a small army, too small, he believed, for the task it had been set, however many American rangers, whom he dismissed as worthless 'canaille', were assigned to it; but the command was an independent one. For, although Jeffrey Amherst, who was to make a simultaneous attack from the south against Montreal, was to have supreme command in America, he was not to have any say in the conduct of the operations at Quebec. Nor, Wolfe was determined, were his three brigadiers to have any say in their conduct either. They were all three older than he was, all three the sons of peers, all three of proven ability and all three soon to be objects of their general's distrust.

For the moment, though, as the British fleet sailed quietly south towards Quebec there were no shadows of these future quarrels to darken the fine, warm days of

ABOVE *A reckless daylight assault on French positions along high cliffs north-east of Quebec was thrown back with heavy losses on 31 July*

RIGHT ABOVE *The taking of Quebec, 'shewing the manner of debarking the English Forces, and of the resolute scrambling of the light Infantry up a Woody Precipice . . . also a view of the signal Victory obtained over the French'*

RIGHT *A portrait sketch by Brigadier Townshend of James Wolfe, the victor of Quebec, which reveals his prominent pale blue eyes and alarming pallor*

early summer. Every day at the mess tables the officers optimistically drank a toast to 'British colours on every French fort, port and garrison in America'.

On the evening of 26 June, however, the voyage came to an end and, as the fleet anchored opposite the Basin of Quebec, these cheerful, confident officers came face to face with the formidable magnitude of their task.

High above them across the river the town stood like a mediaeval fortress. To the left and right, stretching out of sight in each direction, the steep brown cliffs rose sheer from the shallows to the French embankments lining the summit. Scarred here and there by a deep ravine, their face was barren and lifeless until, far away to the east,

to Isaac Barré
from his friend
Geo: Townshend

they were broken open by the roaring torrent of the cataract that pours the waters of the Montmorency River into the St Lawrence, two hundred and fifty feet below it.

It was a magnificent if foreboding landscape, but it was also, as Wolfe was later despairingly to tell Pitt, the 'strongest country in the world'.

The view was shared by the Marquis de Vaudreuil, the Governor of Canada. 'Quebec', he told Versailles with understandable confidence, 'is impregnable.' The Commander-in-Chief, the Marquis de Montcalm, was more circumspect. The position was, indeed, one of great natural strength but, while the English general was free to concentrate his resources behind a single assault on any part of it, the defenders must remain strong everywhere along its extensive front. Certainly the French had almost twice as many troops at their disposal as the British but they were mainly ill-trained Canadians called up at short notice from farms and settlements. With only five regiments of French regular troops, Montcalm did not feel able to share Vaudreuil's blind optimism. He was a man who combined Wolfe's great military gifts with a nature at once warm and noble. Fifteen years older than his adversary, however, he was tired and dispirited by his colonial command and appalled by the inefficiency and corruption of the civil administration with whom he was obliged to work, and whom he suspected of looking to defeat as the only means of covering up their years of swindling which were being investigated in Paris. He longed to return to his estate in the South of France, to a dearly loved wife and children. Before that, though, he assured the Minister of War, he would either 'save this unhappy colony or die in the attempt'.

Wolfe, too, was determined not to return home unless as a victor. Yet victory as the long hot summer days passed by seemed increasingly impossible.

He had begun his operations by seizing the large and undefended Île d'Orléans in the Basin of Quebec and by establishing his base camp there. Then he occupied a high elbow of land, known as the Pointe de Lévy on the south bank of the river immediately opposite the town; and a few days later he took two of his brigades across the St Lawrence and encamped them east of the Montmorency River where they remained for nearly two months.

These two months were fearful ones for Wolfe and for his army. Flies swarmed in the sultry air, buzzing drearily over the cook-houses and latrines, and the men contracted dysentery; rations became short, particularly vegetables, and then they went down with scurvy. When they were not sick they were bored and ill-disciplined and, despite the punishments inflicted, they could not be prevented from getting drunk on the spirits which they got from the women sutlers, the sight of whose petticoats and

View of the SIEGE of QUEBEC.

leather stays, hanging up to dry between the trees, drove Wolfe to fury. Desperately ill himself, he was also painfully aware by the end of August that he had achieved nothing. Montcalm refused to attack him, and the nerve of his men, after nights spent in the outposts surrounded by Indians, unseen and unheard, with tomahawks hanging from their naked thighs and with scalping knives between their painted lips, was beginning to break. He knew he must take the initiative himself.

A reckless daylight assault on the French positions along the high cliffs east of the town had been thrown

The Marquis de Montcalm, the Commander-in-Chief of the French forces in Canada since 1756

Part of Brigadier Monckton's report to William Pitt two days after the battle of 'a very Signal Victory over the French'

back with heavy losses on 31 July; subsequent raiding parties had harried the surrounding countryside but had no effect on Quebec's defences; the constant drills and musketry practice seemed to the men merely a means of keeping them out of mischief. Plan after plan came into Wolfe's restless mind only to be thrown away again. Several times orders for a fresh assault were given and were immediately cancelled. And then at last on 29 August the three brigadiers were ordered to meet at Wolfe's headquarters. He put before them three proposals for a final attack upon the French army east of Quebec before the ice closed over the river again and made further operations that season impossible. None of these proposals appeared feasible to the brigadiers – all of whom now had as little confidence in the general's judgment as he had in theirs – and they suggested an assault further upstream, well to the west of the town. This was an idea which had already occurred to Wolfe but he had abandoned it. Now, as a last resort, he accepted it. 'I have acquiesced in the proposal', he told Pitt. 'And we are preparing to put it into execution.' He kept all the details of the plans he made to himself, however, and without reference to the brigadiers he organized all the complicated marching and embarking orders.

On the morning of 7 September, leaving 1,200 troops on Pointe de Lévy to act as reinforcements should the main assault be successful, he set sail upstream with 3,600 men. Leaning against the rail of a sloop as he peered through his telescope, Wolfe spent the whole day searching for a place to land and by the evening he had found one several miles from the town. He did not tell his brigadiers exactly where it was but gave them instructions to make a general reconnaissance in the area. When they had done so, they were told that the general had changed his mind.

It seems likely that he did so on the advice of an intelligence officer who had learned that a detachment of colonial troops, weak in numbers and morale and commanded by a Canadian officer of doubtful capacity, was defending a cleft in the cliff face only a mile and a half above Quebec known as the Anse au Foulon. Leading up the cliff at this point was a path, broken here and there by felled trees and barricades. It was steep and slippery, but it did seem that it might be possible to clamber up it. This, Wolfe decided, would be the place and in the early hours of the morning of 13 September, after a day had been spent in sailing up and down the river to mislead the sentries on the heights above, the assault boats began to slip quietly downstream on the ebb tide.

Twice they were challenged by sentries, but a Highland officer called back through the darkness that they were taking provision boats to Quebec and no shots were fired. The current was strong when they came round the

Return of the Killed, Wounded and Missing at the Battle of Quebec, September the 13th 1759.

97

Regiments	Colonels	Lt Colonels	Majors	Captains	Lieutenants	Ensigns	Adjutants	Qr Masters	Surgeons	Mates	Serjeants	Drummers	Rank & File	Colonels	Lt Colonels	Majors	Captains	Lieutenants	Ensigns	Adjutants	Qr Masters	Surgeons	Mates	Serjeants	Drummers	Rank & File	Serjeants	Drummers	Rank & File
	Killed													Wounded													Missing		
Major Genl Jeffery Amherst's													2			4								5		52			
Lieut Genl Philip Bragg's				1							1		3		3	1	1							4	1	39			
Lieut Genl Charles Otway's				1									6		2	4								1		28			
Major Genl James Kennedy's													3			1								2		18			
Lieut Genl Peregrine Lascelles's				1									1		2	4	2							1	2	26			
Colonel Daniel Webb's																										3			
Colonel Robert Anstruther's				1							1		8		2	1	1							3		80			
Brig Genl Robert Monckton's													5		1	3	2							2	1	80			1
Colonel Charles Lawrence's																										2			
Colonel Simon Fraser's		1	2								1		14		2	3	3							7		131			2
Louisbourg Grenadiers				1									3		1	4										47			
Totals		1	6	1							3		45		13	26	10							25	4	506			3

Part of Brigadier Townshend's return of British casualties at Quebec: 58 killed and 599 wounded or missing (this part of the return does not include Wolfe and one gunner killed, and five staff officers and seven gunners wounded)

The interior of the Recollect Friars' church, Quebec, after the British capture of the city (one of a series of twelve engravings of the principal buildings in Quebec published in London after drawings made 'on the spot' by Richard Short)

headland and the boats ran fast with the tide. The sailors put out their oars, pulling hard against the rushing water, but they were swept past the chosen landing place. There was no question, though, of wasting time in getting back to it, and volunteers, who were to lead the assault, jumped out and leapt at the cliff. They clambered up so quietly that every one of them had reached the top before the first shots were fired. The post there was soon over-come – most of its defenders ran away – and by dawn 4,441 British troops had scrambled up the cliff while all the guns both in the fleet and on the southern bank kept up a ferocious cannonade.

Montcalm could be in no doubt that Wolfe had secured a triumphant advantage. 'C'est sérieux', he murmured, as he watched the British regiments deploying so skilfully in their long red lines across the Plains of Abraham in front of him. The crack Guienne Regiment, which he had ordered some days before to take up positions here, had been withdrawn and the Plains were, therefore, prac-tically undefended. Not until 9 o'clock was he able to overcome the problems presented by the confusing, con-tradictory and possibly treacherous activities of the civil administration and to draw up his forces in line of battle outside the town.

The early morning rain had stopped and the sun shone brightly down as the French began their advance. The ranks of grey, white and blue figures approached in three main groups with fixed bayonets. In most places they were six deep, but in the centre where the ground was more constricted the line, over half a mile long, was deeper. The soldiers marched forward with an imposing deliberation across the five hundred yards of open ground which separated them from the motionless line of their enemies.

The British soldiers had been lying down to avoid the round shot which constantly bounced at them through the prairie grass and bracken; but now they were stand-ing up, their muskets loaded with an extra ball. When the distance between the two armies had been reduced to a hundred and fifty yards the French opened fire. Several British soldiers fell; and at the sight the advancing troops let out, in curious unison, a shout of triumph and quick-ened their pace. They fired again. More men fell but the ranks closed once more and the British still did not fire back. 'Hold your fire! Hold your fire!' their officers called to them as the French drew nearer.

The advancing ranks, less controlled and orderly now,

RIGHT *A detailed plan of Quebec and its environs, showing the various British offensive operations during the siege, culminating in the battle on the Heights of Abraham above the city*

74

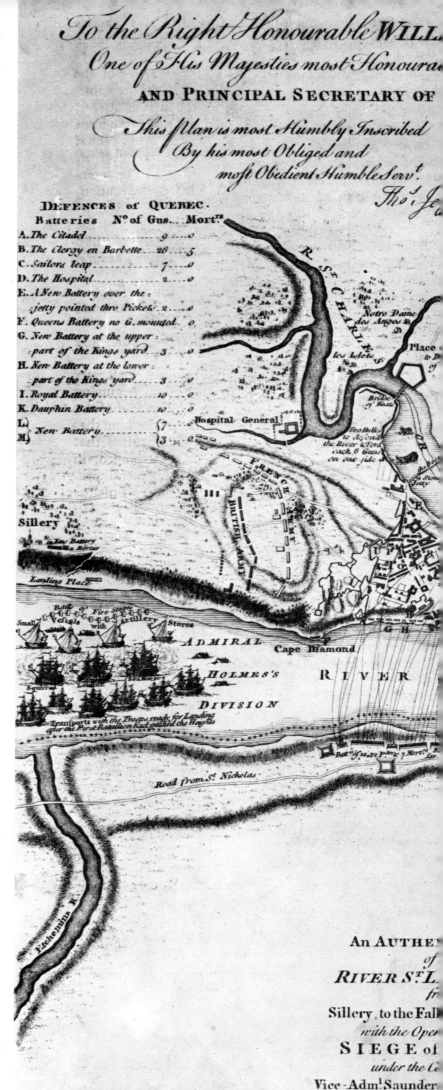

To the Right Honourable WILL
One of His Majesties most Honoura
AND PRINCIPAL SECRETARY OF
This Plan is most Humbly Inscribed
By his most Obliged and
most Obedient Humble Serv.t
Tho.s Je

DEFENCES of QUEBEC.
Batteries   N.o of Gus.. Mort.s

A. The Citadel . . . . 9 . . . . .
B. The Clergy en Barbette . . 26 . . . 5
C. Sailors leap . . . . 7 . . . 0
D. The Hospital . . . . 2 . . . 0
E. A New Battery over the :
   jetty pointed thro Pickets 2 0
F. Queens Battery no 6. mounted 0
G. New Battery at the upper :
   part of the Kings yard . . . 3 . . . 0
H. New Battery at the lower :
   part of the Kings yard . . . 3 . . . 0
I. Royal Battery . . . . 10 . . . 0
K. Dauphin Battery . . . . 10 . . . 0
L. New Battery . . . . {7 . . .
M.}   {3 . . .

An AUTHE
of
RIVER S.t L
fr
Sillery, to the Fall
with the Oper
SIEGE of
under the C
Vice-Adm.l Saunder
down to the
Drawn by a CAPTAIN i

Part of the
Upper River of
St. LAURENCE.

British Leagues

A VIEW
ACTION gained by t
Sep. 13. 1759
QUEB
Brought from
By an OFFICER of

Charlebourg or
le Petit Village

FRENCH INCAMPMENT

Larrey R.

Head

Batteries of 3 Guns Each

The Place where a Feint was
made by the Boats of the Fleet during the
whole night, whilst the Troops landed at Sillery

a Floating Battery

New Battery of 3 Guns

Beauport

New Batteries
of 3 Guns Each

Rafts
of
Fire Stages

FRENCH INCAMPMENT

Intrenchments commanding the Redoubts & Batteries

within Musque

les Batures de Beauport a Shoal Dry at Low Water

THE LITTLE R.

a French Wreck

Buoys that
deceiv'd the Enemy
into which the Boats
Moored that protec-
ted the Fleet
from the Rafts
of Fire Stages

Rafts

New Battery of 3 Guns

Point a l'Essay

the Place
of Attack July
30

LOWER

THE

B A S

ADMIRAL

FRIGATES

SAUNDERS'S

O N

LAURENCE

Point des Peres

Redoubt

BRIG. GEN. MONCTONS CAMP

St. Joseph

Road to Boaumont

POINT LEVY
Blim Cape Lauzon

DIVISION POINT OF ORLEANS

Admiral's Ship

MAJOR HARDY'S
POST

Transports
laid ashore
to clean

PLAN

ENCE

ontmorenci

of the

EBEC

t of

or Genl Wolfe

759.

ajesties Navy

British Miles

Part of the

Transports at Anchor

ABOVE LEFT *His surgeons' efforts were vain, as Montcalm, savagely wounded by an exploding shell towards the end of the battle, shared Wolfe's fate, and died the day after in Quebec, which fell to the British shortly afterwards*

ABOVE RIGHT *A portrait sketch of Wolfe by the Duchess of Devonshire, together with a copy of the lines found in Wolfe's pocket after his death – a fitting epitaph for the victor of Quebec*

were within fifty yards of them before the order to return their fire was given. It was Wolfe himself, bleeding from wounds in the stomach and the wrist and inspiringly elated, who gave the order and all down his line it was repeated and obeyed. The shattering volleys as each regiment fired were so perfectly controlled that a French officer described them as being like the shots from six cannon. Into the smoke the British troops fired again, and so well trained were they that this time, too, the crack of their muskets was like a short, tremendous roll of thunder. Quickly and calmly they reloaded, advanced twenty paces, according to the rules of the drill book and fired once more. For several minutes the firing continued and the balls flew through the smoke into the French bodies behind it; and as the fire lessened and the smoke lifted the British soldiers saw for the first time the havoc that they had caused. When, from the right of the line, Wolfe gave the order to charge, one of the shortest battles in the history of war was already decided.

Isolated groups of brave French soldiers and Canadian snipers held their ground but the main strength of the army was already broken and in flight. And Montcalm,

dying from a savage wound torn in his chest by an exploding shell, could do no more to help them.

Wolfe, too, had been hit in the chest and this, the third wound he had suffered that day, was a mortal one. 'I opened his Breast', a young volunteer remembered when he wrote home, 'And found his Shirt full of Blood At which he Smiled And when he Seen the Distress I was In, "My Dear", said He, "Dont Grieve for me I Shall Be Happy In a Few Minutes".'

Dying the soldier's death he had always hoped for, he summoned with characteristic determination the strength to give a last order so that the French army should not escape across the river to the north. Then he closed his eyes thanking God for his sudden victory.

It was a victory that was almost wasted in the cruel winter that followed, when the British garrison in Quebec was almost annihilated in a still continuing war; but it was a victory which marked a vital turning point in the history of the eighteenth century and decided the fate of North America for ever.

CHRISTOPHER HIBBERT

British troops drilling on the cathedral square; the Jesuits' College and the Recollect Friars' church are in the background (another engraving from the series after drawings by Richard Short)

A general view of the city of Quebec from the Pointe de Lévy, a high elbow of land on the south bank of the St. Lawrence, on which Wolfe encamped during the preliminary stages of his campaign (after the drawing by Richard Short)

1775
Bunker Hill

The American Colonists, by threatening Boston from Bunker Hill, drew out the British garrison who drove them off, though the city was evacuated nine months later

AS THE SPRING DAYS OF 1775 lengthened into summer, Britain's hold on the New World across the Atlantic was suddenly jarred loose. The Captain-General of His Majesty's forces in North America and military governor of the Massachusetts Bay Colony, General Thomas Gage, had striven for years with blundering good will to reconcile the rising exasperation of the American colonists with the inept demands made on their loyalty and their pockets by the royal government three thousand miles away in London. He had been almost too tolerant of the American Whigs and Liberty-Men in their incessant agitation for local autonomy, and he was conscious of his inability with the tiny military forces at his command to restrain the ebullient local population. All attempts to raise a local revenue with which to support the troops and the administrative establishment had been frustrated. Only the previous year three shiploads of tea subject to a nominal export duty had been tipped into the harbour by outraged citizens. In punishment the port of Boston had been closed to commerce.

For months Gage had been warning the home government that they must either abandon the American colonies to their fate or send such massive reinforcements of troops as would overawe the Whigs and their rebellious adherents. In April he had received advice that more troops were on their way. Provincial militiamen were drilling on village greens, hoarding stocks of powder and ball against the day when the inevitable clash must come. The first blood was shed when Gage sent a military column to the villages of Lexington and Concord on 18 April to seize and disperse stores of gunpowder.

In the eighteenth century, the town of Boston occupied a hilly peninsula, connected by a neck only the width of the road with the southern shore of the estuary into which flowed the parallel Charles River in the centre and Mystic River to the north. Boston and the twin settlement of Charlestown were some five hundred and fifty yards apart across the Charles and behind Charlestown three small hills, known as Bunker Hill, Breed's Hill and Morton's Hill, descended from the narrow neck in the west to the harbour in the east. Charlestown had been evacuated and the peninsula itself had become a no-man's-land, since Gage did not have the troops to occupy it and it was in any case dominated by the guns of the British fleet.

Since the two most militant Massachusetts leaders, John Hancock and Samuel Adams, had departed for the endless deliberations of the Continental Congress in Philadelphia; leadership had devolved on the Boston physician Dr Joseph Warren, to whom were joined the Massachusetts volunteer General Artemas Ward, and such French and Indian War firebrands as Israel Putnam from Connecticut and John Stark from New Hampshire. The militiamen were short of muskets, ammunition,

RIGHT *Red-hot shot has set fire to evacuated Charlestown to smoke out American snipers, while the Navy's longboats bring in the second British assault wave; American reinforcements are coming down Bunker Hill to the fort on Breed's Hill*

BOSTON

CHARLES TOWN

View of The ATTACK on BUNKER'S HILL, with the Burning of CHARLES TOWN June 17. 1775.

ABOVE *In April General Gage made his first attempt to nip the Revolution in the bud, sending troops to the villages of Lexington (left) and Concord (right) to seize stores of gunpowder; the Provincial militiamen did not allow them to pass unscathed*

LEFT The Battle of Bunker's Hill *by John Trumbull; at their third assault, by means of a flanking manœuvre and with American ammunition expended, the redcoats finally captured the breastwork on Breed's Hill*

clothing, and the most elementary military stores and could muster only half a dozen cannon. They made up for their deficiencies in numbers and resentment. While their leaders continued to bombard London with protestations of loyalty to King George III and shrill complaints against the Parliament which, by some devious process of reasoning, they considered hostile to them, deferential but continuous communication was kept up with General Gage in Boston.

Gage drew in what military reinforcements he could but at the end of May events had taken a decisive turn. The home government had sent no less than three well-chosen generals to stiffen what they had long come to suspect was Gage's soft backbone. The first was William Howe, who had led the picked detachment up the cliff at Wolfe's Battle of Quebec. The second in rank, Major-General Henry Clinton, had served with distinction in Europe in the Seven Years' War, and the third, Major-General John Burgoyne, 'Gentleman Johnny', a graceful man-about-town, had to his credit a care for the troops under his command rare in his day and age.

It seemed to the three new generals intolerable that an army of British regulars should be bottled up by a rabble of armed peasants. They conceived an elaborate plan for occupying the Charlestown promontory to the north and the Dorchester Heights to the south-east with token forces which would draw the American wings, while the main British force stormed through the narrow Boston neck and across the Charles River to assault and disperse the main American concentration in the centre round the little town of Cambridge.

Artemas Ward, the portly, pain-ridden American Commander-in-Chief, was a defensive-minded man of caution. He knew his troops, although numerous, were ill-equipped, ill-disciplined and virtually without co-

herent leadership. He had placed his one reliable Massachusetts colleague, John Thomas, in Roxbury opposite the Boston neck with nearly half the effective American force. He kept most of the remainder centred round himself at Cambridge. The American regiments, were practically autonomous. Command was exercised by competing colonels, Israel Putnam, Colonel William Prescott, and Dr Joseph Warren. They determined that a challenge must be flung down not only to disrupt British plans but to blood the raw American troops. It was decided to forestall the British by marching Frye's, Bridge's and Prescott's Massachusetts regiments on to the Charlestown Peninsula during the night of 16 June, and throwing up an earthen fort on Bunker Hill.

The three American senior officers who led the troops were by no means novices. Israel Putnam had been a colleague-in-arms of the British regulars during the French and Indian Wars. William Prescott had been offered a royal commission in the war against the French, but had declined the honour in the general resentment against the treatment of provincial officers. With them was Colonel Richard Gridley of Massachusetts, an engineer officer of real accomplishment, who had been responsible for manhandling Wolfe's guns up the Heights of Abraham, but had declared for his countrymen at the outbreak of the present rebellion.

As dusk fell at the end of the long June day, these three mounted the gentle bluff of Bunker Hill and, at Putnam's excitable, stuttering bidding, walked on down the gentle saddle half a mile to the next little eminence, known locally as Breed's Hill. Putnam was insistent that only from here could guns command the harbour. The starlit night, the uncertainty of their position and their officers' unexplained intentions had already unnerved the 1,000 or so militiamen detailed for this exploit. They carried an extraordinary mixture of arms, and very few of them possessed a bayonet. But one thing they did know, how to handle shovel and pick. Two companies were sent down into deserted Charlestown to keep watch and guard against surprise. Four hours later, they had constructed a shoulder-high earthen fort proof against musket and long-range cannon. The digging and clinking of shovel and pick had not gone unremarked in Boston. Clinton had received a vague report of activity on the Charlestown Peninsula, but had agreed with Howe that it could only be a minor demonstration and that the following morning would be early enough for them to take suitable measures.

The guns of HMS *Lively* firing a dawn broadside against the impertinent fort brought them to a different reality. Admiral Graves fluttered signals to her impetuous captain to cease fire. Then, the senior British officers saw with disbelief and astonishment that a perfectly defensible earthwork had been thrown up during the night on the height above Charlestown. Their position had been turned and the threat of bombardment of Boston must be dealt with before their own master plan could be put into operation. Graves was requested to recommence the cannonade, but the cannonballs could be seen bouncing back from its sloping face. General Gage had with him an American loyalist named Abijah Willard. He handed him his glass and asked if he could identify the figure on the parapet. Willard looked, turned to Gage and said it was William Prescott, his own brother-in-law. 'Will he fight?' Gage demanded. 'I cannot answer for his men', Willard replied, 'but Prescott will fight you to the gates of hell.'

The Massachusetts provincials were terrified by the artillery bombardment. Only Prescott's magnificent example maintained their discipline and stilled the panic that followed the early casualties. On the northern side the gentler slope lay completely undefended, open to a flanking movement. Prescott set his tired men to dig a breastwork leading from the fort half-way down the hill.

Howe saw little reason for undue haste: the British regiments must go equipped for a major operation, so his troops were ordered to parade with full equipment and the cooks baked bread and boiled beef for three days' supplies. The ideal manœuvre would be to land at the Charlestown neck and cut off the Americans in the fort, but the triangle between the mainland and the Charlestown Peninsula was filled by a mill dam. Charlestown itself offered endless cover to snipers, while the northern side of the peninsula on the Mystic River was known to consist of extensive mud flats. Howe's choice of the landing point was influenced by the fact that he did not have at his disposal any flat-bottomed landing boats and was dependent on the navy's longboats, which would not be

First Battalion of PENNSYLVANIA LOYALISTS, commanded by His Excellency Sir WILLIAM HOWE, K B.

ALL INTREPID ABLE-BODIED

HEROES,

WHO are willing to serve His MAJESTY KING GEORGE the Third, in Defence of their Country, Laws and Constitution, against the arbitrary Usurpations of a tyrannical Congress, have now not only an Opportunity of manifesting their Spirit, by assisting in reducing to Obedience their too-long deluded Countrymen, but also of acquiring the polite Accomplishments of a Soldier, by serving only two Years, or during the present Rebellion in America.

Such spirited Fellows, who are willing to engage, will be rewarded at the End of the War, besides their Laurels, with 50 Acres of Land, where every gallant Hero may retire. . . . .

Each Volunteer will receive, as a Bounty, FIVE DOLLARS, besides Arms, Cloathing and Accoutrements, and every other Requisite proper to accommodate a Gentleman Soldier, by applying to Lieutenant Colonel ALLEN, or at Captain KEARNY's Rendezvous, at PATRICK TONRY's, three Doors above Market-street, in Second-street.

A finely rhetorical proclamation by William Howe, one of the three new generals sent out from England to assist Gage in suppressing the Revolution

able to negotiate these shallows. Also, such was the ineptitude of Admiral Graves, that no attempt had been made to sound the Mystic River approaches.

It was not until 1.30 pm. that the loaded barges with the first assault wave shoved off. For the landing Howe had combined the ten light infantry and the ten grenadier companies from the regiments in the garrison into special assault corps. These men were the pick of the army. With them in support came the 4th or King's Own Regiment, the 5th, the 23rd, the 38th, the 43rd and the 52nd. The landing was completely unopposed. The light infantry and the grenadiers quickly formed a skirmishing line two hundred yards from the landing point, while the boats returned for the second wave. So confident was

The other side of the coin – an anti-recruiting cartoon, suggesting the real plight of a volunteer, 'Exposed to the Horrors of War, Pestilence and Famine for a Farthing an Hour'

Howe of success that he had his men pile arms and eat their midday meal.

Even as Howe waited, the situation changed to his disadvantage. He could see that his sweep up the peninsula would encounter difficulties on the left flank from the houses in Charlestown and he requested Admiral Graves to give orders to the fleet to set the town on fire. Graves was ready with red hot shot and in no time the houses and steeples were ablaze. But on Howe's right flank the path was less clear than he thought. He caught his first sight of the breastwork and, even as he watched, the greater eminence of Bunker Hill, several hundred yards behind the fort, became crowned with another thousand militiamen.

The British landing had caught the Americans by sur-

prise. As soon as he saw the redcoats massing at Morton's Point, Prescott sent 200 Connecticut men down the steep hill into the open ground beyond the end of the breastwork to advance and challenge the skirmishers. However, Israel Putnam saw that it was madness for them to venture into the open and directed them to man a rail fence about one hundred yards back from the breastwork. He then galloped back to Cambridge and on the way sent a thousand more Connecticut troops over into the Charlestown Peninsula. He also persuaded Ward to send word to John Stark's New Hampshire regiment to make haste over the Charlestown neck. The New Hampshiremen were probably the best marksmen in the American army and the best disciplined. When Stark arrived he could

ABOVE LEFT *William Howe, the British Commander at Bunker Hill, had previously served with Wolfe at Quebec and was shortly to become the Commander-in-Chief of the British forces in America*

ABOVE RIGHT *Israel Putnam from Massachusetts, who had fought with the British in the French and Indian Wars, selected Breed's Hill as the site for the earthen fort which was constructed during the night of 16 June*

The Charlestown promontory, showing the position of the temporary earthwork on Breed's Hill thrown up by the Americans on the night of 16 June 1775, and the rail fence at the foot of Bunker Hill which for so long successfully barred the British advance the next day

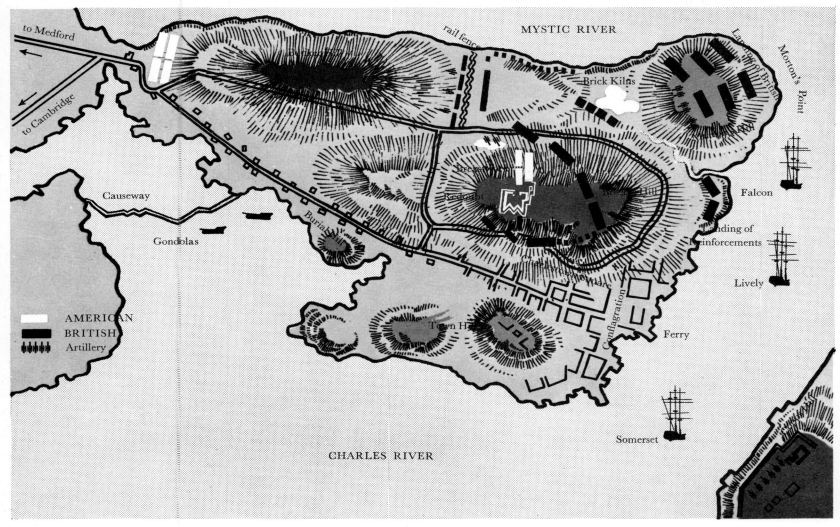

see that the American position could still be outflanked; there were still some twenty feet of river shore unguarded. He set his men to build a stone wall stretching into the river. Prescott's Massachusetts men in the fort had been thinned by deserters and exhaustion. Their morale was only restored by the appearance of Dr Joseph Warren. Prescott offered to serve under him and take his orders, but Warren said that he had come with his musket to fight as a private. His striking figure provided the encouragement the shaken farmers needed.

Howe by now had completed his dispositions, though the troops could not have been worse turned-out for the trial that lay ahead of them: their brilliant scarlet coats made perfect targets and, with their packs, each was carrying a weight estimated at 125 lb while their muskets weighed a further 10 lb.

The light infantry were to move up the river shore against the stone wall and turn the American flank. Howe himself had 37 companies of the grenadiers, the 5th and 52nd regiments, to lead against the rail fence. The left wing was commanded by Brigadier-General Robert Pigot, who had 38 companies of the 38th and 43rd regiments, with more light infantry and grenadiers to lead against the breastwork and the redoubt, while on the far left flank Major Pitcairn and his Marines, with the 47th regiment, were to deal with the threat from Charlestown and turn the fort's left flank.

Slowly and majestically the triple red lines moved up the hill. Howe, able soldier that he was, had left final word with Admiral Graves that the two shallow-draught floating batteries which had been harassing the Americans from the mill pond as they crossed the Charlestown neck, should be brought right round the peninsula into the Mystic River where the guns could be brought to bear on the Americans behind the stone wall and rail fence. What was intended as a military promenade soon ran into difficulties. The waist-high grass concealed ground made uneven by rocks and intersected by low stone walls and rail fences. The British line became badly broken up as the soldiers hacked away at these obstacles. On the left, Pitcairn and the Marines encountered a galling fire from the burning houses of Charlestown and had to refuse their flank. On the northern side, the light infantrymen advanced at their quick pace, confident that a

The raw American troops may have awaited the expected battle in the morning with foreboding, but they tackled more familiar pick-and-shovel work with a will

volley and the bayonet would wreak their accustomed havoc.

Stark had hammered a stake into the shore 40 yards from his stone wall. He warned his men that no shot was to be fired until the front ranks of the British had passed the post. The first volley stopped the light infantry stone dead. As the succeeding companies stepped over their prone bodies, two more unbelievable volleys decimated the British ranks and the rest turned and fled. Howe could hardly believe his ears when the report reached him. Both his flanks were gone, but he urged his own men for-

ward. He roared at them to rely on the bayonet, but as they came within seventy yards of the Connecticut regiment the earth suddenly erupted. Israel Putnam had in his turn been yelling at his men to wait until they saw the enemy's gaiters clearly. 'Fire' bellowed Putnam at last. Safe behind the rail fence 1,500 men fired in unison. The carnage was staggering. Over on the left Pigot and his men suffered the same fate. There was nothing for the British to do but to retire and re-form.

Howe led his men in again with the same result. Three times the general found himself entirely alone, with

While their artillery bombards the American fort, the scarlet-clad British infantry moves slowly and majestically up the hill

everybody around him dead or wounded. Howe essayed a third attack, though many of the grenadier and light infantry companies had lost three-fourths and some of them nine-tenths of their men.

When Clinton saw Howe suffer his second repulse, he sent word to Gage that he was moving and rowed over with more Marines and the 63rd regiment to land nearer Charlestown. Although their losses would have destroyed less disciplined troops, the British were now in a fury to avenge their comrades. Led again by Howe and Pigot, with Clinton in support, they moved forward into the inferno that awaited them.

Howe had kept his head amidst the carnage. His artillery was now up with the forward troops. This time he wheeled left just within musket range of the rail fence, leaving his remaining light infantry to act as a skirmishing line to engage the attention of the Connecticut men, and moved his whole force up the hill to take the breastwork in flank. The manoeuvre worked.

American resistance suddenly collapsed. They had run out of ammunition and powder. With a maniac roar the terrible line of gleaming bayonets was suddenly amongst

'*Bunkers Hill, or the blessed effects of Family quarrels*': a British political cartoon, in which America (left), a Red Indian with toma-hawk and scalping-knife, fights Britannia; Spain supports America, while France stabs Britain in the back (*the figures above are Lords Mansfield, Bute and North*)

A combined anti-recruiting poster and satire of the latest women's fashions in England ('*to Trenton*' is a gibe at Washington's capture of Trenton)

them. Joseph Warren constituted himself the rearguard with a handful of men and the moment the smoke cleared, a single volley dropped him dead. Once through the fort, the redcoats could outflank the Americans, who retreated in surprisingly good order, although the moment they caught up with the shirkers who had been sitting out the battle on Bunker Hill the retreat became a rout. The British in their turn were too exhausted to follow far.

It was a British victory, but not an American defeat. The British casualties were nearly fifty per cent, 226 kil-led and 828 wounded. Twenty-seven British officers were killed and 63 were wounded. The American casualties were about 450, most of them in the final stages, but as they licked their wounds, realization seeped through that this rabble of farmers had not only stood up to the finest infantry in the world, but had inflicted more than twice as many casualties as they had suffered themselves. It was the turning point in the morale of the incipient Revolution.

The British gained no advantage from the sacrifice of so many men. They remained bottled up in Boston and the following March, when the Americans seized and built an even larger fort on the Dorchester Heights, the harbour became untenable. The entire British force, with over a thousand American loyalists, boarded the ships in the harbour and sailed off to Halifax. They never saw Boston again as a British settlement.

BRIAN CONNELL

'*Bunkers Hill, or America's Head-Dress*': *another British cartoon combining political satire and comment on women's hair-styles of the day*

1777
Saratoga

Burgoyne's surrender at Saratoga, mainly the result of inefficient direction of the war from London, brought France and, later, Spain as allies to the Americans

THERE WAS, STRICTLY SPEAKING, no such thing as the Battle of Saratoga. But the capitulation of the British army under Lieutenant-General Sir John Burgoyne which took place at that township on 17 October 1777 marked the turning-point of the American War of Independence. It revived the American cause in a time of darkness and discouragement, and prompted Britain's European rivals, France and Spain, to join forces with the rebelling colonies. This alliance, to which Holland was later added, spelt the loss of the naval supremacy on which all British hopes were founded, and inevitably wrought their ruin.

As we study the campaign which led to this result, there seems to be an inexorability both about its conception and its execution. No individual was entirely responsible for the first of these; it was General Burgoyne himself who submitted to the British Government a plan of campaign along the Lake Champlain–Hudson River line in February 1777, but the idea had already suggested itself to many in America and in London. For the British problem, in overcoming the rebellion of the American colonies, was essentially one of space. Distances were great and frequently across trackless territory, covered with dense forests, split by wide rivers. Only a massive army of occupation, far beyond Britain's capacity, could

LEFT *John Burgoyne by Sir Joshua Reynolds: 'Gentleman Johnny' was a popular, competent officer, with a high sense of duty but, denied the essential co-operation of Howe's army in New York, his Saratoga campaign was doomed to failure*

hold this country in subjection. The alternative was to use sea-power against the heavily-populated coastal strip, and by the mobility which this conferred, to attempt to isolate particular sectors. The most promising of these would be New England, the hot-bed of the rebellion, where secessionist sentiment was at its strongest.

The geography of New England and eastern Canada favoured this scheme; along the whole of the almost three hundred and fifty miles which separated Montreal from New York (both firmly in British hands) lay the great continuous waterways of Lake Champlain, Lake George and the Hudson River. The problems of communication and supply, normally crippling during this war, were thus immensely eased for any British force coming down from Canada. The advantages of this manœuvre were enormous, but all depended on one thing: close co-operation between the Canadian army and the main body of the British forces (some 25,000 men under General Sir William Howe) at New York.

Over the whole drama of Burgoyne's ill-fated expedition lie the shadows of two absent men. In London, the baleful influence of the Secretary for America, Lord George Germain, made itself felt from the beginning. It was he who approved Burgoyne's plan; he who gave the necessary orders to General Sir Guy Carleton, the Governor of Quebec; he who informed Sir William Howe of what was intended; and it was he who entirely omitted to ensure the co-operation between Howe and Burgoyne, on which the whole project depended. It was with Lord

A real representation of the Drefs of An
AMERICAN RIFLE-MAN.

*Though consisting largely of militia, whose quality was unpredictable,
the American army was better suited for fighting in the wild terrain of
North America than the scarlet-clad British troops encumbered both by
heavy equipment and formal European tactics*

RIGHT *An American recruiting notice (its rhetoric is rather more restrained than in its British counterpart), which also includes some
instructions in arms drill*

George's full knowledge that Sir William Howe commenced a series of operations which could only deprive
Burgoyne of the aid from New York on which he counted.
Those operations, in turn, were brought about by the influence of General George Washington, in Pennsylvania.

The year 1775 had ended with the unprepared British
forces locked up in Boston. In 1776 large reinforcements
and new commanders arrived in North America, and the
British Government had high hopes of nipping the colonial rebellion in the bud. An American invasion of
Canada was firmly repelled; the Boston cul-de-sac was
evacuated, and Howe, by a brilliant series of operations,
made himself master of New York. It may be that he

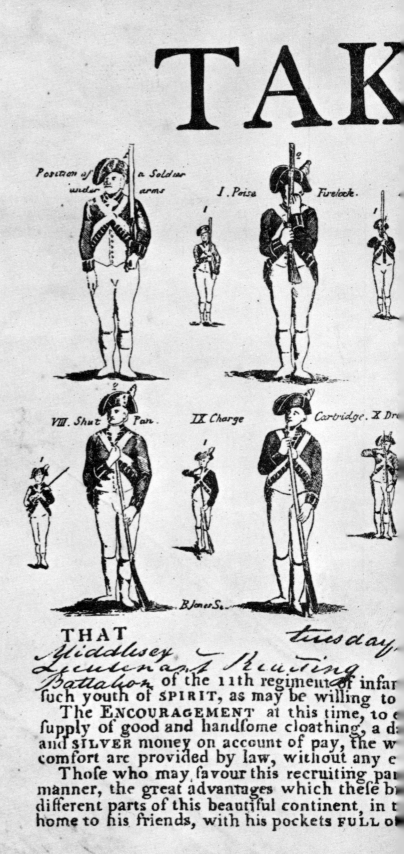

TO ALL BRAVE,
D
IN THIS NEIGHBOURHOOD

GEN

LIBER
OF

TAK

Position of a Soldier
under arms   I. Poise   Firelock.

VIII. Shut Pan.   IX Charge   Cartridge. X Dr

B Jones Se.

THAT   tuesday
Middlesex
Lieutenant Recruiting
Battalion of the 11th regiment of infar
such youth of SPIRIT, as may be willing to
The ENCOURAGEMENT at this time, to
supply of good and handsome cloathing, a d
and SILVER money on account of pay, the w
comfort are provided by law, without any
Those who may favour this recruiting pa
manner, the great advantages which these b
different parts of this beautiful continent, in t
home to his friends, with his pockets FULL of

EALTHY, ABLE BODIED, AND WELL
POSED YOUNG MEN,
HO HAVE ANY INCLINATION TO JOIN THE TROOPS,
OW RAISING UNDER

ERAL WASHINGTON,
R THE DEFENCE OF THE
ES AND INDEPENDENCE
HE UNITED STATES,
ainst the hostile designs of foreign enemies,

E NOTICE,

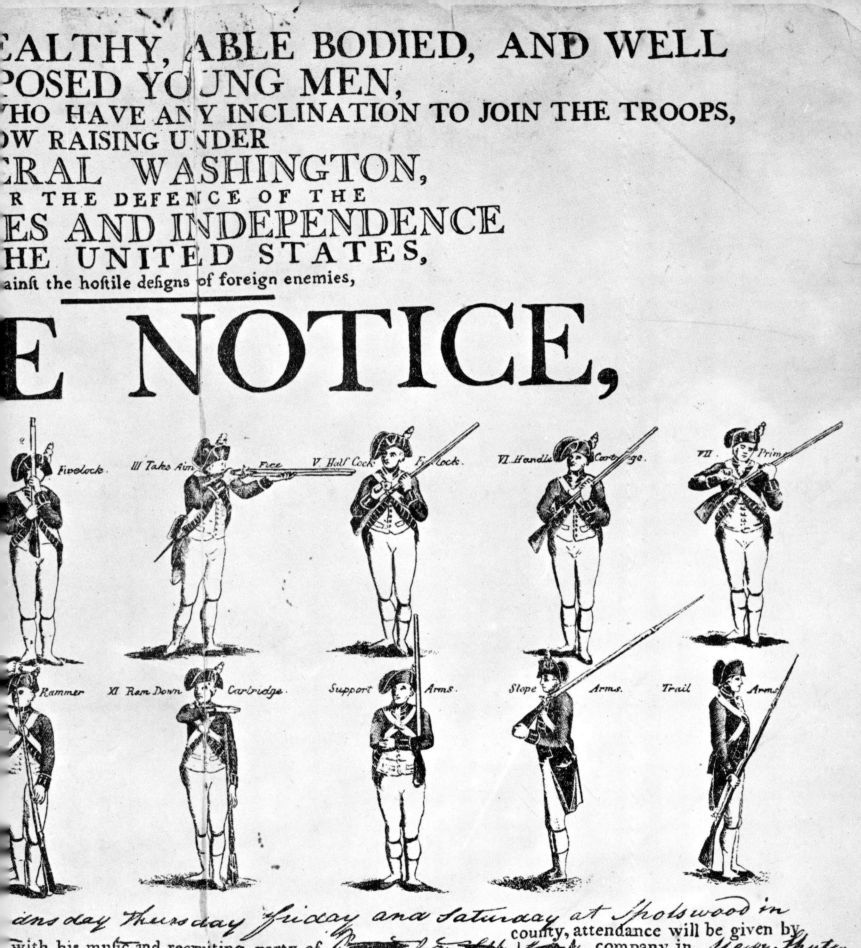

ans day *Thursday friday and Saturday at Spotswood in*
county, attendance will be given by
with his music and recruiting party of ~~Capt~~ company in *Major Shute*
ommanded by Lieutenant Colonel Aaron Ogden, for the purpose of receiving the enrollment of
into this HONOURABLE service.
is truly liberal and generous, namely, a bounty of TWELVE dollars, an annual and fully sufficient
lowance of a large and ample ration of provisions, together with SIXTY dollars a year in GOLD
f which the soldier may lay up for himself and friends, as all articles proper for his subsistance and
e to him.
th their attendance as above, will have an opportunity of hearing and seeing in a more particular
en will have, who shall embrace this opportunity of spending a few happy years in viewing the
nourable and truly respectable character of a soldier, after which, he may, if he pleases return
ey and his head COVERED with laurels.
GOD SAVE THE UNITED STATES.

Benedict Arnold, the hero of Saratoga, is unhorsed as the Americans encounter a group of Major-General Riedesel's Hessians

RIGHT *New England and eastern Canada in 1777, showing the scenes of the various battles of and immediately before the Saratoga Campaign: Trenton and Princeton in New Jersey, Fort Ticonderoga, Bennington and Saratoga*

could have done more, though it has to be remembered that, in conjunction with his brother, Admiral Lord Howe, he was simultaneously attempting to negotiate a settlement with the colonists. But King George III set his face against anything less than complete submission. Thus the year approached its end with British expectations unfulfilled, though damaging blows had been struck at the Americans. Washington, expelled from New York, had escaped by the skin of his teeth into Pennsylvania, where he held his small army together in the depth of winter only by the most indomitable resolution.

It was at this critical juncture that he fully revealed the genius that was in him. When almost any general would

have been satisfied to await better times, Washington decided to hazard everything on a counter-stroke. On Christmas Day 1776, he struck at Howe's detachments along the Delaware River. In icy cold and blinding sleet he fell upon a brigade of Hessian troops at Trenton, and defeated them utterly. A few days later he obtained another success against a second British detachment at Princeton. Thus Washington's skill had ended the year with unlooked-for American successes, and ensured that, when the new year came, Howe would be looking to his left, towards Philadelphia. And so it was; Howe informed Germain that he proposed to make his next campaign in Pennsylvania; Germain, incredibly, approved Howe's intention *within a week* of giving precise orders to Burgoyne and Carleton in an exactly opposite sense.

Ignorant of this, Burgoyne, his subordinate commanders, and his men, were in high spirits as they assembled at the head of Lake Champlain. Carleton, despite the insulting tone of Germain's correspondence, helped Burgoyne to the best of his ability. The latter was himself a competent officer, with a high sense of duty and a great deal of personal magnetism. The generals under him were also able men: Major-General Phillips of the Royal Artillery, who had distinguished himself at Minden; Major-General Riedesel, commanding the German contingent; and Brigadier-General Simon Fraser, a vigorous and gallant leader. One of the junior officers wrote:

> As to our army, I can only say if good discipline, joined to health and spirit among the men at being led by General Burgoyne, who is universally esteemed and respected, can ensure success, it may be expected.

And in truth it may be said that few expeditionary forces have emerged with such personal honour to all ranks as this one, despite the disaster in which it ended.

This efficiency is the more significant because the British Army of the period was far from at its best. All its units were under strength; recruiting was difficult; uniforms were brilliant with scarlet and lace, but utterly unsuitable for the wild terrain of North America; on active service the soldier carried a load of about 60 lb. Yet in some ways Burgoyne's army was extremely modern; having been present at Bunker Hill, he understood the weakness of formal European tactics, and did everything to encourage his officers and men towards mobility and flexibility.

On the American side, conditions were somewhat different. The commander of their forces facing Burgoyne was Major-General Philip Schuyler, a most able officer. Apart from 3,500 men at Fort Ticonderoga, the 'Gibraltar of America', Schuyler's army was scattered in detachments through what are now called Vermont and New York State. Consisting largely of Militia, its quality was unpredictable. Long after the campaign had opened, Schuyler wrote to Washington:

> Too many of our officers would be a disgrace to the most contemptible troops ever collected, and have so little sense of honour that cashiering them seems no punishment.

It speaks volumes for Schuyler's ability that he was able to overcome his army's failings; his efforts would be seconded by those of another brilliant American officer.

On 20 June Burgoyne issued a proclamation which stated:

> The Services required of this particular Expedition are critical and conspicuous. During our progress occasions may occur, in which nor difficulty, nor labour, nor life are to be regarded. THIS ARMY MUST NOT RETREAT.

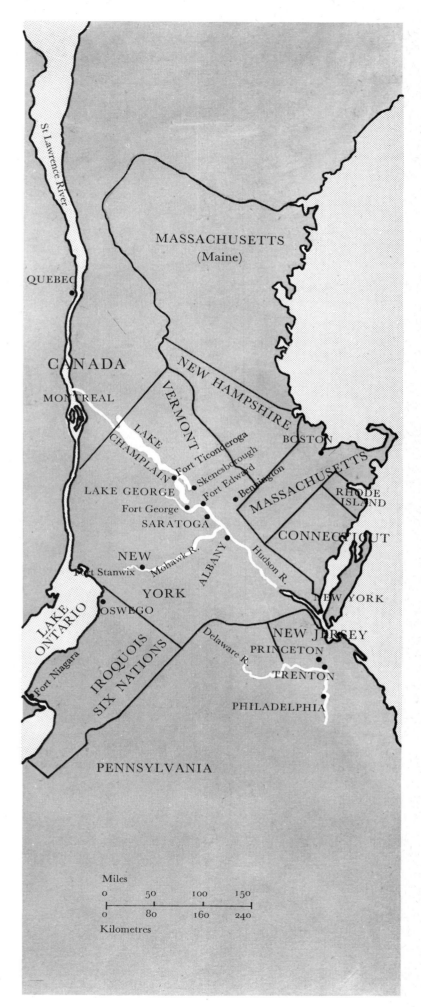

The next day, the whole colourful array set out for Ticonderoga. Five British regiments numbered some 3,700; five German regiments, another 3,000; with officers, artillerymen, Canadians, Provincials (American loyalists) and 500 Indians, the whole amounted to just over 8,000. With them went 38 guns, including heavy pieces and howitzers to reduce the forts in their way. To carry them down Lake Champlain a fleet of three frigates, 20 gunboats and 200 Canadian bateaux had been assembled.

On 3 July Burgoyne appeared before Ticonderoga, and three days later the great fort was in his hands. This was due to the address of General Phillips; noting the dominating height of Sugar Hill, the old Gunner said: 'Where a goat can go a man can go, and where a man can go he can drag a gun'. Phillips forthwith placed a battery on the Hill, and the Americans abandoned the fort. Burgoyne at once broke through the boom across the lake, and pursued the American flotilla so hotly that he almost entirely destroyed it. The garrison retreated by land, and the next day General Fraser caught their rearguard at Hubbardtown. These were picked troops who outnumbered Fraser's brigade by two to one. Yet Fraser was able to hold them successfully until supported by Riedesel, inflicting some 400 casualties for a loss of 140. On 10 July Burgoyne arrived at Skenesborough. In 20 days, at a cost of only some 200 men, he had advanced over 100 miles, captured 128 guns and many prisoners, taken the most important fortress in America, and now stood only some 60 miles from Albany, where he expected to meet Howe's advance from New York.

Yet it was precisely in this moment of triumph that Burgoyne's difficulties began. First, his force was much reduced through having to leave a garrison of some 900 at Ticonderoga. Secondly, his own tactics went far to increase the dangers of this reduction. Far away at Philadelphia, when he heard the account of the campaign's opening, Washington perceived Burgoyne's error; he wrote to Schuyler on 22 July:

> From your accounts [Burgoyne] appears to be pursuing that line of conduct, which is of all others most favourable to us; I mean acting in Detachments. This conduct will certainly give room to Enterprise on our part, and expose his parties to great hazard.

Prophetic words.

Thirdly, there was Burgoyne's decision to continue his advance to Albany overland. The alternative was to sail the bulk of the army back to Ticonderoga, transfer it there to Lake George, and use that waterway to Fort George and the wagon road from there to Fort Edward. Chiefly because of his expectation of receiving much loyalist support in Vermont, he opted against this course, with the most serious results. Finally, while Burgoyne had been seizing Ticonderoga, Howe had been embarking for Philadelphia, and while Burgoyne's men were

A pencil sketch by John Trumbull of Major-General Horatio Gates, the somewhat supine American commander at Saratoga

RIGHT The Death of General Mercer at the Battle of Princeton by John Trumbull; General Washington on horseback directs the battle – an unexpected counter-stroke against the British which helped to ensure that Howe would make his next campaign in Pennsylvania

Benedict Arnold, whose energetic direction of the battle gained success for the Americans in spite of their irresolute commander, Gates

struggling through the forests, Howe's were waiting in their transports for a wind to carry them south. This was the root of Burgoyne's downfall, and the blame must fall upon Lord George Germain.

Transport was Burgoyne's immediate problem. General Schuyler played upon his difficulties with great skill. A British officer wrote from Skenesborough on 17 July:

> We are obliged to wait for some time in our present position, till the roads are cleared . . . every ten or twelve yards great trees are laid across . . .

Sergeant Lamb of the 9th Foot tells us:

> The face of the countryside was . . . so broken with creeks and marshes, that there was no less than forty bridges to construct.

Also, the Americans had swept the country bare; neither food, nor draught animals nor mounts for the Brunswick Dragoons could be procured. Meanwhile the Indians, by their outrages, were thoroughly alienating the population. The march from Skenesborough to Fort Edward, a distance of only twenty miles, cost Burgoyne twenty days.

A long halt followed; Burgoyne would probably now have preferred to swing into Connecticut, but felt that he had no choice. His present preoccupation was supply, and hearing that there was an American depot of horses and cattle at Bennington, over twenty miles from his main body at Saratoga, he detached some 400 men to seize this valuable booty. It was a dangerous move, for which Burgoyne has been much blamed; there is little doubt, however, that he over-estimated the strength of loyalist feeling in this area. Learning of American concentrations, he detached another party of 500 in support. But the leading force was surrounded and destroyed by American Militia; the second might have reversed the issue, but for the arrival of Colonel Seth Warner and his Green Mountain Boys. With this reinforcement, though the British fought until their ammunition ran out, the Americans defeated both detachments. Washington's prediction was fulfilled.

More bad news followed swiftly. As well as the junction with the New York army at Albany, it was part of the British plan to strike in from Oswego, on the banks of Lake Ontario, up the Mohawk River. This diversion, under Colonel St Leger, was also intended to link with Burgoyne. But St Leger's small force (only 850 Regulars,

Canadians and Provincials, with some 1,000 Indians), after an early success, was held up by the log walls of Fort Stanwix. Lacking a battering train, St Leger was forced to invest the fort, and while he was doing so one of the leading actors in the Saratoga drama made his appearance on the stage – Benedict Arnold. By a ruse, Arnold was able to frighten off St Leger's Indians, so that on 22 August the British had to raise the siege and fall back to Oswego. On this same day, which may be regarded as the turning-point of the campaign, Sir William Howe's transports cast anchor in Chesapeake Bay. His design against Philadelphia now became patent. Washington wrote on that day: 'Now let all New England turn out and crush Burgoyne'.

Two days earlier, Burgoyne wrote to Lord George Germain:

> Had I a latitude in my orders, I should think it my duty to wait in this position, or perhaps as far back as Fort Edward, where my communication with Lake George would be perfectly secure;

but his orders were positive to 'force a junction with Sir William Howe'. Accordingly, on 13 September, Burgoyne set out from Saratoga. His army was now reduced to some 5,000 effectives, while the Americans before him numbered about 14,000. Only one advantage had accrued to the British: the replacement of the able Schuyler by Major-General Horatio Gates, an officer of English birth and mediocre talents. But Arnold was also there.

Gates drew up his force at a position called Bemis Heights, overlooking the Hudson River, and commanding the road which ran beside it. Burgoyne, displaying a quick eye for ground, noted that the American position might be turned by its left. On 19 September he divided his army into three columns: Fraser on the right, with the Grenadier and Light Battalions, the 24th Foot and the Canadians and Provincials; Burgoyne himself in the centre, with the 9th, XXth, 21st and 62nd Regiments (the four totalling less than 1,100 men); Riedesel on the left, advancing along the riverside road. Officers and men were in good spirit, but conscious of a desperate adventure.

What followed was Arnold's battle. It was he who recognized the threat of Fraser's flanking movement. He 'urged, begged and entreated' the supine Gates, until at last he won permission to send forward Colonel Daniel Morgan's corps of riflemen and Dearborn's Light Infantry. They clashed with Fraser's column and the British centre at a clearing known as Freeman's Farm, where the bitter fight swayed backward and forward for hours. Hearing that his men were in trouble, Arnold immediately exclaimed: 'By God! I will soon put an end to it'. As more Americans (1st, 2nd, 3rd New Hampshire, the Connecticut Militia, 2nd and 4th New York Regiments, Learned's Brigade) arrived, Arnold swung the weight of

ABOVE LEFT *The Surrender of General Burgoyne by John Trumbull; Gates's promise of a free passage home to Burgoyne and his depleted army was later repudiated by the United States Congress*

LEFT *The burial of Brigadier-General Simon Fraser, the vigorous and gallant British leader who was mortally wounded during Burgoyne's vain second attempt to advance on 7 October (painted by J. Graham)*

A satirical cartoon which ascribes tyranny, failure (at Saratoga) and savage Indian atrocities to the influence of Bute, Mansfield and Lord George Germain, and to the obstinacy of the king.

A political cartoon which includes a reference to Burgoyne's surrender at Saratoga on 17 October 1777, and another to Lord George Germain, who was chiefly responsible for it.

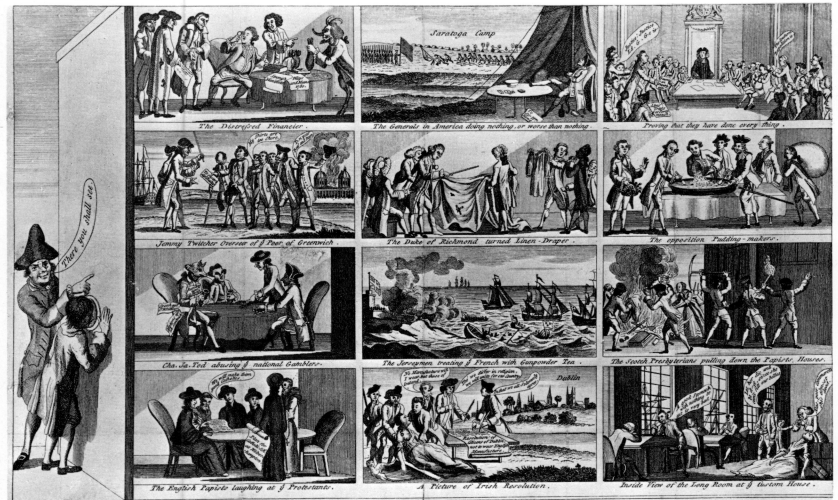

his counter-attack against Burgoyne's centre column. The XXth, 21st and 62nd Regiments (the 9th was in reserve) gave him a hot reception. Sergeant Lamb of the 9th describes the scene:

> Here the conflict was dreadful; for four hours a constant blaze of fire was kept up . . . Men, and particularly officers, dropped every moment on each side . . . Major-General Phillips, upon hearing the firing made his way through a difficult part of the wood to the scene of action, and . . . led up the 20th Regiment at the most personal hazard.

The British Army historian, Sir John Fortescue, wrote:

> Never were troops more hardly tried, nor met their trial more grandly than these three noble battalions, with the forty-eight artillerymen who worked their four guns by their side . . . Again and again the three battalions charged with the bayonet, but Arnold could always bring forward fresh troops to replace those who had fallen.

Both sides were fought to a standstill; Burgoyne had lost about 600 men out of his small force, the Americans about half as many, but enough to daunt their piecemeal attacks. Burgoyne had no reserves, Gates had nearly 9,000. Yet such was the spirit of the former and the feebleness of the latter, that it was the British who camped on the field, while Gates prepared to be attacked again. But the 'victory' was an illusion. Burgoyne now learned that the Americans had cut his communications with Lake Champlain. But knowing too that General Sir Henry Clinton had at last set out from New York to assist him, he felt obliged to hold his ground. Clinton's force did good work on the lower Hudson, but was never adequate to fight its way through to Burgoyne. As the weeks slipped by, Burgoyne became persuaded that he and his army were a deliberate sacrifice. Only such a belief can explain his second attempt to *advance* on 7 October. This time he was only able to put some 1,500 men in the field; the issue was a foregone conclusion. Once again, despite Gates's orders, Arnold was the soul of the battle. Thanks to his energy, the British were driven back to their camp, with further heavy losses, including the brave and talented Fraser, mortally wounded.

The end was now in sight. A miserable week followed for the British troops, reduced to half-rations, soaked by drenching autumn rains. Burgoyne was still looking for opportunities of resuming the offensive, but nothing could alter hard facts. On 12 October he at last decided to abandon his guns and baggage and attempt escape. It was already too late; the Americans were behind him. The next day he sent a flag of truce to Gates, who demanded 'unconditional surrender'. But such was the repute of the British force and its commander that when, on 17 October, they finally capitulated, the American general permitted them to march out of their camp with the honours of war, and promised them 'a free passage . . .

to Great Britain'. On this understanding, Burgoyne's army piled arms; they numbered a bare 3,500 men fit for duty. Later the United States Congress repudiated the Saratoga Convention. The soldiers were not repatriated; many of them died in captivity in miserable conditions extending at times even to deliberate murder. British comment on this has naturally been bitter; but after Saratoga the circumstances were, of course, altered. America now had allies, and could hardly permit these men to be released to fight her friends. This, indeed, was the significance of the Saratoga campaign, the transformation of American prospects which it created. And thus it is rightly counted among the decisive battles of America and of the world.

JOHN TERRAINE

An engraving of a medal struck by Congress in honour of Horatio Gates, to whom Burgoyne surrendered at Saratoga

1781 Yorktown

Admiral Graves's failure to defeat de Grasse in Chesapeake Bay enabled Washington and his French allies to complete the stranglehold on Cornwallis at Yorktown

THE SURRENDER OF A BRITISH ARMY at Saratoga in the October of 1777 internationalized a conflict which hitherto had been limited to Britain's attempt to regain control over the thirteen rebellious American Colonies. France was encouraged to exchange covert for open hostility; and in due course Spain and Holland became her co-belligerents.

As French troops and a French fleet, under the Comte de Grasse, were hastened across the Atlantic, Sir Henry Clinton, in chief command in New York, received fresh orders from Lord George Germain on behalf of the British Cabinet. These instructions directed him to reinforce the West Indies garrisons and then proceed to the support of the loyalists in the Southern States. Having brought his mission to the South to a climax with the capture of Savannah and Charleston, the massing of enemy forces on the Hudson and Long Island sent him hurrying back to his northern base. Lord Cornwallis, at the head of some 4,000 troops, was left to complete the pacification of Georgia and the Carolinas.

In the ensuing campaign the loss of Major Patrick Ferguson and 1,000 loyalists of King's Mountain and the defeat of Lieutenant-Colonel Banastre Tarleton at Cowpens were very largely offset by Cornwallis's narrow but unquestionable victories at Camden and Guildford, exhausting as they may have been to the victors. But although the balance of advantage was slightly in his lordship's favour, the resourceful Nathaniel Greene and his partisan leaders were still dangerously active. More-

over, without the continued presence of British troops in their midst, the allegiance of many of those confidently regarded as loyalists was apt to yield to fear of their patriot neighbours' stored-up vengeance.

It was at this delicate juncture that Cornwallis, befogged by contradictory orders from Clinton and the egregious Germain, resolved, very largely on his own responsibility, to try to consolidate the British position in the South by attempting the conquest of Washington's own State of Virginia, where loyalist sentiment was virtually non-existent. By adding to his own troops the small contingents already operating in this territory, he contrived to muster a force totalling 5,300, including Tarleton's British Legion.

Anticipating a strong Franco-American assault on New York, and in grave anxiety as to continued British dominance at sea, Clinton ultimately sent his subordinate orders to 'take up a defensive station in any healthy position he preferred'. A fresh plan of operations, he wrote, could be worked out between them when the northern base was no longer under immediate threat. His demand for two battalions as reinforcements was subsequently withdrawn.

Terminating his operations against the Marquis de Lafayette, whom he soundly trounced on the James river,

RIGHT *George Washington* by Rembrandt Peale; *the surrender at Yorktown did not end the war, which dragged on for another two years, nevertheless it brought nearer the day that Washington would become the first President of the United States*

Cornwallis moved down to Yorktown. This prosperous 'tobacco township' of some sixty homesteads was conveniently situated on the York river, parallel to and east of the James; and Cornwallis's selection of it as a base was perfectly sound orthodox strategy, since at the tip of the peninsula he could afford protection for the shipping upon which he would rely for supplies and reinforcements.

It was the news that the fleet under de Grasse intended to elude the British squadrons patrolling between New York and the Caribbean, to land a further contingent of 3,200 French troops at the head of the Chesapeake, which spurred Washington and his French colleague, the Comte de Rochambeau, to hasten south. The task of deluding Clinton into the belief that New York remained under close siege was handed over to the somewhat pedestrian but entirely reliable General William Heath. On 30 August de Grasse was as good as his word, and the French troops, together with their artillery, were expeditiously put ashore.

Belated news of de Grasse's movements brought Rear-Admiral Thomas Graves speeding to the Chesapeake. Here, on 5 September, an engagement was fought with the straggling French armada in which Graves's rigid observance of outmoded, over-formalized Fighting Instructions threw away an open invitation to victory in which a Nelson would have exulted. By the day's end the British had lost command of the sea; and with Graves's withdrawal to New York to refit all immediate hope of supporting Cornwallis's defence of Yorktown vanished.

In ignorance of the extent of Graves's setback and therefore in full expectation of early relief, Cornwallis made no move either to retreat southwards or to brush aside Lafayette's inferior force blocking the escape route up the peninsula. By 14 September Washington and Rochambeau had joined the Marquis at the head of 9,000 Americans and 7,000 French auxiliaries. These troops were organized in three divisions, commanded respectively by Lafayette, Thomas Nelson – an erstwhile resident of Yorktown – and that experienced soldier of fortune Baron von Steuben, the Swabian drill-master who had 'bestowed upon the American troops the greatest gift they could have received – the gift of discipline'. The 92 artillery pieces, which included a siege train, were in charge of that born gunner Brigadier Henry Knox.

To oppose this formidable array Cornwallis could muster some 7,500 troops, Navy men, and merchant seamen. In addition to a Guards contingent, the garrison included elements of the 7th, 23rd, 33rd, 60th, 63rd, 64th, and 71st Foot, a handful of gunners, Bose's Hessians, and certain other German auxiliaries, together with a few loyalist Volunteers. From this force some 700 men were detached to hold the Gloucester outpost, three-quarters of a

mile away across the York river. Of the 65 pieces of artillery available, the majority consisted of coehorns, a species of mortar of small calibre, with a few 18-pounders.

Where the potentialities for defence were concerned, Yorktown was not without its merits. Covered both to east and west by swamplands, the terrain that lay in the centre between these two natural obstacles was commanded by three redoubts with a reasonably good field of fire. Additional earthworks covered the marshy approaches. An inner system of defence, close to the township itself, consisted of a stockade, earthworks, and batteries. But the area enclosed by this interior line – 1,200 yards in length by 500 yards in depth – was far too restricted for safety. Matters were not improved by the friable nature of the soil and the lack of serviceable tools. Furthermore, with many refugees as well as the troops to provide for, supplies were barely sufficient to last for three weeks, and were already deteriorating in quality. As early as mid-September one of the General's subordinates had noted in his journal:

> We get terrible provisions now, putrid ship's meat and wormy biscuits that have spoiled in the ships. Many of the men have taken sick with dysentery or the bloody flux and with diarrhœa. Also the foul fever is spreading, partly on account of the many hardships from which we have had little rest day or night, and partly on account of the awful food; but mostly the nitre-bearing water is to blame for it.

The uniforms of Washington's Life Guards (left): white, blue-trimmed coat and white breeches; and of an independent company under Washington (right): blue coat, yellow waistcoat and breeches

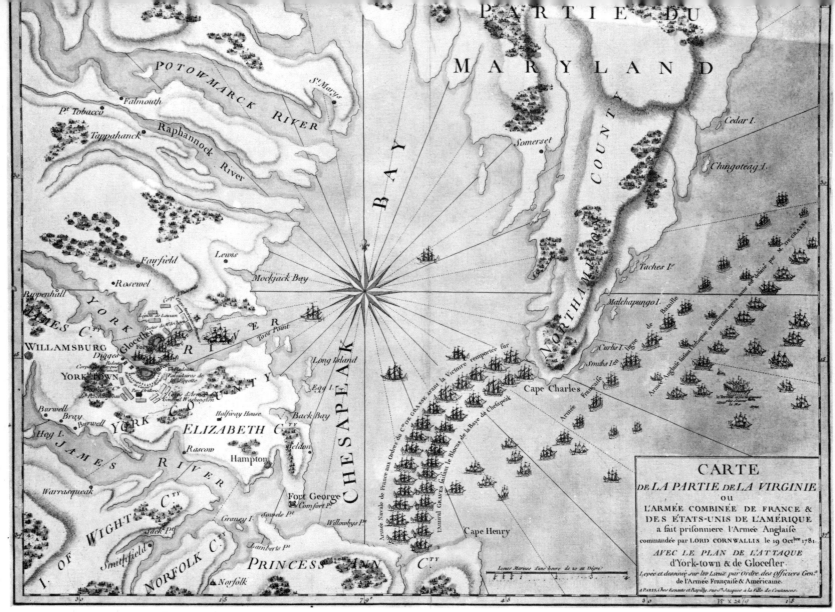

Within the map cartouche:

CARTE
DE LA PARTIE DE LA VIRGINIE
ou
L'ARMÉE COMBINÉE DE FRANCE &
DES ÉTATS-UNIS DE L'AMÉRIQUE
a fait prisonniere l'Armée Anglaise
commandée par LORD CORNWALLIS le 19 Octobre 1781.
AVEC LE PLAN DE L'ATTAQUE
d'York-town & de Glocester.
Levée et donnée sur les Lieux par Ordre des officiers Genx.
de l'Armée Française & Américaine.
A PARIS, chez Esnauts et Rapilly, rue St. Jacques à la Ville de Coutances.

A French plan showing both the final stages of the Franco-American army's siege of Cornwallis's force in Yorktown, and de Grasse's naval victory over Graves's fleet in Chesapeake Bay
BELOW LEFT *The Marquis de Lafayette, whose presence in Virginia, together with that of a considerable body of French troops and a French fleet, was one of the outcomes of Burgoyne's surrender at Saratoga.* BELOW RIGHT *Charles Earl Cornwallis by Gainsborough; by 17 October Cornwallis's position had become desperate and, with no sign of the promised relief from New York, he had no choice but to surrender*

M. LE MARQUIS DE LA FAYETTE

CHARLES EARL CORNWALLIS. 1783.

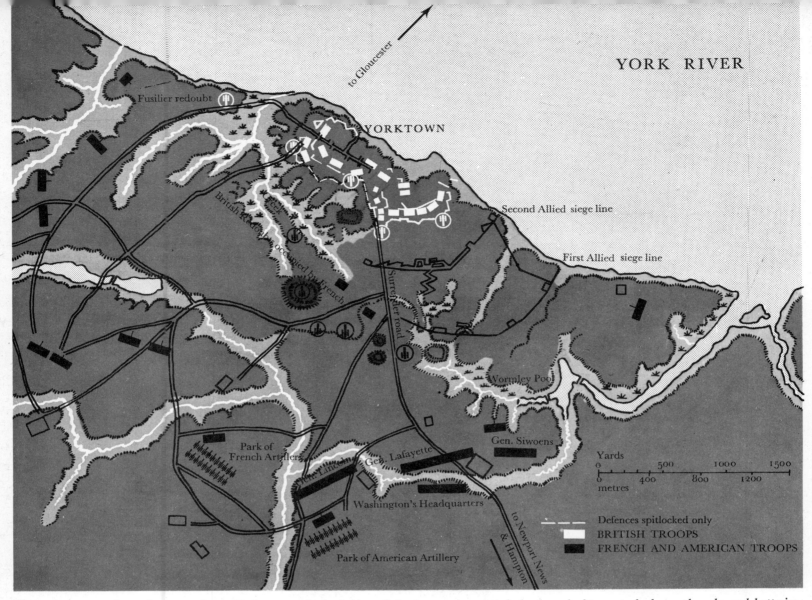

Covered to east and west by swampland, Yorktown at the beginning of the siege was protected also by redoubts, a stockade, earthworks and batteries. As the siege progressed, the redoubts were abandoned to the French on 1 October, the first siege parallels were opened on 6 October, and the second on 11 October

RIGHT *The Comte de Rochambeau (left) and Washington (right, in a long cloak) give their orders for an attack during the final stages of the siege; Lafayette stands behind and slightly to the left of Washington (painted by Couder)*

And the prospect of any improvement in the monotonous and unhealthy diet was, to say the least of it, extremely doubtful.

By 28 September the Franco-American forces were on the move down the peninsula. Although the countryside was flat, it was intersected by several creeks and 'runs' (brooks) which made the transport of artillery particularly laborious. But steadily, inexorably, the allied troops took up position until they stretched in a demilune whose extremities were bounded by the York river, both to the east and west. With the line of investment completed, Rochambeau and the French confronted the British right; the left and the open half mile in the centre being contained by Lafayette, von Steuben, Nelson, and their Americans.

Dawn light on 1 October revealed that the British had abandoned their outer line of defence, where the earthworks linking the three redoubts, having been little more than traced, were quite untenable. Nonetheless, that night Cornwallis wrote assuring Clinton that, providing

relief was not too long delayed, 'York and Gloucester will both be in possession of His Majesty's troops'.

By 6 October the Franco-American forces had opened their first parallel, five hundred yards from Yorktown's inner line of defence. Three days later the guns had been hauled up and the allied bombardment brought heavy fire to bear at a range of six hundred yards; Washington himself plying the linstock to fire the first gun. While Tarleton and his Legion skirmished bloodily with Lauzan's Hussars on the outskirts of Gloucester, the weight and intensity of the cannonade directed at Yorktown's frail defences steadily mounted; Thomas Nelson stoically recommending some of the gunners to concentrate their fire on his own home, as being the most likely location for Cornwallis's Headquarters.

Sheltering in the York river were the 44-gun *Charon*, the *Guadeloupe*, and three transports. As dusk fell the French turned some of their guns on these vessels, firing red-hot shot. The *Guadeloupe* was fortunate enough to find cover behind a bluff, but the other vessels were hulled

ABOVE *A fierce fight for a redoubt, the inevitable outcome of which must bring nearer the day of the British surrender*

LEFT *The Surrender of Lord Cornwallis by John Trumbull; Cornwallis himself pleaded illness, and it was his Second-in-Command, O'Hara, who made formal surrender*

BELOW LEFT *Washington and Lafayette at the Battle of Yorktown by Reuben Law Reed; though painted c 1860, this painting was based on a description of the battle given to the artist by an eyewitness*

BELOW *A British ship set fire by red-hot shot blazes in the York river, while Yorktown is subjected to a heavy bombardment*

before they could slip their cables, and were soon spouting fire from truck to keel

Already the battered state of his earthworks and the rapid dwindling of his meagre reserve of ammunition rendered it difficult for Cornwallis to make adequate reply to the incessant rain of enemy shot. But, confident in Clinton's promise of early support, he fought back grimly. It was a plain question of holding on until the Commander-in-Chief could bring relief or the means of evacuation.

For Washington, time was an equally potent factor, since de Grasse was under orders to return to his West Indies station and could not postpone his departure indefinitely. And it was the French fleet that barred the way to any seaborne sources of relief.

The Americans' inner parallel – opened on 11 October – was soon found to be enfiladed by two redoubts on the left face of the British defences, and it was resolved to carry them forthwith. On 14 October two storming parties, one French and one American, stole out under cover of darkness to deliver the attack. Without waiting for the

Between double ranks of allied troops Cornwallis's army, smartly dressed in new uniforms but with Colours cased, marches along the York-Hampton road to lay down their arms

Another fierce fight for one of the redoubts guarding the British perimeter; with this safely in their hands, the Americans would be another important step closer to the capture of Yorktown, which could not long withstand heavy, close-range artillery bombardment

A French engraving of the British surrender at Yorktown; de Grasse's fleet which deserved much of the credit for this is given due prominence

pioneers to clear the approaches, the Americans, led by Alexander Hamilton, tore their way through the abattis and scrambled up into the redoubt. It was a hand-to-hand tussle, fought out with musket-butt and cold steel; for among many other things the American soldier had learned from the veteran von Steuben was the fact that the bayonet had other uses than to serve as a handy spit for grilling steaks. Had they been reinforced, the British might well have held their own. As it was, after a fierce struggle those of the garrison still left unwounded threw down their arms and surrendered.

If the French took longer over their task it was because they had delayed while their pioneers cleared a way through the abattis in due form. The Gatenois grenadiers had been assigned the post of honour in the forefront of the fray. They had formerly belonged to the old Auvergne Regiment, which had once been commanded by Rochambeau himself, and which, for its heroic gallantry on many fields, had been known as *Auvergne sans tache*. When Rochambeau had addressed them prior to the attack they had promised everything if he would get their old name restored to them. As soon as the abattis had been broken down the Gatenois rushed at their objective with an ardour that even the stout resistance they met with was unable to abate. Overwhelmed by the weight and momentum of the attack, the outpost's defenders were speedily despatched or taken captive. With the redoubts in the allies' hands, the guns in the embrasures were swung about to add their fire to the general cannonade of the crumbling British defences.

The rain of missiles was maintained so furiously that

two nights later a sortie was launched from the British lines on the American works. Led by the two Commanding Officers of the Guards – Abercrombie and Lake – three hundred and fifty men went briskly into an attack that momentarily swept all before it. Two of the redoubts were temporarily won back; eleven guns were spiked, and close on a hundred of the enemy killed or wounded. But the advantage gained could not be held. Allied reinforcements being hurried to the scene, in remarkably short order the raiding party was thrown out of the works they had so briefly repossessed. Roll-call revealed a heavy toll of casualties; and since nothing more effective than bayonets had been employed to spike the guns, they were soon once more in action.

Despite another assurance that relief was being organized – received on 10 October – Cornwallis's situation had so speedily deteriorated as to have become well-nigh desperate. Battle casualties were approaching 500, the sick numbered close on 2,000; food was running short; the defence works had been battered into irreparable ruin; while of ammunition 'only one 8-inch and a little more than a hundred coehorn shells remained'.

In this extremity Cornwallis determined to pass over to Gloucester and fight his way through to the escape route up the peninsula. The attempt was put in hand on the night of 16 October, the embarkation of the Light Infantry, the Guards and part of the 23rd Regiment proceeding as smoothly as the passage across the river. 'But at this critical moment the weather, from being moderate and calm, changed to a most violent storm of wind and rain, and drove all the boats, some of which had troops

111

A nineteenth-century American lithograph of the surrender: besides Washington and Lafayette (on his right) the American group includes Baron von Steuben (extreme left), to whom the fine discipline of the American army was largely due, and Alexander Hamilton (on his right)

RIGHT *The restrained, indeed admonitory, terms of this proclamation suggest that Washington anticipated wild scenes of rejoicing at the news of the surrender*

A detail from an engraving after a drawing by Jean François Renault (Assistant Secretary to de Grasse and Engineer to the French Army at Yorktown); the Hussar de Lauzan is the central figure

Illumination.

COLONEL TILGHMAN, Aid de Camp to his Excellency General WASHINGTON, having brought official acounts of the SURRENDER of Lord Cornwallis, and the Garrisons of York and Gloucester, those Citizens who chuse to ILLUMINATE on the GLORIOUS OCCASION, will do it this evening at Six, and extinguish their lights at Nine o'clock.

Decorum and harmony are earnestly recommended to every Citizen, and a general discountenance to the least appearance of riot.

October 24, 1781.

on board, down the river.' The passage of any further contingents over the wind-lashed stream was obviously out of the question. Neither was it possible, when the storm eventually died down, to bring back those who had already crossed to Gloucester without exposing them to punishing enemy fire.

On the morning of 17 October, with de Grasse still lording it in the Chesapeake and the crescendo of the bombardment steadily mounting, a scarlet-clad figure was seen to clamber up on the hornwork in the centre of the tumbled British defences, to turn and beat urgently on the drum slung at his side. Amidst the din of the cannonade no sound of the drum-beats could be heard. But everyone knew instinctively that the slim figure in the 'bloody-backs'' red coat was sounding the *chamade*.

As the guns fell silent an English officer was brought into the allied lines bearing a formal request for 'a cessation of hostilities, . . . to settle terms for the surrender of the posts of York and Gloucester'.

There was a considerable exchange of correspondence before the terms of capitulation were finally agreed. For on one point Washington had proved obdurate. At Charleston's capture the surrendered garrison had not been accorded the full honours of war. They had been ordered to parade out of the fallen city with their Colours cased and their band playing an *American* march. The British should undergo a similar degree of humiliation.

At noon on 17 October, therefore, the allied forces were drawn up on the York–Hampton road; and between the double ranks of silent men the British and their German comrades, grim-faced but spick and span in newly-issued uniforms, strode out to ground their arms. But to their muted fury, their Colours were cased, and they marched to the ironically appropriate *English* air of *The World Turned Upside Down*.

Cornwallis himself was not present to make formal surrender. Pleading illness, he had delegated that ungrateful task to General O'Hara, his Second-in-Command. And it was to Benjamin Lincoln, a captive at Charleston who had subsequently been exchanged, that he rendered up his sword.

Out in the bay the sloop *Bonetta*, bearing tidings of disaster, was crammed fore and aft with fugitive loyalists; whose fate, had they been allowed to fall into enemy hands, would almost certainly have been the hangman's rope. It must be to Washington's eternal credit that he turned a conveniently blind eye on their entirely unauthorized departure.

About the same hour a belatedly reinforced Sir Henry Clinton set sail from New York, with twenty-six ships of the line and his transports crowded with 7,000 troops. Rarely can a more formidable force have sallied forth upon so futile an errand.

The Yorktown surrender did not end the war, which dragged on aimlessly for another two years. But it sounded the death-knell of Britain's first attempt to create an empire overseas. Forcefulness had been alternated with appeasement until it was too late to pursue either policy successfully. But, regardless of what transpired in the last two years of conflict, the fact is not to be gainsaid that the United States Republic which had been engendered at Saratoga, was brought to birth between the Chesapeake and Yorktown; its reluctant *accoucheurs* Rear-Admiral Thomas Graves and Lieutenant-General Earl Cornwallis.

REGINALD HARGREAVES

'State Cooks, or the Downfall of the Fish Kettle'; an English political cartoon, in which the King and Lord North lament the loss of the American colonies

One of a pair of French prints satirizing the surrenders at Saratoga and Yorktown: Cornwallis is represented as a fox (Burgoyne in the other print as a turkey)

1806

Jena

Jena and Auerstedt were both won by superior French tactics, and Napoleon's determined pursuit of the routed armies ended Prussian participation in the war until 1813

THE JENA CAMPAIGN, which led to the total defeat of the Prussian monarchy, is generally viewed as an encounter between two epochs, in which the old order collapsed before the drive and energy of the new. In the Napoleonic Era the state of Frederick the Great was found wanting; but the events of 1806 are misunderstood unless it is recognized that, even as she fell, Prussia evinced great tenacity, while her conquerors were not as sure-footed as the grandeur of their triumph might suggest. That the two powers were of unequal strength should also be noted, but it was the way in which Napoleon coordinated the political and military means at hand that proved decisive. The *Grande Armée* had more than half won the battles of Jena and Auerstedt before the opening shot was fired, and the climactic 14 October proved of smaller significance than its aftermath.

In 1805 Prussia had remained aloof from the Third Coalition until the chance for successful common action was past, and by her indecision had made the Austerlitz campaign possible. The rearrangement of Germany's political map that now followed worked increasingly to her disadvantage. Austria was temporarily enfeebled; Napoleon's south-German allies gained in strength; Prussia herself was induced to cede her possessions in the south and west, and given leave in return to occupy Hanover, which predictably led to war with Great Britain. Her isolation would have been complete but for her alliance with Saxony and the covert support extended by Russia; but Alexander's armies were still refitting, and in the meantime Napoleon's domination of Germany posed a growing threat to the independence of the state. By the summer of 1806 French pressure had become extreme and, though it would have been wiser to postpone an open break until the Russians could again operate in central Europe, Frederick William mobilized. Fear of the consequence of further passivity and a remnant of faith in the heritage of the Great Frederick pushed the monarchy into disaster. Until the very end there was no formal declaration of war; during August and September Prussian columns gradually moved south, the King and his Commander-in-Chief, the Duke of Brunswick, hoping to the last that Napoleon would negotiate.

After the Campaign of 1805 the *Grande Armée* had not returned to France, but taken up quarters along the Rhine and in southern Germany. Only the Guards had accompanied the Emperor to Paris. When it became apparent that Prussian military preparations were in earnest, the 3,700 men of the Guards Grenadiers and Chasseurs were hurriedly loaded on wagons and transported in relays to the Rhine, where they arrived on 28 September. The regiments had already begun to leave their garrisons; the Emperor now accelerated their concentration towards the north-east. By the first week of

RIGHT *Two of his characteristically superb drawings of French Dragoons by Général Baron Lejeune; there is a world of difference between this entirely realistic representation of the soldier and the glamourized figure of the uniform plate*

October the corps were assembled in lower Bavaria, and began to penetrate the wooded hills that barred the approaches to Saxony and Prussia. The positions and intentions of the enemy could not be estimated with assurance, but lack of information was not permitted to hinder the troops' rapid deployment.

Napoleon's plan of campaign hinged on mobilizing the greatest force possible and then creating an opportunity for its exploitation by advancing on Berlin. Any Prussian move would be interrupted by the need to defend the capital, and once the armies met French numerical superiority should decide the issue. Under the circumstances, an offensive from any quarter promised success; but an advance from the west would have pushed the Prussians back on Berlin and towards possible Russian assistance, while an offensive from the south could be launched more rapidly and stood the chance of separating the enemy from his capital and the Russian border.

The *Grande Armée* advanced in three columns on parallel roads separated by one to two days' march. In the centre, on the Bamberg-Leipzig highway, moved Bernadotte's I Corps, Murat's cavalry, III Corps under Davout, Imperial headquarters and the Guards – together 70,000 men. On the road from Bayreuth to Plauen to their right marched the 50,000 men of IV and VI Corps, commanded by Soult and Ney; to their left, on the Bamberg-Coburg-Saalfeld road, marched the somewhat weaker V and VII Corps under Lannes and Augereau. Together these 160,000 troops formed what Napoleon termed a gigantic battalion square, able to deploy either to the front or flank, each division ready to engage the enemy until others could come to its support. The advance was not without its dangers. During the first stage, until the river Saale was reached, the units were dispersed over an area thirty miles across and fifty miles deep, in terrain that was difficult for cavalry and transport, with few lateral connections between the three roads, making it uncertain that a corps, if attacked, could

Bernadotte, the Commander of I Corps, whose forward units were the first to clash with the Prussians, on the right bank of the Saale on the morning of 9 October

Marshal Soult, the Commander of IV Corps which, with Augereau's VII Corps, supported Lannes' attack on Hohenlohe at Jena

be supported in time. Particularly the left column, weakest of the three and closest to the Prussians, afforded opportunities to an energetic opponent. But the potential advantages of the flank march outweighed its risks, which an overall superiority in numbers made it the easier to accept.

The Prussians had decided to forestall the expected attack by rapidly moving south against the Main, with the hope of defeating the French divisions piecemeal before they could combine. This scheme soon proved to be inoperable. Limited manpower and a fatal tendency to cover every exposed point resulted in scarcely 120,000 troops being available for offensive operations, a total that included 18,000 Saxons. The mobilization of this inferior force proceeded too slowly. When the army reached the northern slopes of the Thuringian Hills at the end of September the enemy was already massed in Bavaria, and the opportunity for surprise was lost. The following week was given over to councils of war. By 8

ABOVE *The Duke of Brunswick, the Commander-in-Chief of the Royal Army, was shot through both eyes at an early stage of the Battle of Auerstedt which, since the King hesitated to assume command, left the Prussians leaderless*

BELOW *Early on 14 October Lannes, supported by Augereau and Soult, extended the French foothold on the Landgrafenberg which he had secured the previous night, thus permitting Napoleon to deploy the remainder of his forces on the plateau above Jena*

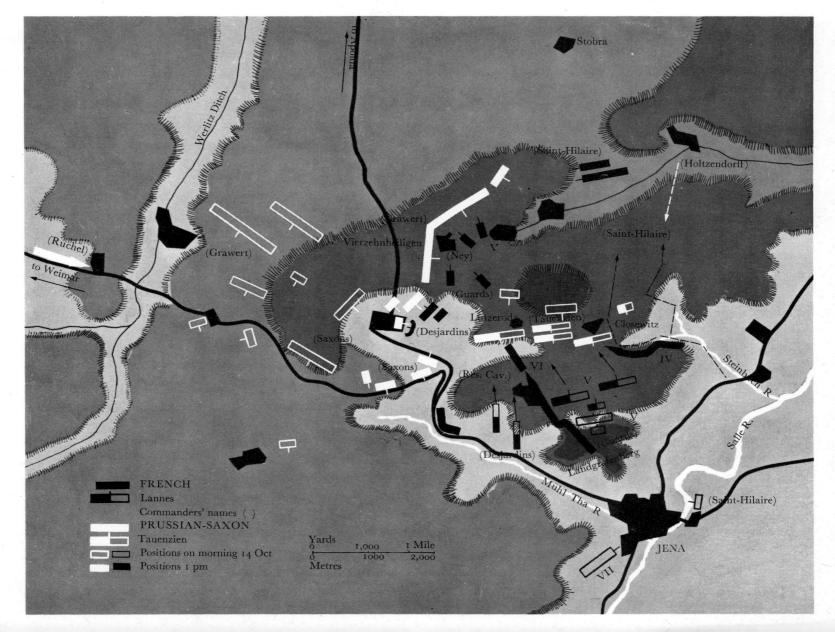

October the main army of 53,000 men, which the King accompanied, and Rüchel's corps still occupied the districts between Eisenach and Erfurth. Twenty-five miles away, along the Saale, stood Prince Hohenlohe's 43,000 men, and smaller detachments were scattered from Meiningen in the south to Magdeburg in the north. Both Brunswick and Hohenlohe remained well to the west of Napoleon's line of advance; only a weak detachment under Tauenzien observed the French approach on the right bank of the Saale, where on the morning of the 9th it was attacked by Bernadotte's forward units and severely mauled.

The King, his commanding generals and their staffs could not decide whether Napoleon should be met head-on, whether the army should take up a flanking position on the left bank of the Saale, or whether it should retreat north to join its reserves and make a stand on the Elbe. At last they determined to concentrate all forces left of the river near Jena, and there await further developments. Few officers, even those who still held to the military ways of the *ancien régime*, felt confident with this temporizing; some were certain that it spelled the end of the army. But even the most progressive among them had not been in combat for over a decade – unlike their opponents, they knew Napoleonic warfare only from study. Not that modern concepts wholly dominated on the French side: in particular there was frequent failure in reconnaissance and communication, and occasionally inadequate staff-work, for which the Emperor himself was to blame since he attempted to do too much himself. But such flaws were made good by a pervasive energy, by the instinctive understanding of war of thousands of veterans, led by a man who recognized the essentials of the problem he faced, and who would allow no side issue to distract either himself or his subordinates from its solution.

On the morning of the 10th, while Tauenzien withdrew towards Jena after his skirmish with Bernadotte, Lannes reached the Saale and immediately attacked Hohenlohe's advance guard on the left bank of the river near Saalfeld. The Prussian commander, Prince Louis Ferdinand, a nephew of Frederick the Great, delayed his retreat too long; his positions were enveloped and he was killed. The news of his defeat and death further lowered Prussian morale, which was already affected by fatigue and loss of confidence. Everywhere the lack of a strong hand was apparent. Commanders and staff-officers went without sleep attending to trifles, while needless marches and counter-marches exhausted the men, some of whom had not drawn rations for days. On the 11th a panic broke out among the troops stationed in Jena; the next day the Saxon contingent threatened to leave unless it was assured of a daily issue of bread. Little of this became known to the French. Napoleon remained in doubt over

Prussian positions and plans, though he imagined Brunswick to be withdrawing to the Elbe, and continued his march north-east to head him off. Not until the 12th did he realize that a large Prussian force still stood between Erfurth and Weimar. The opportunity he sought had come. He swung his right column and the cavalry reserve west towards Jena, which was already being approached from the south by Lannes and Augereau, while ordering Davout north to Naumburg, where he would threaten the Prussian flank and rear, and directing Bernadotte to a central position at Dornburg, from which he could support either Davout or the main force. At the same time, the Prussians finally recognized their peril and decided to march north. Brunswick quit Weimar for Auerstedt, while Hohenlohe remained opposite Jena on the left bank of the Saale with orders not to be drawn into serious fighting until the Royal Army had passed the Unstrut. When Napoleon entered the town on the 13th he believed he was about to attack the assembled Prussian forces. Hohenlohe, in turn, arguing that Napoleon would be at Naumburg to interject himself between the Prussians and Berlin, thought until well after the battle of Jena had begun that he was engaged only by a detached corps.

Opposite Jena the left bank of the Saale rises steeply to a plateau dotted with villages and woods and cut by

LEFT *Gunsmoke begins to cloud the battlefield of Jena, as Napoleon despatches fresh orders to one of his commanders, cavalry and guns are rushed forward, and the Guard observes the inexorable progress of destruction of the old Prussian army (after Swebach)* BELOW *A chivalrous, but idealized French print, which purports to represent the King of Prussia rallying his troops at the Battle of Jena – the hapless Frederick William was, in fact, playing a less useful part at Auerstedt*

valleys to the north and south. On the morning of the 14th Hohenlohe's main body consisting of Grawert's division and the Saxons still faced south along the Weimar-Jena road over which Rüchel's corps of some 15,000 men was slowly approaching. An outcropping of the plateau towards Jena – the Landgrafenberg – had been occupied by Lannes against small opposition; access to the open ground beyond was barred by the thin line of Tauenzien's battalions, their left flank and rear covered by a detachment of 5,000 men under Holtzendorff. A personal reconnaissance on the afternoon of the 13th convinced Napoleon that his first task must be to gain sufficient space on the plateau to permit deployment of large forces. During the night of the 13th to 14th he hurried the remainder of Lannes' corps up the Landgrafenberg, and before sunrise the following morning, with the fog still thick on the ground, he gave the order to attack. In coordinated moves, Augereau in the south and Soult in the north penetrated the valleys that flanked the forward part of the plateau. By 9 am. the villages of Lützeroda and Closewitz had been taken and room was made for the deployment of the regiments that were starting to arrive from the other side of the river. The next French objective was Vierzehnheiligen, a village one and-a-half miles west of Closewitz. Skirmishers advanced over the rolling

ground and were engaged by Prussian light troops, while to their right the retreating Tauenzien was slowly followed by Saint-Hilaire's division, itself for a time heavily engaged by Holtzendorff, who had come down on its flank. By 10.30 he too was forced to withdraw. It was an indication of the gradual breakdown of Prussian operational control that instead of turning behind Vierzehnheiligen where intense fighting was now in progress, Holtzendorff marched to Stobra and Apolda, removing his command from further participation in the battle.

Hohenlohe and his chief of staff Massenbach had only reluctantly realized that they were involved in an all-out fight. When soon after daybreak Grawert wheeled his division left to face the sound of the guns, he had to convince his superior of the need for this change. By 8, however, Hohenlohe had come to sense some of the gravity of his position and sent the first of a series of messages to Rüchel, urging him to hurry. The possibility of withdrawing towards Brunswick's army in accordance with his mission to act as flank- and rear-guard he seems never to have entertained seriously. Instead he busied himself like a regimental officer arranging Grawert's battalions for an attack on Vierzehnheiligen, now occupied by units of V Corps and light infantry of Ney's advance-guard, which had reached the plateau. The fog had lifted by 10,

SLAG VAN JENA. ✻ BATAILLE DE JENA.

d'Oude wagt vegt vol dapperheid,
En vreest voor geen vreedaardigheid.

La vieille garde se bat avec courage,
Et ne craint point le carnage.

De Mameluk in d'aanvals nood,
Vol moed by de Cosakken dood.

Les Mameluks dans les attaques,
Avec courage tuent les Cosaques.

In haast de Dragonder vlugt
Voor d'Housaren, en voor zyn Vaandel dugt.

Les Dragons fuient au grand galop
Pour les Hussards, avec le drapeau.

De Cuirassier op 't klinken der trompet
Vliet tot hulp, en hy den moord'naar plet.

Au son de la trompette le Cuirassier,
Vole au secours et tue le meurtrier.

Te Turnhout, uit het Fabriek en Boek-drukkery van P. J. BREPOLS   N.° 37.

A popular Dutch print consisting of illustrated doggerel verses in alternative Dutch and French texts, which record improbable episodes in the 'Battle of Jena'; the Cossacks and Mamelukes seem purely theatrical, while the 'left-handed' combatants owe this peculiarity to the printer

RIGHT Frederick William III, King of Prussia, whose indecision, together with that of his generals, as to strategy, compounded by their serious tactical errors, precipitated the double disaster at Jena and Auerstedt (painted by Wilhelm Herbig)

OVERLEAF In Thevenin's painting of the Battle of Jena, executed in 1810 for Berthier, Napoleon's Chief of Staff, the Marshal rides immediately behind the Emperor with Murat on his right

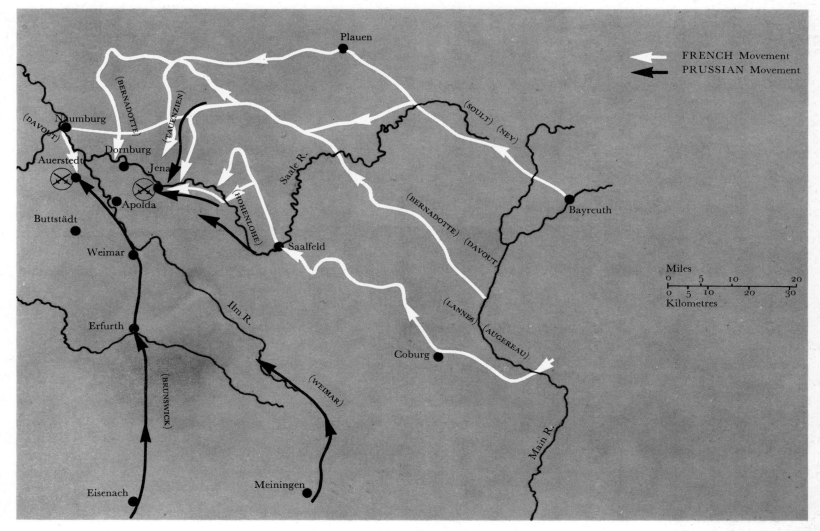

FRENCH Movement
PRUSSIAN Movement

Miles
0   5   10   20
0   5   10   20   30
Kilometres

Napoleon's army advanced in three columns to meet the Prussians; Napoleon himself overwhelmed Hohenlohe at Jena, while Davout defeated the main Prussian army at Auerstedt

LEFT ABOVE *A French print which shows Napoleon's heavy cavalry attacking Prussian infantry and putting it to flight; Frederick Willlam is represented fleeing, hatless, from this battlefield, though he was in fact a few miles away at Auerstedt. The Emperor and his staff can be seen on a slight eminence in the distance*

LEFT BELOW *A German impression of French cavalry types of 1806 (an engraving after a drawing by P. W. Schwarz of Nürnberg); at no other period have soldiers been asked to wear such a bizarre variety of head-dresses*

and the attack started under a bright autumn sky. As the Prussians moved forward they received scattered musket fire, soon they could hear the cries of the tirailleurs pointing out officers to each other, but casualties did not slow the advance. The French were wavering and the moment to fell bayonets was at hand, when the lines were halted, possibly to give Rüchel's men time to arrive. The charge could not have won the day, but possession of Vierzehnheilgen would at least have given the Prussians a more favourable defensive position; as it was the battalions stood on open ground for the next two hours, firing volley after volley at an all but invisible enemy, and slowly being reduced to cinders. In the meantime the build-up of French strength continued. Shortly past noon the Emperor had at his disposal more than 80,000 men; Hohenlohe retained less than 30,000, and Rüchel still had not

arrived. The sky had clouded again from the intense gunfire when Soult began to envelop the Prussians from the north, while in the south Desjardin's division forced a wedge between them and the Saxons. By 1 pm. the French advanced everywhere, and the Prussian and Saxon formations were breaking when Rüchel finally appeared. Instead of deploying defensively behind the Werlitz ditch to give Hohenlohe a chance to re-form, Rüchel advanced in battalion echelons against the oncoming French tide. In half an hour the attack had been smashed, Rüchel himself was mortally wounded, and his decimated battalions joined the thousands of fugitives streaming back to Weimar in almost total dissolution. A battle that could not be won was lost more fully than need be because Hohenlohe fragmented his strength and wasted it in unrelated attacks against an opponent who

Having wasted little time in defeating Frederick William III, Napoleon pays tribute to his redoubtable ancestor, at the tomb of Frederick the Great —
he surely would not have been guilty of the criminal indecision, which invited defeat, or have tolerated the poor generalship from his subordinates,
which set the seal to disaster

French light infantry, entering Leipzig after the Battle of Jena, find provisions, and other delicacies, to their liking; the Negro drummer (left
foreground) would seem to have been recruited during Napoleon's Egyptian campaign

not only had accumulated greatly superior force but knew how to coordinate its use.

At about the time Grawert's battalions were beginning to give way, the main Prussian army fifteen miles to the north was turned back in its attempt to regain its lines of communication. During the night Napoleon had ordered Davout at Naumburg to return south by way of Apolda and operate against the left flank of the Prussians behind Jena. Bernadotte was given the option of joining Davout or continuing to Dornburg; he chose the latter and thus took no part in the battle that followed. His motives have been questioned, but at the time neither he nor Davout realized that the enemy columns moving north were anything more than an advance guard.

The Royal Army had bivouacked near Auerstedt during the night of the 13th to the 14th, and continued its march by daybreak. The commanding officers had failed to secure the defiles towards Naumburg, where French troops were known to be, as they had proved incapable of bringing tactical cohesion to the units that were strung out for miles along a single road. At 7 am., in dense fog,

Engravings of the obverse and reverse of a medal commemorating Napoleon's victory at Jena

A French print of 1806 welcoming Napoleon's victory against the Prussians; this was finally consolidated in the spring of 1807

LES TOASTS.
à NAPOLEON protecteur.   à NAPOLEON vengeur·   à NAPOLEON vainqueur·   à NAPOLEON pacificateur.

the leading squadron of the advance guard encountered fire near the village of Hassenhausen. Both sides hurried troops forward and a pitched battle developed, with the front soon extending hundreds of yards north and south of the village, as Davout and Brunswick attempted to envelop each other's position. Scharnhorst, the Duke's chief of staff, took charge of the left flank; soon afterwards Brunswick was shot through both eyes, and with the King hesitating to assume command operations quickly degenerated into a mass of uncoordinated local engagements. Davout, though hard-pressed, was able to retain control of the battle. The climax came at 10.30. The French left had been partly surrounded and Hassenhausen was evacuated when the 1st Division under Morand reached the front in double time, stopped the enemy's forward movement and in turn advanced beyond the village. This committed Davout's entire corps while the two Prussian reserve divisions had not yet seen action. A counter-attack would at least have stabilized the situation; but Frederick William had lost heart and decided to break off the battle. The Prussians withdrew in fair order, Davout's infantry being too exhausted to follow; but now a final disaster befell them. Instead of swinging north by way of Buttstädt to gain the Elbe, the King panicked and turned south-west to rejoin Hohenlohe. He was still unaware of the disaster at Jena, but under the best of circumstances this move was fatal since it took the army away from Berlin and deep into the French embrace. When news arrived of Hohenlohe's defeat during the night the direction of the retreat was changed first to Erfurth, then to Sommerda. By morning the Royal Army had ceased to exist as a fighting force.

Nothing is more characteristic of Napoleonic warfare – its inadequate reconnaissance, the occasional lack of co-operation and even of competence among subordinates, and at the same time its almost universal energy and the magnificent sense of purpose in the centre – than the pursuit now launched by the Emperor. After his twin defeats the enemy was not allowed to recover. With Blücher's surrender on the Baltic coast three weeks later Prussian resistance west of the Oder and Neisse ceased. To be sure, the war continued through the spring of 1807 in Silesia and East Prussia, but Napoleon's triumph appeared complete. And yet the true victors of the Jena Campaign were not the French. As the destruction of the Holy Roman Empire proved to be a long step forward towards the unification of Germany, so the destruction of the old Prussian army was the necessary condition for the reforms that now began, and that after a few years turned the lessons against the master from whom they had been learned.

PETER PARET

1812
Borodino

*Though Napoleon won this stubborn battle and captured Moscow, his army was decimated during
its retreat both by the rigours of the Russian winter and persistent harrying*

ON 24 JUNE 1812 the Emperor Napoleon with 450,000
men invaded Russia. By early September this polyglot
host faced the main Russian army near the river Moskva.
Thus far the campaign had brought no decisive action.
Sickness had wrought more havoc than battle: the
130,000 men concentrated near the village of Borodino
had numbered 300,000 when they crossed the Niemen.
Thousands of horses had died, and those that remained
were not in the best condition. The soldiers too had
suffered greatly from inadequate rations. The administrative machinery of the French army, always crude in
Napoleon's day, had proved incapable of catering for
so great a force. But it was the weaker men who had suc-
cumbed. The survivors, toughened by their long march,
were to acquit themselves manfully.

Against Napoleon the Russian commander, Marshal
Prince Golenischev-Kutuzov, could pit rather more than
120,000 men, inspired by a patriotic and religious zeal
every bit as strong as the enthusiasm of the French for
their Emperor. The impetuosity of the French was
matched by the dogged courage of the Russians.

The opposing commanders were men of very different
talents. Kutuzov was over seventy and was so stout that
he could mount his horse only with difficulty. Napoleon
too had his handicaps. A heavy cold had almost deprived
him of his voice; worse, his former spirit of enterprise was
somewhat inhibited by the great distance that now lay
between him and his capital, Paris.

The two armies were not unevenly matched.

	French	Russians
Cavalry	28,000	17,500
Cossacks	—	7,000
Infantry	86,000	72,000
Militia	—	10,000
Artillerymen, etc.	16,000	14,300
(Guns and howitzers	587	640)
	130,000	120,000

Napoleon did not enjoy such a superiority as to ensure
certain success in an attack. It behoved him, therefore,
to concentrate against some sector of Kutuzov's line and
crush it before it could be reinforced. The Prince had
obligingly spread out his right wing along the Kolotza
and by so doing had given the Emperor his opportunity.

On 5 September Compans's division stormed an advanced redoubt at Shevardino and on the next day the
Emperor reconnoitred the main Russian position, which
could be clearly seen except where it disappeared into
the forest around Utitza. Kutuzov's left, from that village
to the Kolotza, was obviously more accessible than his
right, but on either side of Semenovskoi the Russians had
hastily thrown up very formidable earthworks, known as

RIGHT *Marshal Prince Golenischev-Kutuzov, the seventy-year old
Russian commander at the Battle of Borodino; Napoleon's mistakes
rather than Kutuzov's good generalship saved the Russian army to fight
another day*

the Great Redoubt and Bagration's redoubts. A frontal attack in this sector was unattractive, even in those days of relatively short-range weapons. Marshal Davout, by origin an infantry officer and a skilful tactician, proposed a major movement via the old Smolensk road and the forest, so as to turn the Russian left flank. This was an excellent plan, but Napoleon rejected it because he was afraid that his enemy would retreat by the Mojaisk road and thus deprive him of his decisive battle. By making a frontal attack he might not gain so easy a victory, but the Russians would be unable to avoid battle. Kutuzov, however, had no intention of abandoning the Holy City of Moscow without a fight.

The artillery, which was to play a tremendous part in the battle, had three main missiles: grapeshot, very effective up to 350 yards, since it had the effect of an enormous shotgun; roundshot, and a crude shell. The normal rate of fire was about one round a minute.

The infantry musket was inaccurate even at ranges up to 100 yards. A trained soldier could fire three rounds a minute, but the proportion of misfires was high. Russians and Frenchmen alike manœuvred in deep columns, relying on the bayonet as much as the bullet. In defence a well-formed square firing volleys could generally keep out cavalry.

The cavalry of both armies relied on shock action. A skilful commander endeavoured to get up speed when he was about 200 yards – half a minute's gallop – from the enemy so as to get his impact before his troopers began to spread out.

The Russian dispositions were purely defensive but, though Kutuzov contemplated no counter-offensive, he placed most of his cavalry in second line about 350 yards

LEFT *General Prince Bagration, the most able and popular of the Russian generals, who commanded the left at the battle, during which he was mortally wounded*

RIGHT *Prince Poniatowski, whose Polish contingent was entrusted with the task of occupying the mamelon of Utitza and turning the Russian left*

behind the infantry with a view to local counter-attacks. The Russian Imperial Guard, in reserve in the centre, was half a mile in rear of the cavalry. During the night before the battle Lieutenant-General Tuchkov (III Corps) was moved from the right wing to the extreme left and posted to guard the old Smolensk road at a work called the mamelon of Utitza.

The Russian command arrangements were unwieldy. Kutuzov intervened but little, leaving the handling of the battle to his subordinate generals, Baron Barclay de Tolly (First Army), who commanded the right and centre, and Prince Bagration (Second Army), who commanded the left. These officers often despatched their orders direct to

Napoleon, flanked by his staff, receives a report from an officer, as the French infantry advances, and cavalry and horse artillery units are rushed to the front; the corpses in the foreground are a mute reminder of the 70,000 casualties, which this battle cost the two armies

divisions without reference to their corps commanders.

Napoleon's plan was straightforward and led to two major offensives and one minor one. On his extreme right Prince Poniatowski (V Corps) with 10,000 Poles was to occupy Utitza and turn the Russian left – the minor thrust. The attack on the Bagration redoubts and Semenovskoi was the main thrust. Davout, who had three divisions (I Corps), was to storm the redoubts, and then Marshal Ney (III Corps) with General Junot and his Westphalians (VIII Corps) under command, was to attack towards the village.

On the left Prince Eugène, the Viceroy of Italy (IV Corps), reinforced by two of Davout's divisions, was to seize Borodino, and then, crossing the Kolotza, to storm the Great Redoubt. The Emperor had in second line the four cavalry corps commanded by Murat, King of Naples, and in reserve the Imperial Guard.

On the evening of the 6th Marshal Berthier, the Chief of Staff, issued orders detailing the dispositions which were to bring two great armies, liberally supplied with artillery, in dense formation, to face each other on a front of three miles. It was a blue-print for carnage.

The night was foggy, but at 5 am. Ney, reporting that the whole army was in position, and eager for the fray, demanded permission to begin the attack. The Emperor was in the saddle by 5.30 am. and rode to the Shevardino redoubt which was to serve as his Command Post. Kutuzov set up his headquarters at Gorki, which afforded him a good view.

At 6 the signal was given and the French opened fire on the Bagration redoubts with over 100 guns but, finding the range too great, moved forward and came into action again at about 1,300 yards. The Russians replied.

Davout made the first attack, sending the divisions of Compans and Dessaix to storm the left of these redoubts. During the next two hours attack and counter-attack of horse and foot swept over the Semenovskoi sector, each redoubt changing hands several times. The guns, ever increasing in number, thundered without respite. Bagration called up Konovnitzin's 3rd Division from the extreme left (II Corps) and from the reserve Prince Galitzin with half the cuirassiers of the guard. As Ney led up Ledru's division in fine style, the chivalrous Bagration rode out in front of his line and saluted the columns crying, 'Bravo, Messieurs! C'est superbe'.

In the bitter fighting Davout had his horse killed under him and was badly bruised, while Compans and Dessaix were both severely wounded. On the Russian side the corps commander, Prince Alexei Gorchakov, was wounded besides both his divisional commanders Voronzov and Neverovski. This prolonged struggle gave Kutuzov time to reinforce Bagration with a corps (II) from Barclay's extreme right. Napoleon too intervened, but less happily. Hearing of Ney's first success – temporary as it turned out – in storming one of the redoubts, he sent Junot's 10,000 Westphalians into the forest to link up the corps of Davout and Poniatowski. They arrived in time to be repulsed by the newly arrived division of the Prince of Württemberg, and their absence deprived Ney of any reserve at the height of his struggle with Bagration.

Meanwhile on the French left the Viceroy had been delayed. Delzons's division after taking Borodino, pushed on too impetuously and ran into Dokhtorov's Corps (VI) in the Russian centre; overwhelming numbers obliged it to retire into Borodino. With three divisions supported by Grouchy's cavalry corps (3rd) Eugène passed the Kolotza

A portrait of Marshal Ney, le brave des braves, *who well earned his title* Prince de la Moskowa *for his part in the main attack on the Russian position*

A Russian hero of the battle, A N. Seslávin, a gallant officer of the Hussars of the Guards regiment, of which Tsar Alexander I was Colonel-in-Chief

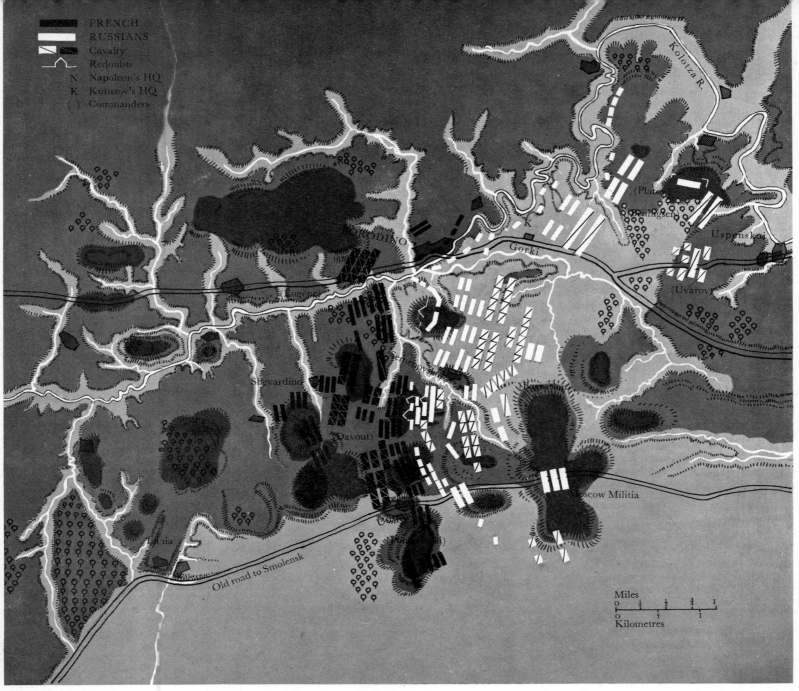

The strong defensive position occupied by Kutuzov's army, together with Napoleon's determination to make a frontal assault on the Russian centre and left, ensured that the Battle of Borodino could not end without heavy losses on both sides

RIGHT Having led a desperate charge, General de Caulaincourt, at the head of the 5th Cuirassiers, is killed as they break into the Great Redoubt (painted by Eugène Charpentier); shortly afterwards Prince Eugène's infantry stormed and captured the redoubt

OVERLEAF The 33rd Regiment have formed square to resist an attack by Russian cuirassiers (part of a panorama of the battle painted by G. Langlois); cavalry did not normally find it profitable to attack squares

BELOW An unusual French print which, besides including the conventional contents of a battle scene, does not draw a veil over its less attractive aspects, the dead and wounded

la Moskowa, le 7 Septembre 1812.

by four small pontoon bridges and made ready to attack the Great Redoubt.

On the Semenovskoi front Napoleon himself, after some hesitation, threw in Friant's division, the reserve of I Corps, which after turning Bagration's right was finally repulsed by Konovnitzin from the smoking ruins of the village. Seeing that Bagration was still getting reinforcements, Ney and Davout now disposed their forces to hold him along the line of the ravine near Semenovskoi. Bagration, hoping to regain the initiative, hurled himself once again at the French line. In the fight that followed he was mortally wounded. The Russians were near the end of their tether, but the impassive Konovnitzin rose to the occasion and rallied them behind the ravine. Dokhtorov now assumed command of the Second Army. At long last the French had won a very real advantage.

On the extreme right Poniatowski had occupied Utitza, but so far from turning the Russian left had found himself confronted by Tuchkov. When eventually Junot appeared and outflanked his opponents the Prince stormed the mamelon. Tuchkov drove the Poles out again, but paid for this success with his life.

Soon after Friant got into Semenovskoi Eugène made a bad mistake, sending the single division of Morand to attack Raievski's corps (VII), part of which enjoyed the cover of the Great Redoubt. This assault was repulsed with loss. Captain François (30th of the Line) clambered through one of the embrasures of the battery just after a piece had been discharged. 'The Russian gunners met us with blows of handspikes and swabs, and we fought hand to hand. They were redoubtable adversaries.'

On the extreme left of the French line a minor episode now had a significant effect on the outcome of the battle. Eugène had deployed Ornano's light cavalry north of Borodino to guard his left flank. Uvarov, wishing to exploit Dokhtorov's earlier success against Delzons, suddenly fell upon Ornano with his 3,000 cavalry (1st Corps), and overwhelmed him. Delzons received the Russians in square and halted them. Meanwhile Count Platov with his 5,000 regular Cossacks worked round the French flank, and Delzons, impressed by this forest of lances, sought help from the Viceroy. In fact the Cossacks did precisely nothing, while Uvarov had no intention of launching his men against squares. Nevertheless Napoleon remained in doubt for about an hour what this incident portended.

Back near Semenovskoi Ney and Murat worked out a

plan to exploit the repulse of Bagration. Murat decided to send two of the cavalry corps across the ravine. Nansouty (1st) fell on the left of Konovnitzin, but the Guard regiments of Ismailov and Lithuania received him steadily in square. When Nansouty had shot his bolt, five Russian cuirassier regiments fell on him and drove him back. Latour-Maubourg struggled across the ravine just south of Semenovskoi but met with no better success.

Even so the position was now extremely serious for the Russians. The Second Army was driven back in the greatest confusion, though Paskievich still maintained his position in the Great Redoubt. The black smoke of hundreds of guns, and the dust raised by continual cavalry charges screened the shattered state of the Russian left from Napoleon. The Marshals did not consider their mangled divisions capable of pushing on without fresh reinforcements. The Emperor still had under his hand the Imperial Guard, nearly 20,000 strong, but he refused to launch it.

The main action now shifted to the Great Redoubt. At 2 pm. Eugène launched three infantry divisions to the assault. Montbrun, one of the great cavalrymen of the Empire, was preparing to second them with the 2nd Cavalry Corps, when a roundshot mortally wounded him. General de Caulaincourt took over the command, and led a desperate charge. Running the gauntlet of massed artillery and infantry, he actually broke into the Great Redoubt at the head of the 5th Cuirassiers and was there slain. His sacrifice was not in vain: favoured by this diversion, Eugène's second attack succeeded, stormed the redoubt and took General Likatschev, badly wounded.

It was now about 3 pm. Although the French left pushed forward as far as the Gorki heights, and although the combat continued until nightfall, the Russians were still able to show a bold front, and both sides, exhausted by eight hours' carnage, were content to cannonade each other.

On the far right Poniatowski, encouraged by Ney's success, attacked the mamelon of Utitza once more, and the Russians fell back upon the Moscow militia, who at least looked sufficiently imposing to convince the French that their enemies still had fresh reserves. During the night Kutuzov drew off his army and a week later the French were in Moscow.

The losses of this terrible day cannot be accurately told. Of the 250,000 engaged approximately twenty-eight per cent were put *hors de combat.* The French lost over 30,000 men and the Russians about 40,000.

The generals suffered severely. The loss of Bagration was a heavy blow to the Russians. Among the wounded were Prince Galitzin, Yermolov, Barclay's chief of staff, and Prince Karl of Mecklenburg. On the French side three generals of division died and eleven were wounded,

LEFT *A detail from Lejeune's painting: Marshal Berthier returns the sword of General Sokereff; Napoleon sends the cross of the Legion of Honour to a dying officer; a soldier, guarding Tartar and Calmuck prisoners, kicks a live shell into a brook*

Napoleon, attended by his marshals and staff, prepares to make his triumphal entry into Moscow, a week after his victory at Borodino; few of the victors were to survive the terrible retreat from Moscow which followed

and these included all four cavalry corps commanders. Thirty-four generals of brigade were hit. The French guns had expended 60,000 rounds and the infantry 1,400,000 cartridges.

If Kutuzov's army survived to fight another day he had to thank his opponent rather than any skilful dispositions of his own. Neither in his prior planning nor in his handling of the battle did the Emperor live up to his reputation. His original layout was faulty. Poniatowski's corps, marching with both flanks in the air was not strong enough for its task, nor was it connected at the outset

with I Corps. To take two divisions from Davout on the very eve of battle and place them under Eugène was a serious error. Had the former disposed of five divisions from the start he could have made short work of the Semenovskoi sector. Little attempt was made to amuse Barclay's army and thus to delay the shifting of reinforcements to Bagration's front.

Napoleon had two great opportunities to destroy Bagration's wing. He threw away the first by not making the initial attack in sufficient force. The second chance was lost when Napoleon failed to reinforce Ney's success at

Semenovskoi by sending in the Imperial Guard, or at the very least the Young Guard. The truth is that he left the conduct of the fight to his generals and that when he did intervene, he did more harm than good. On this occasion the brilliant strategist proved by no means remarkable as a tactician. He certainly appreciated how to use his old arm, the artillery, but for the rest he was content to pile up deep columns of horse and foot and leave his unfortunate generals to sort things out.

From the French point of view the real hero of the day was Marshal Ney, *le brave des braves*, who certainly won his title *Prince de la Moskowa*. On the Russian side one must certainly admire the way in which Prince Bagration won time for Kutuzov to remedy the errors in his initial dispositions. The calm conduct of Konovnitzin during the crisis of the battle was also admirable.

The rest of the campaign of 1812 is another story. Of Napoleon's army that fought at Borodino few indeed were destined to see their native lands again.

PETER YOUNG

1815 Waterloo

*The Hundred Days, Napoleon's final gamble, ended in Belgium when he gave battle
too late at Waterloo, and lost all to Wellington and Blücher*

ON 1 MARCH 1815 NAPOLEON landed near Cannes from Elba with 1,000 men and marched on Paris. Most of the army rallied to his side, oaths of allegiance to the Bourbons were largely broken, his progress became a triumph, and he entered the Tuileries soon after Louis XVIII had fled to Ghent. The Emperor sought to open negotiations with Britain, Russia, Austria and Prussia, but these powers, hastily composing their differences at the Congress of Vienna, pledged themselves to crush Napoleon once and for all. Six armies, comprising over 500,000 men, were to cross the French frontier simultaneously, but this immense force could scarcely be ready to invade before early July.

Napoleon, bending all his energies to confront this formidable coalition, collected money, horses and weapons, set up workshops, and mustered 360,000 troops for the defence of France and the quelling of insurrection. He discarded plans for fighting a defensive campaign in favour of attacking the two most accessible enemies before they could concentrate. If he could dispose of the Anglo-Dutch and Prussian armies strung out over nearly one hundred miles of Belgium, he would then bear down on the approaching forces of Austria and Russia and try either to defeat them or to induce their rulers to make peace.

Wellington, with headquarters in Brussels, had 93,000 men, only 31,000 of them British, the rest being from Hanover, Nassau, Belgium and Brunswick. Blücher's army numbered 116,000. By 14 June Napoleon had concentrated 124,000 troops near the frontier. He should have gathered more, and with such inferior numbers all depended on his being able to strike at Charleroi, the junction of the allied armies, to separate them, to force each to fall back – and so farther apart – along its own line of communication, the one to Ostend, the other through Liége to Coblenz, and then to destroy each in turn. Wellington and Blücher had foreseen this aim and planned to concentrate forward at Gosselies and Fleurus respectively, but the Emperor's extraordinary skill and secrecy robbed them of the three days' warning they counted on. Rumours of French moves had not sufficed to bring their brigades from widely dispersed cantonments.

Early on 15 June French troops crossed the Sambre and drove back to Fleurus Zieten's outnumbered Prussian corps, whose stubborn resistance gained time for Blücher to assemble his other three corps four miles further back at Sombreffe. Meanwhile on the left wing 50,000 men under Marshal Ney advanced cautiously to Gosselies, pushed out the Prussians, but did not obey their orders to seize the vital crossroads to which Quatre-Bras owes its name. Wellington, belatedly informed of the first engagements, still uncertain of the direction of

RIGHT The Duke of Wellington *by Goya (National Gallery)*

140

At a critical moment during the Battle of Ligny, on the eve of Waterloo, Blücher's horse was shot under him; he was stunned and bruised, but the counter-attack enabled his infantry to retreat

Napoleon's main thrust, and very sensitive to a threat to his links with the coast, did not order an immediate concentration on his left flank. Fortunately the Prince of Saxe-Weimar, perceiving the danger, took it upon himself to place his brigade at Quatre-Bras, an action which was confirmed by his divisional commander, Baron Perponcher.

So Ney's forward troops – 19,000 infantry, 3,000 horsemen and 60 guns – were faced that Friday morning of 16 June only by Perponcher's Dutch-Belgian division of 8,000, with 16 guns and 50 hussars. French reconnaissance was most inadequate, especially as Ney allowed

himself to be persuaded by unenterprising subordinates and by his own hard experiences in the Peninsula that he lacked the force to take the crossroads and that the allied position must be typical of Wellington, with most of the troops concealed on a reverse slope. Not until 11 am. did Ney act, and as his infantry were still extended all the way back to the Sambre, results were slow. Moreover, Napoleon's orders had failed to impress him with a sense of urgency.

At 2 the French guns opened fire, the infantry captured two hamlets and, after a fierce struggle, part of the Bois de Bossu. The allied line was in grave danger, but just in time Wellington arrived from his meeting with Blücher at Ligny, a Dutch–Belgian cavalry brigade rode up, and at 3.30 the redoubtable Picton's 5th Division (8,000 British and Hanoverian troops) marched in urgently from Brussels.

For the next five hours fighting was desperate among the trees, in tall standing rye, and among the hamlets. Time and again Wellington's infantry hurriedly formed square to withstand assaults by cuirassiers and lancers. Allied cavalry charged in counter-attack, though usually in vain. But reinforcements were steadily reaching the Duke – all marching or riding to the sound of the guns – until he had 30,000 men on the ground. Eventually weight of numbers and steady musketry prevailed, and after much ebb and flow fighting, the French were forced back. Their casualties totalled 4,000, those of the Allies about 600 more. Though Ney had missed his great chance of breaking through all the morning when his opponents were so weak, he had at least prevented Wellington from supporting Blücher eight miles to the south-east, at Ligny.

The interrelation of the two simultaneous battles is emphasized by the singular fate of d'Erlon's corps. On its way to Quatre-Bras, it was ordered to join Napoleon. The troops reached the edge of the Ligny fighting area, only to receive peremptory orders from an indignant Ney to go instantly to his aid. They arrived too late to affect the Quatre-Bras struggle, and thus marched to and fro between the battlefields without contributing to either.

Blücher had 84,000 men holding a seven-mile front by the Ligny brook. He was expecting Bülow's corps to arrive, but it had farthest to march and had made a late start thanks to imprecise orders. He also had Wellington's promise of support if he himself were not attacked. On the French side were 78,000 troops and 242 guns, 16 more than the Prussians had. Napoleon's plan was to contain the Prussian left, strike at the centre, and force Blücher to commit his every reserve. Then Ney would arrive from Quatre-Bras to surround the enemy's right wing and help clinch the victory. But how could Napoleon calculate accurately either the opposition Ney would meet from Wellington or the time required to overcome

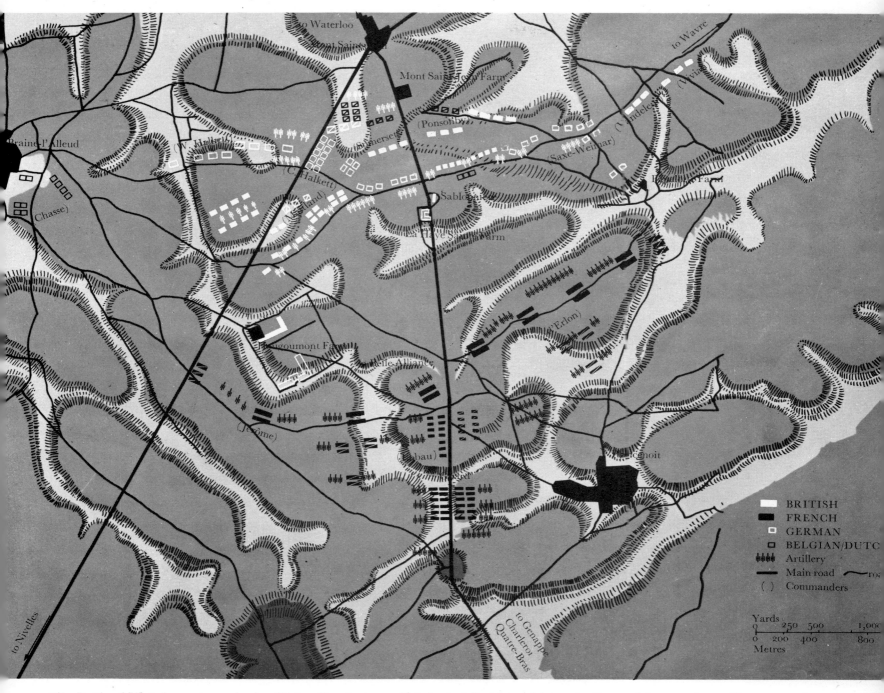

The Battle of Waterloo commenced when Jérôme Bonaparte, on Napoleon's left, advanced to occupy the wooded approaches to Hougoumont in an attempt both to divert attention from the centre, where Napoleon's main assault was to be made, and to draw off Wellington's reserves

A French print, by Bramatti, of different types of Napoleonic uniforms – this was truly the golden age of the military tailor

143

it? He could hope much, but guarantee nothing, and we have seen what occurred. Had he summoned Lobau's reserve corps from Charleroi in good time, he need not have relied upon Ney.

The fighting for bridges, churchyard and fortified farms raged all afternoon. Burning villages kept on changing hands. Corpses choked street, garden and orchard alike. A thunderstorm and failing light heralded the final French assault on the weakened Prussian centre, with Napoleon eager to deal a death blow and so be free to overwhelm Wellington next day without fear of interference. Grouchy had gained ground on the right and was threatening Sombreffe. For the second time the 72-year-old Blücher lived up to his name of *Vorwärts* by leading in person his scanty reserve squadrons in a counter-attack. His horse was shot and rolled on its rider, who, stunned and bruised, was carried to the rear. Despite its bad outcome, this last effort by the Prussian cavalry gained time for the infantry to withdraw. Under command of the Chief of Staff, Gneisenau, the beaten Prussian army retreated on Wavre, sixteen miles to the north, parallel to, not away from, Wellington's line. The Duke called this 'the decisive moment of the century'.

Napoleon, deprived of the decisive victory he had anticipated, was chary of pursuing, for he had received no news from Ney, and Prussian rearguards were holding on to Bry and Sombreffe. So he ordered Grouchy to have

the enemy followed at daybreak, and made no attempt to keep contact with them or to watch the line of their retreat – a costly neglect. Prussian casualties had been nearly 16,000 and 21 guns; a further 8,000 men of doubtful loyalty or sympathetic towards Napoleon, to whom they had formerly been subject, deserted in the night. French losses at Ligny exceeded 11,000.

Next day the French pursuit of both Blücher and Wellington was clumsy, tardy, even apathetic. Vigilance was lacking, co-operation poor. Napoleon, firmly convinced that the Prussians were retreating eastwards and could be discounted anyhow, dawdled inexcusably on the battlefield. When he did go to Quatre-Bras it was to find that Wellington had broken contact behind a screen of cavalry and horse artillery – unseen, unmolested by the torpid Ney. Too late he led the pursuit with blazing energy. Despite torrential rain and a stiff rearguard action at Genappe, the Anglo-Dutch army made its way to the pre-selected ridge of Mont Saint-Jean, thereby keeping level with the Prussians who came to Wavre and near-by villages that evening. Wellington, armed with Blücher's promise to come to his aid next day, stood at bay. As for Grouchy, his commanders fumbled all day, his men marched no more than ten miles, and he called off the pursuit two hours before nightfall, for reasons of rain and muddy tracks, though the Prussians kept going in identical conditions.

RIGHT *Four handsome French prints of elegant uniforms of the age of Napoleon: a Sapper of the Garde Nationale of Paris (top left), a Prussian Grenadier (top right), both by Genty; 2nd and 7th Hussars (bottom left and right), both by Martinet*

OVERLEAF The Battle of Waterloo *by Denis Dighton: Wellington gives orders to an officer, perilously close to a fierce cavalry engagement*

The smoke from four hundred guns partly shrouds the fiercely contested battlefield of Waterloo; in the foreground Lord Uxbridge and the charge of the Horse Guards are prominent

The effective strength of the Anglo-Allied army at Mont Saint-Jean – Waterloo village lies two miles to the north – was nearly 68,000 men and 156 guns; Wellington took a grave risk and deprived himself of another 17,000 troops left eight miles away near Hal on the Mons-Brussels road, to guard against the far smaller risk of a French turning movement. Napoleon, who underestimated Wellington's firmness and tactical skill and Blücher's loyalty to his ally, disposed of about 72,000 men and 246 guns, massed on a three-mile front. The day would have gone better for him had he, a gunner, not accepted the advice that the rain-sodden ground would have to dry out before his artillery could manœuvre, had he insisted upon proper reconnaissance of the allied positions, and had he interfered more with his inadequate subordinates. The day might have been won for France had these commanders known better how to coordinate infantry, cavalry and artillery in their attacks.

Not until 11.30 am. on 18 June did Jérôme Bonaparte's division advance to occupy the wooded approaches to Hougoumont. The objects were to divert attention from the centre where the main assault was to go in and, it was hoped, to draw off Wellington's reserves. It failed, for Jérôme turned what should have been a limited demonstration into an all-out attack which used up more and more battalions and incurred disproportionately heavy loss in the face of superb defence by the Guards and by troops from Nassau and Hanover. Fighting went on most of the day, the château and chapel caught fire, the courtyard gate was almost forced, but the loopholed garden wall proved impassable, and this vital forward bastion of Wellington's front was held.

At 1.30 pm. 80 French guns heralded the main assault in the centre by a half-hour bombardment. Then d'Erlon's 18,000 attacked up the slope in four unwieldly, serried columns. So soft was the ground that many soldiers had their shoes dragged off by the heavy clods. While trying to deploy they were fired at and charged by Picton's division, the General, already concealing a Quatre-Bras wound, being killed. Then the Earl of Uxbridge, choosing well his moment, unleashed Somerset's Household Brigade against opposing horsemen and Ponsonby's Union Brigade against the disordered French columns. Two eagles and 3,000 prisoners were taken, but Uxbridge's impetuous cavalry charged too far and were severely mauled and driven back. Away on the allied left Papelotte Farm was lost and then recaptured.

Ney, angered by the total failure of d'Erlon's attack and seriously misinterpreting through smoke the departure of some British wounded, French prisoners, and

LEFT ABOVE *The staff officer can offer Napoleon no cheerful news; the glum expression on the Emperor's face and the anxious looks on those of his staff show that they realize that they are no longer able to prevent the steady advance of the British line along the whole length of the battlefield (painted by Sir William Allan)*

LEFT *A coloured English print of the battle (after W. Heath); Lieutenant-General Lord Uxbridge is the central figure*

LEFT BELOW *The Evening of the Battle of Waterloo by E. Crofts: the battle lost, Napoleon prepares to flee*

La Garde Meurt et Ne Se Rend Pas *(lithograph by H. Bellangé); had Napoleon thrown in the Guard earlier, instead of waiting till evening, the outcome of Waterloo might have been different*

A Dutch print showing Highlanders presenting captured French eagles to Wellington; the Duke's army included contingents from Hanover, Nassau, Belgium, and Brunswick

empty wagons, now sought to accelerate what he took to be an incipient retreat. For an hour 5,000 cavalry persisted in prodigal attacks. Time and again they lapped ineffectively round the decimated but unbroken infantry squares, until volleys and cavalry charges drove them away. Colours were cut to shreds, and ensigns or sergeants died in their defence. British guns were taken and retaken repeatedly, but were neither spiked nor dragged off as prizes. Orders, trumpet calls, and frenzied shouts of '*Vive l'Empereur!*' could barely be heard through the roar of roundshot, the blaze of musketry, the rattle of balls on helmet and cuirass, and the struggles of sabre slash and bayonet thrust. The smell of downtrodden rye mingled with that of gunpowder. The ground trembled under the hoofbeats of charging squadrons or of rearing, plunging horses: some officers had as many as five mounts shot under them that day.

Time was running short for Napoleon. The Prussians had been sighted at about 1.30 and three hours later Bülow's corps, which had taken no part at Ligny and had been late in starting that morning and delayed *en route*, thanks to faulty staffwork, had 16,000 men and 64 guns engaged. They pressed his right flank; he had to detach Lobau's corps to counter-attack; and as a result the village of Plancenoit was gained, lost and recaptured.

Ney, meantime, had launched 9,000 cavalry on a 1,000-yard front between La Haye Sainte and Hougoumont. Fearful butchery ensued, with successive charges hindered by ramparts of dead horses and then repulsed by musketry. Too late Ney brought up infantry to support his horsemen: when counter-attacked, they gave way and withdrew. But at last the red-headed Marshal gained some success, for soon after Papelotte had been retaken, his mangled divisions finally gained possession of La Haye Sainte. In this central bastion the gallant King's German Legion, after frustrating efforts to storm the barn, twice extinguishing serious fires with kettles of water, and fighting doggedly for many hours, ran out of ammunition. This could not be replenished, and the 43 survivors were ordered to escape.

The allied centre was at once exposed to close-range cannonade and musketry. The troops were exhausted, several units gave way under pressure, and the situation was perilous.

Ney requested more troops to exploit the chance of a breakthrough, but the Emperor testily refused. He was wrong, for had he raised the stakes by committing at least a part of the Old and Middle Guard, this added force must have turned the scales. Instead, Wellington was granted a respite in which to reorganize his line and fill the gaps. Moreover, Zieten's corps came up belatedly on the left, thus releasing two cavalry brigades to strengthen the centre. When, soon after 7 pm., the Guard did advance, it was too late: the chance had gone. The French first echelon was repulsed by Colin Halkett's brigade and a Dutch-Belgian brigade; the remainder

Wellington and Blücher Meeting after the Battle of Waterloo, *an engraving after the painting by Daniel Maclise (in the Royal Gallery of the House of Lords): doubts as to the historical accuracy of this meeting at La Belle Alliance, raised when the painting was exhibited, were routed when Queen Victoria wrote to her daughter, the Princess Royal, in Berlin, and received an assurance that the meeting had taken place from General von Nostitz, Blücher's adjutant*

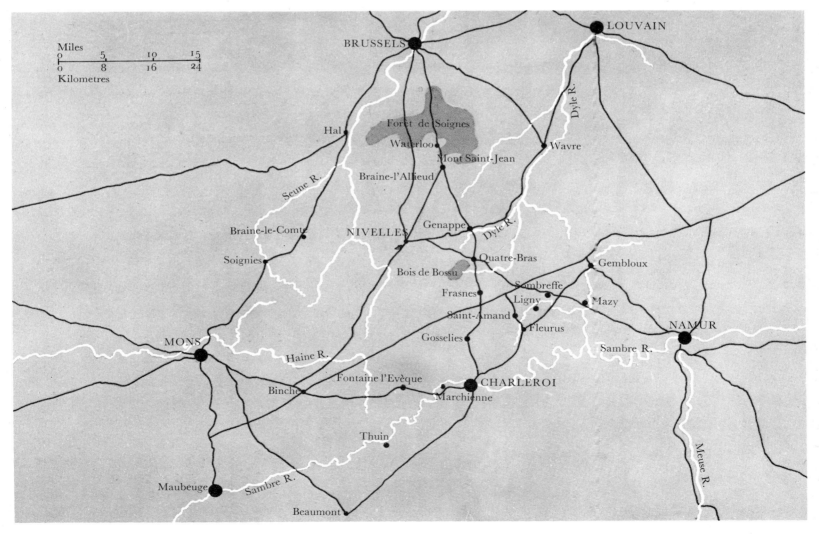

The field of Waterloo on the morning after the battle; Wellington's army suffered 15,000 casualties, the Prussians nearly 7,000, and the French over 25,000

The conclusion of Wellington's report of his victory at Waterloo; the postscript records the death of Major-General Ponsonby, the commander of the Union Brigade

A facsimile copy of Napoleon's letter of 13 July 1815 to the Prince Regent; having abdicated, Napoleon later surrendered to the British Navy after a vain attempt to escape to America

were seen off by Maitland's Guards. Called to their feet by the Duke, who all afternoon exposed himself coolly in one danger spot after another, they fired a devastating volley and drove their adversaries down the slope. The 52nd Foot came in decisively on the flank and aggravated the destruction of France's last hope, as did the cavalry brigades of Vivian and Vandeleur, who charged into the valley. Then Wellington's whole line advanced to victory.

Meanwhile the Prussians, now strengthened by the arrival of Pirch's corps, had penetrated between d'Erlon and Lobau, but the Young Guard valiantly held Plance-noit until nightfall, so preventing Blücher from cutting Napoleon's line of retreat. Three squares of the Old Guard – General Cambronne to the fore – resisted for a while and covered the Emperor's departure; but the rest of the *Armée du Nord* fled in great disorder, with Gneisenau conducting a ruthless nocturnal pursuit as far as Frasnes.

Grouchy, that day, had rejected the urgings of sub-ordinates to march to the Waterloo cannonade, and obeyed Napoleon's first order by advancing to Wavre. Here, on the Dyle, he found the Prussians, but only Thielemann's corps left behind to detain him. When at 5 p.m. a despatch arrived from the Emperor saying that

Bülow was in sight and ordering him to turn and strike this corps in the rear, Grouchy was too involved in fighting his way across the river to obey, though he would have reached the battlefield far too late had he gone. Next morning Thielemann, who had achieved much by holding Grouchy, was obliged by sheer numbers to withdraw, and the French Marshal, on learning of the Waterloo disaster, instantly retreated south with his 33,000 men, skilfully avoided Prussian interception, and brought his force to Paris by a roundabout route.

Whereas the casualties in Wellington's army amounted to 15,000, Prussian losses totalled close on 7,000; French casualties, though harder to calculate, exceeded 25,000, with a further 8,000 men taken prisoner, and over 200 guns lost.

Napoleon returned to Paris still hopeful and ambitious, but his failure to gain the support of the Chambers caused him to abdicate. He retired to Malmaison, but left hurriedly to avoid capture by a Prussian column and, having tried in vain to escape to America, surrendered to the British Navy on 15 July.

ANTONY BRETT-JAMES

An incident during the battle: a French cuirassier and an English Life-guardsman contest a few square yards of down-trodden rye (a whole series of prints published by Thomas Kelly was devoted to this incident)

Rowlandson's cartoon, published two years before Waterloo, showing the confrontation of the Tyrant Bonaparte and the Tyrant Death, 'in a manner which promises a more perfect intimacy immediately to ensue'

COPY

OF THE

Transparency

EXHIBITED AT

ACKERMANN'S REPOSITORY OF ARTS,

During the Illuminations of the 5th and 6th of November, 1813,

IN HONOUR OF THE SPLENDID VICTORIES OBTAINED BY

The ALLIES over the ARMIES of FRANCE,

AT LEIPSIC AND ITS ENVIRONS.

THE TWO KINGS OF TERROR.

1854
Balaclava

This repulse of a Russian attack in the Crimean War is famous for the charge of Lord Cardigan's Light Brigade, which only one-third of his men survived

ON 14 SEPTEMBER 1854 a Franco-British expeditionary force of 56,000 men, together with a Turkish contingent between 4,000 and 5,000 strong, began the invasion of the Crimea. Its objective was the Russians' Black Sea naval base at Sevastopol. Within two weeks the allies had invested the town and occupied the rest of the Chersonese peninsula. It was agreed that the French should besiege the south-western defences of Sevastopol, while the British, whose base was at Balaclava, undertook to prosecute the siege from the south-east and to defend the landward approaches to the allied position.

With the investment of Sevastopol it became apparent that the allied commanders lacked the strength to perform the tasks they had been set. Their forces were too few to maintain the siege and at the same time protect their right flank against the Russian field army. The British Commander-in-Chief, Lord Raglan, gave first priority to the prosecution of the siege. Balaclava was only seven miles away from the divisions on the heights before Sevastopol and, provided he had a few hours' notice, Raglan would be able to bring some of the siege force to the support of the slender numbers guarding his eastern flank. If, however, the allies committed themselves too heavily in defending an attack on their right flank, they might find that they had been made the vic-

LEFT *Lord Cardigan leading the Charge of the Light Brigade, the astonishing, brave and bloody incident for which the Battle of Balaclava is chiefly remembered*

tims of a feint designed to divert their forces from Sevastopol while the garrison (which numbered nearly 54,000) was preparing a sortie.

The problems of defending Balaclava were complicated by the nature of the hinterland. The harbour lay within a narrow gap in the coastal hills; to the north were two valleys, known as the North Valley and the South Valley, running roughly parallel to the coast, and separated by a ridge of low hills called the Causeway Heights. Both valleys were bounded to the west by the Sapounè Heights. Along the far side of the North Valley were the Fedioukine Heights. Four and a half miles to the east of Balaclava, beyond the hills which closed the two valleys in that direction, lay the River Tchernaya.

The Causeway Heights were of great importance to the security of the base at Balaclava. If the Heights went unguarded the Russians could advance unseen along the North Valley, until they had only to cross the Heights to close on the harbour, two and a half miles away.

To give warning of a Russian thrust towards Balaclava and to delay its advance, six redoubts were hastily constructed along the Causeway Heights. These were held by 3,000 Turks with nine 12-pounder guns. Raglan's total effectives had fallen to about 16,000 and few troops could be spared to defend the ground between Balaclava and the Sapounè Heights. The approach to the harbour was guarded by a detachment of marines. A battalion of the 93rd Highlanders, commanded by Sir Colin Campbell, was posted at Kadiköi. A mile and a half away to

'*A split crow Russia fancying himself an eagle, fixed his talons in the fleece of a sheep Turkey – but, neither able to move his prey, nor to disentangle his feet, he was destroyed by the shepherds John Bull and Napoleon III*' (*a* Punch *cartoon*)

The Genoese Castle and part of the harbour at Balaclava, the British base, in defence of which the battle on 25 October was fought (photographed by Roger Fenton, the first war photographer)

'*Lieutenant-Colonel Hallewell, his day's work over*', *a study by Fenton*

the north at the foot of the slope below Redoubt No. 5, were the lines of the Heavy Brigade (commanded by Sir James Scarlett) and the Light Brigade (under Lord Cardigan) which together composed Lord Lucan's Cavalry Division.

By the evening of 24 October, a Russian force numbering 25,000 men and 78 guns, under Count Liprandi, had assembled on the Tchernaya, five miles to the north-east of Balaclava. The British had no lack of warning. Three days before, as the result of a false alarm, 1,000 men of the 4th Division had been marched down from the plateau to the plain of Balaclava and back again. On the night of the 24th, Raglan received a message from Lucan and Campbell announcing that a spy had reported that the Russians were about to attack Balaclava, and this time no action was taken.

Liprandi's troops set out at 5 o'clock next morning, 25 October. Four columns, comprising 60 per cent of his infantry, and half his artillery, were to attack Redoubts Nos. 1, 2 and 3. The mass of the cavalry and artillery marched in support of the columns. Meanwhile, the remainder of his forces would occupy the Fedioukine Heights. About 6 am., the alarm was given to the allied rear and the guns of No. 1 Redoubt opened fire. Confronted by 10,000 men and subjected to bombardment by 30 cannon, the 500 Turks in the redoubt put up a notable resistance. They were driven out at last by a bayonet charge. Their stand had cost them 170 dead and had brought the allies at least an hour's grace. Although he had sent for the 1st and 4th Divisions on receiving the news of Liprandi's advance, Raglan needed still more time to bring up his reinforcements. Their lines were almost two hours' march away, and both divisional commanders were slow to start. The 1st Division, under the

Not melons for the commissariat, but cannons and cannon balls being unloaded on the ordnance wharf at Balaclava

'Captain Walker, 30th Regiment, reading General Orders', attributed to Fenton

The Charge of the Heavy Brigade; the Greys and the Enniskillen Dragoons are featured in this view of the engagement (an engraving from An Illustrated History of the War Against Russia)

The plain of Balaclava, showing the position of the armies immediately before the Charge of the Light Brigade on 25 October 1854

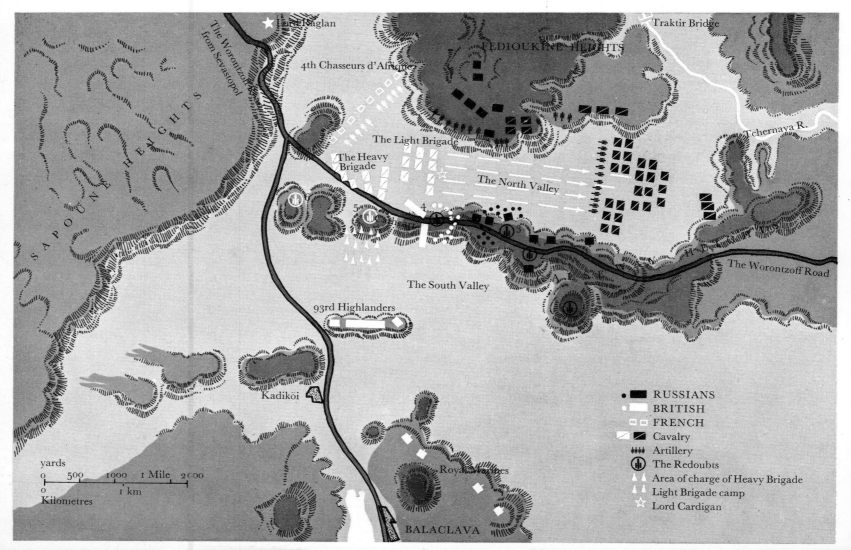

Lord Raglan

Traktir Bridge

FEDIOUKINE HEIGHTS

4th Chasseurs d'Afrique

The Woronzoff from Sevastopol

SAPOUNE HEIGHTS

The Light Brigade

The Heavy Brigade

Tchernaya R.

The North Valley

The South Valley

The Woronzoff Road

93rd Highlanders

Kadiköi

yards

0   500   1000   1 Mile   2000

Kilometres

1 km

Royal Marines

BALACLAVA

RUSSIANS

BRITISH

FRENCH

Cavalry

Artillery

The Redoubts

Area of charge of Heavy Brigade

Light Brigade camp

Lord Cardigan

'A quiet day in the Mortar Battery', by Roger Fenton

Duke of Cambridge, Queen Victoria's 35-year-old cousin, set out half an hour after the arrival of Raglan's aide-de-camp. Sir George Cathcart, with the 4th Division, took a good deal longer to get under way, refusing at first to move at all, on the ground that half of his troops had just returned from a night in the trenches.

Raglan, meanwhile, was observing the Russians' progress in the plain from the edge of the plateau. He was joined there by Canrobert, the French Commander-in-Chief, who ordered two brigades of infantry and two regiments of cavalry to march to the support of the British below. The situation was rapidly deteriorating. Understandably enough, the experience of their comrades in Redoubt No. 1, and the overwhelming strength of the Russian offensive, had been too much for the Turks in the remaining redoubts; they abandoned their posts and made for the harbour. Lucan prudently fell back with the British cavalry towards the foot of the plateau, reserving his force against a thrust on Kadiköi, in front of which stood Campbell's Highlanders and two Turkish battalions. The action was now to take two distinct courses, one in the North Valley, the other in the South Valley. Both valleys were in the view of the spectators on the plateau, but not of the troops on the low ground.

The main body of Liprandi's cavalry and over 30 guns were sent forward up the North Valley. In the South Valley, where a smaller Russian cavalry force advanced on Lucan's retreating cavalry division, the artillery opened fire on the Highlanders and Turks occupying a rise north-east of Kadiköi. When Campbell fell back to find cover, his Turkish troops took fright and fled. Next, five or six Russian squadrons turned southwards *en route* for Kadiköi. At Campbell's suggestion Lord Lucan withdrew again, clear of the Highlanders' front, to a position from which he threatened the Russian flank. As the Russians advanced, Campbell formed the Highlanders in line on the crest of his position – 'a thin red streak topped with a line of steel', wrote *The Times* correspondent. The 93rd's muzzle-loading Minié rifles could be fired about twice a minute, no faster than the muskets of the Napoleonic Wars, but were much more accurate and possessed a far greater effective range. A volley fired at 350 yards' range caused the Russians to halt. Their commander wheeled to the left; then, after a further volley, ordered a retreat.

The progress of the mass of the Russian horse in the North Valley had been checked by the batteries on the plateau. They now turned to their left to climb the Causeway Heights. Between 700 and 800 of the Heavy Brigade were advancing eastwards along the South Valley when the leading ranks of Russian cavalry, 3,000 strong, appeared over the crest of the Causeway Heights on their left. Scarlett immediately ordered his squadrons to form their front facing the slopes and began to dress his ranks in preparation for a charge. What followed was one of the most remarkable small cavalry actions in the history of the British Army.

The Russians resumed their march and were half-way down the slopes when they realized that the British were about to charge. They halted. If the Russians had extended their front and had ridden forward to receive the attack, it is difficult to see how the Heavy Brigade could have avoided being overwhelmed. Instead they themselves paid the price of the excessive depth of their formation. Nevertheless, the Russian front overlapped both flanks of Scarlett's line and his success owed as much to the distribution of his attack as to the effect of the initial shock. Shortly after the three squadrons of Scarlett's first line had ridden into the Russians' front, and the lighter Russian wings began to close on them, separate squadrons struck the front left and right angles of the column. The column was driven backwards up the slope by these repeated blows. It had thus been shaken when Lucan sent the 4th Dragoon Guards in a violent charge against its right flank. This stroke proved decisive. The 4th Dragoons drove straight through the column, which broke its ranks and made off over the hill in confusion. Eight minutes had passed since Scarlett had ordered the charge, but the Heavy Brigade's own disorganization was inevitably too great to allow of a pursuit.

Throughout the short action Cardigan and the Light Brigade had remained immobile 500 yards away, as he had decided he was not entitled to join the struggle on his own initiative. If he had chosen to charge the bewildered squadrons streaming back from Scarlett's onslaught, the Russians' extraordinary reverse would have been transformed into a costly and even more humiliating rout.

Nevertheless, for the loss of 78 killed and wounded the Heavy Brigade had gained a convincing advantage which Raglan now proposed to exploit. The 1st and 4th Divisions would soon debouch on to the plain, and the way seemed clear to regaining the Causeway Heights. He sent an order down to Lucan instructing him to advance his cavalry and recover the Heights, adding that he would receive infantry support. Raglan's divisional commanders, unfortunately, were not men to supply much energy and perception to their directives. Lucan made no move because, as he said afterwards, he could not see any infantry advancing to his support. Cathcart, who thought that the 1st Division should do the attacking, chose to suspend his advance at Redoubt No. 4.

Liprandi too reorganized his forces during the lull which followed the attack of the Heavy Brigade. The squadrons which had received the charge were deployed

R. Caton Woodville's dramatic view of the Charge of the Light Brigade; Lord Cardigan sets an admirable example of coolness to his men

RIGHT *Two lithographs by W. Simpson from* The Seat of the War in the East: *the Charge of the Heavy Brigade (top), and the arrival of fresh troops at Balaclava (bottom)*

at the eastern end of the North Valley with 12 cannon in their front, and three squadrons of lancers on either flank. On the southern slopes of the Fedioukine Heights stood eight battalions, some horse and 14 guns. Along the eastern half of the Causeway Heights the remainder of Liprandi's battalions and their artillery were grouped around the captured redoubts.

Three-quarters of an hour had passed after Raglan's order to Lucan to attempt the recovery of the Causeway Heights when his staff caught sight of what seemed to be Russian preparations to remove the *British* guns from the captured redoubts. Raglan assumed, correctly, that the Russians had been so shaken by the charge of the Heavy Brigade that the threat of attack by the Light Brigade would itself be sufficient to clear them from the Causeway Heights. He now sent Lucan a second order, carried by Captain Nolan, asking that the cavalry should advance rapidly and prevent the removal of the cannon. By omitting to prescribe directions, the new order left Lucan to choose his own line of approach to the redoubts. Lucan was standing on the low ground at the foot of the plateau, and so could not see the Russian gun-teams approaching the redoubts. He should have climbed the slope to gain a view of the Russians' dispositions when he received Raglan's last order. To anyone thinking only of the *Russian* guns in the North Valley Raglan's latest order was an impossible one. Lucan told Nolan so, and insisted, rightly enough, that its execution would lead to serious losses. If Lucan had erred by failing to obtain an adequate idea of the state of the battle, Raglan's newest instructions, for their part, were vague, for they mentioned neither the nationality nor the location of the cannon Lucan was to secure. A long-standing antipathy between Lucan and Nolan prevented the brief conversation which would have sufficed to make it clear to Lucan precisely what he was being ordered to do.

ABOVE LEFT Field-Marshal Lord Raglan *by Jan Willem Pieneman; the British Commander-in-Chief's vague orders were in large part responsible for the disaster which befell the Light Brigade.* RIGHT Sir Colin Campbell, *who commanded the battalion of the 93rd Highlanders which took part in the action (photographed by Fenton)*

LEFT *Another view of the Charge of the Light Brigade, by T. Jones Barker (Lord Cardigan is the central figure); the charge overwhelmed the Russian gunners, but was broken against the mass of cavalry beyond*

BELOW LEFT General Canrobert, *the French Commander-in-Chief.* RIGHT Major-General Lord Lucan, *the Commander of the Cavalry Division (composed of the Heavy and Light Brigades), whose failure to appreciate the state of the battle contributed to the Light Brigade's disaster (engravings from F. N. Nolan's* Illustrated History of the War Against Russia)

The cook-house of the 8th Hussars – one of the two Hussar regiments in the Light Brigade

Lord Raglan, Omar Pasha and General Pélissier at the conference table in 1856 (photograph by Fenton) – Lord Raglan's unmilitary dress contrasts with the ceremonial uniforms of his colleagues

'C'est magnifique, mais ce n'est pas la guerre'; Fenton's re-staging of the second most memorable incident at Balaclava, General Bosquet's comment on the Charge of the Light Brigade

Lucan rode over to Cardigan to give him Raglan's order, and silenced his protests by telling him that they had no choice but to obey. The Light Brigade proceeded to form its ranks for the advance down the North Valley. Behind them Lucan prepared to lead the Heavy Brigade in support. During the first minutes of the Light Brigade's march, the Russians in No. 3 Redoubt, like the spectators on the plateau, believed that the Light Brigade would almost at once veer to the right for the slopes of the Causeway Heights. As Raglan had hoped, the four Russian battalions withdrew to the east of the next redoubt.

By now the Light Brigade was advancing through increasingly heavy fire from both the front, and from left and right. Inevitably the pace quickened and the casualties multiplied, but the squadrons closed their ranks with astonishing coolness. Some of the spectators on the Sapounè Heights were in tears. 'Je suis vieux', said an elderly French officer, 'j'ai vu des batailles, mais ceci est trop.' Lucan decided to withhold the Heavy Brigade from the disaster for which he bore so much responsibility. 'They have sacrificed the Light Brigade; they shall not have the Heavy if I can help it.'

The conclusion of the charge of the Light Brigade was no less admirable, hopeless and extraordinary than its journey to the battery. While some of Cardigan's pitifully thin first line rode into the Russian gunners, others drove back a far larger body of enemy cavalry for several minutes until they in their turn were forced to give ground. A number of Cossacks were repulsed from the battery where Cardigan's second line now arrived to overwhelm the artillerymen before assaulting the cavalry beyond.

A returned hero wearing his Crimean medals: Rough Riding Corporal Swash, of the Royal Dragoons (Heavy Brigade)

The few surviving British cavalry were very soon borne back by the mass of horsemen advancing to their front. The squadrons that had flanked the position were already closing on their rear, but with an inexplicable lack of initiative the Russian lancers allowed them to brush past up the valley. The fugitives had yet to traverse the fire of the artillery to their left. On their right, however, the 4th Chasseurs d'Afrique had silenced the guns on the Fedioukine Heights in a brilliant charge that caused the Russian artillerymen and two supporting battalions to retire without waiting to be attacked. The French had suffered fewer than 40 casualties. Cardigan's losses, though severe, were by no means unprecedented in an action of this kind. Of his 673 men, 113 had been killed and 134 wounded.

Numerous writers have undertaken to distribute the blame for the ordeal of the Light Brigade. Sir George Cathcart, the commander of the 1st Division, has received less censure for his contribution to the allies' virtual defeat at Balaclava. If he had started out promptly that morning, if even he had followed Raglan's directions when he did arrive, there would have been no occasion for the destruction of the Light Brigade. Not only had he done nothing to recapture Redoubt No. 3 before the charge, but he actually refused to occupy the post when the cavalry went forward and its garrison withdrew. Liprandi soon ordered his infantry back to the redoubt.

Even so Raglan and Canrobert disposed of sufficient forces to clear the Russians from the Causeway Heights. This, it appears, is what Raglan intended to do. His colleague argued that if the allies proposed to make an early capture of Sevastopol they could not spare troops to occupy the Heights. The demands of the siege had weighed upon the two commanders throughout the battle. Both had been reluctant to send their infantry very far into the plain. They decided to leave Liprandi in possession of the eastward redoubts, and the action was concluded at about 4 pm. by the reoccupation by the Turks of Redoubts Nos. 4, 5 and 6.

It is perhaps only fitting that the battle of Balaclava should be remembered for no greater reason than the charge of the Light Brigade. The losses of the Brigade fell so heavily on Raglan's slender cavalry force that he was obliged to detach two battalions from the siege force for the defence of Balaclava. Such as it was, the advantage of the day might be said to have remained with the Russians, who could point to the occupation of the three eastern redoubts and the capture of seven guns. In fact, Liprandi had gained little. Within six weeks the Russians had evacuated the redoubts on whose account about 600 men on each side had been killed and wounded.

JOHN NAYLOR

1861
First Bull Run

McDowell's attack on Beauregard's Confederates thirty miles from Washington, the first pitched battle of the American Civil War, failed and the raw Federal troops fled in disorder

THE FIRST BATTLE OF BULL RUN was one of the strangest engagements in the history of modern warfare. Fought by two almost completely untrained armies, it ended with one army completely routed and the other so disorganized that it could not exploit its victory effectively. It had little military significance except that it forced the American people to see the hard realities of a war which they had begun in a mood of romantic enthusiasm, and in the long run it probably helped the losers more than it helped the victors.

The American Civil War began on 12 April 1861 with the bombardment of Fort Sumter at Charleston, South Carolina. Since neither the United States nor the Confederate government was prepared for war, the first three months were devoted by each side to the raising and equipping of troops, and there was no fighting except for minor outpost clashes. By July, however, the impatient Northern public was demanding an 'on to Richmond' move, in the belief that a speedy capture of the Confederate capital would end the war, and Lieutenant-General Winfield Scott, the ageing general-in-chief of the Union armies, reluctantly ordered an offensive campaign. The Federal Army of the Potomac, which would conduct the campaign, was entrusted to Brigadier-General Irvin McDowell.

McDowell's objective was a Confederate army of perhaps 25,000 men under Brigadier-General P. G. T. Beauregard, posted thirty miles west of Washington at the railroad junction town of Manassas, behind a mean-

dering stream known as Bull Run. In the lower Shenandoah Valley, some forty-five miles to the north-west of Manassas, there was another Confederate force of 10,000 led by Brigadier-General Joseph E. Johnston. Johnston could quickly bring his troops to Beauregard's aid by railroad, so it was necessary to pin him down while McDowell advanced on Manassas, and this task was assigned to Brigadier-General Robert Patterson, who had 14,000 men on the upper Potomac river in Johnston's immediate vicinity. With approximately 34,000 men of all arms, McDowell left Washington on 16 July to crush Beauregard.

Military security was rudimentary at that time, and the Confederates had ample warning of the Federal plan. Their first task was to unite the forces of Johnston and Beauregard, and to do this it was necessary to deceive General Patterson. This proved fairly simple; Johnston was a gifted professional soldier, and he was aided by a first-rate cavalry commander, Colonel J. E. B. Stuart, while Patterson was an elderly business man who conceived that his chief duty was to stand on the defensive. Skilful manœuvres by Stuart led Patterson to believe that he was about to be attacked, and Johnston was able to move the bulk of his force to Manassas unobserved. Since

RIGHT *Brigadier-General P. G. T. Beauregard, the Commander of the Confederate army at Manassas, whose plan of attack was endorsed by Brigadier-General Johnston, when he took over the command of their combined forces (portrait by Brady)*

he was senior to Beauregard, on his arrival he would take command of the combined Confederate army.

While Johnston was on the move Beauregard was preparing for McDowell's appearance. Beauregard's army lay just behind Bull Run, the left posted by a stone bridge which carried the main road from Washington across the stream, the centre and right drawn out along an eight-mile front to cover the numerous down-stream fords. Beauregard had no intention of fighting a defensive battle. McDowell was concentrating at the hamlet of Centreville, two or three miles east of the stone bridge, and Beauregard planned to execute a huge left wheel, pivoting on his left at the bridge and sending all the rest across the river to strike McDowell in flank.

McDowell, meanwhile, was planning a similar manoeuvre. It took him the better part of four days to assemble his troops at Centreville – his army, composed almost entirely of militia and the rawest of volunteer troops, found a simple cross-country march almost beyond its powers – and a series of reconnaissances and skirmishes showed him that the Confederate position was too strong for a frontal attack. Leaving a reserve at Centreville, he sent a few troops off to demonstrate at the downstream fords, ordered the division of Brigadier-General Daniel Tyler to move up to the stone bridge, open a bombardment and look menacing, and took everybody else up-

His portrait, in his new uniform, made for his sweetheart, and a Confederate soldier is ready for the war

stream, to cross Bull Run at Sudley Springs ford and sweep down on the Confederate left.

Each commander, in other words, wanted to do the same thing – hold with his left and strike with his right. (Reaching Manassas on 20 July, Johnston could do no more than endorse the orders Beauregard had drawn up.) The only question remaining was which would succeed in striking first.

It is necessary to emphasize again that these armies were desperately, pathetically, unprepared for battle. McDowell, Johnston, Beauregard and their chief lieutenants were of course professional soldiers, graduates of the United States Military Academy, but not one of them had ever seen an army containing more than 10,000 men and none of them had ever actually commanded more than a fraction of that number. Staff services were practically non-existent. The private soldiers had had some company and battalion drill, but they had had no experience whatever in acting by brigade or division; hardly any of them had ever been under fire; and their non-commissioned and company officers were in no better case. Simply to move a brigade or a division by road was a slow, cumbersome process. To get it from marching column into battle line was much harder; and, as the event was to prove, it was all but impossible to withdraw a fighting line from combat and put it into marching formation without seeing it fall completely apart.

So Beauregard's plan for a left wheel evaporated, simply because his staff could not get the orders to the proper commanders. McDowell, meanwhile, before dawn on 21 July, got approximately 12,000 men on the road, took them upstream, crossed Bull Run at Sudley Springs, and sent Colonel Ambrose E. Burnside's brigade in on the Confederate left.

The Confederate left, posted on high ground behind the stone bridge, consisted of 1,100 men under Colonel Nathan G. Evans. Evans got a warning, and he swung his men round to face this assault, sending back frantic calls for help, and somewhere about 9 am. the battle was on, Burnside's men volleying at Evans's, with assorted troops on each side trying hard to stumble into position to help.

It took Johnston and Beauregard a little time to realize that their own attack plan had gone wrong, but at last they caught on and began to shift troops from their extreme right to their extreme left. Evans was driven back, and by noon the Confederates had retreated, down across the shallow valley where the road from Washington went off west and south, and the survivors formed a ragged line on the Henry House hill, just south of the highway. McDowell had got two divisions across at Sudley Springs – those of Colonel Samuel P. Heintzelman and Colonel David Hunter – and a hot, formless, and exceedingly noisy fire fight was in progress. McDowell

Orderlies tend to the wounded, while Federal infantry advances on a Confederate position, in the first important action of the American Civil War

The Confederate Black Horse Cavalry charge Federal Zouaves – both sides introduced a number of colourful units into their armies, of which this Confederate cavalry unit mounted on black horses, and the Federal infantry dressed in uniforms based on those, of Oriental style, worn by the French Zouaves, are typical

RIGHT Confederate cavalry over-run Federal Zouave guns and attack Federal infantry, while other Federal infantry units flee over the Stone Bridge – with raw, untrained troops General McDowell found that an orderly withdrawal to regroup and prepare a new attack was impossible; the unmanageable retreat of the Federal army did not stop till it reached Washington

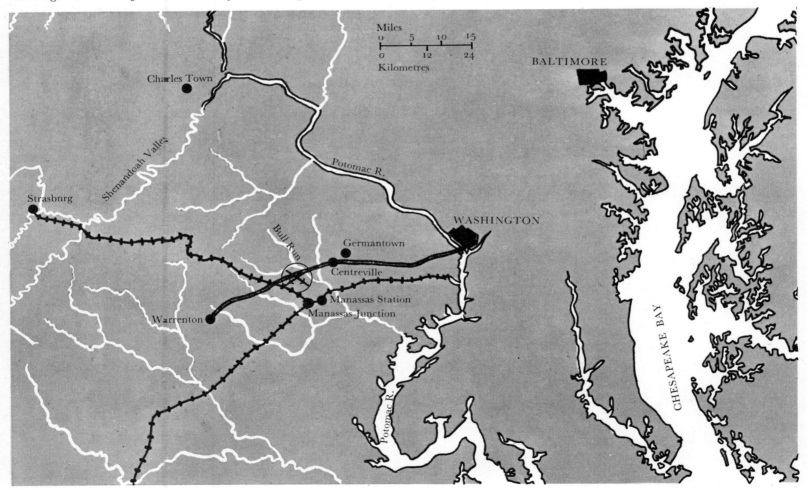

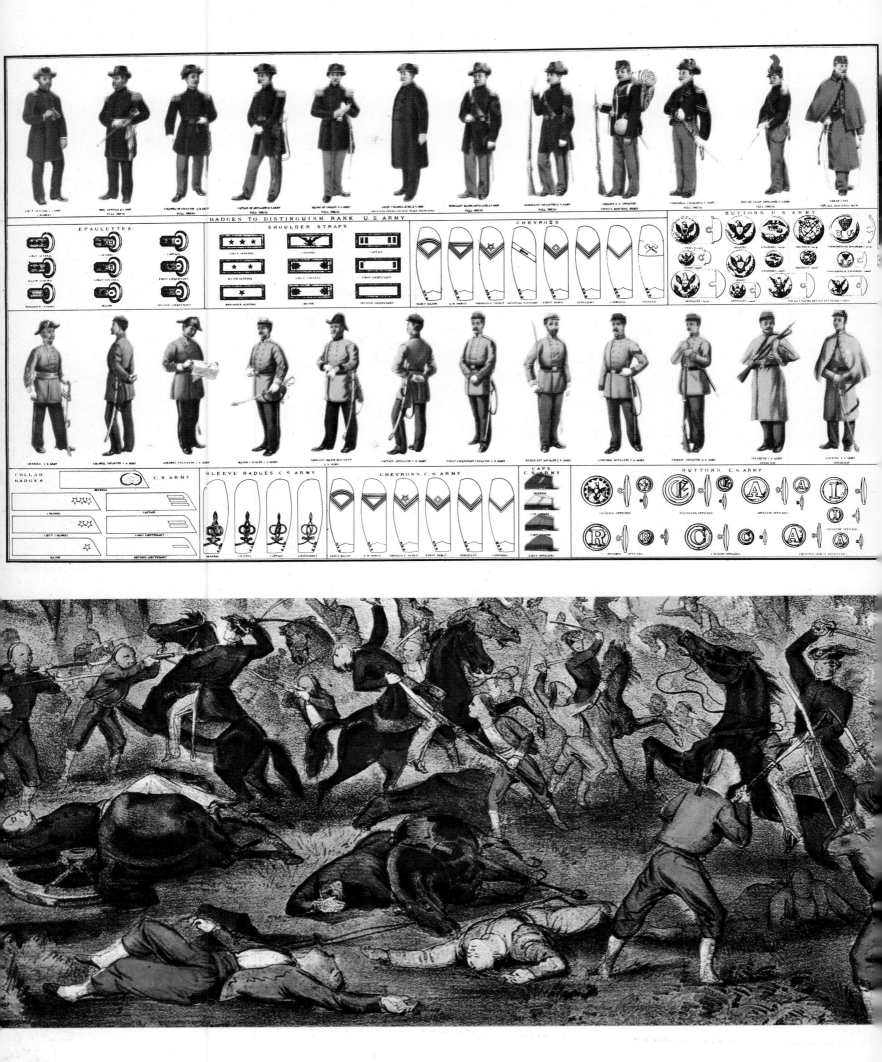

sent forward two regular army batteries of artillery, six three-inch guns in each battery, led by Captains Charles Griffin and J. B. Ricketts, and they plastered the Henry House hill with deadly accuracy while the cumbersome Federal battle line spread itself out for a new assault across the valley.

Johnston was getting reinforcements to the scene; among them, a Virginia brigade under a tough, eccentric and wholly dedicated Scots Presbyterian named Thomas J. Jackson. Brigadier-General Jackson put his brigade in line and kept it there. A despairing Confederate brigadier, Bernard Bee, seeing his own line dissolving, waved his sword toward Jackson's line and told his men to rally there – Jackson was 'standing like a stone wall'. Bee was killed shortly thereafter, but his words took root: from that moment on, Jackson was Stonewall Jackson, a name men remembered.

Federal pressure on the hill was intense, and the Confederates wavered. A red-haired brigade commander in Tyler's division, Colonel William T. Sherman, got his men across the river a little above the stone bridge and joined in the assault. McDowell sent Griffin and Ricketts and their guns across the valley and posted them on the Henry House hill to add weight to the attack, and a complete Union victory seemed to be in the making.

Then the climate began to change. The Federal batteries were too exposed; rifle fire cut down the gunners; and a sudden Confederate counter-attack swept over them and silenced them. Furthermore, the railroad from the Shenandoah Valley came in just behind the Confederate left, and fresh troops that were coming in got off the trains at the precise spot where they could go into action without delay. One of Johnston's brigades led by Brigadier-General Edmund Kirby Smith came on the scene, along with a brigade from Beauregard's right under Colonel Jubal Early, and the Union attack came under heavy flanking fire and slowed to a halt in confusion. A Federal regiment crossing the main highway to support the assault was struck and hopelessly routed by a sharp charge of Confederate cavalry – and suddenly everybody realized that the steam had gone out of the Federal attack and that the Confederates had the advantage.

It was mid-afternoon by now, a hot July day in which thousands of men on each side had stood up to a good deal more hard fighting than anyone had a right to expect; and McDowell saw that he must pull his men back, regroup, and prepare for a new offensive. His flanking attack had not exactly failed but it had not quite succeeded, either, and it was time to reorganize and take stock.

At this point the inherent weakness of an untrained army became the decisive element in the battle.

These Union soldiers could do almost anything except make an orderly withdrawal under heavy fire. When they tried it they came to pieces; and what was meant to be a

LEFT ABOVE *A selection of Federal and Confederate uniforms – cavalry, infantry, artillery, engineers – with details of the distinguishing features between the different ranks and units; this shows quite plainly that neither were the Federals dressed exclusively in blue, nor the Confederates in grey*

LEFT BELOW *Apparently the conclusion of the action, of which the commencement is shown in an earlier illustration – the Federal Zouaves charging and defeating the Confederate Black Horse Cavalry*

Shells burst over advancing Federal infantry – the baptism of fire for 70,000 men, hardly any of whom, officers and private soldiers alike, had ever been in action before

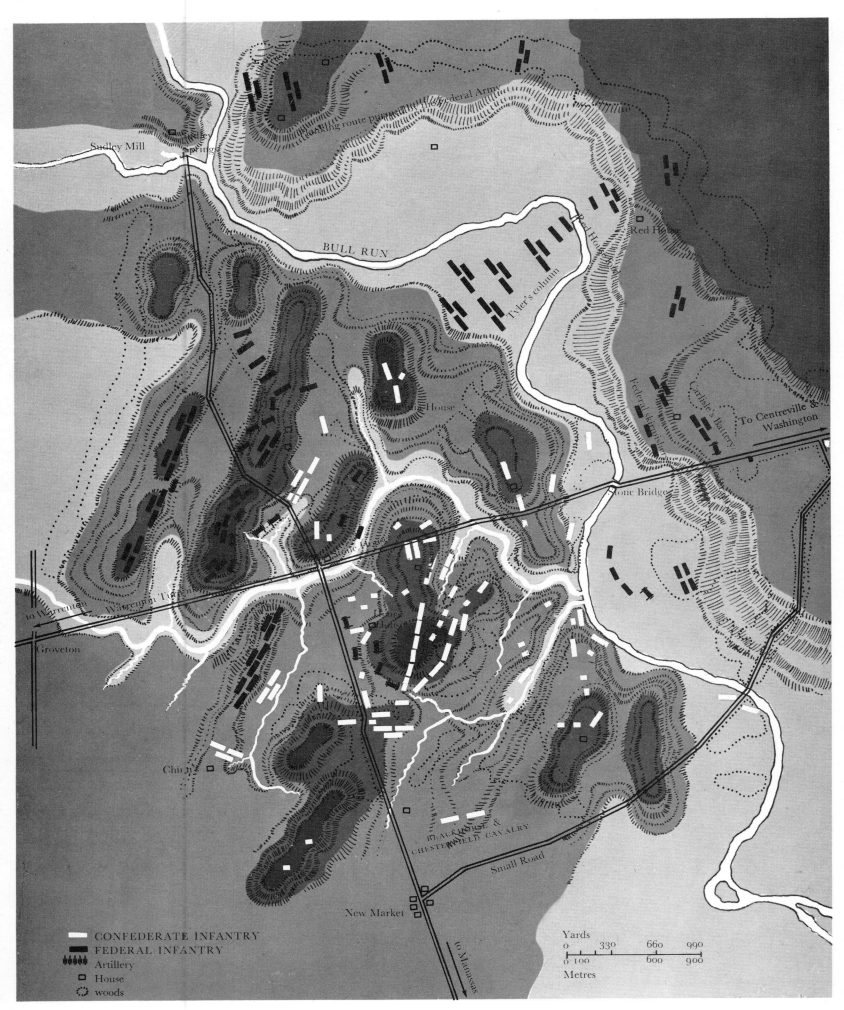

CONFEDERATE INFANTRY
FEDERAL INFANTRY
Artillery
House
woods

Yards
0   330   660   990
0   100   600   900
Metres

simple retirement to a safer position turned into an unmanageable retreat. Regimental formations had been lost. Most of these amateur soldiers would rally if their own officers, men whom they knew by name and sight, rallied them; when squads and companies became intermingled, nobody could take charge of anything, and the Federal retirement from the Henry House hill became nothing better than flight. McDowell had about 12,000 men in this assault, and in a few minutes these 12,000 turned into a mob, each member heading on his own for the rear and hoping to get to a place where he could find his comrades and his officers and get back into some sort of order.

During the next hour the Federals fled from the scene of action – not running, but going to the rear in a way no officers could stop. They went back across Bull Run, found their way to the Washington road, and started back for Centreville; if they were not exactly in a panic they had ceased to be part of an army and had become tired, confused, and distraught young men who just wanted to reach some place where their enemies would not be able to shoot at them.

Then came the strangest element of the whole battle. 21 July was a Sunday; Manassas was not far from Washington; and many hundreds of Washington civilians had taken carriages and picnic lunches and come down, in their innocence, to have the pleasure of watching a battle. They had spread themselves out on the long slopes east of Bull Run, and when the army began to retreat it occurred to all of these civilians that it was time to head for home. So they got their carriages into the road the army was trying to use and set out for Washington at a collective gallop – and what with this multitude of carriages crowding into a road full of artillery, ambulances, army wagons and disconnected foot-soldiers, the highway that led from the stone bridge back to Centreville abruptly became the scene of the father and mother of all traffic jams. A few stray Confederate shells burst here and there, to lend wings to weary feet, a bridge over a little brook collapsed, and the army's withdrawal became a complete rout.

McDowell thought he could make a stand at Centreville. He had 5,000 men in reserve there, a cool battalion of regulars under Major George Sykes was covering the retreat, and the thing might have been done. But the flight of the broken units of infantry was self-accelerating. Nobody would stop at Centreville. Panic had taken charge. The average soldier had no thought for anything but getting back to Washington, and he kept on going, throwing away his weapons and anything that might slow his progress. The greater part of the Union army had simply dissolved, and no power on earth could bring it together again until it had got to the end of the line. Late that night McDowell confessed, in a telegram to Washington, that there was nothing for it but to get back to the capital and reorganize, and the retreat went on all the way to the Potomac.

The Confederate army, which had just won a shattering victory, was little better off. To make an orderly pursuit was as hard as to make an orderly retreat. Stonewall Jackson might announce that with 5,000 fresh troops he could go into Washington and drive the Federal government away; there were not 5,000 fresh troops at hand, and although President Jefferson Davis of the

LEFT *The battlefield of First Manassas, or Bull Run, showing the Confederate positions on high ground west of Bull Run, and the Federal right-flanking manœuvre*

BELOW LEFT *Brigadier-General Irvin McDowell, the Commander of the Federal Army of the Potomac, which was entrusted with the task of attacking Beauregard's army at Manassas.* CENTRE *Brigadier-General Thomas Jackson, who earned his sobriquet 'Stonewall' from his own steadfast conduct at this battle, and from that of his Virginia brigade.* RIGHT *Brigadier-General Joseph E. Johnston, the Commander of the Confederate force in the lower Shenandoah Valley, which combined with Beauregard's army at Manassas to repel the Federal offensive*

A study by Mathew B. Brady of an off-duty moment in a Federal camp – firewood has to be chopped, but there is time for a pipe and a game of cards, which a drummer boy is watching (Brady, like Roger Fenton in the Crimea, was one of the early war photographers)

Confederacy reached the scene and went into conference with Generals Johnston and Beauregard, all of them had at last to admit that the army was too disorganized to follow up its advantage. During the next few days it did manage to send some units forward so far that they could see, from a distance, the dome of the Federal capitol building, north of the Potomac; but to exploit the victory on the evening when triumph was won was out of the question. These men were no better trained or organized than the Federals they had fought. They wandered about their camp, hallooing and rejoicing, and they believed that the war had been won, but they could do no more than that.

What they had done was good enough, it seemed. They had whipped the Yankee invader, capturing 28 guns, 37 caissons and an enormous quantity of small arms,

wagons, rations and odds and ends of military equipment, and they had demonstrated the high qualities of Southern valour. They would rest on that. They could do nothing else.

The figures speak for themselves. McDowell had been able to get perhaps 14,000 men into action, and he had lost between 450 and 500 men killed, more than 1,100 wounded, and upwards of 1,300 in captured or missing. The Confederates had had somewhat lesser losses: approximately 385 killed, 1,500 or 1,600 wounded, and a dozen or so captured or missing. They had the battlefield, the booty and the prestige, and perhaps these would be enough.

Bull Run was followed by months of comparative inactivity. The Confederates established themselves firmly in Northern Virginia, and not until the following spring

did the Unionists make a real attempt to drive them away. Major-General George B. McClellan was called in to supersede the unfortunate McDowell – the man had really done as well as anyone could expect, considering the hopeless condition of the army he had to fight with – and the Federal government buckled down to the task of preparing a properly trained army that could survive the shock of battle. And in the long run, the catastrophe at Bull Run helped the North far more than it helped the South.

To the South it gave over-confidence – the feeling that the war was just about won and that the despised Yankees just could not fight very well anyway. To the North it called for a re-dedication, a shedding of illusions, an end to the old habit of thinking of war in terms of a romantic militia muster. It stimulated the people of the North to

accept the reality of war. They would wait, now, until they had mustered, armed and prepared their strength. From now on they would make war without benefit of romantic illusions. They would stop believing that the enemy would disappear once the United States flag was brought forward.

Meanwhile, the untaught soldier on both sides deserves some sort of commendation. He stood a good deal of hammering before the break came. Under the most inexpert leadership and without preparation worthy of the name, he had stood up to seven hours of hard fighting. Bull Run was the ominous sign that once these armies were properly led and trained they would be prodigious fighting machines.

BRUCE CATTON

1863
Gettysburg

During the three days of the greatest battle in the American Civil War all Lee's attacks, including Pickett's famous charge, were repulsed, and the Confederates had to retire

FOLLOWING THE FEDERAL DEFEAT at Chancellorsville (1–3 May 1863), the Army of Northern Virginia and the Army of the Potomac resumed their positions on opposite sides of the Rappahannock. The Confederate Government now determined to carry the war on to Northern soil by an invasion of Maryland and Pennsylvania. Success in this venture might bring European recognition of the Confederate States, replenish the commissariat, ease Federal pressure on the Southern Armies in Tennessee and at Vicksburg, and strengthen the growing peace-party in the North.

The morale of the Army of Northern Virginia was at its highest. General Robert E. Lee, its commander, was confident that his superb infantry could win any field. In preparation for the campaign, Lee reorganized his Army into three corps (commanded by Longstreet, Ewell, and A. P. Hill) each of three divisions with an average strength of 8,500 men per division. The Army of the Potomac, its morale low after still another reverse, consisted of nineteen infantry divisions organized in seven corps; the strength of the Federal corps and divisions was about half that of the equivalent Southern formations.

Lee was apprehensive lest Hooker might essay another advance over the Rappahannock, but a Federal attack on 9 June was correctly interpreted as only a reconnais-

sance in force and Lee began his march north through the Shenandoah and Cumberland Valleys. Hooker learned of Lee's move on 10 June and asked President Lincoln for permission to march on Richmond, but the latter ordered Hooker to fall back across the Potomac and cover Washington. By 25 June Lee's army was north of the Potomac, Ewell, in the lead, advancing toward Harrisburg, while the other two corps concentrated near Chambersburg. Meanwhile, Hooker had conformed to the Confederate advance and on the 25th and 26th crossed the Potomac near Leesburg; thence three corps fanned out to the north and west while the remainder assembled at Frederick. Lee did not learn until the night of 28 June that Hooker had kept pace on his eastern flank, for J. E. B. Stuart's cavalry, 'the eyes of Lee', had left the main body, crossed the Potomac twenty miles from Washington and set off on a dash clear around the Union Army. Hooker, who no longer had the confidence of President Lincoln, was relieved on 28 June by Major-General George Meade.

The two armies were moving to combat but neither commander was anxious to attack. Lee decided to recall Ewell, who had reached Carlisle, concentrate his forces between Cashtown and Gettysburg so as to threaten Washington, Baltimore, and Philadelphia, and thus force Meade to attack. Meade, moving on the axis Frederick–Harrisburg, selected a defensive position on Pipe Creek, some fifteen miles south-east of Gettysburg, reasoning that Lee would have to come to him.

LEFT *Major-General George Meade, who replaced General Hooker in the command of the Federal Army of the Potomac a few days only before the battle of Gettysburg (portrait by Brady)*

LEFT *General Longstreet, cne of Lee's corps commanders, whose recalcitrant behaviour at Gettysburg, which remains unexplained, went far to frustrating the Confederate design.* CENTRE *General Pickett, one of Longstreet's divisional commanders, who led the famous charge which marked the climax of the battle.* RIGHT *General Sickles, the Commander of III Corps, which formed the Federal left and was badly mauled on the second day of the battle – Sickles himself lost a leg (portrait by Brady)*

On 30 June the twc armies accelerated the march in heat and dust toward the collision at Gettysburg. Lee's main force moved eastward along the Chambersburg turnpike while Ewell hurried south under orders to rendezvous at Gettysburg or Cashtown. To the south-east the Federal left wing, under Reynolds, was advancing behind the screen provided by Buford's cavalry. Late in the day a brigade from Hill's corps, en route to seize a stock of shoes, encountered Federal cavalry west of Gettysburg and fell back to Cashtown. Buford promptly posted troops west and north of Gettysburg and reported to Reynolds that Lee was moving toward the road nexus there. Meade still expected to make his stand at Pipe Creek, while Lee, bereft of Stuart's help and out of touch with the remaining cavalry accompanying Ewell, continued blindly along the Chambersburg turnpike.

At daylight, 1 July, Hill sent Heth's division toward Gettysburg under orders to reconnoitre but avoid a general engagement. Euford had formed his dismounted troopers astride the Chambersburg road along a ridge east of Willoughby Run, with a battery of horse artillery in his centre, and for an hour or so contained the Confederate skirmishers. Shortly after 9 am. two brigades from I Corps reached the Union-held ridge, extending Buford's line. The Confederates soon attacked in force with two of Heth's brigades astride the turnpike and two in support, only to be driven back across Willoughby Run. Now both lines groped in the woods for an open enemy flank. Meanwhile, troops in blue and grey were moving on Gettysburg as if drawn by a magnet. The arrival on the Union right of Rodes's division from Ewell's Corps, and the appearance of Pender's division to reinforce Heth, out-weighed the two divisions of I Corps

which reached the Union line west of Gettysburg. I Corps had been driven back to Seminary Ridge just west of the town when, in early afternoon, two divisions of Howard's XI Corps came up to strengthen the Union right. These reinforcements had barely reached the field when they were forced to wheel northward and face Ewell's corps. Confederate artillery, firing from high ground on the thinly defended angle in the Union line, opened a path for their infantry to flank I Corps while Ewell turned Howard's line from the east. XI Corps retreated in disorder through Gettysburg but re-formed on its reserve division which had deployed on Cemetery Hill just south of the town. I Corps fell back fighting from Seminary Ridge and joined the troops on Cemetery Hill. By 4 pm. Gettysburg and five thousand Federal troops were in Lee's hands. This had been a true meeting engagement. Lee's order for a general attack came only when Early's division of Ewell's Corps debouched from the north. Meade, several miles from Gettysburg, had left Reynolds in charge of the battle and, when the latter was killed, sent Hancock, II Corps Commander, to make the decision as to whether the Army of the Potomac should stand and fight. Hancock deemed the ground on which the Union troops had re-formed to be suitable for defence, and with III and XII Corps already in march, the die was cast. In the late afternoon, however, the odds still were with the South. Lee had some 30,000 infantry and 90 guns in position to press the attack against two-thirds this number of Union troops and cannon, so he ordered Ewell to attack Cemetery Hill 'if possible'. Ewell's failure to resume the battle is one of the major enigmas of Gettysburg. His troops were tired and Ewell used this as an excuse to await the arrival of his third

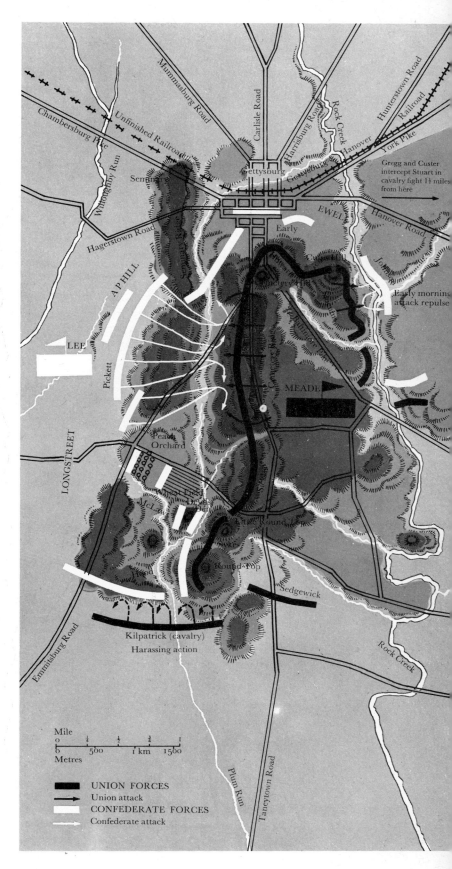

General Robert E. Lee, the Commander of the Army of Northern Virginia, whom the Federals had sought at the beginning of the war for high command in their own army

RIGHT *Lee's main attack on the third and last day of the battle of Gettysburg, and its climax, was Pickett's charge against the Federal centre on Cemetery Ridge*

ABOVE LEFT *Three Federal soldiers and a Negro servant – not a slave, in the North, and Lincoln's Emancipation Proclamation of the previous year would ensure, after the ultimate Federal victory, that there were no more slaves in the South either*

ABOVE RIGHT *The harvest of death: some of those who gave their lives (there were 43,000 casualties) that the nation which, in Lincoln's words, was 'conceived in Liberty, and dedicated to the proposition that all men are created equal' might live*

ABOVE *Two years of war had transformed the raw recruits who had fought at Bull Run into determined veterans, to whom fierce, hand-to-hand fighting, such as this, with bayonet and clubbed musket, was a familiar exercise.*

BELOW *A war artist's sketch, by A. R. Waud, of the Federal position near the centre, with, in the distance, Cemetery Hill (left) and Gettysburg (right), which Lee had captured on the first day of the battle*

A sketch by another war artist, Edwin Forbes, of the Confederate attack on Cemetery Hill on the evening of 2 July, the second day of the battle; General Ewell had been ordered to attack the Federal right 'if possible' on 1 July, and his failure to do so is another of the enigmas of this battle

RIGHT A section from Paul Philippoteaux's panorama painting of the climax of the battle, which shows Pickett's left flank, North Carolina regiments (coming towards the foreground), hurling itself against the Federal 3rd Division

OVERLEAF The Federal centre is pierced, as General Armistead and 150 Virginians (in brown) hurdle barricades and rifle pits, and sweep into the Federal rear; (another portion of Philippoteaux's painting)

division, but when Johnson arrived, an hour before sunset, Ewell gave no attack order.

The ground on which the Federal line of defence would form had the shape of a fishhook. Cemetery Hill marked the bend; Cemetery Ridge, extending to the south, was the shank; Little Round Top, a butt of some 650 feet elevation, formed the eye; the barb was Culps Hill. On the early morning of 2 July Federal troops held only Cemetery and Culps Hills.

Ewell's Corps lay south of Gettysburg with its left flank across Rock Creek while Hill's Corps occupied the northern end of Seminary Ridge. Longstreet's Corps was not yet on the field – two of his divisions (McLaws' and Hood's) had bivouacked only some four miles away, but Pickett's division still was guarding the trains at Chambersburg.

Lee wished to attack the Cemetery Hill position but Ewell was luke-warm to such a venture. Lee decided, therefore, to send Longstreet round to the right in an attack north-east along the Emmitsburg Road designed partially to envelop the Union left and roll up the entire line. Apparently, Lee expected that Longstreet would make this attack early on the 2nd, but Longstreet later would

say that no such order was given. Longstreet's recalcitrant behaviour at Gettysburg has no certain explanation. When Lee disregarded his suggestion that contact should be broken and Meade be turned out of the Gettysburg position by a move on Washington, Longstreet appears to have lapsed into a mood of sullen insubordination, in effect washing his hands of all responsibility. Longstreet tarried through the morning of the 2nd waiting for Law's brigade to flesh out the two of his divisions which had come into position behind Seminary Ridge.

As the day advanced blue-clad troops deployed southward along Cemetery Ridge. By noon, Meade had XII, II, and III Corps on line with I and XI, while V and VI were nearing the field. The Federal left was formed by Sickles' III Corps which he had advanced without orders a half-mile west of the main ridge position. Here he held a dangerous salient: the apex at the Peach Orchard, the right wing fronting on the Emmitsburg Road, the left running obliquely south-east to Devil's Den, opposite Little Round Top.

After marching and counter-marching, Longstreet began his attack about 4 pm., the brigades of Hood's division advancing in successive order of battle from the

National Intelligencer.

Vol. LXIV WASHINGTON MONDAY, JULY 6, 1863. No. 9,504

EXTRA.

GLORIOUS NEWS.

LEE DEFEATED.

GEN. HILL AND GEN. LONGSTREET WOUNDED AND PRISONERS.

THE REBELS RETREATING.

THEIR PONTOON BRIDGES DESTROYED

The holyday taken by our employés on Saturday last prevented the preparation of a regular paper for this morning's issue; but in order to place our readers in possession of all the important information received since Friday night of the progress and successful termination of the great battle which commenced on Wednesday last, near Gettysburg, we issue this extra sheet for city distribution.

The news is such as will cheer the heart of every true patriot. The third day's battle, it will be seen, was decisive as against Gen. Lee, who is now, according to official reports, in full retreat, pursued by our gallant and victorious army. All the battles were severe and well contested—that of Friday was terrific, as well from the heavy forces and large amount of artillery brought into close action as from the sanguinary results of the conflict. We have no time for comment, and can now only congratulate the country and the brave Army of the Potomac upon the fortunate issue of this great struggle with the veteran army of the Confederates, under its favorite and most successful leader.

We insert below the latest official and other despatches received by telegraph since our last publication; and in the succeeding columns we give

This despatch merely states that the enemy had withdrawn from his positions occupied for attack on Friday. The information in the possession of Gen. Meade at the time he wrote did not develop the character of the enemy's movement, whether it was a retreat or a manœuvre for other purposes.

RETREAT OF THE ENEMY.

The two following despatches from Gen. Meade, received at the Headquarters of the Army since the above were prepared for the press, announce the abandonment of Gettysburg by the enemy:

Headquarters Army of the Potomac,
July 4—Noo.

To Major Gen. Halleck, General-in-Chief:

The position of affairs is not materially changed since my last despatch, at seven A. M. We now hold Gettysburg. The enemy has abandoned Gettysburg, leaving large numbers of his killed and wounded on the field. I shall probably be able to give you a return of our captures and losses before night, and a return of the enemy's killed and wounded in our hands.

Geo. G. Meade, Major General.

Headquarters Army of the Potomac,
July 4—10 o'clock P. M.

H. W. Halleck, General-in-Chief:

No change of affairs since despatch of twelve noon.

Geo. G. Meade, Major General.

Reliable information received here yesterday states that Gen Lee's headquarters were at Cashtown on Saturday afternoon, and that the rebels were fortifying at Newman's Cut, in the South Mountains, apparently to cover a retreat.

THE LATEST OFFICIAL DESPATCH.

THE VICTORY COMPLETE

The following official despatch from Gen. Meade, received this morning, shows that his victory over the Confederate army is complete:

Headquarters Army of the Potomac,
July 5—8.20 A. M.

Major General Halleck:

The enemy retired under cover of the night and heavy rain in the direction of Fairfield and Cashtown. My cav-

RETREAT OF THE ENEMY.

Harrisburg, July 3—All the rebel infantry and detachments of cavalry, under Jennings, Imboden, and Fitzhugh Lee, have disappeared from the front, and travel has been resumed between this city and Carlisle.

A despatch from London this morning states that yesterday the rebels left Chambersburg, taking the road in the direction of Gettysburg. Before leaving, they burned the depot and workshops belonging to the railroad. London is fourteen miles west of Chambersburg. The enemy also evacuated Shippensburg yesterday, moving in the same direction.

Harrisburg, July 4—Midnight.—From the latest intelligence received here it is fully believed that Lee has been completely defeated. There has been no fighting today, and the rebel army is endeavoring to retreat through South Mountain Pass and Boonsboro. It is certain that Lee's retreat is already seriously interfered with, and his escape from our army will be a matter of great difficulty. A large force is concentrated here, and ready for offensive operation at any moment. Nearly the full quota of Pennsylvania has been already raised.

Baltimore, July 5—The American has just put upon its bulletin board the important announcement that the rebel army is in retreat, which commenced on Friday night. Many thousands of prisoners and a large number of cannon have been captured.

FRESH IN THE POTOMAC.

Bloody Run, July 3.—A messenger has just reached London from Mercersburg. He left there at nine o'clock this morning. He reports that the Potomac is impassable at the best fords save by pontoons. A portion of Imboden's men retired again this morning from Mercersburg and Cove Gap, going towards Hagerstown. They are reported as being much alarmed at this unexpected rise in the Potomac.

Philadelphia, July 5.—Rain is falling here copiously. There was a severe storm near Carlisle yesterday. It is hoped that the Potomac has been raised by this time, rendering the fords useless.

[A heavy rain also fell in Washington and vicinity last night and this morning.]

REJOICING AT PHILADELPHIA.

Philadelphia, July 5.—The Fourth passed without political demonstrations, both parties having given up their intended assemblages on account of the invasion of the State. The streets were rendered lively by the movement

THE THREE DAYS' BATTLES.

UNOFFICIAL DETAILS.

THE ENEMY DEFEATED, AND HIS DEAD AND WOUNDED LEFT ON THE FIELD.

ABOUT FIVE THOUSAND PRISONERS TAKEN.

Several of the correspondents of the New York press with the Army of the Potomac have furnished accounts, more or less at large, of the engagements on Wednesday and Thursday last. Though all of them are highly interesting, we select the following account from the pen of Mr. G. W. Hosmer as being the fullest and most particular in its statements. His letters are dated "In the Field," near Gettysburg, on the nights of the 1st and 2d instant.

THE BATTLE OF WEDNESDAY.

Gen. Buford's cavalry had previously driven the rebels to the west of Gettysburg, beyond the seminary, and between nine and ten o'clock A. M. the rebels gave his pickets a pretty sharp brush and drove them in.

Gen. Reynolds, with the First Corps, was on the road from Emmettsburg to Gettysburg, *en route* to the latter place, which the road approaches through the scene of the conflict.

BEGINNING OF THE FIGHT.

General Reynolds at once threw forward the first division, under Gen. Wadsworth, which began to drive the enemy from the start. Very soon afterwards the second division of the same corps went on the right of the first division, the third division on the left of the first, and the whole line began to advance.

Nearly west of the town, just in the outskirts, near the seminary, is a large brick edifice. Southward from this runs a piece of woods, and the seminary stands on a ridge which slopes to the west into a little open valley of ploughed fields and meadows, rich with grass and grain. Beyond the valley is a ridge of higher land, thickly wooded. The valley runs in a southwesterly direction, and at its lower extremity is a large farmhouse, near which the Eighth Illinois Cavalry was drawn up in the field, and formed our extreme left. Several farmhouses dotted this same rich little valley.

Across this valley Gen. Reynolds' line advanced some-

ANOTHER ONSET—OUR FORCES FALL BACK.

There is a mysterious fatality connected with the third time; and so, after a lull and period of comparative quiet of twenty minutes, onward for a third time came the rebels, quite as orderly as before, their line of skirmishers firing as they came on. In so great force was this line that it completely overlapped the line of the First Corps on both flanks. Two brigades on the right were quite out of ammunition, and the order was given to retreat on the town; and our boys accordingly retreated in good order, while the rebels rushed forward with yells to our position.

On came the enemy's fourth line, further to the right of the third, in good order, skirmishers ahead, until the position of the seminary was reached, when they came forward with a rush, and occupied a hill we had not deemed it worth while to hold after the other was taken. On also came another line in support behind this, and our cavalry on the extreme left began to retire.

THE FIELD AFTER THE BATTLE.

At this moment the field presented a true war picture. Across the fields to the right came the rebel line, with colors which fluttered in the pleasant breeze; in the centre were two farmhouses, outhouses, and barns in flames, and on the left the column of cavalry in retreat, while beyond all the rays of the sun beat down through the showery clouds and gilded every object with a peculiarly golden light, and over the heavens to the eastward stretched a magnificent rainbow.

The new position of the Third Corps was at a line of stone wall southwest of the town, along the slope of a hill on which is a cemetery. When the First Corps retired to the town the left of the Eleventh was uncovered, and a heavy advance completely on its right flank at the same time compelled it to retire. It affords me pleasure to say that, this corps is reported to have fought well and lost many men. As I was on our extreme left I did not see the fight of the Eleventh Corps.

After our retirement on the town the rebel advance was not pressed further. And so ended a battle that was brought on in the most rash manner, yet which was well fought against a largely superior force, and gotten out of at last much better than we could have expected.

The rebel force fought by us was the corps of Gen. Ewell and that of A. P. Hill. South of the town is a high hill, on which is a cemetery, and this became the headquarters. Its slope to the west was held by the First Corps, and a continuation of hills from it toward the east was held by the Eleventh, while the Twelfth Corps was placed so as to hold both flanks, the first division, under Gen. Williams, being on the extreme right, and the second division, under Gen. Geary, on the extreme left. The

POSITIONS OF OUR FORCES.

Gen. Steinwehr occupied Cemetery Hill, which commands the town, while the fight raged on Wednesday, and at the close of that day's battle the remnants of the First and Eleventh Corps were posted there and a little down the line to the right and left, and there they remained on Thursday at the commencement of the second battle. On the open country to our left lay the Second and Third Corps, and the Fifth was so massed as to fill up the third line. The Sixth was put near to the Fifth when it came up.

On Cemetery Hill we had several batteries, and, indeed, every point that could possibly command a fire was crowned with a battery; for, in addition to the guns regularly attached to the corps, we had up the reserve artillery. Throughout the wide extent of the fields enclosed within our lines ambulances and ammunition trains were packed every where, and it proved that they were all under fire, on Thursday, for the field of fire of the rebel guns opposite our right met that of the rebel guns opposite our left in this enclosed space, and shells exploded every where, and round shot hurtled through the air in every direction.

THE BATTLE OF THURSDAY.

After what had taken place on Wednesday, and with the knowledge of the force that had come up, there was good reason to believe, and all in camp did believe, that Thursday would be ushered in with the noise of battle. Day broke in quiet, however, and breakfast was taken at ease. Now and then there were little disputes between the enemy's pickets and ours in the streets of the town, for we held part and they part, and sometimes a gun in one of our batteries would send an experimental shell towards the enemy's lines. The enemy through all this kept marvellously shy with his artillery, and did not fire a shot, which it was thought indicated that heavy ammunition was scarce in the rebel camp.

During all the earlier part of the day very little was known in respect to the enemy's movements, but it was thought to be clearly made out that he was massing his forces on our extreme right. In view of this additional preparations were made to meet whatever might come in that direction. But there were some who thought that the movements of the enemy towards our right were made only for show and to distract attention from more important points; for such was the nature of the country that, had the enemy really wished to mass his forces there, he could have done it without making a man visible.

AN ARTILLERY FIGHT.

All day more or less picket firing had taken place on our left, and it became pretty sharp between two and three P. M. Some movements were in progress behind this fire, and to develop these Gen. Sickles was ordered to

right but the whole driving toward Little Round Top and Devil's Den in a series of frontal assaults. An hour or so later Law put in his formations, again timing the attack from right to left, first engaging Ward's brigade on Sickles' left wing, then grappling Graham's brigade in a bitter fight at the Peach Orchard. Next, Hood's Corps took a hand. Anderson's division enveloped Sickles' right on the Emmitsburg Road and crushed it, then Wright's brigade attacked in single line straight through the Federal guns on to Cemetery Ridge – but there was no support at hand and the attackers were driven out of the main Union position.

At Devil's Den and the Peach Orchard the Confederate attack had won and held ground. Sickles' Corps, terribly punished by 54 Confederate guns enfilading the angle – Sickles with his leg blown nearly off – fell back through Sykes's V Corps which Meade had hurried up from reserve. None the less, the Union anchor position at Little Round Top was denied Lee. Early in the fight General Warren, Meade's Chief Engineer Officer, observed that only a few Union signallers were on this hill. He seized Vincent's brigade, en route to help Sickles, plus Hazlett's battery of 10-pounders, and sent this detachment up the rugged ascent while Hood's Texans clawed their way along the west face of Little Round Top. The blue-coats held, more Federal troops swarmed on to the saddle south of the hill, and this fight was won.

Longstreet's attack was spent when Ewell finally advanced five brigades against Cemetery Hill and Culps Hill. Most of his guns were silenced in the preparatory artillery duel and although Early's division pressed the attack to within a hundred yards of the Federal batteries on Cemetery Hill the Union right held firm.

The results of the second day's battle gave Lee hope of victory. The successes on the right had brought the Confederate artillery into position for a renewal of the attack by Longstreet. Lee, therefore, planned that Longstreet's Corps, led by Pickett's fresh division, would attack in the morning and that simultaneously Ewell would assail the Federal right. But once again, Longstreet voiced objections. The result was a compromise in which the planned attack would be shifted to strike the right centre of the Union line with Heth's division and two brigades of Pender's division from Hill's Corps joining Pickett as replacements for the divisions of Hood and McLaws.

The battle flared again on 3 July with a dawn assault against Culps Hill delivered by Johnson's division. Attack and counter-attack continued until about 11 am. when Slocum's XII Corps troops drove Johnson from the battle ground.

Meanwhile Longstreet, charged with the main effort, delayed as he had on the 2nd, but in part this may be ascribed to the realignment of Hill's troops. The assault column now forming consisted of ten brigades deployed on a mile-wide front. Lee's design was to breach the Cemetery Ridge position at a point close to the Emmitsburg Road where the ridge dipped slightly; a clump of chestnut-oaks marked the assault objective. Alexander, commanding Longstreet's artillery, would provide support and for this purpose he deployed seventy-five guns along the Emmitsburg Road north of the Peach Orchard. Several hundred yards to the left and to the rear another

LEFT ABOVE *Cushing's Artillery, backing up the Federal centre, is almost totally destroyed, and the remnants are being pulled to safety; Pickett's men began their attack from Seminary Ridge in the distance, and streamed towards the foreground across open fields and past farm buildings on the Emmitsburg Road (another portion of Phillippoteaux's painting)*

LEFT BELOW *First news of the Confederate defeat at Gettysburg which, permanently crippling Lee's army, marked the zenith of all Confederate hopes*

The battlefield of Gettysburg: Little Round Top (left foreground) marks the limit of the Federal left, where a fierce battle was fought on 2 July; the battle on 3 July opened with a dawn assault on Culps Hill (right centre), on the Federal right

A Federal regimental fife and drum corps photographed by Brady; though their music was recognized as a useful aid to keeping up morale, when they reached the front the musicians served as litter bearers and helped evacuate the wounded

A corner of the battlefield after the battle – Trostle Farm House, the headquarters of General Sickles, the Commander of the Federal III Corps; well in front of the Federal lines, it was (as this photograph shows) the scene of a bloody struggle

Brady's photograph of a breech-loading 12-pounder gun; it is an English Whitworth

The fair copy of one of the most famous speeches ever made, Lincoln's Gettysburg Address, delivered at the dedication of the battlefield as a cemetery four months after the battle

sixty-three guns were grouped on Seminary Ridge.

At 1 pm. two guns signalled the commencement of Alexander's artillery preparation. The Confederate batteries fired as rapidly as guns could be swabbed and loaded, but they made poor practice, their shells bursting to the rear of the Union infantry on the ridge. After a duel of 45 minutes, Hunt, the Federal Artillery Commander, diminished his fire to conserve ammunition for the attack he knew would come. This lull on the ridge and the sight of Union guns limbering-up at the chestnut grove prompted Alexander to inform Pickett that the Federal guns had withdrawn, that his ammunition was running low, and that the attack must be made at once. Pickett turned to Longstreet for word to advance but the latter could not bring himself to give the order – Pickett saluted and 15,000 men moved forward from the cover of the woods on Seminary Ridge.

The Confederate left consisted of Heth's division (now commanded by Pettigrew) with its four brigades abreast. Behind came the two brigades of Pender's division led by Trimble. Pickett's division made up the right wing of the assault column with Kemper's and Garnett's brigades forward, followed by Armistead. Wilcox trailed Armistead by a twenty-minute interval.

The Union artillery lay quiet until the first Confederate wave neared the fence along the Emmitsburg Road, then sent volley upon volley of solid-shot and shell into the grey ranks. Five hundred yards from the Union line

Pickett halted and re-formed so as to change his front forty-five degrees to the left; in so doing he closed a growing gap between his own and Heth's division but left Wilcox's and Lang's brigades isolated on his right. Now at short range, musket fire and canister cut down the Confederate ranks. Heth's two left brigades wavered and fell back, but the survivors of the two right brigades and Pickett's division continued on toward the clump of trees, over a stone wall and into Gibbon's division of II Corps with bayonet and clubbed musket. Stannard's Vermont brigade countered by a charge into the gap on Pickett's right and poured a fusillade into the grey ranks. On the Confederate left flank the 8th Ohio Infantry formed a skirmish line in front of the ridge position and delivered a murderous enfilading fire. Now Union infantry poured in from all directions and those attackers who could fell back to Seminary Ridge.

This was the end of the battle. On 4 July, Lee began his retreat from Northern soil, followed at a respectful distance by Meade. The strengths of the two armies at Gettysburg are uncertain but may be reckoned as some 90,000 Federals and 70,000 Confederates. On the third day the Federals employed 220 guns, the Confederates 172. Losses during the battle are estimated as about 23,000 for the North and 20,000 for the South.

HUGH COLE

191

1870
Gravelotte
Saint-Privat

The French under Marshal Bazaine were outflanked on their right, encircled and severely defeated by King Wilhelm's Germans in this episode of the Franco-Prussian War

BETWEEN THE CLOSE of the Napoleonic Wars and the outbreak of the Franco-Prussian, the conduct of war was revolutionized by the creation of the Prussian General Staff; a body of experts who could systematically prepare for war. Thus, in 1870, in order of military responsibilities, General von Moltke, Chief of the German General Staff, took precedence over the Commander-in-Chief, King Wilhelm I.

To Moltke, war was a scientific business, readiness for which demanded incessant study. He was a dedicated military craftsman, and a voluminous writer who, in addition to his many military works, had written a technical book on railways. A defect in his system of command was that it left decisions too much in the hands of subordinates, and at times that was apt to throw a battle out of gear.

Before the war, Baron Stoffel, the observant French military attaché in Berlin, had informed his government that the Prussian General Staff would 'constitute the most formidable element of superiority in the Prussian Army'. But no attention was paid to him, and the French General Staff continued to remain little more than a collection of clerks – '*des bourgeois habillés en militaires*'.

In brief, under Moltke, the German Army may functionally be compared with a clock subject to erratic timing, but which never ceased to tick; and the French Army, under Napoleon III, with an antiquated clepsydra bunged up with silt.

Nevertheless, the French possessed one great asset: the effective range of their rifle, the *chassepot*, was twice that of the German needle gun. Its superiority was recognized by Moltke, but he hoped to discount it by the superiority of the German steel breech-loading field gun over the French bronze muzzle-loader.

Moltke calculated that, at the opening of hostilities, the French would be unable to bring more than 250,000 men into the field against his 380,000. And his study of the French railway system had shown him that, were the French Army to be brought rapidly to the frontier, it would have to assemble in two groups, one at Metz and the other at Strasbourg. He decided, therefore, to deploy three armies—the First (General von Steinmetz), the Second (Prince Friedrich Karl) and the Third (the Crown Prince of Prussia) – in localities from which, should the French decide to invade Germany, they could more rapidly reinforce each other than the two French groups could in either Lorraine or Alsace. Of his intentions he says:

> But above all the plan of war was based on the resolve to attack the enemy at once, wherever found, and keep the German forces so compact that a superior force could always be brought into the field. By whatever special means these plans were to be accomplished was left to the decision of the hour; the advance to the frontier alone was pre-ordained in every detail.

RIGHT *A French 'children's game' which provided an admirable opportunity for satirical comment on the military failure of the Second Empire in the Franco-Prussian War – the unfortunate Bazaine, and Napoleon III's surrender at Sedan received the strongest censure*

Mitrailleuse, gag 20.	Casque Pruss.ⁿ perd 4.	Franc-Tireur, gag. 8.	Bombe, perd 20.	Caisson, gagne 15.	Tambour, gagne 6.	Cantinière, gag 60.	Mobile, perd 4.	Drapeaux, gag 30.	Bateau-Canon, gag 7.
Faidherbe, gag 60.	Prussien, perd 50.	Clairon, gag. 10.	Etendards Pruss.ˢ p. 20.	Sac, gagne 12.	Bavarois, perd 6.	Canon Pruss.ⁿ perd 11.	Turcos, gagne 70.	Fantassin, gag 18.	Chanzy, gagne 20.
Hulan, perd 26.	Fourgon, perd 4.	Marin, gagne 20.	Prince de Prusse, perd 14.	Obusier, gagne 2.	Lancier Franç.ˢ gag 4.	Roi de Prusse, ne gag. rien.	Pompier, gagne 8.	Redoute, gagne 1.	Artilleur, gagne 3.
Forteresse, perd 18.	Tamb. Prussien, perd 25.	Uhrick, gagne 80.	Vaiss.ⁿ Cuirassé, perd 4.	Cuirasse, gagne 30.	Hussard Pruss.ⁿ perd 19.	Casque, perd 1.	Bazaine, perd 100.	Canon Krupp, perd 20.	Blessé, gagne 4.
Trochu, gagne 1.	Zouave & Prussien, p. 12.	Camp, gagne 13.	Bismarck, perd 70.	Casemate, perd 18.	Réquisitions, p. 30.	de Molke, ne gagne rien.	Prisonniers, perd 13.	Bazeilles, perd 9.	Canrobert, gagne 3.
Garibaldien, gag 18.	Off. Français, gag. 3.	Lebeuf, ne gag. rien.	Bomb. de Paris, perd 7.	LA FRANCE, gagne tout.	Can.ˢ Français, gag. 18.	Off. Prussien, perd 7.	MacMahon, gag 100.	Bomb. de Strasb.ᵍ p. 15.	Coup de Feu, gag 17.
Bourbaki, gag. 20.	Attaque, gagne 8.	Zouave du Pape, gag 2.	Ch.ʳ d'Afrique, gag 7.	SEDAN, perd toute la partie.	Garde Nat.ˡ gagne 2.	Hussard Franç.ˢ gag 8.	Sentinelle, perd 3.	Charge de Caval.ᵉ gag 6.	Palikao, perd 10.
Dragon Franç.ˢ gag 17.	Sous la tente, perd 2.	Ballon de siège, gag 2.	Fascines, gagne 2.	Cuirassier blanc, p. 10.	L'Explosion, gag. 3.	Garibaldi, gag. 20.	Souven.ʳ gagne 17.	Après la bataille, perd 3.	Redoute, perd 2.
Prison, perd 8.	Intendant, perd 7.	Fourrageur, perd 6.	Qui Vive, gagne 2.	Volontaires, gag 8.	Chapeau, perd 7.	Pigeons, perd 19.	Trompette, gag 8.	Aide-de-camp, gag 9.	T.-Major, perd 9.
Maréchal, perd 10.	Prince Frederick Ch.ᵖ 6.	L'Exercice, gagne 6.	Matelot, gagne 1.	Sabre & Epée, perd 7.	Cuirassier F.ˢ gag 13.	Képi, perd 8.	La Cuisine, perd 2.	d'Aurelle de Paladine, p. 3.	La Paix, gagne 26.

Ce jeu auquel peuvent prendre part plusieurs enfants, se joue de la manière suivante : L'on découpe les images et on les met ensemble dans une boite, ensuite chacun paie le prix convenu, ce qui forme la caisse. Cela fait, tour à tour chaque joueur tire une image. Si c'est un gagnant, il reçoit de la caisse la valeur qui s'y trouve marquée, si, au contraire, c'est un perdant il est obligé de rembourser à la caisse la perte indiquée. Celui qui tire LA FRANCE gagne toute la partie.

Propriété des Editeurs. (Déposé.)

Fabrique de PELLERIN, Imprimeurs-Libraires à Épinal

LEFT *General von Moltke, the Chief of the German General Staff and the architect of the German victory.* CENTRE *King Wilhelm I of Prussia who, after the successful conclusion of the war, was proclaimed Emperor of Germany at Versailles in 1871.* RIGHT *Lacking his uncle's military prowess, Napoleon III's reign was brought to an inglorious end by the humiliating defeat and surrender of the French armies*

The French plan was highly speculative: it was to deliver an *attaque brusquée* on the Germans before the completion of their own mobilization. 150,000 men were to assemble at Metz and another 100,000 at Strasbourg; they would then move forward, unite, force neutrality on the South German States, link up with Austria, and march on Berlin.

War was formally declared by France on 19 July and when, on 28 July, the Emperor assumed the supreme command, because little had been foreseen or prepared, not a single corps was in readiness. Two, under Marshal MacMahon, were assembling at Strasbourg, and five, known as the Army of the Rhine, under the Emperor, at Metz. Then followed a series of frontier battles in which the French were worsted, and on 7 August orders were issued by Imperial Headquarters for a general withdrawal behind the Moselle. When this became known in Paris, the Ollivier Ministry fell and was replaced by Palikao's. It declared that, should Metz be lost, the capital would revolt.

On 13 August, the Emperor handed over the command of the Army of the Rhine to Marshal Bazaine, a soldier who had seen much active service in Africa, the Crimea, Lombardy, and Mexico. Although he had proved himself a capable divisional and corps commander, he lacked the ability to command an army, let alone a demoralized one. Unfortunately for him, the moment was critical; it would have taxed a consummate general, because on that day the German First Army had reached the river Nied, ten miles east of Metz; the Second had secured a bridgehead over the Moselle at Pont-à-Mousson, seventeen miles south of Metz; and the Third was approaching Nancy and Lunéville. The first two were converging on Bazaine and, though he was unaware of it, when he learnt that Metz was badly provisioned he decided to abandon the line of the Moselle and fall back thirty-five miles to that of the Meuse at Verdun. On 15 August he bivouacked his army around Rezonville and Vionville, west of Metz.

There, early on the 16th, he was surprised by the leading units of III and X Corps of the Second Army, which were equally surprised to bump into him. The desperately fought battle of Vionville–Mars-la-Tour followed and, although it ended in a draw, Bazaine fell back to a position immediately west of Metz. Though he informed the Emperor that he hoped to resume his retreat by the Metz–Montmédy road on the 19th, he decided to stand and fight a delaying action and then seek refuge in Metz. Morally, he was already beaten.

On the 17th, Moltke concentrated his forces, some 188,000 men against his opponent's 140,000. His idea was to drive Bazaine, should he attempt to escape, northward and away from Paris; or, should he intend to stand, to attack him.

The position occupied by Bazaine ran from Saint-Ruffine on the Moselle to Saint-Privat-la-Montagne. Topographically it was divided into two sectors. The left sector south of La Folie farm, followed a wooded ridge between two hundred and three hundred feet above the bed of the Moselle; it was backed by forts Saint-Quentin and Plappeville, and frontally moated by the Mance brook, which ran through a deep ravine; defensively, it was exceptionally strong. North of it, the right sector was for the greater part open country; defensively, it offered a good field of fire, but its outer flank was in the air. Along this front Bazaine deployed his army: on the left Frossard's II Corps; in the centre Lebœuf's III Corps, and de Ladmirault's IV Corps; and on the right Canrobert's VI Corps, based on Saint-Privat, with detachments at Saint-Ail, Sainte-Marie-aux-Chênes, and Ron-

A charge by the Chasseurs d'Afrique over-runs a Prussian gun position during the desperately fought battle of Vionville–Mars-la-Tour, a preliminary to Gravelotte, fought on 16 August 1870; it ended in a draw, but Bazaine retreated

A heroic episode during the battle: the 3rd Battalion of the French 51st Regiment recovers the colours of the 2nd Grenadiers; despite Bazaine's lack of generalship and the eventual outcome of the battle, the Germans as well as the French suffered heavy casualties

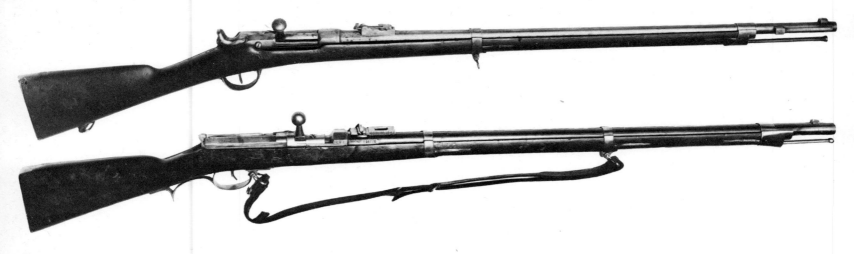

One great asset of the French was the effective range of their rifle, the chassepot (*upper*), which was twice that of the German needle gun (*lower*)

The position of the opposing forces at noon on 18 August 1870, when the Battle of Gravelotte–Saint-Privat commenced with an artillery duel between von Manstein's IX Corps at Vernéville and de Ladmirault's IV Corps at Montigny-la-Grange

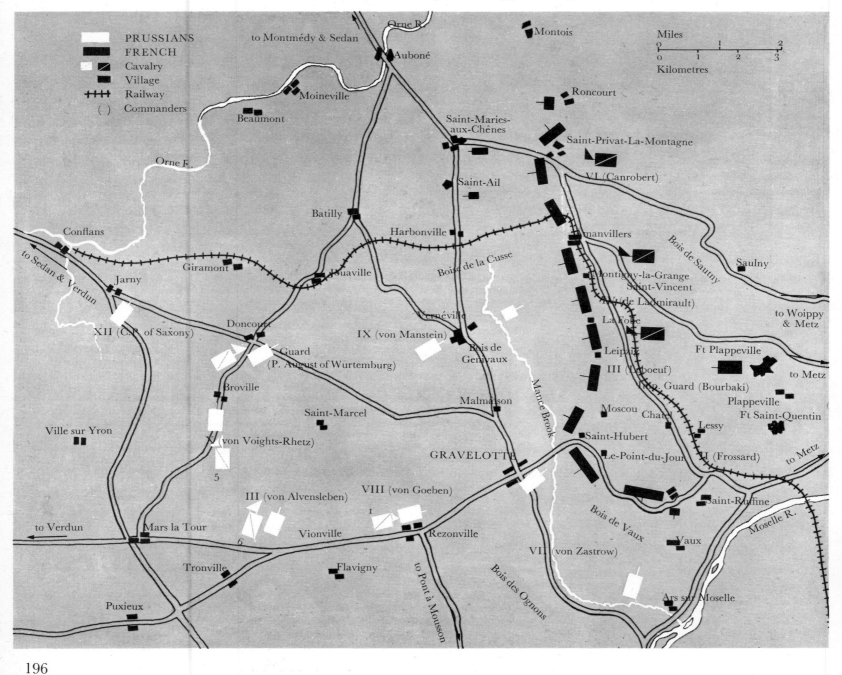

Though the French horse seems to be gaining the advantage in this cavalry engagement at Rezonville, the battle ended in a draw, and Bazaine retreated afterwards (painted by Aimé Morot)

The Cemetery of Saint-Privat by Alphonse de Neuville. Saint-Privat-la-Montagne marked the limit of the French right flank, and was stoutly defended by Marshal Canrobert's VI Corps (a frontal assault on this position cost the Prussian Guard 8,000 casualties in twenty minutes)

court. Army Headquarters were at Fort Plappeville with Bourbaki's Imperial Guard in reserve.

On 17 August, the First Army was ordered to advance its VII Corps (von Zastrow) across the Moselle and contact the French in Bois de Vaux, while VIII Corps (von Goeben) was to hold itself in readiness at Rezonville to move on the 18th to Gravelotte. These two corps constituted the German right, under cover of which the Second Army was to manœuvre northward. Its distribution was: IX Corps (von Manstein) on the right; XII Saxon Corps (the Crown Prince of Saxony) and the Guard (Prince August of Württemberg) on the left; III Corps (von Alvensleben) with X Corps (von Voights-Rhetz) in reserve; and II Corps (von Fransecky) on the road from Pont-à-Mousson, was not expected to reach Rezonville before 4 pm. on the 18th.

At the time, as the result of an unexplained lack of cavalry reconnaissance, all Moltke knew of his enemy was that he was in position south of Point-du-Jour. Therefore, when on the morning of 18 August Prince Friedrich Karl set out northward, he was uncertain whether, should

the enemy attempt to escape, he would have to wheel to the left, or, should he stand, to the right.

When, at 10 am. the French lines as far north as Montigny-la-Grange came into view, Prince Friedrich Karl concluded that he had discovered the actual right flank, and he ordered his army to turn inward. Half an hour later Moltke ordered XII Corps and the Guard to move on Sainte-Marie-aux-Chênes, should the enemy be in retreat; if not, to overlap his flank at Amanvillers. In the latter event, the First Army was to attack east of Gravelotte and IX Corps east of Vernéville. No mention was made of VIII Corps, presumably because for the 18th it had been allotted to the Second Army; but, so it would appear, Steinmetz failed to realize this.

When this order was on its way, the French were reported to be holding Saint-Privat. IX Corps was then instructed to hold its attack until XII Corps and the Guard came up. But Manstein had already set out, and at 11.45 am., before his main body had reached Vernéville, his advanced guard caught sight of the French camps about Montigny-la-Grange, and he impetuously

An illustration which appeared in an English newspaper shortly before the Franco-Prussian War depicting the new French weapon, the Mitrailleuse, an early machine gun like the Gatling gun introduced during the American Civil War

The interior of a French armaments factory devoted to the manufacture of Mitrailleuses and the modification of field guns; at the beginning of the war the Germans had the advantage in artillery – their steel breech-loading gun was a superior weapon to the French bronze muzzle-loader

Railway coaches fitted with hammocks brought into use as annexes to the overcrowded field hospitals in Metz; after his defeat at Gravelotte–Saint-Privat, Bazaine withdrew his army into Metz, where it was besieged and, on 29 October, capitulated

ordered a battery to fire on them. Although taken by surprise, the French speedily retaliated and smothered him with shells; whereupon he hastily called up his leading infantry, who were swiftly brought to a standstill by *chassepot* fire. The engagement then developed into an artillery duel.

When Manstein's cannonade was heard by General von Goeben, he at once ordered the leading units of VIII Corps to cross the Mance ravine and attack the French lines at Moscou and Point-du-Jour; but the French put up so stubborn a resistance that every assault was repulsed, and of their entrenched farms Saint-Hubert alone was lost. In spite of these failures, Steinmetz threw in all available infantry of VII Corps, and by 5 pm., after crippling losses, the attack on the First Army's front petered out.

Meanwhile Bazaine's lethargy was compensating for Steinmetz's costly pugnacity. When he had deployed his army, he left the battle in the hands of his corps commanders and remained in complacent inactivity at Plappeville. Not until 4 pm. did he mount his horse, and then to visit Fort Saint-Quentin on his almost impregnable left flank, which he feared might be turned. On his return at 7 pm., when his right flank was about to be overwhelmed, he sat down to dinner.

When Manstein's attack was repulsed, XII Corps and the Guard were coming up to swing round the assumed French right flank. But by then Prince Friedrich Karl was aware that the actual flank was at Saint-Privat.

Therefore he restricted Manstein's offensive and halted the Guard until XII Saxon Corps came up. It did so about 3 pm. when, under cover of its artillery supported by that of the Guard, Marshal Canrobert's detachments were driven out of Saint-Ail and Sainte-Marie-aux-Chênes. The Guard's artillery was then deployed to the south of the latter and the Saxons' to the north of it. Soon after, the artillery of III Corps reinforced the guns of IX Corps, and by 5 pm. the French artillery was forced out of the battle, and the fire of 180 guns was concentrated on Saint-Privat. The Saxons then advanced on Roncourt to turn the French flank.

At about 6 pm., for reasons still obscure, Prince August of Württemberg decided to launch the Guard in a frontal attack on Saint-Privat. General von Pape, the commander of the 1st Division, expostulated, as he could see that the Saxons were not in position to outflank it, but he was overruled. The assault columns deployed and advanced up the long glacis slope which separates Sainte-Marie-aux-Chênes from Saint-Privat. Met by a withering fire from the French *chassepots*, the result was massacre. Nevertheless the guardsmen pushed on to within six hundred paces of the village: they could go no farther – in twenty minutes they had lost over 8,000 officers and men.

By 7 pm. the Saxons had captured Roncourt and their guns were pounding Saint-Privat from the north, while those of the Guard did so from the west. Caught between two fires, the blazing village became untenable, and Canrobert ordered VI Corps to fall back. Half an hour later,

RIGHT *Marshal Bazaine, the Commander of the Army of the Rhine, a soldier who had served the Emperor Maximilian well in Mexico (the cactus and the map on which Bazaine rests show that Beaucé's portrait is set in that country), but lacked the ability to command an army*

An English cartoon published at the beginning of the Franco-Prussian War, which underlines the ill-preparedness of the French (not one corps was ready when war was declared), and the superior manpower of the Germans (they were able to put 380,000 into the field against 250,000 French)

as the sun was setting, the Guard and the Saxons, followed by a division of X Corps, with drums beating and colours flying, broke into Saint-Privat, but in such confusion that pursuit was impossible. As night set in, in disorderly rout the men of the defeated French VI Corps poured down the Woippy road towards Metz.

An hour and a half later, when a staff officer from Canrobert reported to Bazaine that VI Corps was falling back on Metz, the latter replied: 'You need not grieve over the retreat; the movement we were to make tomorrow morning is now being made twelve hours earlier, and the Prussians have little to boast about in having speeded it up'. Throughout, Metz had been Bazaine's spiritual home.

As we have seen, by 5 pm., except for the capture of Saint-Hubert, all of Steinmetz's attacks had been repulsed. In spite of this, he was determined to renew them, and when General von Fransecky's II Corps reached Rezonville, he appealed to Royal Headquarters to use it. At the time the King was at Gravelotte; he had come there on the strength of an erroneous report from Steinmetz that the heights beyond that village had been carried, and though Moltke disagreed, he placed II Corps at Steinmetz's disposal.

It was about 7 pm. when Steinmetz launched his final assault. Met by intense rifle fire, it was thrown back into the ravine in such confusion that the bulk of the attackers took panic and surged past the King towards Rezonville. Fortunately the discipline of II Corps withstood the rout, and when its leading units had crossed the ravine and deployed, in the closing darkness they saw ahead of them shadowy masses of men which they took to be French. They were units of VII and VIII Corps which had not fled, and the first volley fired into their backs sparked off a still wilder panic. Again Fransecky's men remained unshaken, but all they could do was to occupy the positions the fugitives had abandoned. The 'cease fire' was then sounded, and at 9.30 pm. the battle ended. It cost the Germans over 20,000 killed and wounded, and the French approximately 13,000 besides 5,000 captured.

Meanwhile the King and Moltke had ridden back to Rezonville, where they passed two anxious hours. All troops within thirty-six hours' call had been engaged, and as the rifle flashes seen in the night told them that the French were still in position, there was little prospect of renewing the struggle on the morrow. So far, no news had come in from Prince Friedrich Karl. Then, about midnight, it arrived: Saint-Privat had been taken and the French VI Corps was in rout.

On 19 August, Bazaine withdrew his army into the fortified camp of Metz. There it was besieged, and on 29 October it capitulated.

J.F.C. FULLER

A French print published before the beginning of hostilities, warning the Prussians not to cross the frontiers of France, and threatening war (which was precisely the reaction Bismarck sought)

OPPOSITE ABOVE *An incident during the battle for Saint-Privat: a helmetless French dragoon, with five head wounds, fights on, and here brings down a German lancer*

OPPOSITE BELOW *Repeated attacks by units of General von Steinmetz's First Army were repulsed by the French at Gravelotte on the left of their position, and they suffered crippling losses*

King Wilhelm of Prussia receives the surrender of Napoleon III and his army at the Château de Bellevue near Donchery after the German victory at Sedan

HARPER'S WEEKLY

JOURNAL OF CIVILIZATION

VOL. XLIX. New York; Saturday, June 24, 1905 NO. 2531

W.A.Rogers.

"GOOD OFFICES"

1904
Port Arthur

The six-months' siege of this fortress cost heavy casualties: its fall hastened the end of the Russo-Japanese War upon terms very favourable to Japan

THE JAPAN WHICH FIRST ENTERED FULLY into relationship with the Western world in 1853 was purely medieval. By 1895, however, Dai-Nippon had thoroughly mastered Western techniques; and in her war with China her British-trained navy and German-instructed army won a signal victory which added Korea to the Mikado's cramped and overpopulated domains. But further expansion into Manchuria's Liaotung peninsula was balked by Russia's pact with China and her refusal to withdraw from territory which included the coveted warm-water haven of Port Arthur which, strongly fortified, afforded admirable shelter to the Tsar's Pacific Ocean Squadron.

Negotiations over the disputed terrain were still proceeding when Admiral Togo launched a damaging surprise attack on the Russian warships lying at their Port Arthur moorings. An encounter between the two fleets on the following day ended in the Russian vessels hastily returning to the protection of their coastal defences. Thus early the Japanese had achieved that dominance at sea upon which depended their freedom to land four army corps in and about Pi-tzu-wo. Three of these were to engage General Kuropatkin's field army, concentrated about Liao-yang, while the fourth fought its way down the peninsula to invest Port Arthur.

LEFT *A cartoon in* Harper's Weekly *marking the intervention of President Theodore Roosevelt, which led to the peace negotiations between Russia and Japan after the fall of Port Arthur*

Japan's regular army of 270,000 – with 870 guns – could call on reserves totalling 530,000. Her thoroughly up-to-date navy of 29 craft, including 6 battleships, could be supplemented by 95 slightly older vessels of various classes. Her numerous shipyards could cope with repair work, but were incapable of new construction.

Initially, Russia held Manchuria with a field force of 83,000 – with 196 guns – supported by 25,000 fortress troops and 30,000 railway guards; an army that could be no more than laggardly reinforced from Moscow, 5,500 miles distant, by a precarious single-line railway. The Pacific Ocean Squadron, commanded by the highly regarded Admiral Makharoff, numbered 72 vessels of all denominations. A few craft were detached to Vladivostok from Port Arthur, where the blustering but unreliable General Stössel was responsible for the safety of both the Kuan-tun District and the fortress-haven itself. The whole Liaotung peninsula was governed by the Viceroy, Admiral Alexeieff.

Port Arthur lay in a hollow encircled by a chain of hills broken by the Lun-ho valley, running down to the sea. Its interlocking network of defences included the forts of Chi-kuan-shan on the north-eastern face, Erh-lung-shan and Sung-su-shan on the north, and the dominating strong-point of 203 Metre Hill, facing north and west. An eighteen-mile outer system of defences ran along the Green Hills, with the outworks of Ta-ku-shan and Sia-gu-shan overlooking the terrain towards the port of Dalny.

Naval operations, resumed on 13 April, occasioned less damage to the Japanese fleet than to the Russian, which lost its flagship, the *Petropavlovsk*, and Makharoff, her gallant commander. With the Russians again mewed up behind their booms, the Japanese were free to attempt the capture of Nan-shan – on the isthmus between Kin-chou and Ta-lien-wan bays – and the near-by port of Kin-chou. This would clear the way for a direct advance on Port Arthur. A night and a day's hard fighting enabled the Japanese to overwhelm both objectives, the Russians retiring in a state of confusion only a little worse than that which had characterized Stössel's conduct of the battle.

With the fall of Nan-shan and the occupation of Dalny, the Japanese First and Second Armies faced about to march on Kuropatkin at Liao-yang, the Fourth Army landing to form a link between them. Under General Nogi, the Third Army moved cautiously on the Green Hills. Numerically weaker than the Port Arthur garrison, it awaited reinforcement and the replacement of its siege train – sunk in transit by elements from Vladivostok.

At Alexeieff's insistence, a relief force was detached from Kuropatkin's main body to drive through to Port Arthur. Reaching Te-li-su, it was turned back after heavy fighting; and with its harassed retreat all attempts to succour the beleaguered garrison ended. Kuropatkin was sufficiently hard put to it to hold his own against Field-Marshal Oyama's three Army Corps.

By the end of July Nogi's reinforced Third Army had virtually overrun all Port Arthur's outlying positions at a cost in killed and wounded of 4,885; the Russians losing forty per cent of their forces engaged. On 7 August the first shell from the hostile landward batteries fell in Port Arthur; while preparations were hurried forward to launch an assault on the two buttresses of Erh-lung-shan and Chi-kuan-shan, and the network of field fortifications guarding the key point of 203 Metre Hill, which commanded the town and harbour.

The attack went in on the night of 23–24 August, to be met with a resolute resistance, which owed as much to the untiring exertions of the fortress commandant, Lieutenant-General Smirnoff, as to Major-General Kondratenko and his Siberian Rifles. Thrusting forward in close order, the Japanese, caught in the rays of the defenders' searchlights, were mown down in swathes by concentrated fire. Although the outer rim of the north-eastern defences was taken and held, the Japanese belief that 'the laurel of victory is the bayonet and the war-cry' had failed to make allowance for the effect of machine-gun and magazine rifle fire on troops advancing in close order over open ground, against strong natural positions. Even a 'butcher's bill' of 15,000, as against the defenders' losses of 3,000, failed as yet to force the lesson home.

With Port Arthur and its docks coming under 'remote' fire from newly arrived Japanese howitzers, the Pacific Ocean Squadron received orders to break out and make for Vladivostok. In the ensuing encounter with Togo's watchful squadrons, the loss of the *Tzesarevitch* sent five Russian battleships, one cruiser and three destroyers scuttling back to harbour; the balance fleeing to internment in neutral ports.

The August assault was followed by a lull. With a heavy casualty list and many sick, Nogi needed time for reorganization. But the intelligence that Kuropatkin had

The entrance to Port Arthur (only a quarter of a mile wide), well protected by forts on either side; a Russian warship is just visible outside

The final assault on the Nan-shan Heights on 26 May 1904, whose capture cleared the way for the Japanese advance on Port Arthur

*Japanese infantry waiting to be thrown into the assault on Namako-yama, which fell to them in September after a desperate defence of its peak;
the main Japanese objective during this offensive, 203 Metre Hill (which commanded the town and harbour), resisted capture until November*

Part of the system of siege parallels enabling the Japanese to reach the fort of Chi-kuan-shan, which was mined and finally captured on 18 December

The debris of war: a gun barrel torn from its mountings, a soldier's corpse, twisted corrugated iron – all that remained of the Russian fort of Chi-kuan-shan after the battle was over

been forced out of his carefully prepared positions at Liao-yang was a spur to renewed effort. For to the Japanese people Port Arthur had become a symbol, whose capture would signalize the triumph of the East over the West. Furthermore, with the Baltic Fleet nearly ready for sea, it was imperative to destroy the survivors of the Pacific Ocean Squadron before they could be reinforced.

The September offensive, therefore, was designed to capture the all-important 203 Metre Hill. With unabated ardour the Japanese infantry threw themselves at the Temple and Waterworks redoubts, the struggle swaying to and fro until, at the cost of heavy casualties, the Russians were driven from their trenches. With these subsidiary positions won, the main attack went in with the object of rushing the Hill itself, but the Russians fought back stubbornly. The outer eminence of Namako-yama fell after a desperate last-stand defence of its peak. Try as they might, the Japanese could gain no more than a precarious footing on the lower slopes of 203 Metre Hill, while the casualties they suffered were out of all proportion to the progress made. By 24 September they had been shelled from their exposed positions on the Hill, although they retained their grip on the neighbouring Namako-yama.

On 28 September the besiegers switched their heavy battery fire to Erh-lung-shan and Chi-kuan-shan, towards which they had belatedly started tunnelling operations. Naval batteries concealed behind the village of Sui-shih-ying also inflicted heavy damage on the Russian warships lying helpless at their moorings.

Activities throughout September had been more costly than rewarding. This, however, was inevitable so long as the technique of field operations continued to be applied to the circumstances peculiar to a siege.

A letter smuggled out of Port Arthur in early October revealed that 'our principal forts are uninjured, but the houses in the town are badly damaged, and the harbour works are in sad plight'. Provisions were in as short supply as medical necessities; typhus, scurvy and dysentery were rife, and the hospitals were full of irreplaceable casualties. The Japanese were pounding the whole area with 11-inch shells and the bombs from 110-ton mortars; while the news that the Baltic Fleet had at last set sail was outweighed by the intelligence that in the north Kuropatkin's counter-offensive had ended in failure.

Having at last adopted the 'mole-warfare' technique of spade and mattock, the besiegers succeeded in worming their way further forward. But a concentrated attack launched on Erh-lung-shan and Chi-kuan-shan on 24 October met with no more than limited success. Once again the crowding Japanese were caught in the open by a devastating sleet of machine-gun and rifle fire. The dry ditch of Chi-kuan-shan was penetrated and a few infantrymen actually scrambled over the fort parapet itself. But by failing to destroy the defences on the flank of the fortress, Nogi had put a premium on costly failure. It was still for the engineers and miners to ensure for the assault forces a far closer access to their objectives.

And time was running out. At all costs Port Arthur's fall must be ensured before the Baltic Fleet linked up with the Russian naval elements in Vladivostok and those vessels still surviving of the Pacific Ocean Squadron, which could be destroyed only by 'observed' fire from 203 Metre Hill. On 27 November an assault was thrown in at the Hill which, after a night of savage fighting, at last fell into Japanese hands. Immediately the warships in the basin were brought under a hail of shot that swiftly reduced them to riven, useless hulks.

From early December the battering of Erh-lung-shan and Chi-kuan-shan, and their subsidiary works, took on a new intensity. On the 18th a tremendous explosion burst with the shock of an earthquake beneath Chi-kuan-

Lieutenant-General Anatole Mikhailovich Stössel, the Russian commander of Port Arthur and the Kuan-tun District

General Nogi, who commanded the Japanese Third Army, to which the siege of Port Arthur was entrusted

The fortress of Port Arthur in 1904; its fortifications were constructed by the Crimean veteran, General Todleben, plainly a disciple of Vauban, the seventeenth-century master

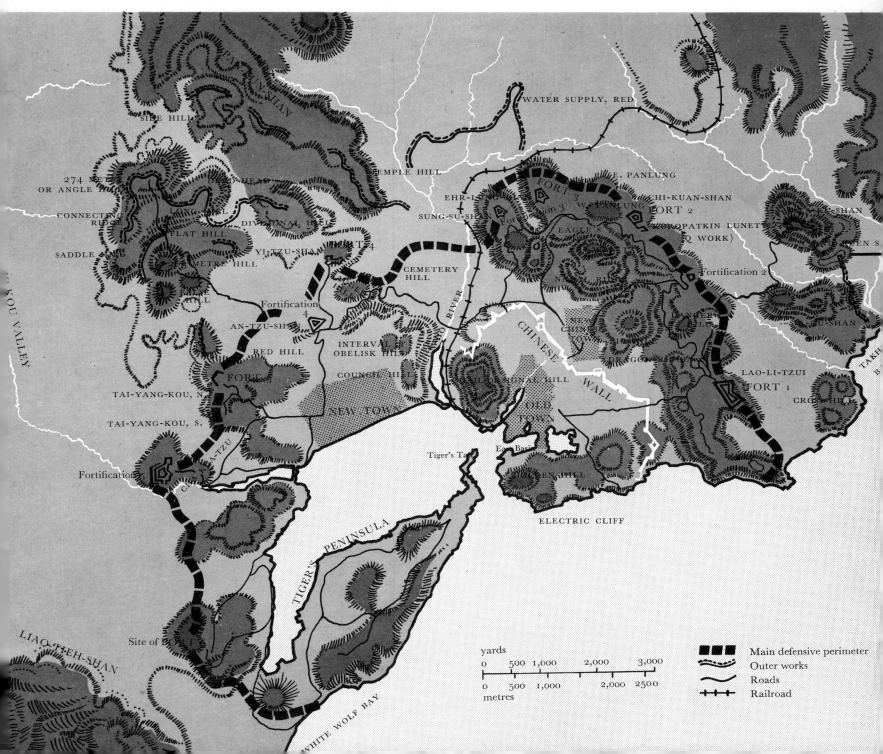

Japanese infantry waiting to go into battle; by the time of the surrender Nogi's casualties numbered nearly 60,000, and sick nearly 34,000

shan. A few minutes later a second explosion sent another spout of smoke and rubble and severed limbs hurtling into the air. Almost before the debris had fallen the Japanese infantry were swarming over the tumbled defences. The garrison, hastily reinforced, fought back gamely, and the assailants' losses from machine-gun fire were heavy until they got to work with grenade and bayonet. Seven hours' grim fighting delivered the battered work into Japanese hands, at a cost of 700 casualties.

Erh-lung-shan had also been mined, and a similar hard-fought struggle ended in its capture. One by one the eastern defences about the Chinese Wall and Eagle's Nest were battered by the guns and overrun by wildly cheering Japanese infantry, whose shrill cries of *Banzai! Banzai!* the wearied, desperate Siberian riflemen had come to dread. Smirnoff was everywhere, and when it was clear that the outer line of works was firmly in enemy hands, he slaved day and night to strengthen the inner ring narrowly enclosing the Old and New Towns. However grim things might look, the fortress commandant was not the man to yield to despair. At a conference summoned by Stössel, Smirnoff and other senior officers

were firm in their conviction that the defence could still be maintained. Enough food remained to sustain life and activity, and there was no shortage of munitions.

But unknown to the majority of his Staff, Stössel was already seeking to negotiate terms of capitulation. Nogi, with his killed, wounded and missing totalling just under 60,000 for operations to date, and with a current sick list of 33,769, was in no mood to be lenient. Thus to all practical purposes the surrender finally agreed upon was unconditional. The Japanese claimed all private and public property in the port, and took into custody as prisoners of war 878 officers, 23,251 of the rank and file, and 8,956 seamen. The care of the 3,387 wounded and 13,613 sick – including civilians – was to be the joint responsibility of the Japanese and Russian medical staffs.

By 3 January Japanese occupation of the haven was completed. But the fall of Port Arthur did not automatically bring the conflict to a close, although there was strong opposition to the war party in Russia, with widespread rioting and the ruthless suppression of public demonstrations.

To Kuropatkin, still holding on south of Mukden, the

collapse of Port Arthur could only presage a steady increase in the forces arrayed against him; and he planned to strike at Oyama's three Army Corps before Nogi's Third Army could be moved up into the line. His offensive was delayed, however, until 26 January, and was then so faultily directed and badly carried out that the Russians were forced to retreat to positions about Hai-ping-kai.

The Russians' only immediate hope of restoring the situation in their favour lay with Rozhestvensky's fleet. But the encounter in the Straits of Tsu-shima only too eloquently demonstrated that men and not ships constitute a fighting marine. Out-gunned and out-manœuvred, 30 out of the 47 Russian pennants were sunk or captured, the remainder seeking safety in flight.

Russia still had a considerable force in the field, but the war was generally unpopular, and there was little prospect that the ineptitude of the High Command, the slipshod staff work, and the fumbling of the 'Intelligence' service – as ineffective as the Japanese espionage organization was efficient – would show any marked improvement. On the other hand, the Japanese had lost 92,800 men – as against a Russian total of 82,000 – and were faced with an imminent shortage in man-power. Moreover, the cartel that controlled international finance was refusing any further loans 'except for purely pacific purposes'. The timely intervention of President Roosevelt, therefore, brought about peace negotiations which accorded Japan the southern half of the Island of Saghalin and granted her the right to lease southern Manchuria from China, while fully recognizing her suzerainty over Korea.

A conflict had ended in which a remote and hitherto unregarded Eastern Power had achieved victory over an empire at least recognized as forming part of the general Concert of Europe. The implications of that victory cast remarkably long shadows. From the teeming *bazaars* of India to the *suks* of distant Africa and the lonely *khans* of the Mandarin Road, the exultant whisper ran that the white man was not invincible. By most Westerners this seething ferment went unregistered. It was left to Kuropatkin to set it down that, 'the cries of "Asia for the Asian" and "Africa for the African" are of serious import for Europe. The danger is approaching, and it is so imminent that the Powers of Europe will be forced to sink their differences and unite to withstand the attempt by these uprising peoples to drive old Europe back into the narrow shell she has long since outgrown'. Subsequent events have clearly demonstrated that at least one individual had the foresight to interpret correctly the writing on the wall.

REGINALD HARGREAVES

General Stössel, the commander of the fortress-haven surrendering Port Arthur to General Nogi, commander of the Japanese Third Army

The Baltic Fleet, on which Russian hopes of restoring the situation in their favour after the fall of Port Arthur were pinned, was all but destroyed at the battle of Tsu-shima; this cartoon in Harper's Weekly *brings home the lesson to the Tsar*

MIKADO: "NOW CAN YOU SEE IT?"

1914
Tannenberg

One of the most complete victories in history was achieved, despite Ludendorff's mistakes, by Russian folly, hunger and disorganization, and the brilliance of General von François

BEFORE THE OUTBREAK of the First World War the Russian General Staff had planned to contain the Germans in East Prussia with a single army, the First, while attacking the Austrians with four armies. It was not until after mobilization that it decided, in order to aid France, to take the offensive in the north with two armies under General Jilinsky, consisting of the First (General Rennenkampf) and the Second (General Samsonov). This would create an immense numerical superiority over the German Eighth Army commanded by General von Prittwitz, who had at his disposal only four corps, I, XVII, XX, and I Reserve, with a single cavalry division, whereas Jilinsky had in the First Army three corps, III, IV, and XX, with five cavalry divisions, and in the Second six, I, II, VI, XII, XV, and XXIII, with three cavalry divisions. On the other hand, the Germans were superlatively equipped and all the corps commanders were highly competent, two of them, Otto von Below and Hermann von François, brilliant, whereas the Russians were primitive, haphazard in method, and were to reveal only in Martos, commanding XV Corps, their one first-class leader. Major-General Sir Alfred Knox, a British representative with the Russian Army, tells us that a colonel in charge of the few cars in the Northwest Army Group – junior officers had to do with dogcarts – could not read a map.

Even the superiority in strength was in part illusory. Though they had in the field some 250 battalions to the German 144, a simple calculation shows that the proportion of guns to battalions was considerably higher on the German side. This was a relatively small handicap by comparison with the ratio of the heavy artillery, in which the Germans were about ten times the stronger. The Russians were short of telephone cable and sent wireless messages in clear to lower formations, either because these did not have the codes or were too ignorant to decipher the orders quickly, and even to the armies in codes so simple that they were quickly broken. On the German side the worst handicap was Prittwitz, an experienced and not undistinguished veteran who had let body and mind run to seed in social life and hunting.

On the morning of 17 August Rennenkampf's III Corps clashed with the German I Corps at Stallupönen, just within the East Prussian frontier. Prittwitz ordered the corps commander, von François, to fall back on Gumbinnen, fifteen miles to the west. He refused point-blank, continued his attack, dealt the Russians a smarting blow, was then pushed back, and reached Gumbinnen with 3,000 prisoners. He had, however, lost seven guns, and the engagement must be accounted a Russian victory.

On the 20th a much more important action was fought at Gumbinnen. General von Mackensen with XVII

Corps and Otto von Below with I Reserve had been ordered up to the support of François, who was left alone until their arrival at noon. The fighting began favourably for the Germans nevertheless. About 8 am. François launched a division of his I Corps in a flank attack, routed a Russian division and, though his own losses were heavy, scattered it and took 5,000 prisoners. Then the situation changed radically. For once the predominance in heavy artillery on the German side was slight, and the Russians stopped Mackensen dead. The whole of his corps seems to have become unsteady, and one division broke and fled in wild disorder. Below, starting late, was not up in time to aid him, and the fleeing division could not be halted until it had covered some fifteen miles. The Russians lost 19,000 men, over 6,000 being prisoners of war, but remained victorious. Knox thought that Rennenkampf had shown pluck and initiative.

An extraordinary drama at German headquarters now opened. In peace-time war-games it had been agreed that if the situation became desperate it would be necessary to retreat behind the Vistula. Prittwitz thought that the time to do so had now come. Samsonov was at last advancing and, since he was a more enterprising man than his colleague, at a very fair pace. Prittwitz telephoned his intention to the Chief of the German General Staff, the younger Moltke. The listener was appalled. A long series of messages passed to and fro, and Moltke finally decided that he had no option but to relieve Prittwitz. His choice of successor fell on the Eighth Army commander's brother-in-law, a retired officer who knew the country

Tsar Nicholas II inspects Russian troops; by comparison with their opponents in 1914, the Russians were primitive and ill-equipped

Army Orders for 26 August 1914, containing Hindenburg's orders for the commencement of the Battle of Tannenberg; the battle opened with a Russian attack early on the 26th, but this was parried by a prompt German counter-attack

BELOW *German infantry, in full marching order, advances through East Prussian woods towards the front; the Russians enjoyed greater numerical superiority, but lacked the appropriate proportion of artillery*

well, Paul von Hindenburg, and he assigned to him as Chief of Staff Erich Ludendorff, who had just distinguished himself on the Western Front at Liège. He was not alone in the belief that Prittwitz must be got rid of. Major-General Grünert, Chief of the Operations Staff, and his much more efficient and enterprising second string, Lieutenant-Colonel Max Hoffmann, agreed with him and saw a far more promising solution. They would play on the impetuosity of Samsonov and the over-caution of Rennenkampf, leave only a screen to watch the latter, and swing the bulk of their strength against the former. There was one other equally important argument in favour of this course, the great chain of the Masurian Lakes, which virtually cut off one of the Russian armies from the other. The danger was that, if Rennenkampf came on, he would be in a position to fall upon their rear, and in view of their numerical inferiority this would be disastrous; but they were ready to accept the risk.

On 23 August at Hanover station Ludendorff picked up Hindenburg, still wearing his outdated uniform. On the way they worked out the details of a plan precisely the same as, though naturally less detailed than, that of Hoffman. It was long believed that the scheme was wholly theirs, and this error started the legend of Hindenburg as 'a sublimated image of the German warrior', just as it was not realized that François was the hero of Tannenberg.

In fact, when Hindenburg reached Eighth Army Headquarters, I Corps was detraining west of Tannenberg. For some time François was in an ugly situation because Below's I Reserve and Mackensen's XVII Corps had to cover something like eighty miles by road, bad road at that. He had to face odds of six to one, and had the worst of the fighting while he remained unsupported. Meanwhile all that was facing Rennenkampf was the single cavalry division, on a front of over twenty miles. Jilinsky, however, was playing into the hands of the Germans by urging the willing Samsonov to push on faster. 'German troops', he telegraphed,

after heavy fighting and the victory of General Rennenkampf, are hastily retiring . . . only inconsiderable forces in front of you. . . . You will advance energetically . . . Your movements directed to meeting the enemy retreating in front of General Rennenkampf and to cutting off his retreat to the Vistula.

Nobody could have been more eager to hurry than Samsonov, but he was now ploughing his way through sand, putting double teams into his guns, short of food and forage, exhausting his troops by marching ten to twelve miles a day. Meanwhile Rennenkampf was living up to form.

Ludendorff, unlike Hoffmann, had been worrying about Rennenkampf in his rear. He ordered François to open the attack on Samsonov on the 25th. From what has

already been said of his character and his previous action, it will not cause astonishment that he refused, secretly backed by Hoffmann. Not even all his infantry had as yet detrained and none of his heavy artillery. Hindenburg, Ludendorff, and Hoffmann then drove out to see him. Ludendorff stormed with anger, but Hindenburg had nothing to say, while François promised that he would fight with the bayonet on confirmation of the order, though one doubts if he meant to. However, Hoffmann, in another car, stopped at a railway station, where he was handed an intercepted message from Rennenkampf which showed that his next day's march would not threaten the German rear, and a second from Samsonov ordering 'pursuit' of the supposedly fleeing XX Corps of General von Scholtz. The first signs of Ludendorff's doubtful

General Rennenkampf, the Commander of the Russian First Army (second from the left), dining with his staff; thanks to Rennenkampf's over-caution and the faulty orders he received, the Germans were able to defeat Samsonov's Second Army before he came to its relief

BELOW *General Erich Ludendorff (left), Hindenburg's Chief of Staff, whose jealousy prevented the subsequent promotion of General von François (right), Commander of I Corps – the real hero of Tannenberg*

German infantry in a defensive position (evidently a trench dug below floor level inside a war-damaged house); the Eighth Army consisted of four corps of infantry and one cavalry division, which faced nine corps of Russian infantry and eight cavalry divisions

The positions occupied by the German and Russian armies on 29 August, the climax of the Battle of Tannenberg (the battle was fought 25–30 August 1914); the strategical advantage which the great chain of the Masurian Lakes afforded the Germans can be clearly seen

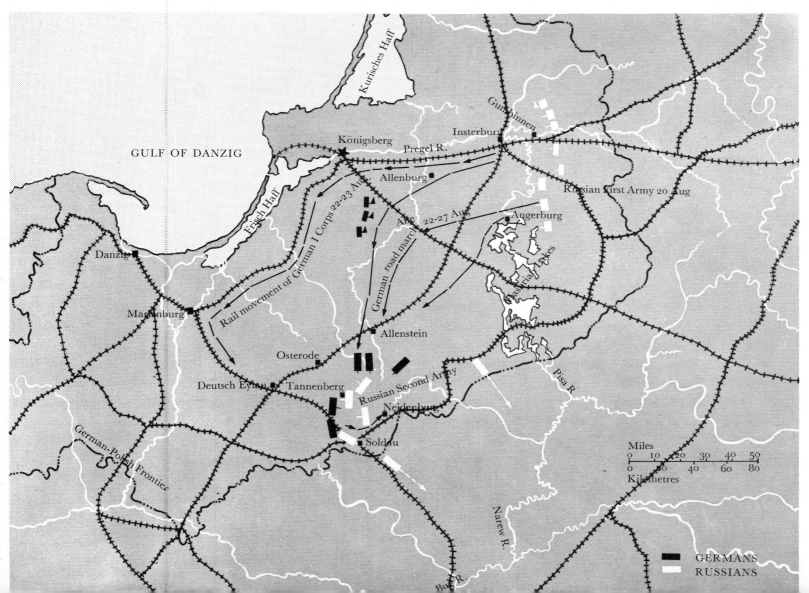

The victors: Hindenburg (centre), flanked by his Chief of Staff, Ludendorff (right, in a cape), and Colonel Hoffmann of the Operations Staff (left, foreground), who devised the plan which brought victory

Destruction in Ortelsburg, near the battlefield of Tannenberg – yet some sort of a makeshift market has been set up again

nerve, which he was to lose so signally in 1918, had already appeared, but so had the promises of fortune. On the morrow Mackensen and Below should be ready to attack Samsonov.

That night Samsonov formed up with XV Corps under Martos and XII Corps under Kliouviev in the centre, to advance on the front Allenstein–Osterode, its right covered by VI Corps under Blagovestchenky, and the left by one division of XIII Corps under Kondratovitch, the other having been assigned to the centre. The attack was launched early on 26 August, but Mackensen fell on one division of VI Corps and a little later Below on the second. Both were driven back in confusion and Samsonov's flank was turned. Martos and his fine corps were fighting splendidly but hard pressed, and Kliouviev took Allenstein, but had to leave it because Martos needed his aid, hoping that Blagovestchenky would take it over, which that commander was in no situation to do. By evening Samsonov, though still partly in the dark, saw that he himself, rather than the enemy, faced a threat. He hoped, however, that Rennenkampf's leading troops would shortly unite with him and that all would then be well.

François was ready by the early hours of the 27th. His heavy bombardment, continued for seven hours, sufficed to drive the Russian I Corps back in confusion after very heavy loss. That evening there were several further panics of a minor sort, not all of them in the Russian ranks.

Jilinsky's eyes were opened at last, and he sent urgent orders to Rennenkampf to attack at once. Even now the contest was not completely decided, but it really was when Rennenkampf was directed to move nearly due west instead of south-west. 28 August was crucial. Ludendorff ordered François to move to the aid of XX Corps, which was under some pressure. Once more he disobeyed, this time not reporting that he was doing so. He thrust straight forward for Neidenburg, and had he not done so it is highly probable that a large part of the Russian Second Army would have escaped the net on the two following days. Nor did XX Corps find any serious difficulty in holding the enemy. The Russians avoided shame – if shame can ever fall on starving troops – by the great fight put up by Martos and Kliouviev, until the latter was enveloped by Below, bursting through a gap at Allenstein. The Russians had suffered a disastrous defeat already, but even at their weariest they were, as always in their history, great marchers. An annihilating victory demanded that they should be herded like livestock into a corral.

Though Rennenkampf was not moving in the right direction, a little further anxiety was felt at German headquarters because he *was* moving, and in great strength. However, news then came in that his progress was too slow and that he had virtually no prospect of making contact with Samsonov. The latter was by now no longer in the dark. His flanks were turned; only two of his corps were putting up what could be called a fight; his communications were to all intents and purposes cut. But, whatever his faults, always a fighting man, he decided to take personal control on the battle-front. He said good-bye to Knox outside Neidenburg, remarking that, though the enemy had had luck on one day, he would have it on another. It was not to be. He witnessed one more pleasing sight, a column of prisoners marching past Martos. Then things went from bad to worse without his being able to exercise any control. Late in the night of 29 August he walked alone deep into the woods and shot himself.

As so often happens, the two good corps were the two left without a chance of escape. Martos and Kliouviev with their remaining troops wandered about helplessly. The former got separated from his men and was captured. Kliouviev shared his fate, but a handful of the survivors of his corps, entrenched all round, held out till the morning of the 31st, the remnant surrendering only when all their ammunition was expended. One last honourable gleam illumined the death of the Second Army. Artomonov had been rightly relieved of command of I Corps, and his first-class successor, the Guardsman Sirelius, broke through the enemy and retook Neidenburg, but could not maintain his hold upon it.

Then came the herding, or what the Germans called 'the day of harvesting'. On the northern side Below's I Reserve Corps, starting with its centre seventeen miles east of Allenstein, pressed south-west, then almost due west, against the fugitives, while farther east Mackensen's XVII Corps dealt with the Russian XV and XXIII Corps. Once again, however, it was François who played the *beau rôle* and made it for himself. His orders had been to keep his station on the right, but he split his corps in two, left half where it was, and strung out the other in a screen of small posts and patrols. His haul of prisoners was immense; in fact it comprised nearly all that were taken with their units, the remainder being for the most part stragglers wandering in the woods and captured after quiet had fallen on the battlefields. His prisoners numbered 60,000 out of a total of 92,000. In round numbers 500 guns were captured.

Only a few words can be given to the operations which followed immediately. Jilinsky was dismissed. Rennenkampf fell back out of reach. Moltke had ordered two corps to cross from the Western to the Eastern Front, an ill-advised decision in view of the critical situation on the former but a godsend to Hindenburg. With their aid he defeated Rennenkampf, but failed in his main object, which was to pin him to the shore and annihilate his force like that of Samsonov. Rennenkampf suffered heavily enough, losing 30,000 prisoners, but shook himself clear and retreated out of reach.

It was a brilliant victory, one of the most striking of the war. It did not, however, damage the Russians to as great an extent as was then believed and has been sometimes since asserted. They were indeed able to invade East Prussia again. It was of course decisive in the sense that, had the Germans lost it, the future course of the war would have been altered profoundly. It certainly affected the Western Front and not only by reason of the two corps sent by Moltke in the expectation that they would take part in the battle though, as we have seen, they arrived only in time to fight in the next. It had one feature which may well be unique. After certain battles victory is attributed to the wrong man; here it was to two wrong men. Neither Hindenburg nor Ludendorff failed. The former was, as ever, rock-like in his personality and a steadying influence upon his emotional subordinate; the latter was quick as lightning, with an extraordinary gift for summing up a situation. But Tannenberg was planned by Hoffmann and mainly won by Hermann von François, whom Ludendorff's jealousy prevented from ever rising beyond the command of a corps, whereas Below became a group commander and one of the greatest generals of the war.

CYRIL FALLS

Russian troops surrender – the magnitude of the German victory is measured by the fact that they took 92,000 prisoners (60,000 of these, still in their units, were captured by von François's I Corps)

The fruits of 'the day of harvesting', some of the great haul of prisoners taken from the Russian Second Army assembled in Augustowo; when he saw that all was lost their commander, General Samsonov, shot himself

RIGHT ABOVE *Russian trenches under artillery bombardment during the Battle of Tannenberg (painted by Max Rabes); the Germans had a much higher proportion of guns to battalions than the Russians, and were ten times stronger in heavy artillery*

RIGHT *Pioneer German units were equipped with 'liquid fire apparatus' (more familiar as 'flamethrowers' later) before 1914, but it was not used successfully until February 1915*

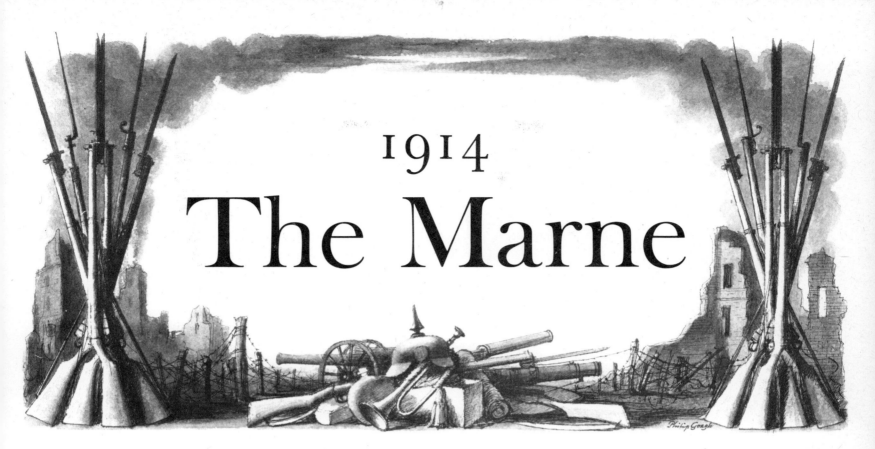

1914
The Marne

After the failure of Plan 17, Joffre rallied the French armies and the BEF and, piercing a gap in the German front, gained a great victory

THE FIRST BATTLE OF THE MARNE changed history as men thought to make it and war as men thought to fight it. This vast, incredibly complex action fought from 5–10 September 1914 was the climax of a military campaign begun on 4 August when Germany invaded Belgium in the first great offensive of the First World War.

The major front of the Battle of the Marne covered over 125 miles – from north-east of Paris to Verdun – with 5 German armies fighting 6 Allied armies, and another 4 armies engaged from Verdun south to the Alps. The Germans marched to the Marne expecting to finish the war within a week; five days later they began a retreat to trenches where they would remain for four years.

What went wrong?

The opening of the western war saw a German battle line stretching almost from the Swiss Alps along the French border through Luxembourg past the Belgian and Dutch borders, some 475 miles of mountains, valleys, hills, and plains. Under a plan drawn up by the military *maestro* Schlieffen and in 1905 bequeathed to his weak successor, Moltke, a small German army was holding the Russians in the east; 2 armies were defending Alsace-Lorraine up to Metz-Diedenhofen; and, stretching from this fortified bastion, 5 other armies, Germany's best,

poised to wheel scythe-like through neutral Belgium into northern France, then sweep down west of Paris on to the French armies – a gargantuan development designed for swift, total victory.

To counter a German invasion the French army, under General Joffre, evolved Plan XVII, a monument to the doctrine of the *offensive à outrance* – the all-out offensive – that held the French army in its tactical grip. Plan XVII called for strengthened covering forces to fight a defensive action along the north-eastern frontier until the thirteenth day of mobilization. Then 2 right-wing armies would attack into Lorraine and 2 centre armies would strike east of Metz. Joffre's left army, commanded by Lanrezac and buttressed by Sir John French's British Expeditionary Force, would attack either into Belgium or straight ahead towards Metz, depending on the route of the German invasion. Simultaneously Russia would send 2 armies into eastern Germany.

The French army commander did not dream that the enemy could muster sufficient strength for a sweep from the north. His error and that of most of his staff and commanders stemmed from the completely mistaken but enduring belief that German reserve corps and divisions were employed behind and separate from their regular forces – the conventional method discarded years before by Germany.

On 20 August the French dream became a nightmare when the disastrous Battle of the Frontiers began. In four

LEFT *Minethrowers, one of the new weapons introduced in the First World War; the colossal concentration – guns, too, were used in this way – added a further dimension of horror to war*

Officers of the 1st Cameronians, in General Sir John French's BEF, confer before the bitter action of Le Cateau, 25 August 1914, during the retreat to the Marne

days Joffre's armies, one after the other, met the enemy and were beaten. By 24 August the battle was over, a fantastic Allied defeat with casualties estimated as high as 300,000, with all the armies in retreat to the Marne.

A good many commanders would have given up. Joffre did not. He sensed that his armies were beaten, but not broken. He knew his terrain and he knew the staying power of artillery, particularly the French 75 mm cannon, the most advanced artillery piece of the day. On 24 August he revealed the secret of the Battle of the Marne to the Minister of War:

> We are therefore compelled to resort to the defensive . . . our object must be to last out as long as possible, trying to wear the enemy out, and to resume the offensive when the time comes . . .

From 24 August to 5 September the French and British retreated, the British stopping to fight the bitter action of Le Cateau, the French the vicious fight at Guise-Saint Quentin. Time and again Joffre attempted to halt the retreat, to reorganize and strike back. Time and again the advancing grey hordes of enemy upset his plans; time and again he faced disaster from the recalcitrant commanders, Sir John French and General Lanrezac, who seemingly loathed each other more than the enemy. He could not persuade Sir John to hold up his withdrawal; he had to threaten Lanrezac into fighting at Guise. Yet with stolid calm he continued to face each crisis as it arose, patching here, plugging there. Evil days these, but patience is said to be its own reward, and Joffre was to find this true.

For while Joffre roamed the battlefield like a frustrated Napoleon, his finger on the precise pulse of his people, his German counterpart was trying to fight a battle from hundreds of miles away. Reports of great victories pouring into Moltke's headquarters, first at Coblenz, later at Luxembourg, lulled him into a false optimism that was to cost him victory and deprive him of command. During those weeks Moltke reduced the strong right wing demanded by Schlieffen from 17 to less than 12 corps. No longer could he wheel west of Paris. But with the fantastic victories claimed by his commanders and with the victory of Tannenberg in Prussia, no longer did this seem necessary. At the end of August, with Kluck encountering only slight resistance, with the British (in Kluck's mind) obviously defeated, the main French strength, Moltke supposed, lay in front of his centre armies. If Rupprecht could break through on the left and Bülow and Kluck on the right, Moltke would win a classic envelopment battle. Kluck already had suggested a change of direction and Moltke now approved: Bülow to march towards Rheims, Kluck toward Compiègne-Noyon.

This was what Kluck wanted and he now pushed his tired army recklessly to the south. When Moltke, suddenly worried by reported French troop movements from east to west, ordered him to 'follow in echelon behind the Second Army' where he would be responsible for the flank protection of the force, Kluck refused the order. Demonstrating the selfish independence that characterized the German commanders, he continued to push his advance across the Marne.

By 5 August Moltke realized the true situation and ordered the two right wing armies to 'remain facing the eastern front of Paris, to act offensively against any operations of the enemy from Paris . . .' Convinced of Moltke's confusion, Kluck decided to let his army reach the day's objective *south* of the Marne, but did order one corps to halt where it stood in the north.

Learning of Kluck's change of direction on 31 August, Joffre followed his subsequent advance with the keenest interest. His patching and plugging had given him two new forces, Maunoury's Sixth Army north of Paris and Foch's Ninth Army in the centre. A visit from the British Secretary of State for War, Lord Kitchener, had also slowed Sir John's withdrawal and Joffre further appeased the British commander by relieving Lanrezac in favour of the dashing Franchet d'Esperey. Trusting that his right and centre armies could hold, Joffre decided to send the Sixth Army against Kluck's right while the BEF and Fifth Army attacked north.

In moving to the jump-off line on 5 September, Maunoury struck Kluck's rear corps commanded by Gronau, who that evening withdrew some six miles to a better defensive position. Kluck did not learn of the action until late in the evening. By then one of Moltke's staff officers, Lieutenant-Colonel Hentsch, sat in Kluck's

The Curé watches as French infantry marches through a village on its way to the front; during the Battle of the Frontiers, 20–24 August, the Allies had lost 300,000 casualties, and Joffre, the Commander-in-Chief, needed all the reinforcements he could get before resuming the offensive

French cavalry are sent to the front by taxicab by order of the Military Governor of Paris – one of the thousand of 'Galliéni's taxicabs'

German infantry advance on foot, while ambulances bring back casualties; the Marne Campaign filled the hospitals of France and Germany, and the German casualties were too appalling to publish

headquarters giving the aloof Army Commander for the first time a realistic picture of the overall situation, in short that all the victories claimed by all the German commanders had been grossly exaggerated and the French army was still very much alive. Kluck now began feeding back a corps to Gronau with plans to send back another on the following day. He would keep one corps in the south until Bülow's army could wheel south-west to screen Paris by extending Kluck's left flank. Simultaneously Moltke's centre armies were attacking to the south-east to open the way for Rupprecht's Sixth Army, struggling since 4 September to push in from the east.

On 6 September Maunoury continued his advance but soon ran into Gronau's new line stretching from Vincy south to the Marne, where the first elements of Linsingen's corps were arriving. Throughout the day the battle roared with one side gaining here, one side there, a vicious but inconclusive fight that left the battlefield strewn with dead and wounded. To the south the BEF moved forward with maddening slowness despite slight opposition. D'Esperey's advance ran into Kluck's two corps on the left while on the right he sent a corps to help Foch whose Ninth Army was caught by Bülow's wheeling movement. Although this slowed d'Esperey's advance, it also disrupted Bülow's movement, an accomplishment whose importance would grow with the hours.

Joffre's centre formed his most vulnerable area, for on Foch's right only a single cavalry division screened the twelve-mile wide Gap of Mailly, and on Langle's right the five-mile Gap of Revigny separated him from Sarrail. Only very hard fighting elsewhere on this line prevented

The Order of the Day for 6 September, the battle's turning-point, when Joffre seized a chance to exploit a weakness in the German position

BELOW LEFT *General Joseph Jacques Césaire Joffre, the French Commander, whose good generalship went far to winning the Battle of the Marne.* RIGHT *General Karl von Bülow, one of the two army commanders on the German right wing, whose independent action led to the German defeat*

The man considered most responsible for the outbreak of the First World War, Kaiser Wilhelm II – here inspecting naval and army officers at Bruges station

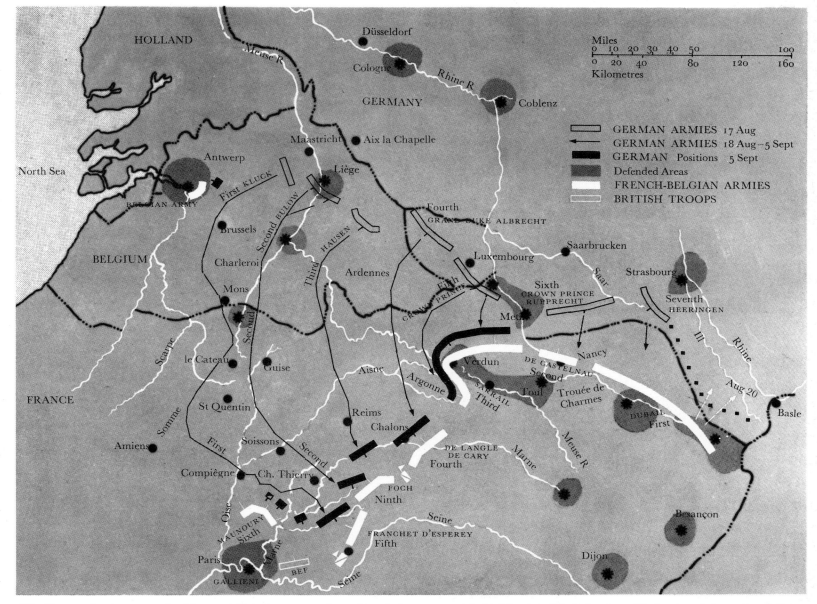

Miles
0 10 20 30 40 50 ... 100
0 20 40 80 120 160
Kilometres

GERMAN ARMIES 17 Aug
GERMAN ARMIES 18 Aug–5 Sept
GERMAN Positions 5 Sept
Defended Areas
FRENCH-BELGIAN ARMIES
BRITISH TROOPS

The Germans' advance to the Marne, which they expected would end the war, was halted by the Allied Armies rallied, after their earlier defeats, by their Commander, Joffre; the subsequent German retreat was the prelude to four years of trench warfare

The No. 1 gun of a battery of French 75-mm field guns has just fired and the barrel is at full recoil; the 75, the most advanced artillery piece of the day, was one of Joffre's greatest assets

French cavalry passing men of the 1st Cameronians in bivouac in a wood after the Battle of the Marne; this campaign saw the end of mobile warfare for nearly four years

Men and horses struggle hard to move a German heavy gun stuck fast in the mud of a rain-sodden field; many guns were abandoned in the retreat to the Aisne

French Chasseurs reconnoitre; the newly invented aeroplane would soon play this role more effectively, and cavalrymen would shortly give up their horses for another new invention, the tank

the enemy from exploiting these gaps that would remain a threat until plugged by two corps marching in from the east.

To Joffre the day gave a slight tactical edge to the enemy, a strategic edge to himself. He was about to be rewarded hugely, if unknowingly, for Bülow, using Kluck's two corps on his right, decided to complete his own wheeling movement on 7 September. But now Kluck, seriously worried about the battle north of the Marne, ordered *these same two corps* to retire ten to twelve miles behind the Petit Morin River. This meant that the gap already existing between Bülow's right and Kluck's left would be considerably widened. To worsen matters, Kluck early on 7 September forced Bülow to send the two corps north.

Here was a decision of paramount importance to the entire battle, a decision made by Kluck and Bülow with no reference to Moltke, and with not even a very clear idea of the enemy's intentions. By transferring these two corps north, the German commanders extended a gap already insufficiently guarded by tired cavalry divisions inadequately supported by Jäger battalions. Coming up from the south, pointed precisely at this gap, was not only the entire British army but, on its right, Conneau's cavalry corps and d'Esperey's Fifth Army.

Joffre correctly recognized this as the key to the battle and in the ensuing days his every moment went to holding in the north, centre, and east while pushing up from the south. It was not easy to hold. Everyone wanted more divisions, troops that Joffre did not possess. When Sarrail complained of his weak left Joffre told him to pull in his right from Verdun, that the bastion could temporarily hold on its own. When Castelnau proposed to withdraw from the Grand Couronné at Nancy, Joffre ordered him to stay where he was. To help Maunoury he brought a division from the east. When it reached Paris on 7 September that city's military governor, the doughty old soldier Galliéni, collected a thousand taxicabs to convoy two regiments to the front – and 'Galliéni's taxicabs' became a household phrase in the history of war.

Joffre was commanding, Moltke was not. Convinced finally that a dangerous gap existed between his right wing armies, Moltke called a staff meeting on 8 September. Someone suggested sending Hentsch to visit the front and determine the true situation. Moltke agreed and gave the staff officer oral orders that are still surrounded in controversy. Allegedly, Moltke told Hentsch that if a retreat were necessary he should influence the movement so as to close the gap between these armies, that is the First Army should withdraw to the line Soisson–Fismes, the Second Army to a line behind the Vesle River.

At Second Army headquarters, Bülow, no longer the victor but a tired old man, told Hentsch:

As a result of all that we have been through and of the hard combats of the last few days, the Second Army has naturally lost a considerable part of its combat value. It is no longer capable of forcing a decisive victory. As a result of the transfer of two army corps from the left to the right wing of the First Army, a gap has been created which forms an immediate danger to the inner wings of both the First and Second Armies. I am informed that enemy columns, brigades or divisions [the BEF and d'Esperey's Fifth Army], are on the march into this breach, and I have no reserves left to attack the enemy or to hold him off . . . It should therefore be considered whether it would not be better, viewing the situation as a whole, to avert the danger by a voluntary concentric retreat of the First and Second Armies.

Their meeting was still going on when a corps commander telephoned to report the loss of Marchais-en-Brie to a French night attack. Montmirail could no longer be defended. Bülow now ordered his right-wing commanders to begin withdrawing to a line some six miles east, which once more widened the gap between the two armies.

Although Hentsch did not again see Bülow, he left the next morning convinced that Bülow was going to retire. At First Army headquarters he explained the bleak situation to Kluck's chief of staff, Kuhl. His pessimism was soon rewarded by the arrival of Bülow's message, '. . . Second Army begins retirement'.

Satisfied that even if Kluck rolled up Maunoury's left he was in no condition to exploit the victory, Hentsch now repeated Moltke's instructions for the First Army to withdraw to the line Soissons–Fismes, where its left would join Bülow's right. Kluck later agreed. In mid-afternoon of 9 September First Army units received orders to break off the action and join a general retreat. Two days later Moltke ordered a retreat along the line.

No one on the French side quite realized what had happened. Not sure of a victory to exploit, Joffre issued conservative orders for 10 September. By that evening he knew the battle was won. After issuing vigorous pursuit orders for the following day he wrote, 'to confirm and exploit this success, the advance must be pursued energetically, leaving the enemy no respite; victory is now in the legs of the infantry'.

The legs of the infantry were either too tired or too confused to conform, nor did low weather followed by high winds and cold, drenching rain help. The pursuit dragged and despite Joffre's best efforts continued to drag. By 12 September Germany's right wing was trickling into prepared defences behind the Aisne. At 1.15 am. on 15 September Joffre telegraphed his commanders: 'It seems as if the enemy is once more going to accept battle in prepared positions north of the Aisne. In consequence it is no longer a question of pursuit but of methodical attack'.

These were momentous words, for they rang down the curtain on a stage of hopes. Act One of the great war

A French soldier stands beside the remains of a German convoy, which demonstrate the effectiveness of the 75-mm gun in action

drama – the campaign of the Marne – was played out. Gone now on either side were any pretensions to swift, crushing victory. Gone now on either side were any illusions of the glory and romance of modern war.

The French won the campaign, but there was little to applaud in the victory. France put her casualties for August and September at 329,000. Britain recorded 12,733. The Germans did not publish their figures, which were appalling. Wounded filled the hospitals in both countries; dead covered the fields of France; tons of matériel and guns had been lost.

Now there would be a pause between the acts, a shifting of human scenery along the stage from the Alps to the English Channel. Then the curtain would rise again. In Act II there would be no more mobile warfare. This time the play would take place in trenches. This time the act would last four years.

ROBERT B. ASPREY

Wounded German prisoners in the hands of French Red Cross; despite Joffre's vigorous pursuit orders, fatigue and bad weather prevented the Allies from following up their victory adequately

1915
Suvla Bay

The landing was successful but, over-cautious, General Hamilton lost a great opportunity, and the Turks, under Liman von Sanders and Mustapha Kemal, easily checked him

THROUGH A QUIRK OF HISTORY Suvla Bay has come to be accounted one of the great and decisive battles of the ages. To question whether this evaluation is merited is but one method by which to view it in perspective.

We know why it is so identified. Prior to Suvla Bay, the Gallipoli campaign, for all of its frustrations, remained a shining hope. Then came what was supposed to be the crowning effort, with the maximum strength of troops available to fulfil an elaborate plan aimed at last to secure an ample and dominant beachhead. But when this mighty effort fell apart among the low ridges just beyond Suvla Bay, the Gallipoli hope expired. Its inevitable sequel was that the campaign to end the First World War quickly by eliminating Turkey and giving a full-armed embrace to Russia was abandoned. Still, within this same thesis, there are reasons to question whether Suvla Bay deserves its high estimation.

Toward the Gallipoli adventure, soldiers and scholars may be of different mind as regards its prospect and promise, but none is indifferent to the argument: Gallipoli has an irresistible allure, it commands the imagination and grips the emotions. More poignant books have been written about it than on the Marne, Gettysburg, or Waterloo. Again we know why. We are struck by *Weltangst* when what is so nobly tried dismally fails.

And we continue to brood over the thought that the Gallipoli campaign was time and again at the threshold of momentous success. That feeling of being almost there persisted from the dark hour when the fleet was turned back from the Narrows. Is there any way of knowing? Two fluke hits killing two capital ships in the first five minutes might have stopped the fleet again in a second try. The same is true of the land battle. We see mainly the glow of opportunity. We discount the vagaries of fortune. There is no way of knowing what might have happened, had what did happen not happened.

But to count Suvla Bay a decisive battle, one would have to assume that Gallipoli failed only by the narrowest of margins, that succeeding, it would have disabled the Central Powers, and that the brightest and best chance was the last great effort. For reasons other than those already outlined, these are challengeable assumptions. They are to be found in the conception of the enterprise at Suvla Bay and the joined fight at Sari Bair, and in the personalities of some of those responsible for their execution. What we know of its consequence is that after Suvla Bay those in England who had been for Gallipoli to the bitter end in the main said: 'That's it!' But if the operation was wrong at its taproots, destined only to be a wasting effort, with no chance of winning through, because of insuperable built-in handicaps, that changes the light wholly. What is wishfully conceived or grotesquely mismanaged has no claim on heaven's help or on redemption due to enemy stupidity.

RIGHT *British horses landed at Suvla; the picture of inactivity represented here was typical of the operation even at its more crucial moments and presaged no other end than the ultimate evacuation*

228

Their defences gradually taking shape, a fatigue party rests; the shipping in the distance is a reminder that the Royal Navy played an exemplary part in this amphibious operation

Suvla Bay has one unique distinction: no other amphibious operation was ever floated from such an inordinately complex and unnecessarily ramified plan. Yet simplicity is a first requirement. Every landing by troops in the face of the enemy is chaotic by nature, rife with disorder, plagued by unanticipated problems. Nothing but first-hand command management may restore balance and drive the flow of force toward the object. Suvla Bay itself was the heart of this over-elaborated undertaking. Troops had to succeed there. The commanding ridges inland had to be secured so that a perimeter with depth of position behind it could be maintained, or the explosion out of Anzac Cove and the demonstrations elsewhere would never deliver the expedition into the Promised Land. But one would never guess that from the plan, which by its very diversification thinned high command attention to the break point. Why the Staff thought that the landing at Suvla Bay, the break-out from Anzac Cove and the attack from Cape Helles all had to be synchronized, or rather, timed to one another over several hours of one night, baffles common understanding. The motive for so doing was to get the Turk off balance. But covering feints in war succeed more rarely than bluffs in draw poker. Further, when one attacks everywhere, the enemy resists everywhere, and his command is constrained to sit back and await positive information about

A 60-pounder gun in action at Cape Helles; on the night of the landing at Suvla the six divisions here were ordered to create a diversion by making a limited attack against the nearby village of Krithia

where the real threat is developing. One negative consequence of the plan's ramification was to overload the man at the top who by nature was unsuited to this terrible burden. General Sir Ian Hamilton's attention should have been riveted on the ridge mass around Tekke Tepe and Anafarta spur inland from Suvla, which if not quickly won and held, doomed his whole enterprise. He might have sustained a defeat of the forces who strove so heroically to gain the high ridges dominating Anzac Cove and still have claimed a shining victory.

It would have needed some other general. The best and bravest have mortal limitations. Fortunate are the few whose weaknesses are never laid bare by the demands of a particular field. Sir Ian was a leader of vast courage, soldierly imagination, and scholarly depths. He is still revered; few other leaders came through the Gallipoli fire unsinged. Aged 62, greatly-travelled, a keen observer of armies over the world, he was a celebrated author. The great commander and the gifted writer are not necessarily two different fellows. But Sir Ian had the habit of essaying faultless prose amid the conduct of operations, instead of paying single-minded attention to the battle. And he was more interested in analysing and recording his own reactions than in writing clear-cut orders based upon fullest possible knowledge of the developing situation. There is never time for both; no proper commander has that much genius, that much energy. Sir Ian used his Staff too little; his personal interventions in the battle tended to come too late. But what is more striking is that, throughout the Gallipoli campaign, the plans of his headquarters were never based on a realistic appreciation of men's powers under stress. By aiming too high on paper, they sowed the seed of battle disarrangement.

So it was at Suvla Bay, and we come now to the situation on the Gallipoli peninsula at the beginning of August 1915, the first anniversary of the start of the war. By then Sir Ian had either on base or in transit 13 divisions or approximately 125,000 men to expand his holdings ashore. Though the expedition stayed chins up, it had now to break out or eventually perish. Its forces hardly more than finger-held the harsh edge of the shore. At Anzac Cove, the beachhead was a shallow crescent about 2,000 yards long, just off the shore, its entrenched perimeter enclosing less than 400 acres. The Turkish line was literally on top of these trenches, much of the way within easy grenade-lob distance from above, which kept the garrison under siege. Any bodily exposure drew instant fire. Yet within this shallow crater- and diggings-pocked warren, 17,000 Anzac soldiers survived by struggle, or died in repelling the immediate Turkish enemy, threefold as numerous. At Cape Helles there were six divisions, or 35,000 soldiers, also just barely ashore. The beachhead on the snout-shaped end of the peninsula had

General Liman von Sanders, the German commander of the thirteen Turkish divisions in the Gallipoli peninsula (photographed here during a later assignment in the war, at Haifa)

General Sir Ian Hamilton, the British Commander-in-Chief, being rowed ashore with his Chief of Staff, General Braithwaite; much of the blame for the failure at Suvla must be apportioned to Hamilton

more than double the area of Anzac Cove but was little less desperately placed. Greater tenacity than was displayed by these men in clinging for months to graveyard ground is not to be found in the annals of war. Both positions were intrinsically hopeless and their succour depended on staging a major diversion which would ease the pressure on them.

Opposite these forces garrisoning the peninsula were 13 Turkish divisions, three containing Anzac Cove, five against Cape Helles, three at Kum Kale, three at Bulair and two south of Gaba Tepe. They were ably directed by the German General, Liman von Sanders. Among the Turkish commanders, Colonel Mustapha Kemal, a star slowly rising, was the catalyst of inspired action. In the vicinity of Suvla Bay there was only a minor troop body,

called the Anafarta Detachment, embodying three rifle battalions, a squadron of cavalry, a labour battalion and 19 artillery pieces. But that is more than enough weapon-power to instil the shock fear which paralyses unseasoned troops.

There were better reasons than the light manning which made Suvla Bay the chosen spot for landing. Besides affording secure anchorage for the invasion fleet, it was to the eye the one fair target on the peninsula: steep-to ridges did not directly command the shore; a salt lake more than one mile wide lay straight inland from the Suvla beaches, but this was known to be dry in summer, and Sir Ian intended that the assault waves should swing round the edges of the parched flat. There was room to deploy at Suvla; the extreme spaciousness of the front

The Turkish defences at Suvla Bay were lightly manned, but the chief reasons for its choice for the landing were that it afforded a secure anchorage for the fleet; that the nearest ridges could not command the shore; and that there was room to deploy

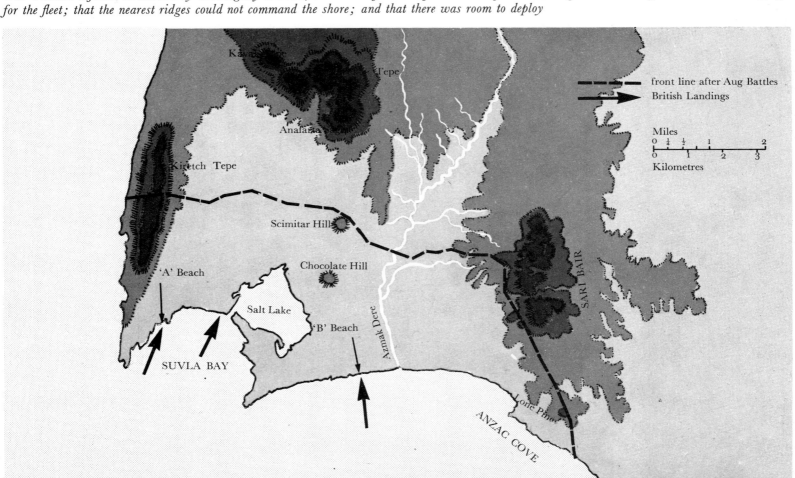

promised to deny the enemy any concentrated target.

Before June ended, planning was well along. On the appointed night the six divisions at Cape Helles were to make a limited attack against the near village of Krithia. The Anzac Force, augmented by one and a half divisions fresh from Britain, were to feint toward the knob called Lone Pine, then under cover of dark, drive for the commanding ridge of Chunuk Bair. The landing at Suvla from small boats was scheduled for one hour later, or 10.30 pm., just in time to beat the rise of a waning moon. By midnight the Allied front would be in full eruption all around.

Wonders were accomplished in the safeguarding of this multiple-chambered surprise. The reinforcement at Anzac Cove – men, animals, and vehicles – had to be smuggled ashore at night by the Navy in stealth and silence, then kept hidden by day during the preceding weeks so that the Turks would not come alert to the build-up. Somehow it was done, though the beautifully contrived deception deserved a better return by the Army for naval prodigiousness. With hardly more trouble, the sea service, given Sir Ian's blessing, might have shifted places between the Anzac Force and the 25,000 untried soldiers shipped from Britain. That would have delivered dependable strength against the decisive target; the attack out of Anzac Cove could have been given more moderate limits, or restrained to await opportunity. (But it failed anyway, and these are not new suggestions.)

To command the corps going in at Suvla Bay, Lieutenant-General Sir Frederick Stopford was sent from England. Old for his 61 years, kindly, complacent, remote from troops, he had never commanded in combat in his life. Kitchener picked him because he was senior; there couldn't have been a sorrier choice. By comparison with him, the ranks had at least youth in their favour. They had never felt fire. Their junior leaders were equally ignorant of the very special tactical problems of the venture – shore organization, preserving identity and control by night.

Where lies their unique complexity? Even the tac schools barely skim the surface and staff colleges ignore it. So to spell it out: command power derives only from recognition of authority; in daylight, the face, manner, gesture, and spoken word convey it. Men see and know

their chief; any good junior leader may memorize the faces and names of 200 men within 40 days. But in that same period he will not be able to identify more than 10 to 12 of them by voice. We all have this low ceiling and there is no help for it.

Yet in the dark all is dependent on voice recognition. Let troops become scrambled and authority evaporates. Leaders hesitate to give orders, not knowing whom they address. Men will not obey, not knowing who speaks. Worse swiftly ensues. For it is starlit truth that men endure battle and achieve unity of action only out of faith and confidence in each other. Where there is no recognition the current dies.

No more wretched scene may be imagined than such a breakdown by night on a strange beach under fire. Each man feels lost in the crowd and his personal panic is exacerbated by the bedlam confusion of the whole milling mass. There is no brake against mounting terror and the physical depletion which this induces. We can pass by the other excessive pressures earlier in the ordeal – the enervating heat during the mount-up, the churning approach by the small boats, the vomiting of frightened men, the awful sweat of anticipating the unknown. Dropped to the nadir of demoralization, the troop body loses its will, its energy, its legs.

This is the fate into which Hamilton, Stopford, Hammersley, and their fellow commanders delivered 25,000 soldiers at Suvla Bay shortly before midnight on 6 August. We have learned much since about these motor forces which was not known at the time of Gallipoli. So in justice to them, it must be said that they probably did not understand what they were attempting (the impossible) or one commanding voice would have cried: 'Stop!' (No, I cannot agree with my great friend, J. F. C. Fuller, that it was 'an ingenious plan'. It was a nightmare. At the decisive point, it ignored the fundamentals.)

I am reminded of Masefield's words as he closed his powerful essay on this whole campaign: 'So courage failed, so strength was chained'. Tragic is the only word for it. As the result of the basic blunder at Suvla in the end everything failed. And it need not have happened. But at least in so far as the Suvla landing is concerned – in trying to give the great effort a future – it was beaten before the start.

Suvla Bay seen from Anzac Cove: the lines of Kiretch Tepe Sirt can be seen in the distance with the Salt Lake in front of it; over 40,000 Allied soldiers fell here during the battles in August 1915 – the price paid for 'five hundred acres of bad grazing ground'

Three wounded Turkish prisoners are brought in; the youth of their escorts draws attention to the fact that of the troops sent in to Suvla 25,000 were untried, and freshly arrived from England

A captured Turkish sniper brought in under guard; he is camouflaged by an ingenious Jack-in-the-Green arrangement of foliage attached to his uniform

There was relatively little Turkish fire against the landing mêlée, but it was enough. Such was the inertia that settled on troops from their night of shock that a score or more of Freybergs and Unwins would have been needed next morning to spark the determining number and boot them along from the shingle and the flats to the not distant high ground. (It only took about forty-seven to generate action out of stagnation at Omaha Beach.) But at the working level there were too few of these stalwarts whose drive is as prodigious as their instinct for doing the right thing. A few brave parties struck out eastward; the mass stayed inert not far from blue water. They were still scrambled, still dazed, worrying about getting properly assembled. And some were probably a little euphoric, what with the coming of day and the withdrawal by the Anafarta Detachment. But there was now a worse drag. They had made shore with only a canteen of water apiece, long since drained dry. Parched men can't swallow salt; saltless, dehydrated, they reel on the edge of sunstroke and cannot march. The whole being becomes flabby. For lack of water the corps could not get going again. Water tankers arrived off shore that afternoon; no means existed for getting the water distributed. The tactical details pale into insignificance beside the appalling fact that, given two days as a gift, the Turks closed first in strength on the near-by ridges above Anafarta Sagar which all along beckoned to this stranded corps. Incredible? Not at all, when we get the picture of Stopford, dawdling on his command ship, then crippled on a stretcher ashore, distant from the wrought confusion, sending back congratulations to Major-General Hammersley for getting his division ashore, seemingly unconcerned about what he does with it after. Here is a general definitely not commanding. But when Hamilton belatedly gets up to him, he neither takes over this sector of the battle nor relieves the man who is toying with it. It's the old chain-of-command hesitation waltz, a gentleman's glide when the going is good, but a burlesque turn when the life of an army is at stake.

Out of Cape Helles the corps commander did not carry out the limited holding attack toward Krithia as ordered. Overreaching, he tried to capture both the village and Achi Baba. So doing, he paid for his failure with the loss of half of the force of 4,000.

There are no braver tales in war than that of the gallant try for break-out by the forces of Anzac Cove. Wrote Ashmead-Bartlett: 'It was launched against positions the like of which had never been attacked before under modern conditions of warfare'. Masefield, Moorehead, and others have paid eloquent tribute to the superhuman valour attending this intricate, over-demanding operation. Deathless courage was abundant. But more so was death. And glorious failure is failure still. The strike for the commanding ridges missed, partly because men lost their way, baffled by the twisted ridge folds in the dark.

There and at Suvla the fighting continued for about a week. When the fire sputtered and died, Anzac Cove was just a little roomier, the sector extending eastward to enclose Lone Pine and northward to tie-in, near Azmak Dere, with the Suvla beachhead which now ringed the salt lake and anchored on Kiretch Tepe. The British clung to Chocolate Hill. The Turks had Scimitar. More than 40,000 Allied soldiers fell during the August battles, the greater number of them cut down in the fighting around Anzac Cove. It was the price paid, as one general put it, 'for five hundred acres of bad grazing ground'.

Stopford was sent home. Hamilton remained, not to muddle through, but to muck it up at least one more time and to be superseded before the evacuation. What followed for the Gallipoli Expedition were months of misery and tedium, hard duty and the grinding gamble to stay alive against odds, all of it anticlimactic. It is infinitely trying on soldiers when the idea settles that though the game is not over there are no longer prizes to be won.

Failure at Suvla made inevitable the ultimate evacuation. Pride postponed it for a little while. Fate, and good staff work, made possible its astonishing success. But even that deliverance could not write a happy ending.

S. L. A. MARSHALL

1917
Caporetto

An Austro-German force, breaking through the Italian left on the Isonzo, inflicted a disastrous defeat on General Cadorna, forcing him to retire to the Piave

THE CRIES OF 'TRENT AND TRIESTE' from the Italian crowds who speeded their army to war with Austria in May 1915 presented it with a task beyond its powers, for antiquated equipment and deficient numbers would confine it to a single choice of objective. The risk of an Austrian descent from Trentino, the most coveted and Italian of the 'unredeemed' provinces, upon the flank of an offensive for Trieste seemed to dictate which that must be; but a drive into the high Alps did not attract the Comando Supremo. Cadorna had long decided to ignore the dangers and allurements of the Trentine salient and to mount his initial offensive on the river Isonzo where, for fifty miles between Carnia and the sea, the mountain frontier relaxed a little and allowed a route eastwards over the barren plateaux of the Carso and the Bainsizza towards Trieste and the distant Russian armies in Galicia.

The terrain is, however, only comparatively easier and the first assault made inconsiderable gains. The nine battles which followed during the next two years achieved little more. In the Sixth Battle, in August 1916, the Italians, returning invigorated by their skill in holding an Austrian thrust from Trent, carried the line beyond Gorizia and on to the Carso, but the next four battles relapsed into painful attrition. The Eleventh Battle in August 1917 was more successful. In eleven days' fighting the Second Army, under the energetic leadership of General Capello, broke across the upper Isonzo and established a line on the Bainsizza, driving the Austrians from the last of their prepared positions and leaving them

the most precarious hold upon this vital abutment. Despite losses now approaching one million, the Italian army was larger than ever before, its leaders believed its spirit was as resolute and a twelfth offensive seemed at last to assure an advance to Trieste. Unfortunately for the Italians, this appreciation was accepted equally readily by the Austrians, who now decided to send for help.

As early as 26 August, while the Eleventh Battle was still in progress, the Austrian Emperor wrote to the Kaiser: 'The experience of our eleventh battle convinces me that the twelfth will be a very hard task for us ... [We] believe that it is best to overcome the difficulties with an offensive'; but he asked for no more than the loan of German artillery and the relief of Austrian by German divisions in Russia. German intervention against Italy, attracting comparable French and British support, might compromise the hope of a separate peace with which Austria comforted herself in her time of troubles. Ludendorff, impatient of any distraction when a winter victory in the East and a spring offensive in the West seemed at last within grasp, was uncooperative. The Austrians' departure would eliminate his tiny strategic reserve which had heavy calls upon its service: the coming reduction of Riga, and thereafter the extinction of Rumania. He withdrew his refusal only after Krafft von Delmensingen, sent

RIGHT *An Austrian gun emplacement in the mountains, where General Krafft von Delmensingen decided to launch a surprise attack on the Italian Second Army, and force the whole line to retreat*

to inspect the Isonzo front, had convinced him of Austria's urgent need and the swift conclusion of the Riga battle (1–5 September) had interposed a breathing space.

Discussions were therefore resumed, but in a familiar spirit of mutual distrust and dislike. Ludendorff was quite unwilling to accommodate his none too steadfast allies in a 'national' offensive and resurrected the plan for a joint offensive which the Austrian staff had suggested as an alternative to Verdun in 1916. He suppressed, however, that part of it which called for a simultaneous descent from Trent and rejected new Austrian proposals, notably those of Major-General Krauss, to fix the objectives in Southern France. Italy, in his view, was a secondary theatre and so inappropriate for a decisive stroke, whether or not the force could be made available. He wanted no more than a limited and largely German offensive to cobble together the Isonzo front, German because he despised Austrian methods and limited because he needed the troops for work elsewhere. The Austrians, who were in no position to bargain, finally acquiesced in the loan of seven divisions for a quick push to the Tagliamento, thirty miles westwards.

In the middle of September these divisions, now formed with eight Austrian into the Fourteenth (German) Army, completed a circuitous assembly in the valleys of the Drave and Save, sixty miles east of Caporetto. All were lavishly provided with artillery, trench mortars and pack transport and the quality of the individual units, many of them mountain regiments, was high (the Austrian mountain divisions were particularly good, whereas the German Alpenkorps – a division – had no recent experience of this sort of ground). Otto von Below had come from the west to command with Krafft, the expert in mountain warfare, as his Chief of Staff. Two of his corps commanders, Stein and Berrer (the victor of Riga) were German, two, Scotti and Krauss (a brilliant soldier), Austrian.

Yet, despite the calibre of the army, Krafft had warned that success in its mission lay 'only just within the borders of possibility'. It would merely waste its force in an orthodox assault to regain ground on the Bainsizza and must pin its hopes upon a strategic surprise elsewhere. Fortunately he had discovered a quiet and weakly garrisoned sector on the upper Isonzo which seemed vulnerable to mountain troops. At Plezzo the river ran across the lines, turning sharply south-west behind the Italians at Saga to emerge again into Austrian territory at Tolmino. Simultaneous thrusts along the valley from the northern and southern bridgeheads, to meet near Caporetto, would bite out fifteen miles of the Italian positions, marooning the defenders on the Monte Nero heights. If the Fourteenth Army could then scale the Stol and Colovrat ridges which formed the western edge of the basin and

General Luigi Cadorna, the Italian Commander-in-Chief, who, after months of painful attrition, had been successful in August 1917 and, until von Below struck, had real hopes of reaching Trieste

RIGHT ABOVE *The front line on 23 October 1917; in the early hours of 24 October von Below's Fourteenth Army delivered a surprise attack on five tired and unready divisions of Capello's Second Army*

RIGHT BELOW *German riflemen and light machine-gunners, reluctantly lent by Ludendorff to the Austrians for a quick push to the Tagliamento – in fact, it reached the Piave, thirty miles beyond*

General von Below, the German Commander of the Fourteenth Army (composed of seven German and eight Austrian divisions), which, in a fortnight, wrung from the Italians the painful gains of two years of war

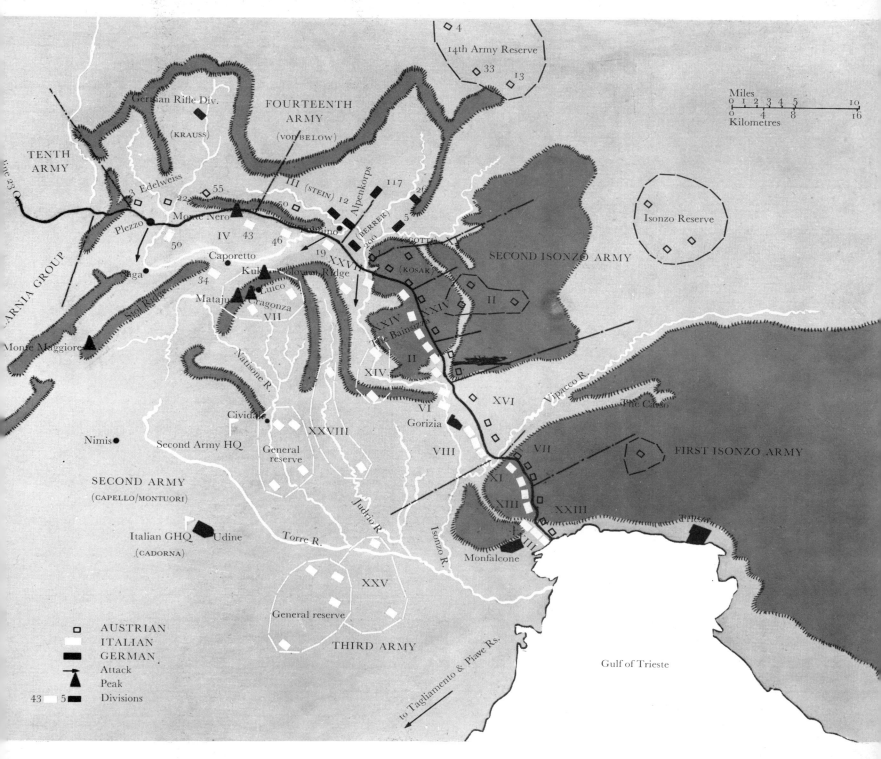

TENTH
ARMY

German Rifle Div.

FOURTEENTH
ARMY
(VON BELOW)

(KRAUSS)

3 Edelweiss

55

22

III (STEIN) 12

Alpenkorps

117

50

26

5

Plezzo

Monte Nero

(BERRER)

200

5

50

IV 43 46

Tolmino

XXVII

KOTTA

SECOND ISONZO ARMY

CARNIA GROUP

Caporetto

19

(KOSAK)

Isonzo Reserve

Aga

34

Stol Ridge

Kuk
Luico
Giovanni Ridge

XXVI
XXIV
Bainsizza

II

Monte Maggiore

Mataju
Cragonza
VII

XIV
II

Natisone R.

XIV
XVI

Vipacco R.

The Carso

VI

Gorizia

Cividale

XXVIII
VIII

VII
FIRST ISONZO ARMY

Nimis
Second Army HQ

General
reserve

XI

Judrio R.

XIII
XXIII

SECOND ARMY
(CAPELLO/MONTUORI)

Isonzo R.

Italian GHQ
Udine
(CADORNA)

Torre R.

Monfalcone

to Tagliamento & Piave Rs.

XXV

General reserve

THIRD ARMY

Gulf of Trieste

14th Army Reserve

4

33

13

Miles
0 1 2 3 4 5   10
0   4   8   16
Kilometres

AUSTRIAN
ITALIAN
GERMAN
Attack
Peak
43 5 Divisions

Austrian infantry off duty outside their fortified position in the mountains near Tolmino; it was from this area that the Fourteenth Army's attack was launched towards Caporetto and beyond in the early hours of the morning of 24 October 1917

Italian troops re-grouping; although their commanders were confident, the mood of the men (losses now approached one million) was uncertain and, wrongly deployed and quite unready for the blow which was about to fall, many panicked and the front collapsed before von Below's attack

place itself across the valleys of two parallel rivers, the Judrio and Natisone, it would take in flank the bulk of the Italian Second Army further south and force the whole line into retreat.

The Italians entrusted security in the area to the normally unavoidable warnings which offensives gave in preparation, but the Germans hoped on this occasion to forestall counter-measures by a new tactical method, recently visited upon the Russians at Riga and shortly to dismay the Allies in the West, which substituted sudden unregistered bombardment and supple infiltration for the lengthy fire-plans and rigid attack schemes of previous practice. The Fourteenth Army spent the next three weeks in surreptitious rehearsal of these new techniques. When ready, it was to move up by night marches to camouflaged positions in the zone of attack. Its presence was meanwhile covered by wireless deception and strong air patrols.

Despite these precautions, rumours of the offensive came early to Cadorna. By 18 September he was already sufficiently apprehensive to cancel the twelfth offensive and start defensive preparations; but he did not suspect German intervention and could not yet usefully redeploy. At the beginning of October, however, it became clear that the enemy was thickening on the Second Army Front and in the weeks following a stream of deserters, mainly men of the national minorities whose arrival always heralded an attack, brought increasingly precise intelligence. On 21 October, two Rumanian officers disclosed in detail plans for an offensive 'from Plezzo to the sea', but he could not believe that anything more than a secondary attack threatened in the mountains. He diverted one brigade northwards but had by then allotted the bulk of reserves to Capello's southern wing and did not change their dispositions. Capello, moreover, resented any dispersal of his offensive concentration on the Bainsizza. He hoped still to reap some profit from the coming battle and argued for holding the troops forward and mounting a spoiling attack. Cadorna was for thinning out the front line and using the artillery to break up the attack as it developed; but despite a show of acquiescence by Capello, who was conveniently if genuinely ill during October, the bulk of his infantry (231 out of 353 battalions) and much of his artillery was in the front line on the eve.

Although they differed over the deployment of their troops, neither commander questioned their spirit. Cadorna, the grim attritionist, was insensitive to such things, Capello felt only his own unshaken resolution. Yet the mood of the men was uncertain. Heavy and prolonged loss and miserable conditions had brought the French army to the verge of dissolution six months before. The Italians had suffered as badly but in an aggressive war which now daily divided the nation more deeply, which

An Austrian 30·5-cm mortar in its firing position; the hurricane bombardment which opened the Battle of Caporetto – itself a new tactic which assured surprise – largely obliterated the Italian first line

the Pope and the Socialists indifferently condemned and which was for most too far from home. If they had never been asked to believe that 'the homeland is in danger', it was unsurprising that for many Treves' cry 'Next winter not another man in the trenches' had about it the ring of good sense. Infirm of purpose and wrongly deployed, they were quite unready for the blow about to fall. Five tired divisions were to suffer a surprise assault by a select fifteen, seven of them German whom the Italians had never met before, who on the night of 22 October arrived unseen at the start line and lay up to await zero hour.

The morning of 24 October was misty with cold rain in the valleys and snow showers on the peaks. At 2 am. a hurricane bombardment opened, at first with gas which the primitive Italian respirators could not filter out and

General Krafft von Delmensingen, the expert in mountain warfare who was appointed Chief of Staff to von Below – here photographed during an earlier command on the Roumanian front, November 1916

then with high explosive. Italian counter-fire was fitful and when the infantry assaulted at 8 am. they found the first line largely obliterated. From Plezzo, Krauss's troops quickly reached Saga and by evening were struggling for a foothold on the Stol. In Stein's sector, the Alpenkorps immediately cleared the foot of the Colovrat and opened the valley to the advance of the 12th Silesians, who met only one Italian platoon on the road to Caporetto and at dusk had reached the valley of the Natisone. Thus by evening, the Fourteenth Army had seized the triangle Plezzo-Saga-Tolmino and were poised to break over the lip. The Berrer and Scotti groups, driving along the southern arm of the Isonzo defile from Tolmino, were threatening large numbers of the Second Army on the Bainsizza who still held on to Monte Globocek but had lost Monte Jessa, the dominating feature of that part of the range. Only Conrad's Tenth Army and Boroevic's Second Isonzo Army on the flanks had failed to make progress.

The Comando Supremo had realized by late afternoon that the situation was grave but had difficulty in obtaining any clear picture of it. Communications were intermittent at best and there was no news of the 43rd and 46th divisions west of the river nor of the 19th at Tolmino. But it still seemed possible to contain the break-in along the Stol and Colovrat and Cadorna ordered the immediate occupation of Monte Maggiore, the hinge of this line, by Alpini from the Carnia Zone. He also arranged for five divisions from army reserve to move up, two to Globocek and three to Nimis, to hold the heads of the Judrio and Natisone and called four divisions from Third Army and Trent which would take longer to arrive. Less optimistically, he sketched in two alternative and wider lines swinging back from Maggiore towards the plains and sent orders that the Tagliamento be prepared for defence.

On the morning of the 25th, the true nature of the

A shattered gun in its mountain emplacement after the tide of war has swept over it; the Italians lost 3,000 guns, as well as 265,000 men (and 40,000 casualties besides)

King Victor Emmanuel III (right) watches infantry marching to the front; in the long term this defeat brought more benefit to Italy than the victory to their opponents

crisis became more apparent. As the reinforcements from army reserve moved forward they found progress impeded by parties of their own troops already in retreat and, occasionally, by enemy ambush. There had clearly been a panic in the first positions and the enemy had infiltrated deep behind the lines. The northern and southern thrusts had made contact behind Monte Nero, the valleys had been lost and the remaining points of resistance were isolated on the heights, unable to influence the course of events below. At noon, before his final retirement sick, Capello arrived at Cadorna's headquarters to advise withdrawal, at least to the Torre and perhaps to the Tagliamento. Cadorna agreed but then hesitated and later accepted the opinion of Montuori, Capello's successor, that resistance might be prolonged. Enemy progress seemed slower and the orders for retreat, although prepared, were not issued. Neither commander grasped that the enemy were coming on along the crests,

particularly behind the northern flank of Third Army, south of Tolmino. The passes through the Colovrat were also under fierce attack by units of the Alpenkorps. One of these, a three-company group of the Württemberg Mountain Battalion led by Erwin Rommel, had predictably taken the lead and by evening on 25 October had seized the Kuk, opened the Luico pass and bluffed into surrender after a short fight 2,000 men of the 4th Bersaglieri Brigade, who were advancing to reinforce. During the night, Krauss's 22nd Division took the Stol and Rommel drove his group to the summit of Monte Cragonza, the key to the Italian third position along the northern arm of the Colovrat, capturing a further 1,600 men. The Fourteenth Army's haul of prisoners now amounted to some 30,000, mainly men found dazed in the first position or surrounded later, but confusion and despair were also infecting the oncoming reserves. During the third day, 26 October, Austro-German progress con-

Italian trenches on the Piave; in the event of a retreat, Cadorna ordered the Tagliamento (the Fourteenth Army's original objective) to be prepared for defence – but, when the retreat was a reality, it could not be brought to a halt before the Piave

A stranded dinosaur fails to arouse the interest of an old man, some children and a horse in Zampichia – an Italian 30·5-cm gun found abandoned by the advancing Fourteenth Army

Alpenstocks identify these men being ferried across the Isonzo near Canziano as mountain troops, to whom von Below gave a vital role (note the thorough destruction of the bridges)

tinued. Krauss, brushing aside resistance, passed his divisions over the barrier of the Stol, Rommel secured the Matajur, the last objective on the Colovrat, and the 200th and 117th Divisions advanced to within five miles of Cividale, Second Army Headquarters. Further south, Berrer and Scotti took Monte Globocek and invested Monte Corada, the Second Isonzo Army penetrated to the Italian second position on the Bainsizza and the First Isonzo Army reported that the Italian Third Army was breaking contact on the Carso. The Isonzo front was now in ruins but it was not until midnight that Cadorna, who had spent the day in impotent attendance upon garbled scraps of information which told only of further enemy success and an epidemic of surrender, recognized the inevitable. News then came of the fall of Monte Maggiore and at 2.30 am. on 27 October the orders for retreat went out.

It had already been in progress for some time. Some units clung on without hope of relief, the Alpini on Monte Nero dying almost to a man, and others held together and fought bitterly in the rearguard but the bulk of the Second Army poured down without check to the plains. The Carnia Group and the Third Army, by extending their flanks, constricted the pursuit, which was itself hindered by confusion, lack of transport and Austro-German disputes. But the surprise at Caporetto had done its work and neither the Torre nor the Tagliamento provided a refuge. Krauss, determined to evade Ludendorff's guillotine, found a footing at Cornino on 5 November and the Italians were driven back again. It was not until the line of the Piave was reached on 7 November, as new divisions of recruits were hurried to the front and Allied divisions arrived from France, that the Italian army came to rest. During its ordeal, it had suffered 40,000 casualties, lost 265,000 men, 3,000 guns and much matériel to the enemy and seen the painful gains of two years of war swallowed up in a few days.

Yet, by a curious reversal, the experience of Caporetto served the Allies better than their enemies. While it led Ludendorff still further away on his vain pursuit of tactical means to victory and drew Austria into a fifth and fatally injurious year of war, it brought to the Italians a firm sense of national unity and purpose and to the Allied leaders, meeting at Rapallo in the aftermath of defeat, the opportunity to found the international command which their generals had so long and unwisely resisted.

JOHN KEEGAN

Cadorna's message to the troops after the catastrophe, calling on them to rally and remember the enthusiasm of May 1915, when crowds sped the army to war with Austria with cries of 'Trent and Trieste' – in fact Caporetto did restore Italian national unity and purpose

UN TELEGRAMMA

" Siamo in un'ora decisiva. Ancora una volta ripeto: " *Ogni viltà convien che qui sia morta* ". Non solo sulla prima linea ogni debolezza sarebbe tradimento: si armi ciascuno, soldato o cittadino, della suprema volontà di vincere e avremo la vittoria. Si fondano tutte le classi e, tutti i partiti che sinceramente amano la Patria in un solo impeto di orgoglio e di fede per ripetere come nelle giornate memorabili del maggio 1915 al nemico CHE ASCOLTA IN AGGUATO: **L'Italia non conosce che la via dell'onore!**

1940
The Crossing
of the Meuse

*Despite the respite of the 'phoney war', France and England were unprepared for the German assault:
its success led swiftly to the fall of France*

THE GERMAN ATTACK in the West, which had been postponed twenty-nine times since October 1939, began on the morning of 10 May 1940. The plan had been shaped by General Halder, Chief of the Army General Staff, in conformity with ideas suggested by Hitler and Lieutenant-General von Manstein. This plan, in contrast to the Schlieffen plan of 1914, placed the centre of gravity of the forthcoming German attack not on the northern, right wing, but much further south. As the number of divisions on each side was approximately equal the German thrust could be concentrated on the weakest point in the Allied line.

The German invasion of Belgium and Holland was intended to compel the Allied Supreme Command to throw the British Expeditionary Force and First and Seventh French Army hastily into Belgium. Once this had occurred, the main German attack would be directed through the Ardennes towards the Channel coast, in order to drive a wedge between the main French Army and the British, and to create a large cauldron in the area of Belgium and northern France.

The plan assigned the larger part of the German armoured forces to Army Group A (Colonel-General von Rundstedt). In the north stood Army Group B (Colonel-General von Bock), with only two armoured divisions

LEFT *Motorcyclists of 7th Armoured Division in Dinant; with the bridges destroyed, the Germans crossed the Meuse in rubber dinghies, (at first tanks crossed only by night and one by one)*

(3rd and 4th) of XVI Corps under General Hoepner, besides its infantry forces. Army Group C (Colonel-General Ritter von Leeb) in the south consisted only of infantry formations and was not to attack before 14 June.

Army Group A was reinforced by an Armoured Group under General von Kleist. It was the first massive armoured formation in the history of warfare, and consisted of XIX Corps (General Guderian), XXXXI Corps (General Reinhardt) and XIV Corps (General von Wietersheim). In these three Corps there were five armoured divisions and three mechanized infantry divisions, and they were placed under the command of Twelfth Army. On the right wing of this force two more armoured divisions were at the disposal of Fourth Army. While the 3,142 tanks of the Allies were dispersed along the whole front, the 2,580 German tanks entered the battle as a concentrated force.

The main German thrust was directed against Ninth French Army of General Corap. The condition of this Army, revealed by a parade in November 1939, prompted the Commander of II British Corps, Lieutenant-General Sir Alan Brooke, to make some unflattering remarks about it in his diary. Its main elements had taken up position within and behind the hills of the Ardennes, a part of the front which the French High Command assumed to be fairly safe. The crossing of the Ardennes by armoured formations was regarded as a technical impossibility, although Captain Liddell Hart had drawn attention to its feasibility before the outbreak of war, but his

LEFT *Major-General Erwin Rommel, the Commander of the 7th Armoured Division who, as his future opponents with hindsight would have expected, played a conspicuously successful part in the Meuse operation.* CENTRE *General Guderian, one of the greatest German armoured commanders of the war, who commanded XIX Corps, which was given the task of crossing the Meuse at Sedan.* RIGHT *General von Kleist, the Commander of the massive armoured formation (XIX, XXXXI and XIV Corps) which gave to Army Group A a concentrated force of over 2,000 tanks*

premonitions had been attributed to an excitable imagination. The French Command was therefore utterly bewildered when the full extent of the danger became evident on 14 May.

In preparation for the operations of the armoured formations under von Kleist, the two armoured divisions of Fourth Army (Colonel-General von Kluge), which were integrated in XV Corps (General Hoth), carried out a diversionary attack across the northern part of the Ardennes in the direction of Dinant. Still further to the north, the fortress of Eben Emael had to be rendered harmless in order to allow the German troops to enter Belgium without hindrance. The German High Command hoped that the battle would develop into mobile warfare instead of becoming bogged down in trench warfare. In these circumstances, the necessity for speed of action was paramount.

For the capture of Eben Emael, the cornerstone of the Franco-Belgian lines of fortification on the eastern frontiers of both countries, a special task force, named 'Assault Group Koch', had been created in November 1939. This force was given the task of landing in gliders on top of the fortress, in order to avoid betraying their approach by the noise of engines. The destruction of armoured cupolas with hollow charges had previously been practised on old fortifications in Czechoslovakia. Nine transport gliders succeeded in landing on top of the fortress at about 5.30 am. on 10 May. The troops first

attacked the infantry weapons and armoured cupolas which could rake the fortress area. The anti-aircraft positions were captured after a short struggle, but the battle for Hut 25 required harder fighting. In ten minutes fifty-five soldiers from the gliders had overcome nine works. Seven steel turrets had been blown up and nine 7·5 cm guns in three casemates destroyed. Two other groups of the assault force were assigned to capture what were in fact dummy positions. This was the only hitch in the whole operation.

It became obvious that work 24 could not be captured and a charge of dynamite was placed in its two-barrelled gun and exploded. The final success of the assault was in large part due to the fact that the garrison, confined in their holes like mice, did not receive any effective help from outside to dispose of the cats waiting in front of their holes. The explosions in the ventilation plant and the destruction of the entire artillery led to panic among the garrison and the few counter-attacks from outside had no effect upon the situation. During the morning of 11 May Lieutenant Witzig (today a Lieutenant-Colonel in the German Federal Army) was relieved and, at about 12 noon, the fortress of Eben Emael capitulated, after its Belgian commander had committed suicide. The casualties in Assault Group Koch were six dead and nineteen wounded, while the Belgians lost about one hundred men. The remaining 1,100 were taken prisoner. Since the bridges over the River Meuse at Vroenhoven and Veld-

Machine-gunner's eye view from a German bomber attacking an Allied column; during this operation the Luftwaffe's superiority was a vital element in the build-up of the ground forces

Hitler decorates three Eben Emael heroes; the capture of this fort was a brilliant conception, faultlessly executed

wezelt also fell into German hands without damage, the German troops were able to enter Belgium with great speed.

On the following day, 12 May 1940, a spearhead of 7th Armoured Division reached the River Meuse at Dinant in pursuit of the French 1st and 7th Cavalry Divisions. The French succeeded in blowing up the bridges at Dinant and Houx before the very eyes of the German troops, who were therefore obliged to resort to rubber dinghies to effect a crossing.

By the morning of 13 May 78th Artillery Regiment had taken up positions to support the infantry forces of 7th Armoured Division, 6th and 7th Armoured Grenadier Regiments and 7th Motorcycle Battalion. Men of this Motorcycle Battalion had in the meantime discovered an undamaged weir, which they used for crossing the river in small groups during the night. However, their numbers were insufficient for a large bridgehead on the further

Some of the 1,100 prisoners taken at Eben Emael; landed by glider on top of the fortress, the special task force, having destroyed the armoured cupolas, had the garrison at their mercy

The German-Luxembourg frontier in the early hours of the morning of 10 May 1940, when the much-postponed attack in the West was finally launched; these flimsy barricades were no obstacle

When the bridges were destroyed, the Germans crossed stretches of water – here a Dutch canal – by rubber dinghies; these are so close together as to suggest that artillery attack was not expected

The obstacles removed, German tanks advance through Sedan; this was the objective of Guderian's XIX Corps, to whose 1st and 10th Armoured Divisions it fell, with little resistance, on 12 May

bank. The first attempts to cross the river in daylight had failed when the divisional Commander, Major-General Rommel, whose name was not yet well known, arrived at the front line. He personally took over command of 7th Grenadier Regiment. Covered by the fire of a handful of tanks, a larger bridgehead was now built up. The other Armoured Grenadier Regiment had meanwhile also succeeded in crossing the river further downstream. The larger part of 42nd Anti-tank Battalion was immediately ferried across. This move was of particular importance since it was only possible to take the tanks across the river one by one during the night.

On 14 May the tanks, about thirty in number, which had so far been ferried across the west bank of the Meuse, began the attack under the command of Colonel Rothenburg. Rommel took part in the attack, but the tank in which he was mounted was soon hit. He was lightly wounded in the face and the tank had to be abandoned. A further attack during the evening secured a launching base for an advance on 15 May which was designed to enlarge the bridgehead to a very considerable extent.

Like most German commanders of armoured troops, Rommel again chose to lead his men from the front, leaving his G-3, Major Heidkaemper, with the divisional staff further behind. After a short fight near Flavion, 25th Tank Regiment pushed forward towards Philippeville and the garrison was quickly forced to surrender. As the Germans nowhere encountered any strong resistance, 7th Armoured Division was able to extend the breakthrough to a depth of twenty miles. The speed of their attack had prevented 1st French Armoured Division from mounting a counter-attack and had already outflanked the new defence positions of Ninth French Army.

By the evening of 12 May, 1st and 10th Armoured Divisions of XIX Corps had already reached the River Meuse at Sedan, and the French, offering hardly any resistance, had been pushed out of the town. X French Corps, under General Grandsard, which had been allocated to this front, consisted of two divisions (55th and 71st), neither of them in the best fighting trim, and a good, active infantry division (3rd North African). Grandsard had not expected an attack, believing that the German artillery was not sufficiently strong to provide the necessary cover. In fact, a large number of the German guns were stuck in the congested streets, but the Luftwaffe were able to silence the French artillery. This greatly assisted the soldiers of 1st Armoured Grenadier Regiment. Shortly before, they had been obliged to make for cover, but were now able to cross the river with remarkable speed in full view of the French dugouts. When the sun set, the strategically important heights on the far bank of the river had been captured, and the regimental commander, Lieutenant-Colonel Balck, could greet

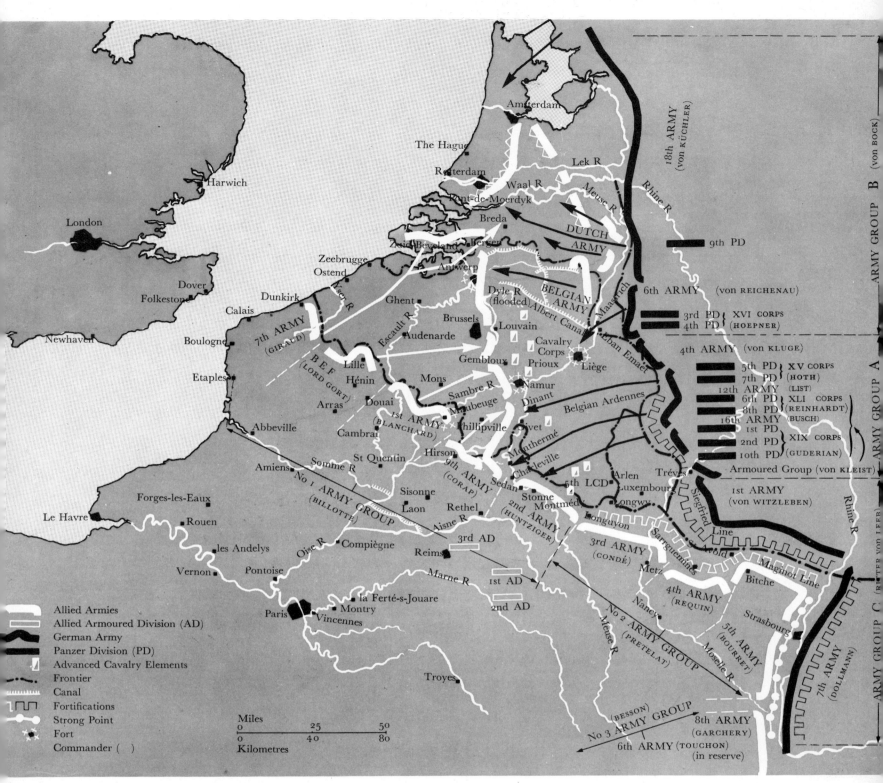

The opening of the German offensive in the West, 10–12 May 1940: Hitler's plan was first to encircle the Allied forces in Belgium, then to move south to destroy the remainder (note the heavy concentration of armour in the central sector)

General Guderian, who had hastened to the front, with his own words: 'Boat trips on the Meuse are forbidden!'. It had all gone so easily. Of course, if the French counterattack had been mounted more quickly, the situation could have become critical. 1st Armoured Grenadier Regiment had had to face the enemy at the start without the support of tanks. When a French armoured brigade began its attack on 14 May, the first tanks and 37th Anti-tank Battalion had already gained the far bank of the river. The tank battle at Bulson ended in favour of the German 1st Armoured Division. The natural obstacle of the valley of the Meuse and the strong fortifications had been surmounted so rapidly that it appeared to General Guderian almost miraculous.

German artillery moves forward in close support of the armoured divisions, the guns too being towed by armoured tracked vehicles; French stupe-faction at the nature of the German threat was increased by their assumption that the Ardennes were impassable to armour

Their divisional commander, Rommel, inspects (and photographs) men of the 7th Armoured Division bridging the river Ourthe near Beffe in the Ardennes, a shallow river, but the only water-crossing of consequence they encountered between the German frontier and the Meuse

On the following day the bridgehead was enlarged and consolidated by the capture of the surrounding heights at Stonne, so that the infantry divisions, which followed up quickly, could pour through the gap which the tanks had torn in the French centre near Sedan.

If von Kleist's armoured formation is regarded as a huge dragon, its head (XIX Corps) lay at the beginning of the campaign on the west German frontier, and its tail (XIV Corps) across the Rhine in the area bounded by Herborn-Butzbach-Friedberg. The middle of its body was formed by XXXXI Corps under General Reinhardt. It was Reinhardt's hard lot first to march on overcrowded roads – what a boon that the superiority of the Luftwaffe was assured! – behind Guderian's Corps, and afterwards to take up his position on the right of the Corps for the simultaneous attack at Monthermé, while Guderian was about to cross the Meuse at Sedan. Only 6th Armoured Division was available for this attack, since the other two divisions of the Corps remained immobile in the congested streets.

During the evening of 13 May, 4th Armoured Grenadier Regiment and parts of 57th Armoured Reconnaissance Regiment succeeded in crossing the river in rubber boats. Here, too, the bridge had been blown up, but so inadequately that it was possible to erect a temporary gangway over its ruins. The commander of 42nd French Colonial Half-Brigade, Lieutenant-Colonel Pinsun, who was taken prisoner, declared at his interrogation that the cold weather had rendered some of the fuses useless.

The terrain at Monthermé, with its deep-set river valley skirting a mountain, resembled the landscape of the River Moselle – a factor which, of course, favoured the defence. Because the troops which had so far crossed the river were too weak in numbers, 1st Battalion of 4th Armoured Grenadier Regiment, which arrived on 14 May, was immediately sent across the Meuse. Corps Headquarters ordered the breakthrough to be attempted during the afternoon of this same day. All the protests of the commander of 4th Armoured Grenadier Regiment, Colonel von Ravenstein, and of Major-General Kempf were in vain. In fact, the attack came to a halt, but it widened the bridgehead considerably, and the tanks were able to cross during the night. The guns of 76th Artillery Regiment had destroyed the most important French communication centre, cut a number of telephone wires which were fixed on poles high in the air and had killed the sector commander together with several of his staff. The normal transmission of orders could not be restored until the following morning.

With the help of reinforcements which had arrived during the night, a decisive breakthrough was achieved through the fortified line of Bois de Roma on 15 May. When the Grenadiers of 4th Regiment reached the road

to Charleville, their regimental commander loudly called: 'Boys, that was the last line of bunkers! We're through!' In the evening the first elements of 6th Armoured Division stood at Montcornet, the furthest point reached by any German troops at that stage. For Major-General Kempf the advance of more than forty miles on a single day marked the climax of his armoured career.

To sum up the results of the fighting between 12 and 15 May: the French front had been unhinged at four important points. For von Kleist's armoured formation the way to the Channel lay open. 2nd Armoured Division reached the mouth of the River Somme on 20 May, and on 19 May General Giraud, the new commander of the defeated French Ninth Army and his staff were taken prisoner by 6th Armoured Division. The Armies of the Allies had been split in two.

All the preliminary conditions for the knockout blow of Operation Sickle had been fulfilled. But when Hitler and von Rundstedt, who were worried about the exposed southern flank of Army Group A, and were planning the second half of the campaign, called a halt to the advance of the armoured divisions on 24 May, the British Navy was able to rescue the larger part of the British Expeditionary Force.

JOACHIM RÖSELER

The map Rommel drew showing how, on 16–17 May, he exploited his initial success; it brings out the extraordinary depth, narrowness, and audacity of his thrust – from Cerfontaine to Le Cateau

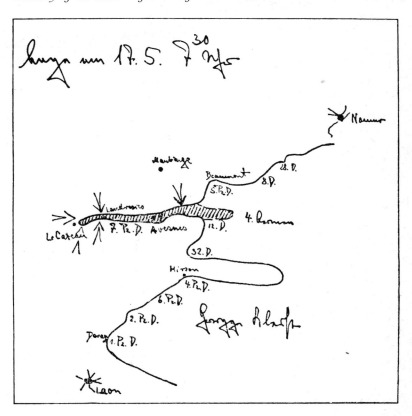

1942
Stalingrad

The heroic Russian defence of this city against the Germans, which cost both sides appalling casualties, was one of the turning points in the Second World War

ALTHOUGH, IN THE EARLY MONTHS of 1942, the German armies had been forced back at many points along their 1,200-mile front in Russia, Hitler believed that his adversaries had expended the bulk of their reserves in this relentless, hammering effort to regain lost ground. 'The Russians are finished', he told his Chief of Staff. 'In four weeks' time they will collapse.' That summer Germany and her allies had over 3,000,000 fighting troops available in the east; and the time seemed ripe to destroy what remained of the Soviet defence potential. Once Russian forces west of the Don had been defeated, and the Crimea neutralized, Hitler aimed to secure vital oil supplies in the Caucasus and also to capture Stalingrad, thereby closing the Volga and protecting the left flank of the Causasian offensive. Despite contrary advice and the General Staff's strong opposition to these over-extended objectives, the Führer ordered simultaneous attacks against Stalingrad by Army Group B, which would then send troops down the Volga to Astrakhan, and by Army Group A far southeast between the Black Sea and Caspian. Four Rumanian, Italian, and Hungarian armies would follow on a broad front.

The Russians struck first, on 12 May near Kharkov, and were repulsed with heavy loss; but, by delaying

Hitler's offensive for a month, they gained a long-term advantage. When the Germans did advance, their progress was at first slower than anticipated, Sevastopol resisting siege for a month; but once beyond the Don, Army Group A, under Field-Marshal von Kleist, advanced with great momentum and reached Maikop on 9 August, only to find the oilfields wrecked. An advance along the Black Sea coast met with little success, and the German spearhead got no further than the Caucasian foothills. Eventually the intervention of winter and the arrival of fresh Russian soldiers brought Kleist's columns to a halt.

Further north, on Army Group B's front, the Fourth Panzer Army fought its way over the Don and reached the heights of Kotelnikovo, seventy miles south of Stalingrad. On 23 August the Sixth Army advanced, under the command of General Friedrich Paulus, a fifty-two-year-old Hessian who had been its Chief of Staff in France in 1940 and afterwards Quartermaster-General of the Army Staff. Tall, thin, quiet-spoken, he was later described by General Guderian as 'the finest type of brilliantly clever, conscientious, hard-working, original and talented General Staff Officer'. Paulus's formations moved across the open, almost treeless steppe between the Don and the Volga, encountering little resistance until they sighted the skyscrapers and factory chimneys of Stalingrad.

For three days the Luftwaffe systematically bombed the city, which stretched in a narrow band for some twenty miles along the western river bank. Incendiaries

LEFT *Russian soldiers fight desperately to deny the Germans even the shells of buildings, practically all that remains standing in Stalingrad after incessant bombing and shelling*

General Andrei Yeremenko (left), who was appointed to command the Stalingrad Front, consisting of the Fifty-seventh, Sixty-second and Sixty-fourth Armies, and General Rokossovsky (right), the commander of the Sixty-fifth Army, which formed the northern pincer in the encirclement of the German Sixth Army

The party representative and political commissar on General Yeremenko's three-man military council, Nikita Krushchev, talking to fresh re-inforcements coming into Stalingrad

soon had the many wooden houses ablaze; dockyards were set on fire; burning oil storage tanks belched out choking black smoke. Of the population of half a million, many of whom worked in factories, foundries and ship-building yards, tens of thousands were rendered home-less, while thousands were killed or injured. And when the Soviet authorities decided to evacuate the women and children and old men, these refugees were bombed and machine-gunned on the two-mile river crossing. When the Germans dropped mines in the Volga, hoping to close the river and so strangle Stalingrad, men of the naviga-tion service hunted and destroyed the mines.

The Russians formed a Stalingrad Front under General Andrei Yeremenko, with the Fifty-seventh, Sixty-second and Sixty-fourth Armies, of which the second was led by Vasily Zhukov, a tough, thickset, loud-laughing peasant's son who had worked as an apprentice in an armaments factory before joining the Red Army in 1918. Thereafter he had seen service in Spain and Finland and in the de-fence of Russia. A civil defence council was set up, and Yeremenko's three-man military council was fortunate to have as party representative and political commissar the courageous and extremely energetic Nikita Khrush-chev, then aged forty-eight. Their principal aim was to prevent the Germans reaching and crossing the Volga, and with this latter threat in mind Yeremenko even had his engineers destroy a pontoon bridge which they had just built in record time.

The Germans made extensive gains on 14 September and captured the dominant Mamaiev Hill, continued possession of which would probably have enabled them to shell river traffic to a standstill. But that night General Rodimtsev's Guards Division crossed the Volga under fierce shellfire, after making several forced marches, and next day recaptured the vital feature and evicted the enemy from the precipitous river bank.

Desperate fighting continued, street by street, house by house, even room by room – a hand-to-hand struggle for every square, canal, factory, cellar, gutted building

and ruined wall. Soviet soldiers used sewers to get behind their opponents till girders were rammed down manholes to block their route. At fearful cost the Germans ad-vanced about a thousand yards towards the Volga, re-gaining Mamaiev Hill and seizing the great Tractor Plant. Some 45,000 Russians, inspired by the order: 'Stalingrad will be saved by you or wiped out with you', were left clinging to four separate and narrow bridge-heads on the river. That the Sixth Army did its utmost to capture the rest of the city is shown by the fact that General Gurtiev's Siberian Division defending the Red October Factory was subjected to over 100 assaults in the course of a month, and on one day alone German tanks tried 23 times to oust the tenacious defenders. Suc-cess was near; yet, whereas the Russians constantly brought up new forces, only a trickle of reinforcements reached the German units. Hitler went so far as to an-nounce that Stalingrad was virtually in German hands: only a few pockets held out, and these had not yet been destroyed because he wished to avoid a second Verdun, preferring to attack with small assault groups. The troops involved were not amused. As for the Russians, they hung on doggedly, awaiting their turn.

Indeed, for days past their commanders had been pre-paring a two-sided concentric blow aimed at encircling the Sixth Army. On 19 November Rokossovsky's Sixty-fifth Soviet Army broke out of its Don bridgehead by Kremenskaya, eighty miles north-west of Stalingrad, and attacked south across the great loop of the river towards the weak Third Rumanian Army guarding Paulus's left flank. At the same time another powerful Russian force swept out of the Beketonskaya bridgehead six miles south of the city against the Fourth Rumanian Army. Here too they broke through and headed north-west for the Don at Kalatsch, where the two Soviet armoured spearheads met and, thanks to a ruse, captured intact the bridge on which the Germans relied for supplies.

As a result of this great pincer movement, at least 230,000 German and Rumanian troops, a fighter wing

In a city with a population of half a million, tens of thousands of whom were made homeless, and thousands killed or injured, the soldiers fight doggedly on amongst the rubble

The Germans did their utmost to capture the whole of Stalingrad, but 45,000 Russians, like these four, held out with grim determination, and would not let them pass

A German machine-gun crew (left) searches for a new target in the ruins of Stalingrad. German soldiers find shelter in a bomb crater (right) – a photograph published in a Berlin newspaper on 1 October 1942

German soldiers inspect the useless ruins of a factory in Stalingrad, once vital to Soviet industry, destroyed by the Russians before they were forced to relinquish it

The tide turns and, with a potent ally in the Russian winter which Napoleon before had confronted to his cost, the Red Army advances (a still from a Russian film)

View from a German tank patrolling a ruined street in Stalingrad; no traffic was to pass along the tram-lines in this great industrial city for many months to come

Well and warmly clad in white camouflage clothing, specially trained Russian ski-troops advance to the front line for a night assault on the German communications far behind the front line

A German tank hits a mine during General von Manstein's attempts to bring rescue to the beleaguered German Sixth Army inside 'Fortress Stalingrad'

A Russian trench mortar crew, coming under heavy fire, advances to take up a new position on the Stalingrad front

and a Croat regiment were trapped between the Don and the Volga in a pocket measuring thirty miles across and twenty-five from north to south.

When Hitler learnt of the encirclement and heard his Chief of Staff, Colonel-General Kurt Zeitzler, propose that the Sixth Army be allowed to fight its way out to the west, he banged his fist on the table and twice shouted: '*Ich bleibe an der Wolga*'. On 22 November he designated Stalingrad as a Fortress which must be held – a decision deeply influenced by Göring's unwarranted assurance that his Luftwaffe could supply the huge garrison with the minimum requirements of food, fuel and ammunition – 500 tons a day.

It was widely believed, not least by the commander of Army Group B, Freiherr von Weichs, that to supply over twenty divisions by air was not feasible, and it will be seen that his gloomy but realistic appraisal proved correct. Weichs supported a break-out plan for the Sixth Army, and by 24 November Paulus had for this purpose assembled 130 tanks and 17,000 troops as a first wave, with a second of 40,000 men. When he informed Hitler that the Army would inevitably be destroyed unless the attacking Russians were themselves attacked at once, the Führer refused. That same day Weichs took the grave personal risk of ordering Paulus to break out, but Hitler, who had his own liaison officer and signals section installed at Sixth Army Headquarters, by-passed Army Group B and forbade a break-out, promising instead supplies and eventual relief.

He next summoned General Erich von Manstein, whose army had captured Sevastopol in June, and ordered him to take command of the newly created Army Group Don, comprising the Sixth Army, the Fourth Panzer Army, and the two Rumanian armies. If anyone could restore the perilous situation, it was the iron-nerved, blunt, but brilliant Manstein.

For Operation *Winterblitz* he planned to cut from south to north a corridor through which the Sixth Army could be replenished and thus enabled to hold out longer. This much Hitler had agreed to; but it was also in Manstein's mind to have Paulus push southwards to support the rescue bid, and then, having restored the Sixth Army's mobility with stocks of fuel, he would fetch the troops out from the 'cauldron'. On past form the Führer seemed unlikely to consent to such an evacuation.

On 12 December General Hoth's reinforced Fourth Panzer Army struck north from Kotelnikovo and at once met fierce opposition from Vatutin's tanks and infantry. It fought forward across the Aksay river and reached the Myshkova on the 19th after a tremendous tank battle for the village of Werchne Kumskij. Hoth's spearhead was now only thirty miles from the southern edge of the Stalingrad front, and the beleaguered troops, hearing distant gunfire, allowed their hopes of salvation to rise; but German strength was dwindling fast, while the Russians were able to replace their losses, especially in tanks.

Manstein now ordered Paulus to break out. Under pressure Hitler agreed to this on 21 December, but at

Russian infantry, with close artillery support, advances across open country near Stalingrad

The decisive turning-point in the Battle of Stalingrad came in mid-November 1942, when Soviet forces north-west and south of Stalingrad broke out of their bridgeheads, met at Kalatsch (thus cutting the German supply line), and completed the encirclement of 230,000 German and Rumanian troops

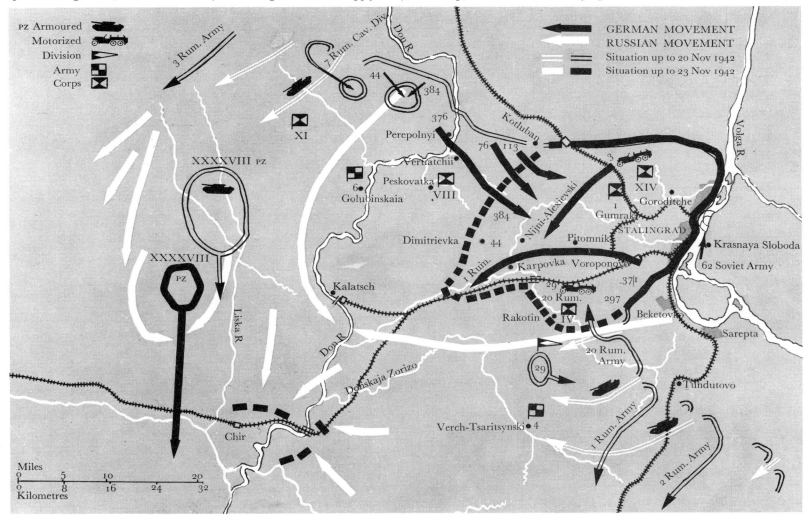

once vitiated the whole plan by insisting that the Sixth Army must simultaneously continue to hold its existing fronts, already hard pressed. To do both was impossible. Though Paulus collected his sixty remaining tanks and hundreds of lorries, he found that his armour had enough fuel for at most twenty miles – and the gap was thirty. What if Hoth failed to make further progress; or if his own troops became stuck half way? Of course the risks were immense, but not to use this slender last chance meant resigning all hope of saving the trapped army. Paulus was in two minds, unless Manstein could extract from Hitler permission for a total breakout: by 22 December he had not yet succeeded. With Paulus the fuel shortage counted; so did the influential views of his Chief of Staff; also his undue trust in promises of improved air supply, his inability, from within the 'cauldron', to assess the overall picture along the southern front; above all his rigid sense of duty and obedience. The testimonies of Manstein and Paulus conflict on this breakout issue, the one implying that another commander might have chosen to present Hitler with a *fait accompli* and risk the consequences, the other feeling that independent action might lead to an even greater catastrophe.

Meanwhile a new and admirably timed Soviet offensive, having smashed through the Italian Eighth Army on the middle Don and advanced south towards Millerovo and Tatsinskaya despite heavy fighting on the line of the River Chir, was threatening Manstein's left flank and promptly sealed the fate of the Sixth Army. Manstein was compelled to detach part of Hoth's force to meet the fresh threat and build up a new front to cover Rostov, whereupon the depleted Fourth Panzer Army was driven back over the Aksay to Kotelnikovo. The rescue attempt had failed, at a cost of 300 tanks and 16,000 men. Now Army Group Don was obliged to retreat towards Rostov, and Army Group A, also in peril of encirclement, had to do likewise from the Caucasus.

Inside the irrevocably isolated 'Fortress Stalingrad', now taken under Hitler's personal command, most of the Germans were, unlike their opponents, without mittens, felt shoes, padded jackets, thick stockings and fur coats, thanks in part to Hitler's assurance that when winter came all fighting would be over and that an army of occupation required no special winter clothing, in part to a breakdown of the railway system and the marooning of the Sixth Army's winter supplies in sidings far from Stalingrad. Cold outside, the men were cold within as well, for lack of hot meals – fuel was at a premium – and even of food of any kind. The air lift was failing so lamentably that many had already been reduced to eating half-starved horses. On 5 December 300 tons were flown in, and this total remained a record. So much for Göring's guarantee of 500.

Miserable-looking German soldiers with woefully inadequate clothing to withstand the severity of the Russian winter – Hitler's over-optimism and a breakdown of the railway system were to blame

A Russian sniper (note the telescopic sights) who, besides wearing white camouflage clothing himself, has bound his rifle in white also

Not nearly enough aircraft were available. Most of them had to fly at least 130 miles, and some as much as 200, to reach Stalingrad from suitable airfields, and by the month's end several of the best runways had been lost to the Russian advance. Too often the pilots had to land amid the hazards of deep snow, bomb craters, and damaged planes. They had also to beware constantly of icing-up and of the new Soviet fighters. Eventually this airlift was to cost the Luftwaffe 536 transport planes.

On 8 January Generals Rokossovsky and Voronov addressed surrender terms to Paulus, and he rejected them, whereupon the Russians launched their final offensive. Levelled specially at the western and southern sectors, their attacks burst in at several points, for Paulus no longer had reserves with which to contain them or to fill the gaps, and by now most of his heavy weapons were immobilized for lack of petrol. Moreover, when a German regiment was forced to withdraw to a new defence line, the troops found no trenches or dugouts, only the snow in which they tried to scratch fox-holes. Though many Russian tanks were knocked out, many more rumbled forward and could not be stopped by exhausted men who, suffering from severe malnutrition and frost-bite, were crushed to death like beetles.

The daily average of airlift supplies having dropped to 42 tons, on account of terrible snowstorms and Russian anti-aircraft fire, Hitler instructed Field-Marshal Milch, Göring's deputy, to take personal charge, but it was already too late. Once Pitomnik airfield was lost, on 18 January, most landings had to be cancelled and the inadequate stores dropped by parachute. For a week the Luftwaffe managed a daily drop of 20 tons, but when the last aerodrome, at Gumrak, fell into Russian grasp, this figure slumped by two-thirds. The end was in sight.

On 24 January Paulus, who had moved his headquarters into the basement of the ruined Univermag department store in the central Square of the Fallen Soldiers, signalled to Hitler that as the troops lacked ammunition and food, and as 18,000 wounded were without drugs or dressings – up till the loss of Gumrak airfield some 30,000 wounded men had been flown out to hospital – further defence was senseless, effective command no longer possible, and collapse inevitable. From his headquarters 1,300 miles away the Führer refused to allow surrender. The Sixth Army, he still insisted, would hold its positions to the last round and the last man.

Four days later the Russians broke through to the Volga from the West. Whole German battalions were annihilated or just went silent. Three divisional commanders, deliberately presenting an obvious target as they fired at the oncoming enemy, were killed; and another general shot himself. On 31 January Paulus – he had just been promoted to Field-Marshal, Hitler declar-

Having appealed in vain to Hitler a week earlier for permission to surrender, on 31 January 1943 Field-Marshal Paulus finally took it upon his own responsibility; he is seen here arriving for interrogation by Generals Voronov and Rokossovsky

ing that there was no record of a German marshal being taken prisoner – surrendered. When interrogated personally by Voronov and Rokossovsky in their blockhouse headquarters, he asked only that the sick and wounded should be treated well. The last pocket of resistance gave up on 2 February under massive assault.

Twenty-four generals were numbered among the 90,000 prisoners. Some 140,000 Germans and Rumanians must have perished in battle or from cold, hunger and disease. The booty captured by the Russians or found destroyed included 60,000 vehicles, 1,500 tanks, 6,000 guns and 7,000 motorcycles.

Stalingrad, one of the most appalling and costly reverses ever suffered by German arms, marked the turning-point in the struggle between Hitler's Third Reich and the USSR.

Thereafter, except for three notable German counter-offensives during 1943, initiative remained with the Russian commanders all the way to Berlin.

ANTONY BRETT-JAMES

1942
Alamein

Ten days' strenuous fighting brought Montgomery victory and forced Rommel – hitherto virtually unbeaten – to retreat: it was the prelude to German expulsion from North Africa

THE SECOND BATTLE OF ALAMEIN began at 9.40 pm. on 23 October 1942 with a tremendous British bombardment of more than 1,000 guns. Line upon line of infantry advanced at a pace of fifty yards to the minute to the first minefields – over a mile from the start line – the Highlanders cheered on by the wail of bagpipes. Soon the bright moonlight was obscured in a pall of smoke and dust, and confusion descended upon the orderly lines. So was the battle to continue; confusion worse confounded by the almost featureless nature of the desert. Even more than in most battles must historians of Alamein avoid distorting reality by conveying a false impression of orderly progress controlled by a chain of command.

The victorious British generals at Alamein were the Commander-in-Chief, General Alexander, and the Commander of the Eighth Army, General Montgomery, both of whose appointments dated from mid-August. Rommel's drive towards Alexandria had been decisively checked by General Auchinleck at the beginning of July, in the first battle of Alamein, and his successors undoubtedly profited from the subsequent influx of men and matériel. But, although the road had been made easier for Montgomery, the crucial problem remained: the destruction of the Axis forces was more than just an 'epilogue' to Auchinleck's successes.

Second Alamein deserves its place in the historical list of 'decisive battles' because it finally ended the Axis threat to the Suez Canal and, on a longer view, cleared the way for the opening of a second front in Europe. Tactically, however, this was not the most interesting of the desert battles owing to the disparity of the opposing forces and the restrictions on generalship imposed by the terrain.

In the summer of 1942 Tobruk had fallen, but lack of supplies prevented Rommel advancing to the Nile Delta. Thereafter the tide turned against him. His communications by land and sea were overstretched and ill-protected. But fundamentally his predicament was political. Hitler always regarded the North African theatre as a sideshow, and the almost miraculous success of the Afrika Korps – originally intended only to provide a backbone for the disintegrating Italian army – encouraged in Berlin and Rome the delusion that Rommel could conjure victories out of the air.

The comparative strengths of the Allied and Axis forces at the beginning of the battle have been surprisingly neglected, for they are essential to an appreciation of the conduct and outcome of the conflict.

Rommel commanded barely 200 German tanks, of which only 38 were Mark IVs with first-class 75-mm guns, and 300 M.13 Italian tanks, the negligible fighting

RIGHT *General Bernard Montgomery, the Commander of the Eighth Army, observes the progress of the Battle of Alamein from a Grant tank*

Rough notes used by me for my address to all senior officers before the Battle of Alamein (code name "Lightfoot")

Address to officers — "Lightfoot" 19/20 Oct 1942

1. Back history since August. The mandate; my plans to carry it out; the creation of 10 Corps. Leadership — equipment — training

2. Interference by Rommel on 31 Aug.

3. The basic framework of the Army plan for Lightfoot as issued on 14 Sep. To destroy enemy armour.

4. Situation in early October. Untrained Army. Gradually realised that I must recast the plan so as to be within the capabilities of the troops. The new plan; the crumbling operations. A reversal of accepted methods.

5. Key points in the Army plan. Three phases.
   30 Corps break-in.
   10 Corps break through. } Fighting for position and
   13 Corps break in.   } the tactical advantage.
   The dog-fight, and "crumbling" operations.
   The final break of the enemy.

6. The enemy
   His sickmen; low strengths; small stocks of petrol, ammunition, food. Morale is great, except possibly Italians.

7. Ourselves
   Immense superiority in guns, tanks, men. Can fight a prolonged battle or will do so.
   25 pdr 832
   6 pdr   753   1200 tanks (470 heavy)
   2 pdr   500
   morale on the top line.

8. General conduct of the battle
   Methodical progress; destroy enemy part by part, slowly and surely.
   Shoot tanks and shoot Germans
   He cannot last a long battle; we can.
   We must therefore keep at it hard; no unit commander must relax the pressure; Organise ahead for a "dog-fight" of a week. Whole affair about 10 days. (12).
   Don't expect spectacular results too soon. }
   Operative from firm basis.   } If we
   Quick re-organisation on objectives.   } do all this
   Keep balanced.   } victory is
   Maintain offensive eagerness.   } certain.
   Keep up pressure.

12. Morale measures to get it. Addresses. Every soldier in the Army a fighting soldier. No non-fighting men. All trained to kill Germans. My message to the troops.

11. The issues at stake.

10. The troops to remember what to say if they are captured. Rank, name, & number.

B. L. M.

Montgomery's pencil notes of his address to officers before the battle, which show that he did not expect a quick, easy victory; the British superiority in guns, tanks and men, and their abundant supplies (Rommel was desperately short of petrol) would tell in the end

A tank of the Afrika Korps in action; the almost miraculous success of the Korps encouraged Hitler and Mussolini to believe that Rommel could conjure victories out of the air

Field-Marshal Rommel, the German Commander-in-Chief, and some of his staff inspect a knocked out British tank; at Alamein Rommel commanded 500 tanks (300 of which were Italian), against 1,100 British

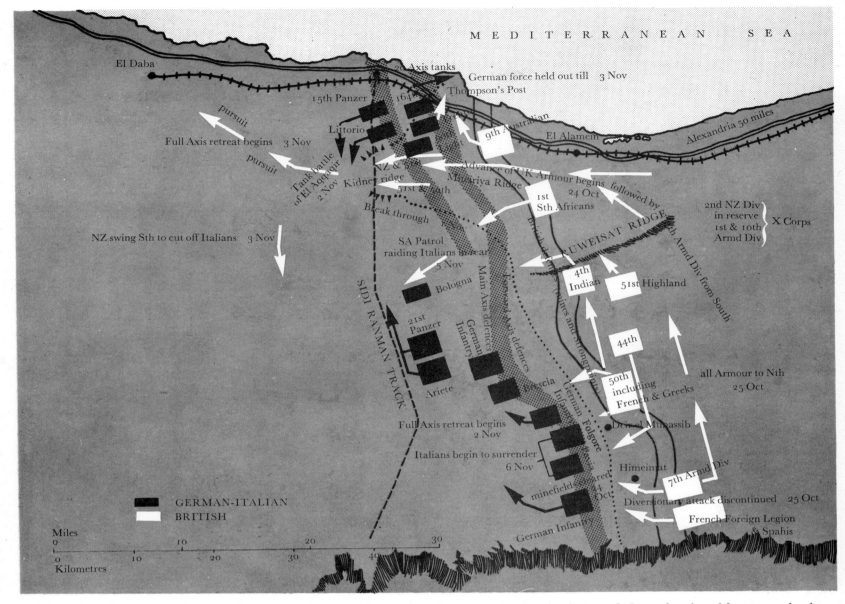

The various phases of the Battle of Alamein, fought 23 October–5 November 1942, showing the changes of plan enforced on Montgomery by the initial failure of his attack; quicksands prevented him from employing classical desert tactics and turning the southern tip of the German defences

OVERLEAF As the barrage lifts, after many hours of relentless air and artillery bombardment, out of the smoke and dust of mortar fire suddenly bursts the infantry – British infantry charge a German position

value of which was epitomized in their nickname of 'self-propelled coffins'. Montgomery had more than 1,100 tanks at the front and almost as many in reserve in depots and workshops. Of those fit for action 270 were Shermans and 210 Grants, both armed with 75-mm guns. Axis fighting strength in troops was approximately 108,000, but rather more than half of these were Italians. Allied fighting strength was 220–230,000. Rommel's air support consisted of 129 German and 216 Italian aircraft in Africa. Montgomery, from Egypt and Palestine, could call on almost 900 aircraft. Moreover, whereas Axis supplies, in petrol particularly, were being reduced to a trickle – only 70 tons arrived for the whole army on 27 October – the Eighth Army, enjoying the security of the Cape route, was gaining vastly in strength.

The situation of the Alamein position was in one res-pect unique in the desert war. Forty miles of almost featureless desert are here bounded by impassable barriers at either end: by the Mediterranean in the north and by the quicksands of the Qattara Depression in the south. Hence classical desert tactics of turning the southern tip of defences could not be employed. Continuous defensive works resting on minefields up to five miles deep con-verted this natural bottleneck into a formidable 'line' which could not be breached by strategic surprise. For once, armoured mobility was likely to have less effect than carefully trained infantry supported by superior fire power. With the enemy driven on to the defensive by shortage of supplies, Montgomery was able to plan a set-piece battle in which his distinctive traits as a general would be at a premium. Rommel's task, on the other hand, was uncharacteristically defensive: to prevent a

break-through at all costs. Knowing the British propensity to concentrate their artillery fire close to the attacking infantry, he retained only a thin screen of troops in the forward minefields and strengthened the main defences further back. Close behind the latter the Axis armoured divisions were held in readiness to 'plug the gap' at any point along the front.

The factor of morale, as in most battles, was of vital importance at Alamein. Without doubt Montgomery's cocksure, ebullient personality had a tonic effect on the Eighth Army. Through extensive use of propaganda – such as the cancellation of all 'withdrawal orders' – and through personal addresses, the new commander impressed on everyone his own unshakeable conviction that the coming battle would be fought on his terms, and that victory was certain. He also insisted on placing hand-picked men in nearly all the key positions. By contrast the morale of the Axis troops, even the Germans, was falling with the realization that the last hope of reaching the Nile was gone. Rommel himself was in poor health and somewhat dispirited by the lack of co-operation from Hitler and Mussolini. His absence on sick leave from 23 September to the evening of 25 October increased Montgomery's advantages in the opening stage of the battle.

After Rommel's repulse at Alam Halfa, Montgomery drove his troops through seven weeks of intensive training in preparation for the coming battle. The crucial problem in the opening phase of the battle was to clear a passage through the minefields and pass through the narrow channels a mass of armour in precise order; and all in about ten hours of darkness.

The constant arrival of new units and the need to rest others caused Montgomery to carry out a great reshuffling after Alam Halfa, the chief purpose of which was to form X Corps, to which he gave the vital role in the Alamein offensive of exploiting the break-through to be engineered on the ground by the infantry of XXX Corps.

Command in the air, elaborate use of camouflage and dummy vehicles, and an exceedingly thorough security system successfully blinded General Stumme, Rommel's deputy, as to the time and precise location of the 'break-in' attempt.

Montgomery's original plan had been to strike simultaneously on both flanks with the object of destroying the enemy's armour. Early in October, however, the slow progress of training caused him to change his conception of the battle because, in his own words, 'I was not satisfied that we were capable of achieving success in a plan so ambitious'. In the revised plan the first objective was to destroy the enemy holding troops (mostly unarmoured) in order to deny him secure ground essential for launching an armoured counter-attack. The idea, therefore, was 'to aim first at the methodical destruction of the infantry divisions holding the enemy's defensive system'. An essential factor for the success of this process of 'crumbling' or attrition was that the British armour should speedily pierce the enemy minefields in order to hold off his anticipated armoured counter-attack on 24 October. The main attack was to be made by XXX Corps (General Leese) in the north on a front of four divisions (from north to south 9th Australian, 51st, 2nd New Zealand and 1st South African) with the aim of forming two corridors through the minefields. Immediately behind them X Corps (General Lumsden) would pass through the corridors and get to grips with the enemy armour. In the south XIII Corps (General Horrocks) was to launch a diversionary attack.

The twelve days' battle naturally falls into a number of phases, though to call those 'stepping stones' as did General de Guingand, Montgomery's Chief of Staff, in his book *Operation Victory* suggests that the battle progressed more closely according to plan than was actually the case.

The first phase was that of the 'break-in' starting on the night of 23 October and lasting until 26 October. Although most of the units comprising XXX Corps reached their objectives by dawn on 24 October, they were too exhausted by unexpectedly stubborn resistance to assist an armoured break-out. In any case, the task of clearing, marking and keeping open the corridors proved too much for X Corps' engineers. Some parties were delayed when their mine detectors would not work and tanks were knocked out by scattered mines. At dawn only one route through to Miteiriya Ridge was entirely free from blockage and none of the armoured units had broken out. XIII Corps had also made little progress in the southern sector.

At one point it looked as if the British armour might have to be withdrawn and rested, but Montgomery overruled his armoured commanders. The advance along the congested corridors continued in the face of the devastating fire of German 88-mm anti-tank guns. By 26 October the two British armoured divisions had still not broken clear of the enemy defences, although the leading section of 1st Armoured Division had reached the end of the northern corridor by the evening of the 24th. Both sides lost heavily in tanks in desperate fighting around 'Kidney Ridge', known to the enemy as Hill 28. After three days of fighting the British had already lost 200 tanks, roughly the German total at the beginning of the battle. It was becoming clear that to continue the frontal attack under concentrated fire would be to jeopardize the victory which superior forces had seemed to guarantee.

Montgomery realistically accepted the failure of his original plan. He drew 1st Armoured Division and 24th

A long line of British tanks moving up to the front: besides 1,100 at the front, Montgomery had as many tanks in reserve in depots and workshops, so that he could afford to 'trade' tanks at the rate of three to one until the German armour was completely destroyed

Silhouetted against a moonlit sky, punctured by flashes from guns continuing the bombardment, a British infantryman prepares to charge the battered German lines

One of the more than a thousand guns that took part in the night bombardment which preceded the British infantry attack at the beginning of the battle of Alamein

A German heavy machine gun position, part of the elaborate system of defences which the Eighth Army had to penetrate before they could really get to grips with their opponents

Under cover of a dense smoke screen, infantry of the 9th Australian Division approach a German strongpoint; the Australians' task was to attack in the north and break through on to the coast road

Men of the Middlesex Regiment behind a Vickers gun in a forward position; British fighting strength was over 220,000 – approximately double that of the Axis

With tapes marking the lane along which vehicles will later advance, Sappers sweep for mines; Montgomery required two corridors through the minefields which were up to five miles deep

Montgomery's main tank strength was in his 210 Grants (of which this was one) and 270 Shermans, which were both armed with 75-mm guns – Rommel possessed only 38 Mark IVs which also carried 75-mm guns

Armoured Brigade back into reserve, brought 7th Armoured Division into the northern sector (in response to the move northwards of 21st Panzer Division), and handed over the southern corridor to XIII Corps so that the battle-weary 2nd New Zealand Division could rest and regroup.

The basic feature of the second plan was that 9th Australian Division would strike northwards at right angles towards the coast and then turn west to break out along the coast road. This attack began on 28 October but failed to achieve the break-out. The Australians did not quite reach the coast road and on 29 and 30 October were hard put to hold their ground against repeated counter-attacks.

A third plan was devised after Rommel had blocked the coastal road by bringing up 90th Light Division from farther south. In conjunction with another thrust to the north a second attempt was to be made to break out westward led by Freyberg's New Zealanders. Operation 'Supercharge' was scheduled for 31 October but had to be postponed twenty-four hours, because the New Zealand Division was exhausted and dispersed.

Meanwhile, by 29 October, the Axis troops had been so heavily punished by the Allied Air Force and artillery that Rommel was contemplating withdrawal to the Fuka position, some fifty miles back. He dared not risk a move, however, until the enemy was committed to a breakthrough attempt; otherwise with most of his infantry unmotorized and the tank disparity now 90 to 800 his whole army might easily be surrounded in the open desert.

Operation 'Supercharge' was launched on the night of 1–2 November only to be held up in front of the German anti-tank screen. The British suffered a numerical reverse in the tank battle of Tel el Aqqaqir, but owing to their overall superiority this was actually a step nearer victory. By the evening of 2 November Rommel was reduced to about 30 effective tanks. Complete annihilation must result unless he could effect a withdrawal the following day. On 3 November an unequivocal order from Hitler forbade the retreat that had actually begun. Montgomery was given an additional thirty-six hours to accomplish the destruction of Rommel's army. The final break-through was achieved early on 4 November by Montgomery skilfully switching his attack slightly south of the enemy anti-tank screen. The cardinal question now was whether a costly slogging match could be transformed into a complete victory by the cutting off and capture of the retreating enemy.

The pursuit got off to a slow start when its spearhead, 8th Armoured Brigade, halted for the night of the 4th before cutting the coast road. Poor traffic control and an underestimation of Rommel's speed resulted in two time-wasting coastward swings on 5 November: by 10th Armoured Division to Ghazal, and 1st and 7th Armoured Divisions to Daba, some ten miles further west. Meanwhile the New Zealand Division was making a broader sweep through the desert to trap Rommel at his first intended defensive position of Fuka. Just south of Fuka the New Zealanders were delayed by what appeared to be a virgin minefield but which was in fact a dummy one laid, ironically, by the British four months previously to cover their retreat in the opposite direction. Rommel meanwhile decided that the position was untenable and again slipped away successfully. After two days' delay due to heavy rain 10th Armoured pressed on to the fourth 'trap', Mersa Matruh, which was reached early on 8 November only to find that the majority of the retreating Germans – though fewer Italians – had escaped.

The unduly cautious follow-up of victory has been attributed to the heavy rain on 6 and 7 November which turned the coastal road into a morass. This overlooks the fact that the pursued were similarly delayed. The real opportunity had been missed early on 5 November when 1st and 7th Armoured Divisions were not redirected towards Mersa Matruh.

Alamein was won at comparatively high cost. Allied casualties (killed, wounded and missing) totalled 13,500. The Germans lost 9,000 (dead and prisoners) and the Italians 17,000. Allied losses in tanks, 600, exceeded the combined Axis total; indeed the latter had not that number to lose. Against the Germans the Allies were strong enough to 'trade' tanks at the rate of three to one until the enemy's stock was eliminated; and, moreover, were able to repair a considerable number which were only lightly damaged. When allowance has been made for the strength of the Axis defences it was still a remarkable achievement for them to have held out for twelve days against such heavy odds, especially in the face of relentless bombardment from the Air Force and artillery.

Alamein, unlike many decisive battles, was not a close run thing. In the opening phase it seemed possible that the British would squander their great matériel superiority, but Montgomery desisted in time from trying to force his armour through congested corridors under concentrated fire. With his adoption of more flexible tactics the eventual outcome was assured; lack of petrol was in itself sufficient to deny Rommel even the hope of staving off defeat.

As to the strategic significance of the victory, Stalingrad rather than Alamein probably marked the decisive moment for Germany. The immediate effects of the battle are to be seen in the security of Malta and the Suez Canal and, most important, in the success of TORCH, the invasion of North Africa. In the Mediterranean theatre Alamein, though costly, was far from a barren victory.

BRIAN BOND

Trucks taking British troops through a minefield corridor come under heavy shell fire; Alamein cost the British 13,500 casualties, the Germans 9,000 dead and prisoners, and the Italians 17,000 – Rommel's speed and the over-cautious British pursuit enabled most retreating Germans to escape

1942
Guadalcanal

The ejection of the Japanese from this island in the Solomon group by the US Marines and Army,
with naval and air support ended a hard fought campaign

IN THE MIDDLE OF 1942 there were only three mobilized divisions in the South-West Pacific area and, if the Japanese had managed to isolate it by taking possession of, say, New Caledonia or Fiji, they would have had Australasia at their mercy. As early as January they had occupied New Britain and in May they had taken over Tulagi – a small island with a fine natural harbour that lay twenty miles north of Guadalcanal in the strip of water known as the 'Slot' that lies between the two main island chains of the Solomons. In reply the Allies took up forward positions on Rennell and San Cristobal in the Solomons and began building airfields on Espiritu Santo and Efate in the New Hebrides. Then Tokyo's time-table of conquest was dislocated by naval defeats in the Coral Sea and near Midway Island and this gave the Allies a chance to seize the initiative.

Accordingly, on 2 July the United States Joint Chiefs of Staff ordered the preparation of the first step towards the capture of Rabaul, which was to be a landing, scheduled for 1 August, on Tulagi. They also advanced the western boundary of the South Pacific Command under Vice-Admiral Ghormley to longitude 159°E, thereby creating a precedent that was important in helping determine that subsequent amphibious strikes should be conducted predominantly by Marines rather than soldiers and across the Central Pacific rather than through the Dutch East Indies. This new boundary embraced the island of Guadalcanal, which was fortunate because on 4 July a reconnaissance bomber that had been blown off course brought back evidence that the Japanese were constructing what came to be known as Henderson airfield near Lunga Point on the north-east side of that island. It was correctly estimated that if this work were not molested it would be completed by the middle of August and so, in an amended invasion plan, Guadalcanal was made the principal objective. Fortunately, the very gentle grass-covered slopes that made the Lunga delta about the only area on Guadalcanal suitable for airstrips also made it a good venue for an amphibious assault, whilst the muddy effluent maintained a large gap in the coral reefs that otherwise extended almost all round the coast.

Haste, inexperience, and inadequate resources made the planning of the expedition an orgy of improvisation, muddle, and delay. Appallingly bad maps resulted, for example, in Alligator Creek being described as the Tenaru River throughout the campaign and in a calculation being made that the dominant feature of Mount Austen could be taken on the first day, whereas, in fact, it was not captured for months. Intelligence estimates of the opposing forces were likewise poor, ranging from 3,000–8,000 crack troops, whereas in fact there were a

LEFT *An American camp in the jungle on Guadalcanal during the rainy season, when as much as eight inches of rain might fall in a day, and rivers could rise as high as seven feet above normal in two hours*

US Marines land from assault boats during a critical phase of the battle for Guadalcanal, during November 1942; only after three months were Marines replaced by soldiers, since the island was within the area of the South Pacific (Naval) Command

mere 500 combat men and 1,500 pioneers. Also the three regiments of General Vandegrift's 1st Marine Division were not brought together until the main rehearsal which was, in part consequence, a complete failure.

Nevertheless, early on 7 August the task force entered the Slot under an almost total cloud cover and landed 2,500 men on Tulagi and two neighbouring islets and one and a half times that number on Guadalcanal. They enjoyed the actual or potential protection of the 300 shore-based aircraft, 3 carriers, 1 battleship, and 45 cruisers and destroyers which the Allies had assembled within the theatre, but they were threatened by local Japanese air and naval forces that included 150 land-planes and 28 cruisers and destroyers and which could be backed up by the 5 carriers and 2 battleships located at Truk. Throughout the campaign the tussle for the command of the sea and the skies had a controlling influence on the outcome of the fighting ashore.

Though fierce resistance, which lasted for one or two days, was encountered on the other islands the Japanese forces on and around Henderson Field melted into the jungle immediately, leaving behind a near-to-complete runway and an elaborate complex of aerodrome installations and equipment. By 11 August the Americans had rendered the airstrip usable in good weather. Just over a week later it became the base for 40 combat planes and thenceforward was never entirely lacking operational aircraft.

Meanwhile, however, the Americans and the Australians had temporarily lost naval command of the Slot. This was the result of a surprise attack during the night of 8 August on the six cruisers screening the beachhead. Four of them were sunk and because of this and of a few sporadic air raids and imaginary fuel shortage the American carriers were withdrawn the following day and the expeditionary transports were obliged to follow suit.

American light tanks, moving up to assist hard-pressed infantry, emerge from the jungle; within a month of their first landings, the Americans had established 11 battalions of infantry and raiders, 5 of artillery and 1 of light tanks on the island

A captured Japanese 70-mm gun, which was later destroyed by the Marines, as they were not able to take it back to their own positions

Unfortunately, unloading operations had been considerably slowed down by beach congestion and so most of the cargo ships retreated whilst still three-quarters full. Only eighteen spools of barbed wire were landed and no guns of a calibre larger than 105 mm.

It was, therefore, inevitable that the troops ashore should rest on the defensive awhile. A line of foxholes and machine-gun nests was constructed along the coast from Alligator Creek to a point two miles west of Kukum and behind it was concentrated a reserve consisting of one of the rifle battalions and all the field artillery. The landward sector was left to be controlled at that stage by what proved to be some very successful fighting patrols.

As soon as it heard of the landings the Japanese High Command ordered the diversion of formations equivalent to three divisions from the objective of capturing Port Moresby to that of recapturing Guadalcanal and during the next three months these units were consumed piece-

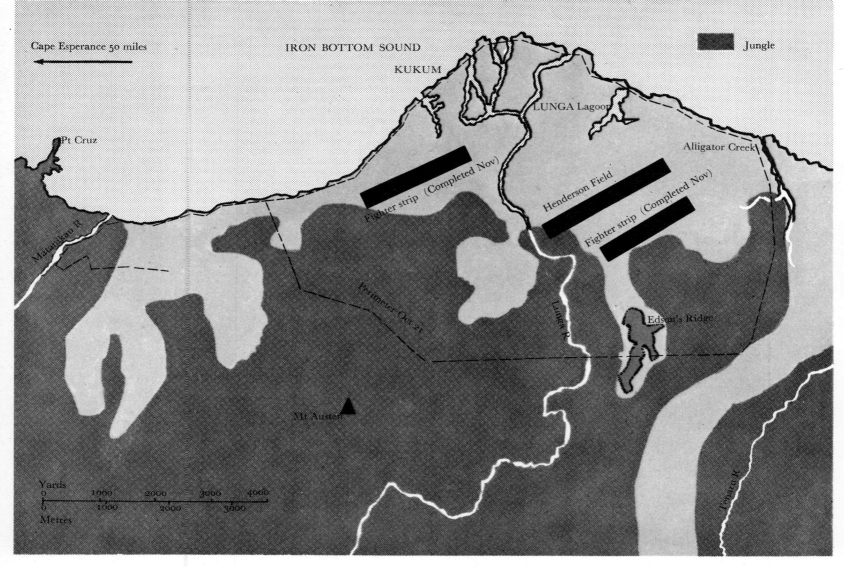

Jungle

The perimeter of the American beachhead on Guadalcanal on 21 October 1942; by this date the threat of a Japanese amphibious landing had lessened, but Henderson Field remained vulnerable to bombardment by Japanese warships

Details of Japanese uniform and equipment which appeared in an American official publication intended for use for identification purposes – as even this admits, Japanese 'uniform' could be very unorthodox and might not appear to follow any regulation pattern

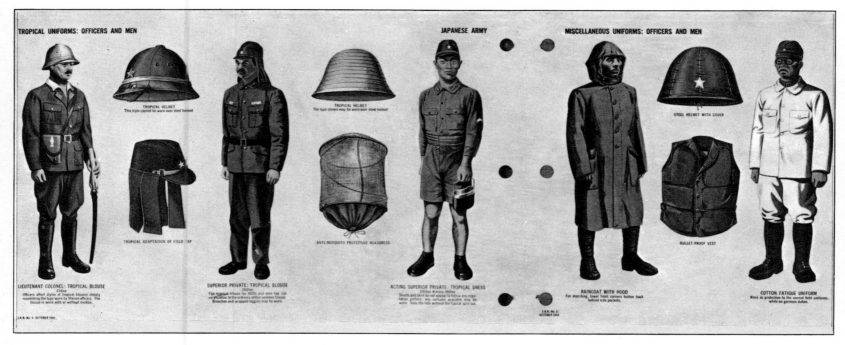

meal in this endeavour. The first major probe was by 1,000 men of Ichiki brigade, whose attempt to storm the Alligator Creek sand-bar on the night of 21 August was nipped in the bud by an artillery barrage and by an enveloping movement by the reserve infantry. It was followed by the much more powerful thrust made on 12 September which resulted in the 'Battle of Edson's Ridge'.

By this time the beachhead forces had been built up to 11 battalions of infantry and raiders, 5 of artillery, and 1 of light tanks. A perimeter had been established to landward of which the central feature was a grass-covered ridge held by two companies of parachute marines and Colonel Edson's raider battalion. All round the ridge were steep ravines filled with thick jungle and it was through these that the Japanese attacked on two successive nights. Their second assault nearly threw the outnumbered Marines off the crest of the ridge but reserve companies were fed in and behind them the gunners fired over 2,000 shells in area bombardments of suspected Japanese concentrations. As soon as dawn came 'Airacobras' from Henderson Field strafed the remnants of the attacking force. In this battle nearly 2,000 out of the 9,000 Japanese then on Guadalcanal became casualties. The Americans killed and wounded amounted to about 200.

Meanwhile the sea and air battles continued. Late in August the United States Navy turned back large Japanese sea-borne reinforcements and sank a light fleet carrier, but in so doing lost one large carrier and had heavy damage inflicted on another. Then during the last half of September the Japanese put ashore in a series of nocturnal dashes almost the entire Sendai division together with some 150-mm guns. As a result their force level on Guadalcanal rose to 20,000 against the American 15,000. On the other hand, the Marine Corps had now assembled within the perimeter some 5-inch gun batteries, enough trucks to lift a battalion simultaneously, and over 50 aircraft. By the time two more airstrips were opened in the middle of November the size of this 'Cactus Air Force' had risen to over 100 planes.

As the strength of American forces rose the danger of a Japanese amphibious landing inside the beachhead receded and so the chief direct threat from the sea became that of the bombardment of Henderson Field. During the second week in October a bitter conflict was waged as Japanese battle squadrons sought by night to render the aerodrome inoperable. They chose to come at night because it was then that Henderson Field was relatively most vulnerable, being a large and static target, the Cactus Air Force least effective, and the Japanese numerical superiority in torpedo boats and qualitative superiority in torpedoes of most value. These factors were felt to outweigh the possession by the Americans of a few crude search radar sets. The Japanese immobilized many planes during successive shellings of the airstrip, for in the course of one of them a battleship delivered over 1,000 14-inch shells against it and these were backed up by many smaller rounds and by bombs. On 16 October, however, two American destroyers fired 5,000 5-inch shells against the main Japanese supply dumps and destroyed stores which, unlike the planes of the Cactus Air Force, could not be readily replaced. The damage they did gravely handicapped subsequent Japanese ground operations.

A month later there was fought another, and this time very decisive, series of sea–air engagements that came to be collectively known as the Battle of Guadalcanal. It followed a build-up of forces within the theatre by both sides. The Japanese concentrated nearly all their 38th Division at Rabaul and located some 200 land-planes within striking distance of Lunga Point. Their available ships included 5 battleships, 60 cruisers and destroyers, and 11 transports. The United States Navy squadron included 2 battleships and 1 carrier and the troop reinforcements available included a Marine and two army regiments. The latter belonged to the American National Guard Division, the other regiment of which had landed on Guadalcanal in October to provide the first active United States Army representation in the campaign. In early November both sides had 30,000 troops ashore and so, if either had been able to move in all the reinforcements it had mustered without compensating increments on the part of its opponents, the local balance of power would have been tipped decisively.

Vice-Admiral Halsey who replaced Vice-Admiral Ghormley in November, when a very decisive series of sea-air engagements were fought, which both prevented the Japanese landing re-inforcements on Guadalcanal and finally secured American command of the local sea areas

A fighting patrol sets out into enemy territory; during the early days of the American offensive on Guadalcanal, the US Navy temporarily lost control of the sea, and so the land forces were obliged to rest on the defensive, indulging only in patrol activity

Marines laying steel matting along an airfield runway; airfields were essential both for bringing in supplies and for the maintenance of the island's own 'Cactus Air Force'

A well placed Marine gun position concealed behind camouflaged sandbags, which was originally constructed by the Japanese but captured and put to use by the Americans

BELOW *A Japanese troopship sunk by the stern off a Guadalcanal beach during the engagement of 13–15 November, when 10,000 out of 15,000 Japanese re-inforcements were drowned*

BELOW *'Veterans of the Tenaru River fight' – the photograph caption records an error produced by the appallingly bad maps used at the outset (the 'Tenaru River' was, in fact, Alligator Creek)*

Once again the central theme was that of the Japanese trying to immobilize the American airstrips before running their reinforcements in. This time, however, they fatally overestimated the effectiveness of their bombardments and advanced their slow and cumbersome transports prematurely. They were hammered unmercifully by Henderson Field planes and only 5,000 of the 15,000 soldiers on board escaped drowning. At the same time the Imperial Japanese Navy lost two of the battleships and with them all hope of challenging the growing American command of the local sea areas.

In early October the Marines established some positions on the steep banks of the lower Matinakau so as to prevent the enemy from using the sand-bar to move his heavy artillery up and so as to put behind them some stretches of open country that would have made good attack assembly areas. The Sendai Division promptly made preparations for a counter-attack by pushing three companies back across the river to form a bridgehead through which might be channelled larger forces. However, the two Marine battalions digging in on the eastern bank dislodged them, while three more battalions began an enveloping movement upstream. Heavy shell-fire and concern about their seaward flank inhibited the Sendai response and they retired in confusion. Three weeks later they returned to mount a big flank attack on the Marine positions, but the approach march for this was thrown out of gear by exceptionally heavy rainfall and by the jumbled terrain, and soon petered out.

By now the incidence of malaria within the 1st Marine Division was soaring as a consequence of weeks of continual effort and privation and so just before the Battle of Guadalcanal they were relieved by the 25th Army Division, though General Vandegrift was not replaced as local ground commander by a soldier in the person of General Patch until 9 December. Meanwhile an American regiment carried out a sweep eastwards from the perimeter to cover a prolonged fighting withdrawal action of a raider battalion that had been landed twenty-five miles along the coast with the original object of constructing yet another landing-ground. The idea was Admiral Ghormley's and reflected his view that the function of the Marines was to effect a series of small-scale lodgements intended to facilitate the exercise of naval power. It was not until November, when he was replaced by Admiral Halsey, that there was an officer in flag command who comprehended fully the importance of strengthening and expanding the Lunga perimeter.

General Patch waited a few weeks to allow his new troops time to acquire experience and the Japanese time to feel the effects of malnutrition and inadequate medical treatment. Then on 19 January he began a two-division drive towards Cape Esperance which was the northern-

most point on Guadalcanal. The main Japanese forces fell back, but they left behind small pockets, located often on the reverse slopes of steep ridges, which offered fierce resistance and so, despite the introduction of flame-throwers, the average rate of advance was only one mile a day and this meant that mopping up was not complete until 2 February. The Japanese were left enough time to organize an evacuation and in fact got 13,000 men off. That this was possible across waters then dominated by eight American capital ships seems surprising, but part of the explanation is that this was another period of exceptionally squally, thundery, weather. The rest of it consisted of a deception plan that lured the United States Navy into thinking that it was reinforcement and not withdrawal that was being contemplated.

With the conclusion of the Guadalcanal campaign the initiative in the Pacific War passed to the Allies. This was not only because the Japanese had endured about 30,000 casualties and had suffered a serious territorial loss. It was also because the myth that they were invincible in the jungle had been dramatically and unequivocally shattered.

NEVILLE BROWN

Admiral Nimitz decorates Marine and Air Force personnel during a visit to Guadalcanal in October; Major-General Vandegrift, the Commander of the 1st Marine Division stands behind him

1944
Saint-Lô
Falaise

Following the successful Normandy landings, Eisenhower directed the main American attack towards Saint-Lô, while the British and Canadians trapped 100,000 Germans in the Falaise pocket

ON 6 JUNE 1944 GENERAL MONTGOMERY's Twenty-first Army Group threw five divisions on to the beaches of Normandy, while airborne troops secured the flanks of the landings. By the end of the day they had torn the German coastal defences apart; three days later, as reinforcements poured in, they formed a continuous front with a depth of between four and fifteen miles, stretching from beyond the river Orne in the east to near Montebourg in the Cotentin Peninsula. On the right was General Bradley's American First Army, on the left Dempsey's British Second Army.

The opposing Germans were handicapped by a complicated system of command. The German ground forces in the west were commanded by Field-Marshal von Rundstedt. Under him, but with an elastic directive from Hitler which made him something more than a subordinate, Field-Marshal Rommel commanded Army Group B on the most threatened coastline. Yet another headquarters, Geyr von Schweppenburg's Panzer Group West, commanded half the armoured divisions in Rommel's area under Hitler's direct control (Geyr was to be recalled in July for criticizing Hitler's dispositions, and was succeeded by Eberbach).

The formation defending Brittany and western Normandy was the Seventh Army. At the Orne Fifteenth Army took up the task, with its main strength in the area opposite the Straits of Dover. For the Allies it was vital to prevent a rapid shift of forces from Fifteenth Army into the area of the bridgehead. This was largely achieved, partly by air attacks on bridges and railways, but still more by a deception plan which persuaded the Germans till the middle of July that a second landing was intended in the Pas de Calais. Thus, through the rest of June the Allies were able to consolidate and expand; to secure the Cotentin and the port of Cherbourg; and to win space for the deployment of reserves and the construction of airfields. At the same time Montgomery had to retain the initiative, to avert an enemy counter-stroke, and prepare his own break-out.

Montgomery's intention was to make his break-out on the right. He realized that the Allied landing point would force the Germans to form front to a flank. Their communications ran eastwards through Paris; and to contain the bridgehead they had to form a front parallel with their lines of communication. Thus an allied breakthrough in the east at Caen would lead them straight on to the German line of retreat and supply. Here, on their inner flank, Rommel must hold the vital hinge or risk annihilation. Here he must mass his main strength. If Montgomery could maintain a firm eastern flank and press the Germans hard, he might so upset their balance as to give the Americans in the west their opportunity.

RIGHT *Allied air superiority ensures the orderly advance of American armour through a shattered French village in Robert Capa's photograph taken during the battle for Saint-Lô*

LEFT *Three Allied commanders, Generals Patton (Third Army), Bradley (Twelfth Army Group) and Montgomery (Twenty-first Army Group).* CENTRE *Field-Marshal von Rundstedt, the German Commander-in-Chief.* RIGHT *Field-Marshal Rommel, the Commander of Army Group B, inspecting coastal defences before the Normandy landing*

The First Army would thrust southwards for the Loire; and, while a fresh American army cleared Brittany, the main front would wheel eastwards, and thrust the Germans back against the Seine. In such a war of movement the Allies could exploit to the full their superior mobility on the ground and their overwhelming power in the air.

From the first the Germans reacted as Montgomery knew they must. Though the failure to capture Caen on D-day denied the British and Canadians the elbow-room of the open country to the south-east, the Germans threw in all their armoured reinforcements against the British end of the line. The British front was taken over by Panzer Group West, renamed Fifth Panzer Army in the course of the battle; and within four days of the landings all the three Panzer divisions which had reached the front were committed piecemeal to hold off the British attacks.

Hitler struggled to keep his armour out of the defensive battle. On 17 June he ordered the Panzer divisions to be relieved as fresh infantry came up, and collected for a planned counter-offensive. Simultaneously, however, he insisted that the line must be held tenaciously to prevent the Allies from emerging into the open country to the southward and developing a war of movement. Thus the Germans could only disengage their armour if Montgomery yielded the initiative; and this he did not intend. Already a British thrust towards Villers-Bocage had drawn a fourth Panzer division into the line as it arrived from Belgium; and on 25 June a new thrust began which carried a spearhead across the Odon and gained the dominating crest of Hill 112. Here a ferocious fight developed. The Germans had already thrown in the last reserves of I SS Panzer Corps to hold the attack; and to regain the vital hill Rommel committed all the fresh armour which was arriving: two SS divisions from southern France and Belgium, and II SS Panzer Corps which had been speeding from the Russian front. On 29 June heavy counter-attacks developed against the British salient. All were smashed. Thus the last German hope of breaking the Allied bridgehead with armoured reinforce-

ments was forestalled. On 1 July, the day when II SS Panzer Corps was finally repulsed, Bradley's Americans captured Cherbourg and turned southwards against the main German front.

In three weeks of hard fighting little ground had been gained except in the severed Cotentin; but the German armies' balance had been upset. Elements of eight Panzer divisions had been committed against the Allied left, and none had appeared against the Americans. The time for the break-out was approaching.

The ground on Bradley's immediate front was far from ideal. If he was to forge ahead before the Germans could switch their armour from the British front, he had first to gain a start-line where the going was good. In the coastal sector with its hedgerows and marshes, ground could be won but slowly and at heavy cost, while further east towards the Allied centre the thick impenetrable country of the Normandy *bocage* was ideal for an infantry defence. Bradley's plan was therefore to push his right forward to the Saint-Lô–Coutances road, before he launched his break-out.

Bradley's attack began on 3 July; and, as it developed, the Second Army opened a costly attack in the east to pin the main enemy forces. Dempsey's troops fought their way through elaborate defences to enter Caen on the 9th; and on the following day a second bitter struggle opened for Hill 112.

Bradley's push, however, made slow progress. In the coastal sector the Americans met such difficulties that on 10 July he broke off the attack and changed his plan. Instead of taking Coutances and launching his break-through on a wide front, he would make it on a narrow front just west of Saint-Lô. The code name of the operation was COBRA.

Even to reach the modified start-line, the First Army faced many days of bitter fighting. The delay was disquieting. The German command was beginning to see the American threat and to shift armour westwards from the British front as it was relieved by fresh infantry.

Montgomery had promised Bradley that the British would continue to hold the German strength in the east, and a further effort was required: this was the controversial operation called GOODWOOD.

COBRA was now timed for 19 July. To hold off the German armour, Second Army would open a heavy attack against II SS Panzer Corps west of Caen on the night of the 15th, followed by a major effort with three armoured divisions on the 18th from the narrow bridgehead east of Caen. At first Montgomery hoped to push his armour down the road towards Falaise; but before the attack was launched it became clear that Bradley would not be ready for COBRA by the 19th. Second Army would therefore have to hold the Germans for many days longer, and at the same time maintain its own balance in the eastern bastion unaided. The initial objective was limited to the high ground six miles south-east of Caen.

The opposition was stronger than had been realized. Two German corps held the Caen sector in a massive five-layered system of defences, backed by three armoured divisions, two battalions of Tiger tanks, and most of the heavy multi-barrelled mortars in Normandy. The open country, favourable in other circumstances for rapid movement, provided a glacis for the fire of the long-range anti-tank guns of III Flak Corps, posted in the defended villages and woods. Cramped by the narrow bridgehead, the British failed to get their rearward troops forward with sufficient speed, and the attack lost its impetus as German reinforcements rushed in.

GOODWOOD was a tactical failure, but strategically it succeeded. The Germans, expecting a further assault, brought in fresh troops from east of the Seine and shifted a Panzer division east from the Caumont sector. Thus, when COBRA was at last launched on the 25th, the German army was completely off balance. 7 Panzer and 7 infantry divisions, many of them relatively fresh, faced the 14 divisions of Second Army, and were buttressed by all their Tiger battalions and heavy mortars. Against

21 American divisions were 2 Panzer divisions, 1 Panzer Grenadier division without its tanks, and 6 exhausted infantry divisions made up largely of remnants and oddments. Before dawn on the day of COBRA a Canadian Corps launched a new attack south of Caen: a few hours later Bradley struck at Saint-Lô.

Bradley's new plan was to punch a hole clean through the German defences on a six-thousand-yard front, using three infantry divisions in line with an exploiting force of two armoured and one motorized division behind them. Immediately before the attack the front line was drawn back, and nearly three thousand aircraft plastered the German defences with thousands of fragmentation bombs. Two-thirds of the defending division was knocked out. Pockets of resistance still held out amidst the devastation, and the first day's advance was slow. But by nightfall General Collins guessed that his VII Corps was practically through the German defences, and early the next morning he launched his exploiting force. By the third day, when the Germans at last began to try to shift their armour westwards, the whole right wing of First Army was in rapid movement. On the 30th it swept into Avranches, at the apex of the Gulf of Saint-Malo. Ahead lay open country.

At Avranches the character of the battle changed. A single corps instead of an army was launched into Brittany, and the main American forces, pushing through the Avranches bottleneck with extraordinary speed, rushed south and south-east through lightly defended country towards Nantes, Angers, and Le Mans. This spectacular role went to General Patton's newly committed Third Army, whose three fresh corps ate up the ground towards the Loire.

Montgomery's wheeling movement was now under way. If the Germans had accepted the logic of the situation, they would have attempted an orderly withdrawal to the Seine, swinging their line back on the Caen pivot. To prevent this, Montgomery was preparing a fresh blow

An American vehicle, struck by artillery fire, blazes on the road to Saint-Lô on 20 July 1944, as General Bradley makes his final preparations before launching Operation COBRA

The gun crew clamp their ears to avoid concussion, as an American 'Long Tom' (a 155-mm gun mounted on a Sherman tank chassis) blasts off a shell against German positions

at their inner flank; but before he could strike, the Germans themselves sealed their fate by launching their armour westwards in a forlorn offensive.

The plan was Hitler's. A great armoured force was to be launched through Mortain to sever Patton's communications at Avranches and roll up the Allied front. Von Kluge, who had succeeded von Rundstedt, was attempting to hold a British attack at Vire which threatened to cut off Seventh Army. But under a hail of telephone calls from Hitler's headquarters he succeeded in assembling four battered Panzer divisions which he launched on the night of 6–7 August. By midday the attack was halted. Had it struck further south, it would have found undefended country and might have cut deeper. But its whole tank strength was less than eighty; one of the attacking divisions was still engaged in a defensive battle and never advanced; and against the confident American counter-dispositions and the devastating hail of missiles from the air the offensive could in no circumstances have succeeded.

That night the Canadians attacked again down the Falaise road. On the next day, the 8th, Patton's XV Corps reached Le Mans and a momentous decision was taken. Bradley realized that by launching his armour westwards von Kluge had exposed his armies to encirclement. If Patton's force were wheeled north towards Alençon and Falaise, the Germans might be trapped in a pocket. With Eisenhower's promise that the troops could be supplied by air if necessary, he telephoned Montgomery and got his agreement. A new pattern developed.

Operation COBRA, *Bradley's plan for a break-out on a narrow front just west of Saint-Lô, punched a hole clean through the German defences; within a week the right wing of his First Army had reached Avranches*

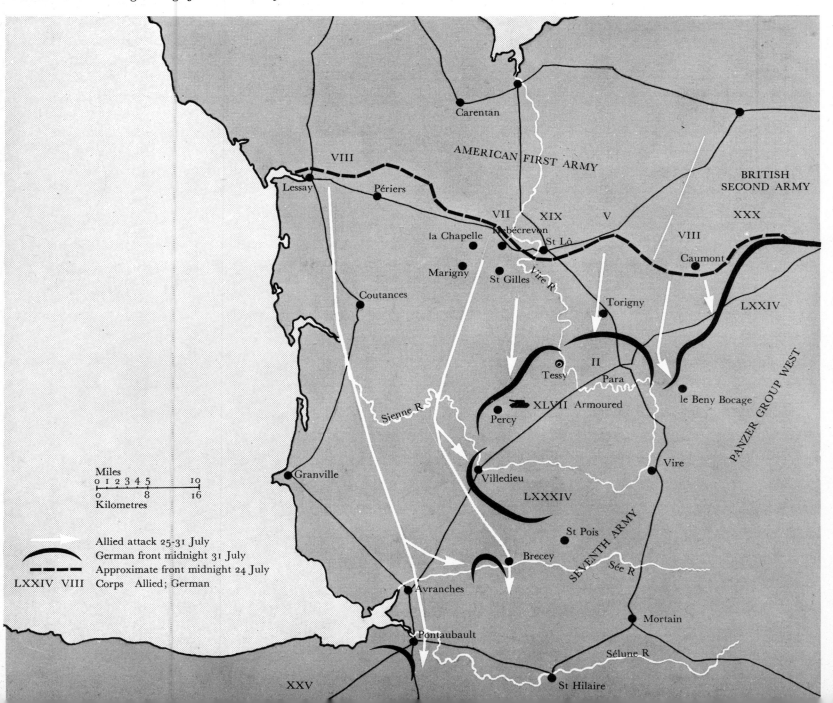

A Sherman tank in Montgomery's command speeds through Cahagnes on the advance towards the Odon; by pressing the Germans hard Montgomery gave Bradley the opportunity to make his break-out

US Signal Corps wiremen file through rubble-strewn streets to install communications in newly captured Saint-Lô on 20 July 1944; the ruined buildings bear witness to a successful air bombardment

The character of the battle changed after the capture of Avranches: Patton's Third Army rushed south and south-east with extraordinary speed and, after the capture of Le Mans, Bradley gave orders for a double envelopment south of Falaise

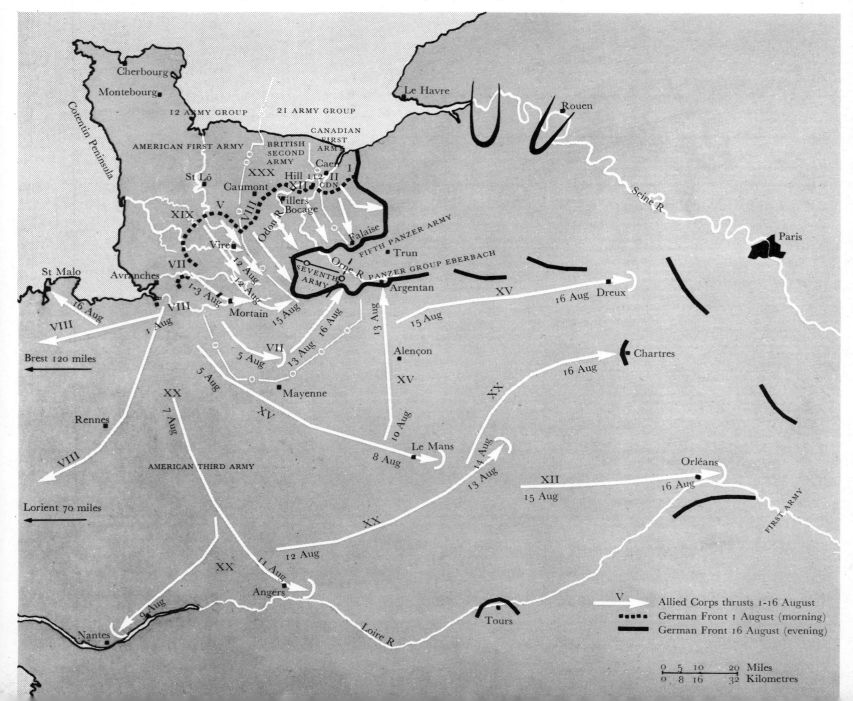

Instead of a wheeling pursuit on a broad front, the Allies would attempt a double envelopment south of Falaise. It was an astonishing concept. The Allied right wing, originally facing south, would swing through a half-circle to face northwards. Its supplies would follow it through that semicircle from the small and devastated ports of Normandy.

To succeed completely the Allied envelopment required a rapid closing of the pincers and careful co-ordination of the two jaws. Unfortunately, Haislip's XV Corps was delayed for a few vital hours by confusion on the roads south of Argentan, enabling German armour from Mortain to arrive and check its advance, while in the north the Canadian thrust towards Falaise still met strong and stubborn opposition which two inexperienced armoured divisions were unable to prise loose. And the Allied command was in a stage of transition which weakened the chain of authority and caused its wheels to hesitate.

With the advent of Patton's Third Army at the beginning of August a new Army Group, the Twelfth, was formed under Bradley's command, consisting of the First and Third American Armies. Montgomery remained in command of Twenty-first Army Group, with Second Army and the newly arrived First Canadian Army. It was intended that Eisenhower should eventually assume command of the ground forces. But till the Normandy battle was over Montgomery retained a measure of tactical control. It was a curious arrangement for conducting a battle. No longer truly in command, Montgomery was responsible for co-ordinating boundaries with an equal. With the delicate honour of Allies to be placated, it was a difficult situation for both Montgomery and Bradley; and, brooding over them, the enigmatic Eisenhower gave little help. If the closing of the Falaise gap gave rise to sharp polemics, it is remarkable that they were not still more bitter.

One decision which caused much criticism was taken by Bradley on 13 August. Only thirteen miles separated Haislip's American corps from the Canadians, and no one expected the weak German front to hold. But Bradley suddenly halted Haislip. Without consulting Montgomery, he ordered him to resume the drive to the Seine. The bulk of XV Corps drove through undefended country to Dreux, while the southern pincer stood still.

In the event Bradley's decision may not have had much effect, since most of the Germans were still in the pocket. Only on the 16th, when the Canadians entered Falaise, did Kluge order a general withdrawal. On the 19th the Canadians and Americans met at Saint-Lambert, a village south of Trun, and stretched a tenuous line across the German rear. Adventurous bands still found their way eastwards to the Seine, but most of Seventh Army

British soldiers survey a road east of Chambois completely blocked by wrecked transport vehicles abandoned by the retreating Germans after a successful RAF attack

RIGHT *Wrecked German tanks and corpses litter a battlefield after the Allied breakthrough (painted by Ogden Pleissner); by the end of August the Allies had lost 210,000 casualties, the Germans many more*

RIGHT BELOW *RAF rocket-firing Typhoons add their contribution to the punishment of German armour fighting in the Falaise area (painted by Frank Wootton)*

and much of Fifth Panzer Army were lost. In the Argentan–Falaise area 50,000 prisoners were taken, and 10,000 dead were counted. No census was made of the horse-drawn vehicles which choked the lanes; but more than 3,000 tanks, guns and lorries were counted.

This was not the end of the German ordeal. When Patton had diverted XV Corps northwards to Argentan, he had maintained the eastward drive with two other corps, leaving his flank on the Loire to the protection of air patrols. These forces were now driving across the German rear further east, narrowing their Seine crossings to the stretch between Rouen and the sea. Seven Panzer divisions got only 1,300 men, 24 tanks, and 60 guns across the river. With losses like these there could be no stand on the Seine, and the pursuit continued relentlessly to the gates of the Reich.

To the end of August the campaign had cost the Allies 210,000 casualties. The German losses are impossible to estimate. The whole campaign in the west, including a subsidiary invasion of southern France, cost 500,000 men, of whom 200,000 were lost in the coastal fortresses. The matériel losses were immense. By holding an inflexible line across the *bocage* and taking the offensive when all was lost Hitler, like Napoleon at Waterloo, had spent his last farthing, and was left without resource to limit the catastrophe.

PIERS MACKESY

1944
The Ardennes

Von Rundstedt's counter-attack, aimed at Antwerp, achieved initial success, but delayed the main Allied offensive by a mere six weeks, at the cost of heavy German casualties

THE SUDDEN THUNDER of a thousand guns that broke the silence of the fog-shrouded Ardennes hills in the dawn of 16 December 1944 sounded more than just a rude reveille for stunned American soldiers. It shattered the delusion that the German Army, after catastrophic defeats in the summer and autumn, was finished and could not rise again.

The German offensive plunged the Allied armies, commanded by General Dwight D. Eisenhower, into the gravest crisis since the Normandy invasion. The impact was all the greater because Allied intelligence had utterly failed in its estimates. Even today, it seems incredible that the Germans could have assembled without detection 250,000 men and thousands of tanks and guns in the relatively small area of the Eifel, west of the Rhine. Actually, Allied air reconnaissance had spotted suspicious road and rail movements, and prisoners and civilian border crossers had reported large concentrations, even the imminence of an attack. But Allied headquarters saw only what they wanted to see. Rigid German security measures, in combination with an elaborate cover plan, fitted all too well into the picture of a German Army reduced to merely reacting to Allied moves.

Ever since the invasion in Normandy, Hitler had been

LEFT A column of black smoke rises from a blazing American tank in Robert Capa's photograph of one of the casualties in the great German winter offensive. INSET *The debris of another tank battle near Bastogne (painted by Bernard Arnest)*

determined to recapture the initiative. At Mortain, he had attempted to check the Allied breakout, in Lorraine to halt Lieutenant-General George S. Patton's tank race to the Rhine. He failed both times. Only after the theatre commander in the West, Field-Marshal Gerd von Rundstedt, had worked the miracle of stabilizing the front along the German frontier in September was Hitler presented with a situation that offered him the opportunity for a major counter-offensive.

Since July, Hitler had scrupulously gathered a formidable strategic reserve of 250,000 men, organized in a score of infantry and more than half a dozen panzer divisions and a host of supporting units. But he was caught in the vice of a two-front war. In addition to Eisenhower's seven armies, he had to consider the enormous mass of the Soviet Army, poised to strike from positions on the Vistula.

Hitler had neither the time nor the temperament for a waiting game. He was, in his words, 'sick of the rot of barren defence' and determined to 'achieve a decisive turn of the war', or lose all. Limitations of time and resources kept him from taking the chance of throwing his last reserve against the Russians, who could frustrate a quick victory by sucking the German forces into an endless campaign. But on the western front, Hitler might, by one bold stroke, eliminate half of Eisenhower's force and possibly compel the Allies to withdraw from the Continent. Then he could deal with the Russians.

For the tactical application of his strike, fate seemed to

offer just the right spot. The Ardennes, in the corner of Belgium east of the Meuse, was the weakest sector in General Eisenhower's line. No more than a hundred air miles to the north-west beckoned the great port of Antwerp, vital to the supply of the Allied armies. Toward that objective, Hitler would hurl Army Group B (Field Marshal Walter Model) with 3 armies and 26 divisions. Once the rapid thrust had leaped the Meuse between Liège and Dinant and reached Antwerp and the Scheldt Estuary, 4 Allied armies would be caught in a giant Cannae trap. A subsidiary attack from the area of Roermond was to tie down Allied forces north of the projected breakthrough.

The deceptively simple plan was a splendid expression of Hitler's vaulting ambition. Success depended on an extended spell of bad weather that would ground Allied air forces, a factor of awesome unpredictability. Von Rundstedt and Model warned Hitler that the distant objective of Antwerp was out of proportion to the available means. But the time had long passed when Hitler could be influenced by logical reasoning.

On 16 December, Hitler's Ardennes offensive, thrice postponed, jumped off against an 85-mile sector held by 5 American divisions of Lieutenant-General Courtney H. Hodges' First Army. In the north, the first assault waves of SS General Sepp Dietrich's Sixth Panzer Army rushed forward in the eerie illumination of hundreds of searchlights. To the men of Major-General Leonard T. Gerow's US V Corps, the white-sheeted figures appeared to be so many phantoms. But they were real, the spearhead of Dietrich's thrust toward Liège. After the unbelieving 99th and 2nd Divisions had recovered from the first shock, they fought with every man and weapon. Their artillery gave them magnificent support. Favoured by the rising slopes of the Elsenborn Ridge, they turned back wave after wave of Dietrich's panzer army during three crucial days of fierce battles and denied the Germans access to the only direct route to Liège and the Meuse. Only one armoured task force broke through the Losheim Gap on the Sixth Panzer Army's southern boundary. This lone force drove on toward Malmédy, Stavelot, and Stoumont, threading its way through the deep-cut valleys and over the hills, feeding on captured supplies, and missing only by a hair's breadth the largest Allied fuel dump in the west and General Hodges' headquarters at Spa. Then, on 19 December, it was stopped. Model's right wing, his strongest army, had failed.

It was General Hasso von Manteuffel's weaker, but better led, Fifth Panzer Army that achieved a breakthrough. To win tactical surprise, Manteuffel forwent preparatory artillery fires. He attacked with closely coordinated armour-infantry teams and penetrated Major-General Troy H. Middleton's thinly-spread US VIII Corps positions. With one corps on his right, Manteuffel encircled two regiments of the inexperienced US 106th Division on the frosty heights of the Schnee Eifel. Farther south, he launched his main attack with two panzer corps abreast. He smashed through the depleted US 28th Division and drove to the outskirts of Houffalize and Bastogne. The force of these blows shattered Middleton's VIII Corps.

General Erich Brandenberger's Seventh Army had been assigned the mission of protecting the south flank of the German main thrust by gaining defensible positions extending from Luxembourg to the Meuse. But his army was weak. After only modest gains in the first few days, Brandenberger's divisions ran afoul of the US 4th Infantry Division and a combat command of the 9th Armoured Division. Only on his right was Brandenberger able to keep pace with Manteuffel's advance.

By 18 December, the failure of the Sixth Panzer Army

BELOW LEFT *US artillery shells positions occupied by the Sixth Panzer Army; three crucial days of fierce fighting stopped the panzers' thrust towards Liège.* RIGHT *German infantry rush across a Belgian road blocked with damaged vehicles; Hitler contrived to assemble 250,000 men and thousands of tanks and guns for this offensive without detection*

had ruined Hitler's chances of reaching Antwerp. Even Manteuffel's Fifth Panzer Army had fallen behind schedule. His breakthrough, furthermore, was too narrow to be fully exploited. Having made no provision for failure, Hitler was trapped by the inflexibility of his own plan. But he decided to exploit Manteuffel's breakthrough. To feed it, he cancelled the subsidiary attack from Roermond and shifted those forces and Dietrich's armour south. This might widen the breakthrough area. The change in plans was fraught with an accumulation of 'ifs'. If the fog and low clouds over the Ardennes would continue to shield German movements against air attack; if the terrible congestion on the winding mountain roads of the Ardennes could be dissolved; and if the Allies were slow in reacting; then there still might be a chance of at least reaching the Meuse.

Near Reims, meanwhile, Eisenhower had correctly judged the offensive to be more than a mere spoiling attack. His first reaction was to pinch off the German penetration by a wide double envelopment converging on Bonn and Cologne. But as the crisis deepened and the thrust threatened to rip his front apart, Eisenhower settled for a more modest counter-move. He cancelled his planned offensive to the Rhine and ordered all available reserves, British and American, to be gathered at once. He intended to hold the shoulders of the penetration at any cost and prevent the Germans from crossing the Meuse. Then he would strike back from the shoulders and eliminate the salient. To shore up the crumbling lines of Middleton's corps, Eisenhower directed Lieutenant-General Omar N. Bradley, commanding the 12th Army Group, to send one armoured division from the north and one from the south against the German flanks. To General Hodges he despatched his only ready theatre reserve, the XVIII Airborne Corps. When it appeared that

Model might split Bradley's army group, Eisenhower placed all US forces north of the breakthrough under Field-Marshal Montgomery's 21st Army Group, leaving only Patton's Third Army under Bradley. Thus did Eisenhower personally take charge.

To preserve the integrity of his forces, Eisenhower was prepared if necessary to yield space. For a counter-attack against the German southern flank, he had directed Patton to disengage his army opposite the Saar and wheel it ninety degrees to the left for a thrust to the north. The 6th Army Group in Alsace would have to conform by taking over Patton's sector and giving up some of the hard-won terrain in Alsace, even Strasbourg. In the emotionally charged atmosphere in Paris, General de Gaulle's resistance to the decision threatened to split the Allied coalition. Largely because Hitler hesitated to exploit this moment of Allied weakness, only the northern corner of Alsace was evacuated and Strasbourg was saved.

Even before the first stop-gap measures could begin to influence the course of the battle, small groups of brave men had done so by clinging to critical features all along the ridged and furrowed face of the Ardennes. They slowed the German advance and gave the first American reserves a chance to make a stand at two crucial points. At Saint-Vith the 7th Armoured Division delayed the fall of the city until 21 December. The sacrifice of elements of the 10th Armoured Division held up Manteuffel's armour long enough to allow the 101st Airborne Division to enter Bastogne on the 18th and organize its defence sufficiently to turn back the first German attack on that vital road centre next day. The heroic action forced the Fifth Panzer Army to detour around Bastogne and leave forces behind for an encirclement, forces that Manteuffel desperately needed for his further advance. On 22 December the Germans threatening the annihilation of Bastogne

BELOW LEFT *A reconnaissance patrol of the 7th Armoured Division, which had been forced to surrender the city on 21 December, re-enters battle-scarred Saint-Vith.* CENTRE *Infantrymen of the 3rd Armoured Division advance on the run under a fierce barrage of shellfire in Mont-le-Ban on the northern flank of the German salient.* RIGHT *German infantry advancing past burning vehicles*

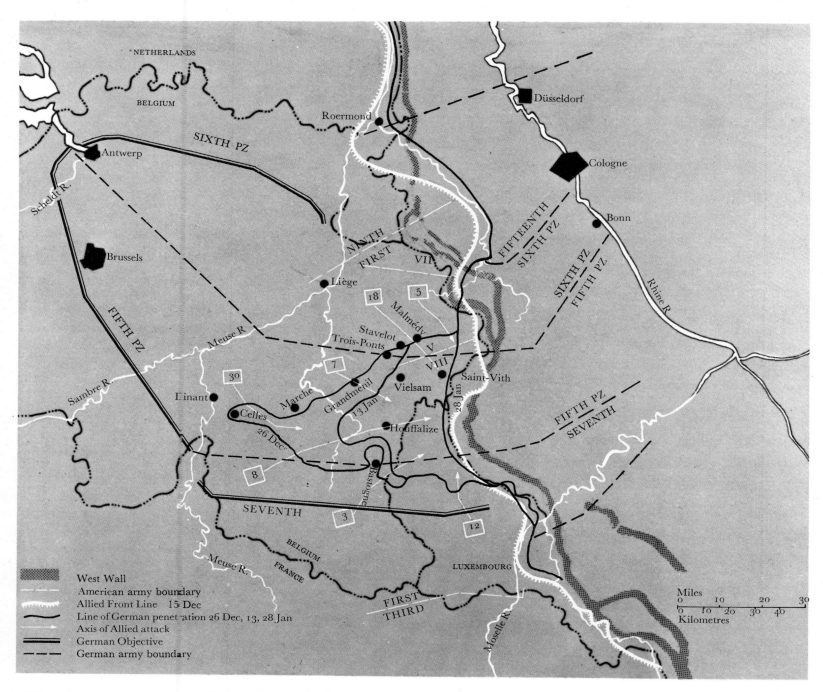

Hitler's deceptively simple plan to eliminate half of Eisenhower's forces, which he hoped would compel the Allies to withdraw from the Continent; and Eisenhower's counter-attacks, after Hitler had lost the initiative

demanded its surrender. Brigadier-General Anthony Mc-Auliffe's defiant answer, 'Nuts', epitomized the indomitable American fighting spirit. The irony of the situation was that the Germans could not carry out their threat, nor could the Allied garrison, fast running out of supplies, have held the city in the face of a determined assault.

The gallant defence of Bastogne narrowed the German advance, but could not stop it. Manteuffel's two panzer corps continued their westward drive. On the right, the Sixth Panzer Army once again was on the move. On Christmas Eve, Manteuffel's 2nd Panzer Division's spearhead reached the heights overlooking the Meuse, near

the village of Celles. Exposed in flank and rear because other divisions had failed to keep abreast, the point of Hitler's offensive, within sight of its objective, stood alone. It went no further.

At this crucial moment, the weather changed. Hundreds of Allied fighters and bombers rose into the clearing skies and pounced upon the hapless Germans. They bombed and strafed forward positions, the endless columns that clogged roads clear back to the German border, and the airfields, rail lines, depots, and dumps. Transport planes in the nick of time resupplied Bastogne.

By Christmas Day the Allies at last had drawn a tenuous cordon around the serrated salient of the Ardennes.

On its southern edge, General Patton was on the attack to relieve Bastogne. Slowly his III Corps, flanked by VIII and XII Corps, was gaining against stiff opposition. Along the northern rim, General Hodges had placed three of his corps – V, XVIII Airborne, and VII – and at the Meuse stood the British XXX Corps. Montgomery, finding Hodges' centre still fragile, ordered a withdrawal from a pocket at Vielsalm to a shorter line between Trois-Ponts and Grandménil. Before striking, Montgomery was ready to fall back even farther.

On Christmas Day the US 2nd Armoured Division (VII Corps) cut off, then crushed, the advanced elements of the 2nd Panzer Division at Celles. On the 26th, the reverse at the tip of the bulge flared to the flanks. At Marche and Grandménil German efforts to widen the penetration were frustrated; and at Bastogne the first tanks of the US 4th Armoured Division broke through to the besieged city.

The first phase of the battle was over. Hitler had lost the initiative, although he was unwilling to admit it. He projected yet another set of grandiose schemes: capturing Bastogne, outflanking the First Army by a hook to the north, reinstating the supporting attack from Roermond, launching a New Year's offensive into Alsace, and lashing out against Allied airfields with a thousand planes. Hitler was playing with little tin soldiers. The Alsace and air offensives both fell short of their objectives. In the Ardennes, Hitler could apply his remaining strength only to Bastogne. It became the fulcrum on which the ultimate outcome of the battle would turn.

Eisenhower, meantime, had ordered Bradley and Montgomery to attack. Hodges' First Army was to strike from the north; Patton, who had never stopped in his drive, was to continue it. The two armies were to join hands at Houffalize and at Saint-Vith, thus slicing the German-held bulge into pieces.

Patton had been finding the inheritance of Bastogne an increasingly heavy burden. At the end of the year, the corridor to the city was still no wider than a mile. Two German corps were doggedly clinging to its shoulders. As Patton made his plans for the northward thrust, Manteuffel, on Hitler's orders, was bringing up new forces to cut out the festering sore on his south flank. The two attacks collided on 30 December. For days the battle raged with mounting bitterness, swaying back and forth, at times in utter confusion. Heavy snowfalls and icy winds decimated the ranks where the battle already had taken its heavy toll. When it was over, Hitler's Ardennes offensive was dead.

The rest was anticlimactic. Hodges, after laborious regrouping, joined the attack on 3 January 1945. On the 9th, Patton shouldered his way out of the sack of Bastogne. Fighting a skilful and determined delaying action,

and aided by the weather, which had again closed in, Model, a master at improvization, managed to extricate the bulk of his forces before they were trapped. Grudgingly, Hitler had permitted limited withdrawals on 8 January. On the 13th he authorized a general retreat. The day before, the Russians had launched their great winter offensive that was to carry them in the spring to the gates of Berlin. Hodges' and Patton's armies at last made contact at Houffalize on the 16th. Bradley again assumed command over his First Army and within the next two weeks flattened the bulge.

On 28 January the Battle of the Ardennes was over. Like a gigantic magnet, it had drawn 33 Allied and 29 German divisions into the greatest of pitched battles on the Western Front. The costs were appalling: almost 100,000 German and 75,000 Allied casualties, hundreds of German tanks, vehicles, guns, and planes, many of them abandoned for lack of fuel or minor defects. It was a savage, merciless struggle, erupting on occasions in atrocities, yet bringing to the surface islands of mutual respect, mercy, and human dignity. Acts of heroism and cowardice, both went unnoticed under the awesome shadow of events. Most men simply did their duty. For many an American soldier Normandy had been the initiation. In the Ardennes he came out as the man who fought and stood his ground against fearful odds, in seemingly hopeless situations.

An Army broken in body and spirit retreated to the German positions of old. The men, having been led to believe that this last desperate effort would bring an end to the war, knew that ahead lay only the long night of total defeat. Hitler, too, knew that the end was near. He had gambled all – and lost.

CHARLES V. P. VON LUTTICHAU

General Eisenhower, the Supreme Allied Commander, with (left to right) Lieutenant-General Bradley, Commander of the Twelfth Army Group, Air Chief Marshal Tedder, Eisenhower's deputy, Field-Marshal Montgomery, Commander of the Twenty-first Army Group, and Lieutenant-General Simpson, Commander of the US Ninth Army

The Development of Fortifications

From earliest historical times soldiers have used fortifications to strengthen important positions and to support their field armies. The evolution of the art of fortification has therefore been continuous, inevitably reflecting the current developments in weapon technology and the Art of War. In particular, the increasing range and destructive power of artillery weapons have compelled military engineers to adapt their permanent fortifications to meet the new conditions, and similarly the improvements in field guns and in the accuracy and rate of fire of small arms have caused alterations in the design of field defences.

There are two distinct types of fortification and one additional, hybrid variety. First there are 'permanent works', normally constructed in time of peace on a large scale by Governments anxious to protect vital strategic areas against sudden attack; coastal and frontier fortifications often belong to this category. 'Field defences', on the other hand, are usually hastily extemporized to meet a particular tactical situation during hostilities, normally taking the form of earthworks or trenches. Thirdly, there is a category which may be described as 'semi-permanent' – defences which contain elements of both the main types of fortification.

All fortifications are designed to perform certain basic functions, although priorities alter with changing circumstances. First, there is the element of fire-power; it is axiomatic that all sectors of the defence perimeter should be covered by fire, and every position must be designed to afford the defenders the freest possible use of their weapons. Secondly, there is protection; this can be achieved either directly by the use of earth parapets or concrete overhead cover, or indirectly, through the employment of camouflage or distance. Thirdly, comes the task of obstruction, achieved by ditches, wire entanglements, minefields and obstacles of all kinds covered by fire,

designed to slow down the enemy's advance, impede his use of weapons, and delay his arrival at hand-to-hand grips with the defenders. It is not unknown for priorities to conflict; for instance, the requirements of protection and weapon employment may not be easy to reconcile, and consequently, a carefully balanced compromise has to be devised to suit the particular circumstances.

Although weapons and materials may alter beyond all recognition with the passage of time, rudimentary principles underlie the construction of all good fortifications. The most important of these are simplicity, strength, provision of clear fields of fire, careful adaptation of defence schemes to the configuration of the ground, and utmost economy in the use of manpower.

For nearly two hundred years the name of Vauban was practically synonymous with the development of fortification. This is somewhat ironic for, although his place in history rests on his reputation as an engineer, the French Marshal was, in fact, far more interested in the problems of active warfare. His achievement in the sphere of fortification was to perfect the work of others, and although his many admirers and imitators subsequently attempted to distil his work into the so-called 'three orders' of military architecture, he insisted that every town or position be regarded as a unique fortification problem.

To counter the effects of smooth-bore cannon, capable of firing cast-iron shot to a maximum range of 600 yards, he perfected the system of the bastion trace invented by his predecessor Pagan, making the widest possible use of cross-fire to sweep the approaches to a distance of 800 yards, and employing elaborate series of supporting defences to protect the parapets from direct assault. The all-important angle bastions were massive constructions of earth and stone, dominating the intervening parapets and generally standing to

a height of 17 feet over the lip of the 'glacis' – a killing ground purposely cleared of all forms of cover. Between the glacis and main trace was an 18-foot ditch, and it became the almost invariable practice to build 'tenailles', 'demi-lunes', 'hornworks' and 'ravelins' within it to protect the curtain walls and bastion salients. A further refinement was the construction of 'counterscarp galleries' within the outer face of the ditch from which musketeers could sweep the foot of the parapets. Generally speaking, engineers abandoned vertical walls for banked fortifications, striving to achieve depth rather than height, a standard thickness for curtain walls being 18 feet of packed earth faced with stone. Fortifications of this type became increasingly complex, with the disadvantage that it became ever more difficult for the garrison to concentrate at a threatened sector owing to the complication of internal communications. In the days of comparatively rudimentary gunnery investments were often lengthy affairs, but Vauban's perfected system of breaching and approaching the enemy fortifications with parallel and approach trenches, using sap and gabion, became standardized European practice for over two centuries.

So deeply did Vauban's influence permeate the conduct of defence and sieges that many of his successors contented themselves with copying his methods wholesale. Nevertheless, certain improvements in profile and trace did appear over

Star Trace (Mid-18th C.)

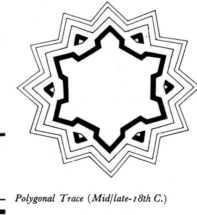

Polygonal Trace (Mid/late-18th C.)

the following one hundred and fifty years, most of them made necessary by the considerable improvements in the artillery arm introduced by such experts as the Frenchman, de Gribeauval. Even during Vauban's lifetime, the Dutch engineer Coehoorn taught the need for maximum firepower rather than elaborate earthworks, while the German Rimpler experimented with the use of a central bastion within the enceinte. Not all the changes were for the better, however; some experts advocated the use of a 'star trace' which produced strong cross-fire, but almost precluded outward fire and exposed the parapets to an increased danger of enfilading. Such 'geometrical' systems often ignored the natural configuration of the ground.

Other developments were more successful; Chasseloup-Laubat experimented usefully with placing ravelins beyond the glacis to increase the area of cross-fire. The most important innovation, however, was the gradual development of the 'polygonal trace' which dispensed with the use of angle-bastions, replacing them with bombproof 'caponiers' in the ditch. The Prussian, Landsberg the Younger, was one of the first to suggest this system, but its strongest advocate was Marc René Montalembert. He was also the great protagonist of 'active' defence and all-round fire, designing long stretches of low parapet and placing cannon in successive tiers of casements to improve the volume of outward fire. His ideas were largely copied in a simplified form by Carnot, but the system reached its perfection under the German school. Although there was a growing realization that simplicity and strength were the most important principles, many French engineers remained conservative in outlook, and employed the ancient bastion-trace until as late as 1870.

Long before 1870 it was becoming clear that the bastion-trace was obsolescent in the face of rifled artillery with a range of 1,500 yards, and a new form of permanent fortification was evolved in the detached fort. Outlying defences had to be placed at ever-increasing distances from the place defended to keep the enemy's guns at a distance. As the construction of a continuous enceinte was by this time prohibitively costly, this led to the employment of chains of detached forts relying on fire-power to command the intervals between them.

Although Vauban had experimented

The Vauban Bastion Trace (Late 17th C.)

ravelins and horn-works

glacis · counterscarp step · ditch · bastion

counterscarp gallery

▲ caponiers at foot of wall

Torres Vedras Redoubt (1809)

with such an idea at Toulon, Wellington's famed Lines of Torres Vedras form perhaps the most striking example of the use of strings of such works instead of a continuous line of ramparts and ditches. More than 100 redoubts were built to command the 30-mile width of the peninsula. Linz and Paris were fortified thus between 1830 and 1844, but the new system reached its fullest development in the new defences of Antwerp (commenced in 1859), which comprised a 9-mile 'polygonal' enceinte divided into 11 fronts with a citadel on the northern side, supported by 14 detached forts with inundations to the north and west.

The detached fort system, however, did not long match the developments in missile-firing weapons using high explosive shells. In 1904, the six uncompleted forts of Port Arthur's main defence perimeter soon crumbled under the fire of the Japanese 11-inch howitzers. The system came abruptly to a conclusion in 1914 when Liège, Namur and Antwerp were rapidly overrun by the Germans, and the whole future of permanent fortifications was apparently placed in jeopardy.

The lessons of Port Arthur reinforced the 'redoubt and trench' school of thought first expressed in the Rumanian Sereth Line (built 1889–1902), and in 1905 the German Schroeter advocated the use of low-lying defences contained within a 1,200-yard wire perimeter protected by a 20-foot deep ditch; within this area were sited infantry and artillery positions individually wired-off and provided with deep underground galleries for protection. The first 'Feste' redoubts were constructed at Metz, and their principles became widely copied.

In 1914, the French abandoned the Verdun fortresses after the loss of Maubeuge in eleven days, but they were subsequently re-occupied two years later when it was noted that German shells were having little noticeable effect on the steel artillery cupolas. However, the role of the fortress had changed; it was no longer an island of resistance, but a strong sector in a vast, integrated and connected system of trenches and redoubts. The advantages conferred by field fortifications were now very evident. The result was almost four years of trench warfare and stalemate on the Western Front, although three new weapons of war made their appearance, namely aircraft, tanks and gas, two of which were probably capable of ending the deadlock if properly employed. These developments foreshadowed another radical change in the Art of Fortification.

During the inter-war years, considerable thought was applied to the problems of fortification. The Germans and, to a lesser extent, the British became aware that the advent of tanks and aircraft implied the end of static warfare, and paid comparatively little attention to permanent defences. In Russia, too, the climate of opinion was in favour of 'scorched earth' policies and the utilization of wide open spaces, supplemented with field defences. Only the French totally misread the lessons of 1918 and placed their faith in massive fortifications capable of fantastic fire-power. The Maginot Line was a series of large ferro-concrete and steel fortresses, shell-proof and tank-proof, containing heavy guns and being provided with underground shelter-galleries and connecting tunnels. However, there was little defence in depth, and only in 1939 were field-works constructed in the intervals and covering the rear. In the event, the Maginot Line was never finally tested, for it reached only as far North as Valenciennes, and in May 1940 the German forces swept round the northern flank with ease.

The obsolescence of permanent fortifications faced by the modern techniques of blitzkrieg war was convincingly shown in Poland and Belgium; the fortress of Westerplatte near Danzig was pounded into submission after six days of bombardment and assault, and the reputedly impregnable fort of Eben-Emael near Maastricht was stormed by German paratroopers and special engineers within forty-eight hours.

Faced by these new circumstances, the bulk of fortifications followed the field pattern; the principal requirements were all-round defence, adequate camouflage, cover from air attack as well as conventional artillery bombardment, and above all security against tanks. Self-sufficient enclaves of weapon slits and gun positions, surrounded by wire and minefields became the standard form of fortification used by British forces in both the Western Desert and Burma. The Japanese went in extensively for strong bunkers associated with weapon slit positions, and under jungle conditions this type of defence proved extremely hard to crack.

As the Germans were forced on to the defensive in Italy, they made use of defended river lines to hold up the Allied advance; their strong positions behind the River Garigliano (the 'Gustav Line') included the natural fortress of Cassino, and further north the Gothic Line also proved troublesome. The most notable characteristic of these positions was depth – successive series of minefields, pill-boxes and fortified villages.

To protect 'Festung Europa', Hitler's engineers devised the 'West Wall' along the coasts from Holland to Spain. The ports were heavily protected with guns and inland flooding, and to protect the intervening stretches of coast the Germans used a variety of beach-obstacles and wired the overlooking cliffs. Further back a line of defended localities commanded the beach exits, and between two and five miles inland a second belt of strong-points was sited, all containing artillery and minefields, flooded areas and wire for local protection. American experience on Omaha Beach showed how formidable these defences could be, but fortunately for the allies large stretches were incomplete on D-Day.

DAVID CHANDLER

Defences of Antwerp (Detached Forts) (c 1859)

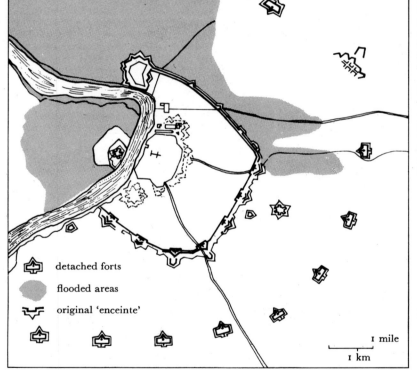

detached forts

flooded areas

original 'enceinte'

1 mile

1 km

Section of Maginot Line Fortress (1939)

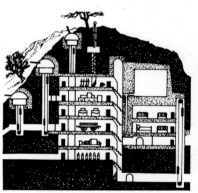

Omaha Beach Defences (1944)

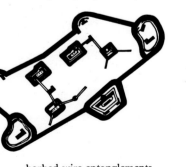

high water mark

low water mark

pill-boxes

sea wall

wire

cliff positions

underwater and waterline obstacles

minefields

Retractible Armoured Gun-Turret (1860)

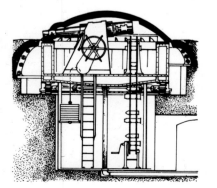

German Festé Redoubt (Early 20th C.)

barbed wire entanglements and ditches

The Development of Uniforms

Introduction

The 'Uniform Plate' shows, as a general rule, a regulated dress with everything correct and the soldier or officer turned out exactly as the designer of the uniform, the tailor and the sergeant-major in barracks would have him.

All too many of us have had experience of active war service and know that a soldier seldom appeared as he was designed to look, and that a soldier turned out as he felt he would be best equipped to deal with circumstances and his own personal demands – or with a hostile individual or machine. However, he might subconsciously preserve some respect for uniformity with his comrades. On the occasion of a ceremony, inspection or 'triumph' a Commanding Officer contrived to achieve uniformity and a turn-out approximately conforming to regulation.

In this collection of figures I have felt it necessary to compromise, my intention being to present a figure that shows the characteristics of the soldier's dress or uniform at the period of each battle – what the soldier should have looked like if high command, the artist and the uniform pundit had control, and not how he appeared, in fact, at his dirtiest and most unorthodox. A Scot in the Crimea, a Russian at Stalingrad, a Frenchman in the retreat from Moscow or in the trenches in Flanders, really might look much the same and I would fail to demonstrate any development of uniform.

An apology may therefore be necessary for what the realist might regard as a too theatrical treatment and the uniform fan 'inaccurate'. However, the soldiers pictured were issued with uniforms and equipment much as those shown, and one can be more certain with the later figures than with the earlier. Documentation for the earlier is sparse and unreliable, so common sense and experience must combine to penetrate the superficiality of the handsome and romantic plate or battle print of the past.

A. E. HASWELL MILLER

1 Rocroi *1643*

A Musketeer. At this time uniforms did not exist. So far as we can gather, difficulties in distinguishing friend from enemy were frequent, notwithstanding the adoption of something in the nature of an armband, scarf or cockade of a certain colour. Small branches of foliage might also be employed. Hanging from the shoulder belt are the 'Twelve Apostles', ingenious containers of measured charges for the musket. Between the fingers of the hand holding the rest is the match

2 Blenheim *1704*

British Infantry. Regiments were uniformed by their colonels, whose names they bore as titles. Numbering or regional designations were not employed. Such regulations as existed were rather approximate, but regiments were distinguished by facings of different colours – a 'Royal' regiment having blue

3 Poltava *1709*

Russian Officer. An army of western pattern had only recently been created, clad mainly in green. From some not very reliable evidence it might appear that some – possibly Guards – formations wore red

4 Rossbach *1757*

Prussian Cavalry – *Belling* Hussar. The Hussar – Hungarian Light cavalry – had become fashionable in armies outside Hungary, the dress having an obvious appeal. Although 'Hussars' are named in the Order of Battle of the Jacobite forces in the 1745 Rising, the British Army did not have Hussar regiments until the beginning of the nineteenth century. On the *Flügel Mütze*, or wing cap, is the device of a complete skeleton. This is one of the prototypes of the many 'Death's Head' regiments common to various armies but particularly the German – and discredited by Hitler's employment of the device for his SS formations

5 Quebec *1759*

British Officer of Infantry. When serving in distant campaigns, uniform regulations drawn up in the 1740s would tend to lapse. This officer felt more comfortable with a light fusil and bayonet; and a short 'hanger' replaces his sword. Parading at home the officer would be armed with an 'espontoon', a kind of partisan or pike. The uniform remains loose and practical. The waistcoat might be more elaborate than the coat, which could be quite a plain article on service

6 Bunker Hill *1775*

British Light Infantryman. A flank company of an infantry battalion was differently trained and equipped from the rest of the battalion. A leather cap was worn, of varying pattern in all regiments – and sometimes improvised. The jacket had short tails, and short gaiters were usual. Regulation dress seems to have largely disappeared as the war went on, this figure presenting few or limited irregularities

7 Saratoga *1777*

Grenadier Officer. The right flank company was the Grenadier Company wearing a high pointed cloth cap with a high, fur-edged front with a metal plate at the base. Officers carried a fusil. The colours of facings, and the pattern and arrangement of the laced button-holes on lapels and cuffs would vary according to regiment

8 Yorktown *1781*

Revolutionary Infantry Private. The pattern of the uniform of the revolutionary corps naturally followed that of the British army, but it was in general blue in colour with white facings. There was however a great deal of variety, especially among irregular corps, possessing few characteristics of conventional military uniform

9 Jena *1806*

Prussian Cuirassier Officer. By now the easy and reasonably practical uniform had become more formal. High close collar and tight sleeves and breeches seem to belong more to the parade ground than the field. The heavy straight sword, large boots and white uniform are typical heavy cavalry characteristics in central Europe

10 Jena *1806*

French Infantryman. The French Revolutionary soldier was extremely sketchy in dress, albeit wearing many articles of more elaborate uniforms. The sloppy cocked hat, worn in a manner no others appear to have copied, and the striped or checked trousers, or overalls, of very arbitrary style disappeared with the rise of Napoleon, when military tailoring became an industry

11

12

13

14

15

16

17

18

19

20

21

22

11 Borodino *1812*
French Dragoon. Dismounted and in some adversity but shown nearer regulation state than many contemporary documents suggest was common. He carries the valise from his saddle as a knapsack. The 'Grecian' helmet remained with comparatively few changes, but with variations according to the type of corps wearing it, as a functioning headdress up to 1914, and indeed is still worn as the headdress by the Garde Républicaine in ceremonial dress

12 Waterloo *1815*
French Infantry – Grenadier of the Guard. Only a small patch of the original Grenadier Cap (a conical cloth one), with the badge of a grenade, is visible, as it is by now almost entirely covered with fur. Whether of intent, or as a subconscious policy, the high headdress goes far in the intimidation of any enemy, suggesting as it does a super-human and impersonal creature. Oddly enough, below the hand-pouch may be seen the off-duty cap: the neatly rolled white 'night cap' from which the massive furred grenadier cap sprang. He might wear white breeches and gaiters in place of trousers

13 Waterloo *1815*
French Infantry – Voltigeur. Typical of the French Infantry full dress uniform. The colours of the plume, collar, patch on cuff, epaulette strap and fringe all had their significance, indicating type of infantryman, battalion of regiment, brigade, etc. Within a decade or so there were many changes, shape of shako, of badge; and there were periodic changes to an all white uniform with coloured facings

14 Waterloo *1815*
British Dragoon, Royal Scots Greys. Except for the Grenadier Cap (worn as an honour, as taken from the French), the uniform is a typical heavy Dragoon pattern of service dress. The grey overalls are literally 'over-alls' covering and protecting breeches and stockings

15 Balaclava *1854*
Private of the 93rd Highlanders (renowned as 'The Thin Red Line'). He is shown too properly dressed, it may be. But there probably were some who took part in the action thus. As an alternative to the costly and precious feathered bonnet, a 'glengarry' would be worn. Contemporary photographs, few but admirable, show that, although the British soldier appeared on the scene correctly attired according to the coloured uniform prints of the period, he was also the most irregular as soon as conditions proved his uniform and equipment unserviceable

16 Balaclava *1854*
Troops of a Russian Regiment. Contemporary photographs suggest an army superior to its opponents in personnel and equipment. The Uhlan or Lancer shows the imposing Polish *tschapka* or lancer cap covered by waterproof as it would be on service. The lancer tunic was probably replaced by a plainer short shell jacket

17 First Bull Run *1861*
Cavalry Officer, Confederate States Army. This figure in the grey uniform, which is popularly regarded as that of the South, is a somewhat dandified type. At the outset the Southern Cavalry were superior to the Northerners and their quality was reflected in their uniform. By the end of the war there would be little of this elegance left

18 Gettysburg *1863*
Sergeant, Zouaves – Union Army. Although the accepted convention is that the Union Army was clad in blue with a kepi and the Confederate in grey with a felt hat, a great variety of uniform was, in fact, worn. This figure, based on a contemporary painting, records a Zouave corps. It must be remarked that blue is the one colour lacking

19 Gravelotte – Saint-Privat *1870*
Prussian Cuirassier. The white uniform with facings of regimental distinguishing colours was worn from the 1840s up to 1914 with little more alterations than those dictated by fashion

20 Gravelotte – Saint-Privat *1870*
French Zouave. The Zouaves were a comparatively new branch of the infantry dating from the 1830s. The uniform underwent few changes up to 1914, by when there was no turban over the *chechia* or fez, and plain white gaiters were worn. Other corps with similar exotic dress were the Turcos in light blue and the Spahis (cavalry) with red jackets and light blue Turkish trousers

21 Port Arthur *1904*
Japanese Infantry. The Japanese were now equipped in the German pattern with little elaboration and no headdress of full dress type. Officers however in ceremonial dress had a uniform somewhat French in character with a stiff kepi carrying a high white plume. In cold weather heavy dark grey greatcoats with hoods were worn

22 Tannenberg *1914*
Russian Infantry Officer. The Russian service dress was of a greyish khaki; headdress a peaked cap with an oval cockade or in winter a grey fur cap. The officer is in a semi-service dress which could be worn when not in action. This method of slinging the sword was peculiar to the Russian army

23 Tannenberg *1914*
Trooper, *Totenkopf* Hussar Regiment. A trooper of the 'Death's Head' Hussars – of which there were two Prussian and one Brunswick regiments – in the handsome field grey correct hussar pattern as worn in the *Ausmarsch*. Before long these uniforms were replaced by plainer issues suitable for all branches. At first the peacetime full dress headdress was worn, covered in grey which would be adjusted, in appropriate situations, to exhibit an impressive device, if such were worn

24 The Marne *1914*
French Infantry. The French began the war clad practically as on manoeuvre and, beginning with khaki or grey covers to headdress, gradually became uniformed in 'horizon' blue, dark grey-blue or khaki, according to the arm of the service. The *poilu* shown begins to exhibit the altered shape of the French infantryman which had changed little since 1870

25 The Marne *1914*

German Infantry. Full dress *Piekelhaube* with spike, was covered, unless out of actual service, and a new field grey uniform of the same shape as full dress had been prepared in good time for the *Ausmarsch*. As opposed to the French, the Germans of all arms appeared as prepared to the last degree of the *praktisch*. Nevertheless – a curious phenomenon – no army changed as little in appearance during the war as the British

26 Suvla Bay *1915*

Australian Light Horse, dismounted. The Australian forces were uniformed in a particularly comfortable and practical blouse-jacket of a more buff colour than the British (and New Zealand) greenish khaki. Units wore coloured formation signs on sleeve and headdress and coloured lines in the puggaree indicated the regiment

27 Suvla Bay *1915*

Turkish Infantry. Properly dressed, the Turks might appear in longish skirted tunics of grey-green of German pattern, but all kinds of material – drab, yellow or grey – and pattern were employed. The headdress here is the 'Enver helmet', a rather untidy endeavour to comply with the Moslem prohibition against shading the eyes and at the same time to afford more protection than that given by fez or kalpak

28 Caporetto *1917*

Italian Infantry. Caporale Maggiore of Bersaglieri. The grey-green service dress was devised several years before 1914 and, like the British, underwent no alterations during the war – proving indeed so satisfactory that it survived to the Hitler-Mussolini war. The steel helmet, of French pattern, was adopted, like all those of the combatant armies, by 1916 and, in the case of the Bersaglieri, adorned by the bunch of cock's feathers, as worn in their full dress felt hat dating from the 1830s

29 Stalingrad *1942*

Russian Infantry. The imitation fur cap with red star badge, a smallish peaked cap, a fore and aft field cap and steel helmet were all typical of the Russian headdress. The very long grey greatcoat and felt boots are peculiar to the Soviet soldier

30 **Stalingrad** *1942*
German artillery Officer. Rather properly dressed for Stalingrad where the Germans were somewhat *in extremis* and would more typically appear in balaklava and steel helmet, greatcoat and plenty of stick grenades

31 **Alamein** *1942*
British Infantry, Highland Regiment. The khaki drill tropical uniform remained unchanged from that worn for some ten years previous to the war. Details such as the formation sign worn on shoulder strap were new and the web equipment with clumsy large pouches gave the soldier a somewhat different shape from that of the 1914–18 war. For the first time the Highland soldier was persuaded to discard the kilt on service although mysteriously kilts would appear at any 'triumph'

32 **Alamein** *1942*
Indian Infantry. The Sikh Bren-gunner is shown in ordinary universal battle dress, worn in cold weather. Sikhs were the only Indian troops to retain the *pagri* or turban invariably, and all their hair, the beard being neatly rolled. Unlike certain other Indian troops, such as Punjabi Musalmen, the Sikh wore no conical cap around which the *pagri* was tied

33 **Alamein** *1942*
German Artillery Officer. Perhaps imitating the British, the German in North Africa self-consciously dressed the part of the unorthodox anti-regulation swashbuckler. The exaggerated peak of the cap is very typical of the Afrika Korps, as are the wide trousers tied at the ankle – in this case aping the French Spahi fashion

34 **Guadalcanal** *1942*
US Infantry. The soldier would be more frequently wearing his steel helmet or its 'liner' of the same shape. The American equipment was such that great variation in methods of carrying gear was possible. Gaiters were discarded, as soldiers in Guadalcanal were frequently in water

35 **Guadalcanal** *1942*
Japanese Infantry. A very nondescript uniform. The soft cotton peaked cap was generally even more shapeless than shown here. In full dress the German type of peaked cap with coloured band was worn, but otherwise a particularly wide variety of practical outfits for all conditions of warfare were remarkable for their uninspiring character

36 **Saint Lô-Falaise** *1944*
German SS Officer. The *Waffen SS* (termed by the American authorities Elite Guards) were, when possible, clad in black uniforms, decorated with skulls and crossbones, or some other sinister device. In the field they had different devices on helmet, forage cap or field cap, black patches on collar with death's head and rank badges of SS. The *Hoheitsabzeichen*, worn by the Army proper on the right breast, moved to the left upper arm and a band on the forearm bore the title of the formation

37 **The Ardennes** *1944*
US Infantry. Normal khaki battle dress, neatly tailored with additional gadgets, showed up the British 'poor relation' variety. Equipment similarly offered all conceivable possibilities to the individual, who could adopt his own ideas of comfort in carrying his necessities. The helmet had a lightweight lining which was hard to distinguish from its outer steel form

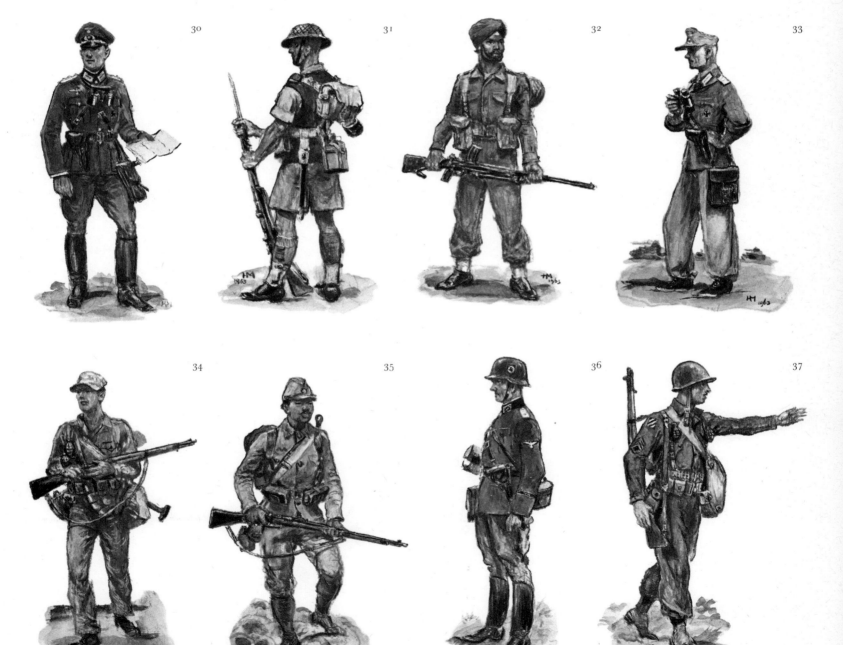

The Development of Tactics

The means by which soldiers seek to achieve their ends in battle are called tactics. In attack or defence, advance or withdrawal, skirmishing or patrolling, the tactician strives to crown the efforts of the strategist, whose task it is to conduct the campaign as a whole. The good tactician, for example Wellington, may ultimately have the advantage over a great strategist, such as Napoleon.

The main factors which influence tactics are ground, weapons, armour, means of movement and of passing information and orders (communications).

Ground – A tactician uses cover to protect and conceal his forces, and obstacles to impede the movements of the enemy.

Weapons – Weapons fall into two main categories: those for shock and those for missile action. In our period the former include pikes, halberds, swords, lances, and bayonets: the latter, muskets, rifles and, in primitive armies, bows and slings (cannon, etc, are not discussed in detail in this section). The most important characteristics of firearms are their range and their rate of fire. These govern their tactical employment.

Armour – Armour may be used either to protect the person or a vehicle. Its chief disadvantage is that its weight tends to restrict mobility.

Movement – Mobility, which means speed and lightness, has always been of great importance to the tactician, since it enables him to surprise his enemy, and to employ his reserves to the best advantage. The horse, the railway train, the motor vehicle, the tank, the aeroplane have all made their contribution at different periods.

Communications – The commander's task is to control his forces. When armies were small and fought in close order with short range weapons, this was done mainly by gallopers. Even then it was difficult. As weapons improved, armies tended to deploy more widely and it became increasingly difficult for the commander to know what progress his troops had made and to influence the battle. The telephone and the wireless have done a great deal to offset this tendency.

In the middle of the seventeenth century armies consisted of horse, foot, dragoons, and cannon.

The normal cavalryman was armed with a sword and a pair of pistols, and wore a pot helmet, back and breast plate, and a buff coat. Exceptionally he was armed with a lance, or wore three-quarter armour. He relied sometimes on shock action, charging at speed, a method favoured by Gustavus Adolphus, Condé and Rupert; sometimes on missile action, firing from the saddle and wheeling off to reload.

The infantry regiments consisted of musketeers and pikemen, in the ratio of 2 to 1. This was very inconvenient, partly because the whole unit was not armed with the same weapon, and partly because the pikemen in their armour were less mobile than the musketeers. As the musket was inaccurate and took a long time to load, the infantry was rather less valuable than the cavalry.

Dragoons were mounted infantry, who usually fought on foot.

Artillery, though useful in battle, was seldom able to play a decisive part. The equipment was heavy and the means of traction, usually horses pulling tandem, but sometimes oxen, was inefficient. There was as yet no battery organization. In addition to this immobility, the rate of fire was slow. Missiles used were roundshot and caseshot. It was difficult to observe the fall of shot over about 1,000 yards, which limited the range at which roundshot was employed. Caseshot was used at pointblank range, and was useless over 350 yards.

By the time of the War of the Spanish Succession (1702–13) the infantry had become much more effective, owing to the introduction of the bayonet, which made every musketeer his own pikeman. The pikeman disappeared from the battlefield, leaving the infantry far more mobile and hard-hitting. In the French Army the regiments drew up four deep and fired a rank at a time. A British regiment, however, was divided into 18 platoons, three deep. Six platoons fired at a time, thus getting a concentrated fire at certain points of the enemy front.

The cavalry remained much as they had been in the middle of the seventeenth century.

Guns were used on an increasing scale, but the equipment was not greatly improved until the last half of the eighteenth century.

With the introduction of the iron ramrod (about 1720) the rate of fire of infantry greatly increased, so that Frederick the Great could say that a Prussian battalion was a moving battery. His men could probably fire three rounds a minute.

The introduction of Grenadier companies, one per battalion, gave the infantry a corps d'élite, particularly useful for storming parties in siege warfare, though the actual grenade does not seem to have been used very much between 1713 and 1914.

Cavalry came to rely more and more on shock action, charging from about 200 yards at speed and rallying after the mêlée to charge again.

One may say that by the middle of the eighteenth century the three arms – Horse, Foot, and Guns – were all equally useful in their ways, though the infantry were gaining ground steadily. The artillery were about to see a period of marked improvement, and the cavalry were virtually standing still.

The introduction of light infantry, partly due to the fighting in the Seven Years' War and the War of American Independence, led to great improvements in infantry tactics. Open order fighting and the use of cover were no longer frowned upon. This tendency was developed by the Armies of the French Republic, who relied on swarms of skirmishers backed by columns rather than the formal formations dear to the continental armies.

The Napoleonic Wars saw tremendous advances in the use of artillery, partly because Napoleon was a gunner and partly because the Russians offset the poor manœuvring powers of their infantry by the use of great numbers of cannon. At Eylau and Borodino the power of their artillery was most impressive.

The main infantry formations of the period were column, line, and square. Column was best for rapidity of movement, line for fire, and square for resisting cavalry, though it offered a splendid target to the artillery.

The French liked column formations, heralded by swarms of skirmishers. They found that their heavy columns would often go through an enemy line like a steamroller. This did not work against the British, especially under the Duke of Wellington. He met the enemy skirmishers with his own light infantry; concealed his line, usually on a reverse slope, until the last possible moment, and protected his flanks with natural obstacles, guns, or cavalry. He relied on firepower to repulse the shock action of the French columns.

There are very few instances of cavalry breaking squares during the Napoleonic Wars, though Garcia Hernandez is one.

By the middle of the nineteenth century rifled firearms with a greatly increased range were revolutionizing the battlefield. In the later years of the American Civil War field works were common; heavy casualties drove the troops to depend more and more on the axe and the shovel. Cavalry, though still valuable for recon-

Battle of Naseby, 1645

The British Attack, Ramillies, 1706

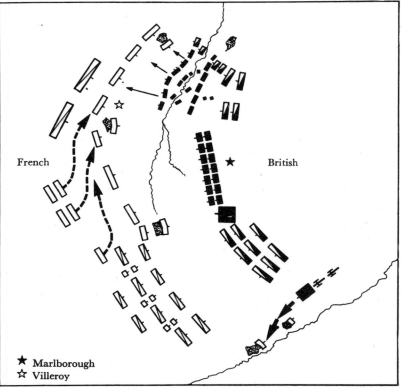

French

British

★ Marlborough
☆ Villeroy

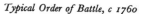

Typical Order of Battle, c 1760

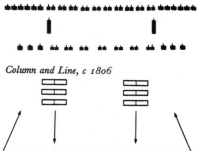

Column and Line, c 1806

300

naissance and raiding, began to disappear from the battlefield, though they still had private battles such as Brandy Station.

These tendencies were accentuated in the Franco-Prussian War. The attack of the Prussian Guard at Saint-Privat showed the danger of an advance across the open in close formation against modern firearms – a lesson the Germans had plenty of time to forget before 1914. At Rezonville the French and German cavalry had an old-fashioned mêlée on the grand scale without undue damage to either side, but at Sedan the gallant General Gallifet and his Chasseurs d'Afrique could make no impression at all on the Prussian infantry. The *arme blanche* was losing ground.

The experiences of the South African and Russo-Japanese Wars left the armies of the great powers relatively ill-prepared for the problems of 1914–18. The limitations of cavalry were ruthlessly exposed by actions such as Haelen 12–13 August 1914, where the pride of the Prussian Garde Kavallerie Division was shattered by a Belgian force which, except for the Guides, consisted largely of reservist infantrymen. Faced with the machine gun, barbed wire, and pillboxes, the infantry took to trench warfare of a type that had not been familiar since the great sieges of Marlborough's day. Four years of war taught the infantry to find the enemy's flank in the attack, and to use the technique of fire and movement, covering each forward movement by carefully sited machine guns.

Infiltration was a feature of the great German offensive of March 1918. The forward waves bypassed strongpoints, leaving them to be mopped up by the supports and reserves. Defence in depth and the all-round defence of each position was the answer to this technique.

Control was one of the great problems of the First World War. In a big attack commanders seldom knew precisely where their forward troops had got to. Telephone with its vulnerable line was only a partial answer. Wireless was still in its infancy.

The 'Blitzkrieg' of 1939 and 1940 heralded a new epoch. The German armoured

Confederates Attacking Federals, c 1860

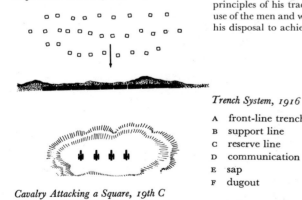

Cavalry Attacking a Square, 19th C

forces, using Stuka dive-bombers in place of close artillery support, carved deep into the lines of their less mobile Polish and French opponents. The use of parachutists added to the confusion these tactics caused. But the Blitzkrieg was less effective against a fully motorized army, particularly when command of the air was seriously disputed. Thus despite many successes, the Afrika Korps eventually met its match in the Eighth Army, notably at El Alamein, a battle in which the British were not ashamed to employ some of the techniques of the First World War; for example the barrage of 1,000 guns which began the offensive and the relentless attrition of the 'break-in' and 'dog-fight' battles that followed. General Montgomery was quick to reorganize his army as a balanced force, forbidding the unorthodox formations known as 'Jock columns'.

Throughout the war the Germans showed great skill in supporting their tanks with batteries of anti-tank guns. They went in for very heavily armoured tanks, while the Allies favoured large numbers of more mobile tanks – notably the Sherman.

In Normandy in 1944 the Allies enjoyed almost complete air superiority. In consequence they were able to seal off the battle zone by destroying the bridges over the rivers Seine and Loire, to protect the flanks of the bridgehead by dropping three airborne divisions, and to attack German armour with rocket-firing Typhoons capable of knocking the turret off a 'Tiger' tank.

In the Second World War both sides, but especially the Allies, made much use of special forces for airborne landings, commando raids, and sabotage.

As technology advances war sees many changes. Tanks take the place of cuirassiers; hussars fight not on horseback but in armoured cars; an army's transport is powered not by hay but by petrol.

Fashions come and go. The great Duke of Marlborough would not have felt at sea before Messines in 1917; Gideon understood well enough the technique of a night raid; the Roman soldier, like the musketeer of Blenheim, could combine both shock and missile action. Above all the tactician's art, assuming that he knows the history and the principles of his trade, is to make the best use of the men and weapons that he finds at his disposal to achieve his aim.

PETER YOUNG

Trench System, 1916

A front-line trench
B support line
C reserve line
D communication trenches
E sap
F dugout

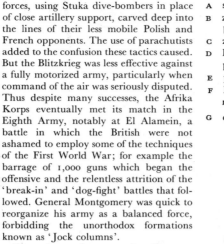

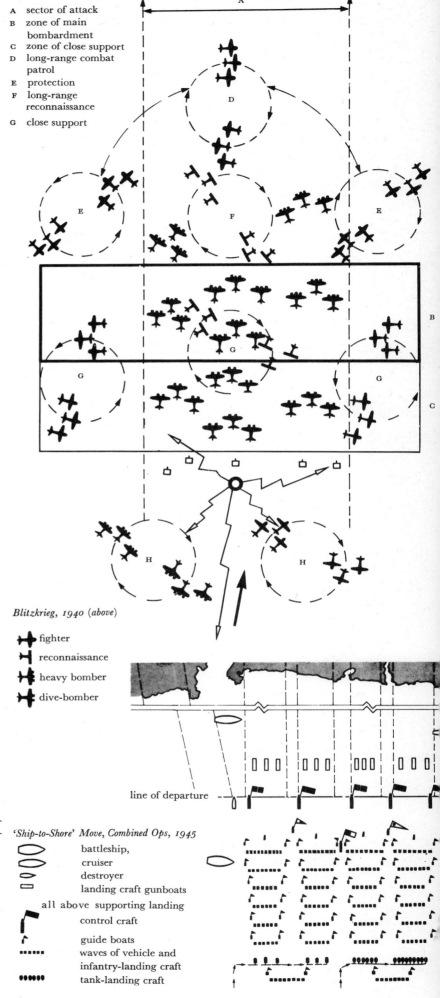

A sector of attack
B zone of main bombardment
C zone of close support
D long-range combat patrol
E protection
F long-range reconnaissance
G close support

Blitzkrieg, 1940 (above)

✈ fighter
✈ reconnaissance
✈ heavy bomber
✈ dive-bomber

line of departure

'Ship-to-Shore' Move, Combined Ops, 1945

battleship, cruiser
destroyer
landing craft gunboats
all above supporting landing
control craft
guide boats
waves of vehicle and infantry-landing craft
tank-landing craft

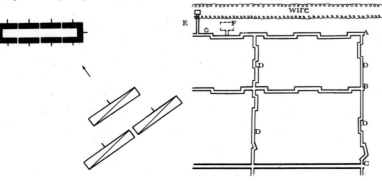

The Development of Artillery

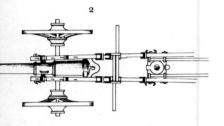

Till Stuart times the mind of the military commander was obsessed by the theory of investment. Wheeled gun-carriages were therefore heavy and crude although their principles followed present day practice. Manœuvreability was not recognized till about 1680 when the limber was introduced. Field artillery, however, still remained cumbersome and inefficient. The English first used artillery as a mobile weapon at Blenheim and, realising its advantages, the authorities introduced the battalion gun, a 3-pounder allotted to infantry battalions. In spite of his enlightened ideas on the value of gun-fire, Marlborough had to endure the inconveniences suffered by his predecessors.

By the beginning of the nineteenth century, gun-carriages, though lighter, had not advanced in design, and the next fifty years brought little improvement. About 1867, Dr C. W. Siemens suggested that recoil might be controlled by the resistance of water flowing through an orifice; thus was the hydraulic buffer born. About 1890, a spade under the trail was incorporated to check recoil. The most successful carriage embodying these principles was the famous French '75' to which a shield was added in 1902.

In 1881, the adoption of breech-loading guns for field artillery gave improved ballistics. This necessitated further refinements in field-gun carriage design. New equipments followed, such as the 13-pounder and 18-pounder, which embodied the independent line of sight and the layer's telescope. Afterwards split trails and independent traversing became standard practice. Finally, gun carriages, like the 25-pounder gun-howitzer, were equipped with pneumatic-tyred wheels.

1 Guns Static *1640*
French Eighth Cannon (Saker). Muzzle loader. Calibre 3·75 in. Point blank range 500 yards, extreme range 5,300 yards. Fighting position front line. Rate of fire 250 rounds per day. The heavy and unwieldy carriage made it difficult to manœuvre, but at this time mobility had not been seriously considered

2 Mobility *1750*
French light cannon, 6 pdr. Muzzle loader. Calibre 3·75 in. Point blank range 450 yards. Fighting position front line. By this date mobility had been recognized as desirable, and an embryonic form of horse artillery was taking shape in most European armies

3 Rifling and Breech Loading *1860*
British Whitworth, 12 pdr (as used in the American Civil War). Breech loader. Calibre 2·75 in. Range 3,000 yards at 5° elevation. Fighting position back. Rifled breech loaders gained over smooth bore guns in muzzle velocity, range, accuracy, time of flight and rate of fire

4 The Machine Gun *1862*
American Gatling gun. Calibre ·58 in. Range 1,000 yards. Fighting position front line. Rate of fire 350 shots per minute from its 10 barrels. Invented by Dr Richard J. Gatling of Chicago, based on the idea of a fifteenth-century weapon, the machine gun considerably altered the tactics of the battlefield

5 The Hydraulic Buffer *1897*
French '75'. Breech loader. Calibre 75 mm. Range 7,000 yards originally, increased to 11,000 yards during the First World War. Fighting position back. Incorporating the new and important principle of the hydraulic buffer to check recoil, it combined a very rapid rate of fire with great accuracy

6 Indirect Fire *1900*
British 15 pdr, Mark I. Breech loader. Calibre 3 in. Maximum range 6,500 yards. Fighting position back (normally). Rate of fire 5–6 rounds per minute. Guns were now sited in concealed positions, which required an entirely new sighting system (for the layer could no longer see the target), and an observation officer in front to direct the fire

7 Control of Fire by Telephone, Heavy Concentration of Fire *1914*
British 18 pdr, Mark I. Breech loader. Calibre 3·3 in. Maximum range 8,000 yards. Fighting position back. Rate of fire 10–12 rounds per minute. Fire was now directed from an observation post by the battery commander using field telephone, and massed gunfire was employed – e.g. for softening up processes

8 Control of Fire and Movement by Wireless, Complete Mechanization *1940*
British 25 pdr gun/howitzer. Calibre 3·45 in. Maximum range 13,400 yards. Fighting position back. Rate of fire 12–15 rounds per minute. Observation was now partly from aircraft, communication was by wireless, and guns and stores were all mechanically hauled

O. F. G. HOGG

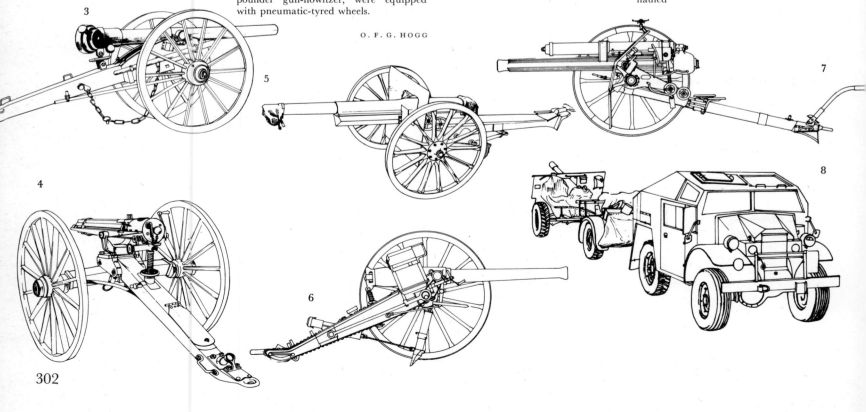

The Development of Small Arms

The design of military firearms has been influenced mainly by the needs of fire-power and accuracy. The heavy matchlock musket of the seventeenth century had to be fired from a rest, and loading, which took two to three minutes, was performed under the protection of pikemen. Towards the end of the century, the musket was reduced in size and armed with a bayonet, and the inconvenient matchlock was replaced by the flintlock. The flintlock musket remained in service with little alteration until the 1830s when it was fitted with a percussion-cap lock. All these muzzle-loading muskets were smoothbore, and although capable of two or three shots per minute were effective only up to fifty yards.

The long-barrelled sporting rifles used by the American settlers in the War of Independence at ranges up to 200 yards drew attention to the value of long-range accuracy, and afterwards rifles were put to limited use by most European armies. But the muzzle-loading rifle needed a skilled marksman, and it was not until the introduction of the self-expanding Minié bullet in 1849 that the rifle became the universal weapon. As a muzzle-loader, however, its rate of fire was still restricted, and it was left to the Dreyse needle-fire rifle, adopted by the Prussian Army in 1841 and employed with great effect in the Austrian War of 1866, to prove the superiority of the breechloader firing a self-igniting cartridge. Improved metallic cartridges led to the development of fast repeating guns operated mainly by lever and bolt actions. Finally the explosive power of the cartridge was harnessed to work the rifle automatically and at great speed.

H. L. BLACKMORE

1 Dutch matchlock musket *c. 1640*
Weight 15 lb. Calibre ·80 in. Slow-burning match was kept in special holder, then fitted in jaws of cock when needed. Pressure on trigger brought burning end into priming powder. Accessories include rest, bandolier of wooden containers holding a charge of powder, bullet bag and small priming flask

2 British flintlock musket *c. 1800*
Weight 10 lb. Calibre ·75 in. Known as the 'Brown Bess'. Cock held a flint which on striking steel and pan-cover produced spark. Paper cartridge containing powder and ball carried in leather pouch. Part of powder used as priming, the paper forming a wad round ball

3 American flintlock rifle *c. 1770*
Weight 10 lb. Calibre ·40 in. Known as the Kentucky rifle, but developed mainly in Pennsylvania. Features are long barrel and small bore. Accessories shown – cow-horn powder flask, bullet mould, square flints and linen or leather bullet patches (kept in decorated patch box in butt). Bullet was wrapped in patch to fit tight into barrel grooves

4 French Minié rifle *c. 1850*
Weight 10 lb. Calibre 18 mm. Fired by hammer hitting percussion cap on barrel nipple. Final development in series of expanding bullets. In previous attempts bullet hammered by rammer on edge of breech chamber (Delvigne) or on central pillar (Thouvenin). The hollow Minié bullet is shown with the iron cup in its base before and after firing

5 German needle-fire rifle *M 1841*
Weight 10¾ lb. Calibre 15·43 mm. Official name, *Zündnadelgewehr*. Breechloader with bolt-action and self-igniting paper cartridge invented by Johann Dreyse (1787–1867). Needle on bolt passes through powder to ignite percussion pellet in base of bullet. No ejection necessary as cartridge paper consumed by explosion

6 American Dragoon revolver *c. 1850*
Weight 4 lb. 2 oz. Calibre ·44 in. Invented by Samuel Colt and modified by Captain Walker in 1847. Hammer has to be pulled back to revolve cylinder containing six shots. Swivelled loading rammer under barrel. Shown fitted with detachable shoulder stock. Used by US cavalry and Texas Rangers in Indian and Mexican Wars

7 American Spencer carbine *1860*
Weight 7½ lb. Calibre ·56 in. Patented by Christopher Spencer in 1860. Nick-named 'Horizontal Shot Tower'. Tubular magazine in butt holds seven metallic rim-fire cartridges. Lever-operated rolling-block breech ejects empty cartridge case and loads new bullet. Could fire 30 shots per minute. Contributed to Union victory in American Civil War

8 British Lee-Enfield rifle *1902*
Weight 8 lb. Calibre ·303 in. Short magazine model. Incorporated fast Lee bolt-action and box magazine holding ten centre-fire cartridges, re-filled by clips of five. Sword bayonet clips on muzzle. Accurate up to 2000 yards. Used by British troops in both World Wars

9 German Machine Pistol *M 38*
Weight 9 lb. Calibre 9 mm. Nick-named 'burp' gun. Designed in 1938 for parachute troops (note folding shoulder stock) but the type was used extensively in World War II. Easily-made pressed-steel body with simple blow-back action, using popular 9 mm. cartridge. Accurate up to 200 yards. Issued with six spare magazines each holding thirty rounds. Cyclic rate of 500 shots per minute

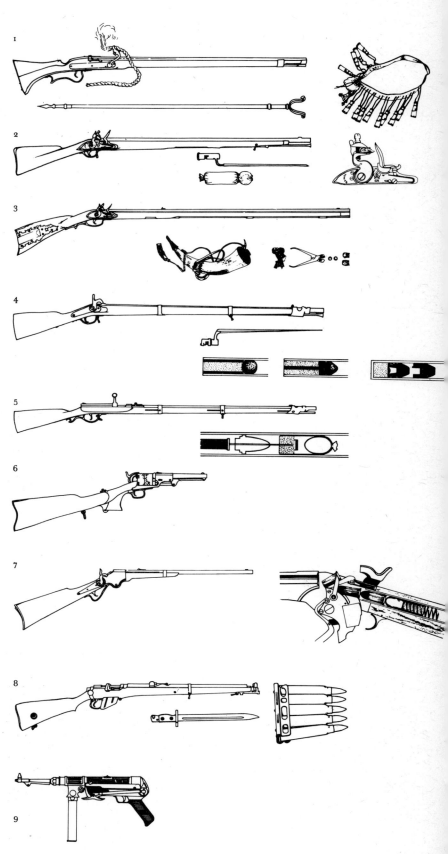

Acknowledgments

The following illustrations were specially drawn for this book:
the battle plans, maps and the illustrations on pages 292–3, and 300–3 by Brian Keogh
the decorative headings at the beginning of each battle by Philip Gough
the drawings of uniforms on pages 294–9 by A. E. Haswell Miller

The editor and publishers wish to express their gratitude to Lieutenant-Colonel C. B. Appleby, the Director of the National Army Museum, Sandhurst, Colonel Jacques Jousset, Conservateur du Musée de l'Armée, Paris and the late Major J. P. Kaestlin, the Librarian of the Royal Artillery Institution, Woolwich, for their help in preparing this book.

The illustrations reproduced on pages 42 and 61 are reproduced by gracious permission of Her Majesty The Queen. The editor and publishers thank the following owners and collectors for permission to reproduce the paintings, photographs and other objects from their collections reproduced on the following pages: The Marquess of Anglesey, pages 34–5, 36, 146–7; A. E. Haswell Miller Esq, pages 143 (bottom), 145, 165; The Hudson's Bay Company, page 33; His Grace The Duke of Marlborough, pages 40–1; Major-General R. C. Money, pages 222, 225 (bottom), 226 (top); Field-Marshal The Viscount Montgomery of Alamein, page 262 (top); Dr Peter Paret, pages 117 (top), 126 (bottom); Herr Manfred Rommel, pages 250 (bottom), 251; The Commanding Officer, School of Electrical and Mechanical Engineering, Bordon, Hampshire, page 162; P. S. Winkworth Esq, pages 68, 73 (bottom), 77.

The remaining illustrations are reproduced by courtesy of the following museums and institutions: the Abby Aldrich Rockefeller Folk Art Collection, Williamsburg, Virginia, page 108 (bottom); the Archiv für Kunst and Geschichte, Berlin, page 152 (bottom right); the Bayerisches Nationalmuseum, Munich, pages 213, 219 (top); the Bibliothek für Zeitgeschichte, Stuttgart, pages 244, 246 (left and centre), 247 (bottom), 248 (top two and bottom); the Bibliothèque Nationale, Paris, pages 18, 27–9, 44–5, 46 (top), 47 (right), 49 (left), 52, 53 (top), 55 (top), 56 (bottom), 64 (top), 105 (bottom left), 118–19, 120, 127, 129, 132 (bottom), 148 (centre), 149 (left), 193, 195, 202, 203 (top), (Collection Hennin) 30, 64 (bottom left and right), 124 (bottom), (Collection Druène) 54 (left), 56 (top left and right), 57; the British Museum, London, pages 9, 10 (left), 11 (left), 12 (left), 60, 62 (top), 65, 66, 84 (left), 83, 84 (top left and right), 88, 89, 96 (bottom), 100 (top), 113, 119, 126 (top), 161, (Crookshank Collection) 69 (top – on loan to the Royal Military Academy, Sandhurst), 111, 144, 149 (right), 150–1 (top), 152 (top); the Collection Raoul et Jean Brunon Marseille, page 226 (bottom); the Civica Raccolta di Stampe Bertarelli, Milan, page 124 (top); Messrs William Collins, pages 251, 262 (top); the Department of the Army, Washington, pages 15, 280 (left), 281, 283

(top right), 285 (top), 286 (inset), 288 (left), 291; the Department of Defense, Washington (Marine Corps photographs), pages 272–3, 276 (top, and centre left and right); the Department of the Great Patriotic War, Moscow, pages 252, 254 (right), 255 (top left); the Domaine de Grosbois, Boissy-Saint-Leger, pages 122–3; the Frick Collection, New York, page 90; Gettysburg National Military Park, pages 185–7, 188 (top); the Heeresgeschichtliches Museum, Vienna, pages 24 (bottom right), 34 (left), 37; the Historisches Museum, Schloss Rastatt, pages 10 (right), 196 (top), 203 (bottom), 215 (bottom right), 218 (bottom), 219 (bottom), 220; the Imperial War Museum, London, the endpapers, pages 11 (right), 12 (centre), 13 (centre and right), 14, 223 (top), 224 (bottom right), 229, 230, 231 (top left and right), 232, 233, 240 (left), 246 (right), 247 (top), 248 (third from top), 255 (centre two left), 256, 256–7 (top), 259, 261, 262 (bottom left and right), 264–5, 267–9, 280 (centre), 283 (top left), 284, 285 (bottom), 288 (right), 289; the Kungl. Armémuseum, Stockholm, pages 12–13, 45 (right), 47 (left), 48; the Library of Congress, Washington, pages 76 (left), 85, 86–7, 94, 105 (top), 109, 110 (bottom), 112 (top and bottom left), 170 (top), 171, 172 (bottom), 173, 183 (top), 189, 191 (left); the McCord Museum, McGill University, Montreal (Notman Collection), page 69 (bottom); the Metropolitan Museum of Art, New York, page 96 (top – gift of Robert W. de Forest, 1906); the Musée d'Arras, page 197 (bottom); the Musée de Condé, Chantilly, pages 16, 22–3, 25, 26 (bottom); the Musée de Gravelotte, page 199 (bottom); the Musée de la Guerre, Château de Vincennes, page 224 (top); the Musée de l'Armée, Paris, pages 131 (left), 133, 134–5; the Musée de Malmaison, page 130 (bottom); the Musée de Versailles, the jacket, pages 21, 24 (bottom left), 26 (top), 50, 53 (bottom left), 54–5 (bottom), 59, 107, 110 (top), 116, 136, 194 (right), 201; the Musée du Louvre, page 197 (top); the National Archives, Washington, (US Signal Corps photograph) page 104, (US Signal Corps photographs, Brady Collection) 167, 175, 176–7, 180 (right), 181 (left), 190 (top), (War Department General Staff Collection) 182 (top right), 190 (bottom); the National Gallery, London, page 141; the National Gallery of Canada, Ottawa, page 70; the Nationalmuseum, Stockholm, pages 49 (right), (Drottningholm Castle Collection) 46 (bottom left), (Svenska Porträttarkivet) 46 (bottom centre and right); the National Portrait Gallery, London, pages 53 (bottom right), 76 (right), 105 (bottom right); the Österreichische Nationalbibliothek, Vienna (Bild-Archiv), pages 215 (bottom left), 224 (bottom centre), 235,

236, 237 (bottom), 238 (top), 239, 240–1, 242 (bottom left and right); Ogonyok, Moscow, pages 130 (top left), 131 (right); the Parker Gallery, London, pages 79, 154, 160; the Pennsylvania Academy of the Fine Arts, Philadelphia, page 103; the Prado, Madrid, pages 19, 24 (top); the Public Record Office, London, pages 38 (top), 72 (bottom), 73 (top), 152 (bottom left); the Royal Military Academy, Sandhurst, page 98 (bottom); the Staatliche Schlösser und Gärten, Potsdam-Sanssouci, page 62 (bottom); the Schwarzhaupterschatz, Riga, page 44 (left); the Victoria and Albert Museum, London, pages 153 (right), (Apsley House Collection) 121, 148 (top), 163 (top left); the Walker Art Gallery, Liverpool, page 148 (bottom); the Yale University Art Gallery, pages 80, 97, 98 (top), 108 (top).

The photographs reproduced on the following pages were loaned or obtained from the following sources: Associated Press, London, pages 255 (third from top right), 258 (top), 275, 277; Bildarchiv Foto Marburg, page 44 (left); MM J. E. Bulloz, Paris, pages 27 (top), 107, 115, 129, 130 (bottom), 197, 199 (top); Messrs Culver Pictures, New York, pages 71, 74–5, 92, 92–3, 100 (bottom), 101, 103, 112 (bottom right), 138–9, 168, 169, 178, 180 (left and centre), 182 (top left), 184, 188 (bottom), 191 (right), 204, 206 (left), 207, 208, 209 (top right), 210, 211 (bottom), 242 (top), 270, 273 (bottom), 276 (bottom left); the John Hillelson Agency (Magnum Photos), London, pages 279, 286; Casa Editrice Il Saggiatore, Milan, page 124 (top); the Imperial War Museum, London, pages 222, 225 (bottom), 226 (top); Keystone Press, London, pages 255 (top three right), 276 (bottom right), 280 (right); the London Electrotype Agency, pages 206 (right), 211 (top); the London News Agency, page 273 (top right); the Mansell Collection, London, pages 39 (left), 53 (bottom centre), 61, 72 (top), 81 (right), 82, 116 (left), 130 (top right), 153 (left), 156 (left), 182–3 (bottom), 194, 198, 200; Federico Arborio Mella, Milan, pages 238 (bottom), 241 (right), 243; the Parker Gallery, London, pages 68, 73 (bottom), 77; Pictorial Press, London, page 254 (left and centre); Planet News, London, pages 255 (bottom left and right), 258 (bottom); the Radio Times Hulton Picture Library, London, pages 142, 156–7, 157, 159, 163 (top right), 164, 209 (top left), 224 (bottom left), 227; Ridge Press, New York, page 172 (right); Ullstein Bilderdienst, Berlin, pages 214, 215 (top), 216 (top), 217, 218 (top), 223 (bottom left and right), 226 (centre), 250 (top); the Victoria and Albert Museum, London, pages 40–1.

The following illustrations were photographed by these photographers: Messrs

John Akerman, pages 158 (top), 163 (bottom left and right); Alinari, page 53 (bottom left); Messrs A. C. Cooper, pages 33, 42, 60, 69 (top), 79, 98 (bottom), 121, 143 (bottom), 145, 148 (top), 154, 162, 285 (bottom); A. de Cusati, pages 80, 97; Messrs John R. Freeman, pages 9, 10 (left), 11 (left), 12 (left), 62 (top), 65, 66, 81 (left), 83, 84 (top left and right), 88, 89, 96 (bottom), 100 (top), 113, 119, 126 (top), 144, 150–1 (top), 152 (top), 153 (right), 161; MM Giraudon, pages 16, 18 (top), 22–3, 25, 26 (bottom), 44–5, 116 (right); Sophie Renate Gnamm, page 219 (top); Ian Graham, pages 34–5, 36, 146–7; Heinrich Hoffmann, pages 244, 246 (left and centre), 247 (bottom), 248 (top and bottom); Studios Josse-Lalance, jacket, pages 21, 59, 122–3, 133, 134–5, 136, 201, 202; Photociné Pichonnier, page 199 (bottom); Société Française de Microfilm, 224 (top); Jean-Pierre Vieil, pages 52, 53 (top), 55 (top), 56 (bottom), 193, 203 (top); the Ziegler Studio, pages 185–7, 188 (top).